THE ELECTIONS OF 2020

THE ELECTIONS OF 2020

Edited by Michael Nelson

University of Virginia Press • *Charlottesville and London*

University of Virginia Press
© 2021 by the Rector and Visitors of the University of Virginia
All rights reserved
Printed in the United States of America on acid-free paper

First published 2021

9 8 7 6 5 4 3 2 1

Library of Congress Cataloging-in-Publication Data

Names: Nelson, Michael, editor.
Title: The elections of 2020 / Edited by Michael Nelson.
Description: Charlottesville : University of Virginia Press, [2021] |
Includes bibliographical references.
Identifiers: LCCN 2021058763 (print) | LCCN 2021058764 (ebook) |
ISBN 9780813946184 (paperback) | ISBN 9780813946191 (ebook)
Subjects: LCSH: United States—Politics and government—2017- |
Presidents—United States—Election—2020. | Elections—United States—History. |
Mass media—Political aspects—United States. | Political campaigns—United States.
Classification: LCC E912 .E44 2021 (print) | LCC E912 (ebook) |
DDC 324.973/0905—dc23
LC record available at https://lccn.loc.gov/2021058763
LC ebook record available at https://lccn.loc.gov/2021058764

CONTENTS

PREFACE

THE ELECTIONS OF 2020 is the tenth in a series of postelection studies that began in 1985 with *The Elections of 1984*. In the midst of endless discussion and debate in the larger political community about what happened in each of these elections and why, the constant purpose of these books has been to bring to bear the deeper and broader perspectives of political scientists.

In nearly all of the previous books in this series, the story of the election ended for all intents and purposes on Election Day in November. Even the one exception—the historically close contest between George W. Bush and Al Gore in 2000—was resolved peacefully through a gradual process of recounts and court cases and, once resolved, was gracefully conceded by the loser.

The 2020 presidential election was different. Although Democratic nominee Joseph Biden took the lead as the returns came in on election night, November 3, Republican president Donald J. Trump made a statement claiming, "This is a fraud. . . . Frankly, we did win this election." Five days later, when Biden's victory—by 306–232 in the electoral college and 81 million to 74 million in the national popular vote—was sufficiently indisputable that every major news organization declared him the president-elect, Trump persisted in maintaining that he was the true victor. He incited his supporters: to file lawsuits challenging the results; to disrupt the official casting of the electoral votes in the state capitals on December 14; and then, on January 6, to "march over to the Capitol" and "fight like hell" to prevent the final tallying of the electoral votes by a joint session of Congress. The march degenerated into a violent occupation of the building. Trump was impeached by the House of Representatives for "incitement of insurrection" on January 13, 2021, one week before his term expired, and acquitted by the Senate on February 13 when the 57–43 majority for conviction fell ten votes shy of the constitutionally necessary two-thirds majority.

Multiple Republican officials, including the eighteen state attorneys general who filed a lawsuit to overturn the results in six states that Trump carried in 2016 but lost in 2020 and the majority of GOP members of Congress who formally protested the counting of the electoral votes on

January 6, participated in Trump's fact-free campaign to overturn the election. In contrast, multiple Republican state and local election officials, state governors, state legislative leaders, and state and federal judges (including Trump's three Supreme Court appointees) refused to support their fellow partisans' efforts to steal the election. On January 20, 2021, Biden was inaugurated as the forty-sixth president of the United States.

Charles Hunt and Candis Watts Smith, the newest contributors to this quadrennial series of postelection studies, were not old enough to read the first book when it was published, thirty-six years ago. With this tenth volume in the series, they join an all-star team of political scientists to bring further insight into modern American politics.

Two members of that team—Paul Quirk (on the presidency) and Gary Jacobson (on Congress)—have been part of it through all ten elections, as have I (on the setting of the election). Others have contributed to previous editions, such as Nicole Mellow (now joined by Smith, on voting), Marc Hetherington (on the general election), and Andrew Rudalevige (on the meaning of the election). Still others have offered their insights for nearly as long to other works before becoming part of this one—William Mayer (on the nominating contests) and Marjorie Hershey (on the media)—or longer—Gerald Pomper (on sixty years of electoral politics). Hunt is a new and welcome addition on the important subject of campaign finance.

At the time of the 1984 volume's publication, the Republican Party was in the midst of a winning streak that included victories in five of the six presidential elections from 1968 to 1988, with four of those five victories taking the form of landslides. Even so, the Democratic Party maintained equally solid control of Congress throughout this period.

Much clearly has changed in American politics since this series began. For one thing, starting in 1992, Democratic presidential candidates have won five of eight elections. They also won the national popular vote while losing the electoral vote in two of their three defeats (2000 and 2016), the first time such anomalous outcomes had occurred in more than a century. Meanwhile, the Republicans won control of Congress in 1994 and have controlled one or both chambers for all but six years since then.

Divided government—when the president's party does not also control both the House of Representatives and the Senate—not only has been the normal governing situation in Washington for more than a half century but also has become more consequential. When this series began, enough Democrats in Congress were moderate conservatives and enough Republicans were moderate liberals that a basis for bipartisan cooperation between the branches sometimes could be found. Over time, the movement of southern conservatives into the GOP and northeastern and Pacific coast liberals into the Democratic Party has transformed both parties into ideological monoliths. The creation and proliferation of hyperpartisan cable news networks, websites, and social media has helped harden the lines of division, as has the rise of ideologically charged independent political groups with broad legal license to flood the electoral system with money.

The elections of 2020 manifested all of these developments in the American political system. Although his predecessor as the Democratic nominee, Hillary Clinton, lost the 2016 election to Republican Donald Trump despite winning the national popular vote, Joe Biden managed to win both by carrying all her states while eking out victories in several states she lost, notably Michigan, Pennsylvania, Georgia, Wisconsin, and Arizona. Biden's fellow Democrats hung on to a slim majority in the House despite losing several seats, while the Republicans did the same in the Senate.

The Elections of 2020 chronicles and analyzes what happened in 2020 while placing it in broad historical and political context. As in all previous volumes of the series, the authors' purpose is to shed the focused light of political science on events that may otherwise seem like a diffuse blur of confusing incidents. In every case, the authors' presentations offer clearly written accounts of complex developments.

As editor and coauthor, I, along with my colleagues, hasten to thank Richard Ellis for his timely and insightful review of the manuscript, and the marvelous team at the University of Virginia Press who shepherded it into print, design, and distribution. In particular, we especially thank the University of Virginia Press's acquisitions editor Nadine Zimmerli, as well as her associates Helen Chandler and Charlie Bailey; editorial, design, and production staff Ellen Satrom, Anne Hegeman, Cecilia Sorochin, and Niccole Coggins; marketing staff Jason Coleman, Emily Grandstaff, and Emma Donovan; and at Westchester Publishing Services, Deborah Grahame-Smith.

THE ELECTIONS OF 2020

The Setting

WHO CAN BE PRESIDENT?

Michael Nelson

Every four years, candidates, consultants, commentators, and, yes, political scientists proclaim the historic nature of the current presidential election. America stands at a crossroads, we solemnly intone, and our nation is at a critical turning point. Usually we are wrong. Most elections are fairly ordinary affairs. But not the elections of 2020.

As is typical when a president's first term draws to a close, little suspense attended the Republican Party's renomination of Donald Trump. But when the field of Democrats seeking to challenge him in 2020 formed, it became clear that it would offer the party's voters a choice among the most diverse array of candidates in history. This was no fluke, either of the year or the party. In 2016 the GOP field was nearly as diverse, including two Latino Americans (Senators Marco Rubio of Florida and Ted Cruz of Texas), an African American (surgeon Ben Carson), an Indian American (Louisiana governor Bobby Jindal), and three candidates from the private sector (Carson and business leaders Trump and Carly Fiorina). The 2016 Democratic contest featured Senator Bernie Sanders of Vermont, bidding to become the first Jewish American president, and former secretary of state and New York senator Hillary Clinton, who became the first woman nominated for president by a major party.

Four years later, Democrats offered their voters an even broader range of candidates, accurately reflecting a party whose members are about 60 percent women, 40 percent people of color, and nearly 10 percent LGBTQ.[1] In terms of social characteristics, nearly all previous presidents were white male married Christians older than forty and younger than seventy. (Barack Obama, an African American, and James Buchanan, a lifelong bachelor, were the only exceptions.) But the field of twenty-eight candidates for the 2020 Democratic presidential nomination included six women, seven candidates of color, four candidates older than seventy, three younger than forty, two Jews, a Hindu, and a gay man. Among the leading contenders were Elizabeth Warren, a seventy-one-year-old woman; Joe Biden, a seventy-seven-year-old man; Bernie Sanders and Mike Bloomberg, both of them seventy-eight-year-old Jewish men; Pete Buttigieg, a thirty-seven-year-old gay man; Kamala Harris, the daughter of a Black father and an Indian mother; and Andrew Yang and Tulsi Gabbard, two Asian Americans.

By the end of the nominating contest not one of the seven Democrats who won the most votes in the primaries and delegates to the party's national convention fit squarely within the white-male-married-Christian-forty-to-seventy template that marked every president and major party opponent from George Washington in 1789 to George W. Bush in 2004.

In terms of career background, the Democratic field in 2020 was also pathbreaking. To be sure, it featured a vice president and multiple senators and governors—the traditional stepping-stone offices to a major party nomination for president. These included former vice president Biden; governors Jay Inslee of Washington, John Hickenlooper of Colorado, Steve Bullock of Montana, and Deval Patrick of Massachusetts; and senators Warren of Massachusetts, Harris of California, Sanders of Vermont, Amy Klobuchar of Minnesota, Corey Booker of New Jersey, Kirsten Gillibrand of New York, and Michael Bennett of Colorado. But the field also contained candidates from nontraditional positions: seven current or former members of the House of Representatives, five current or former mayors, and three candidates from the private sector. Of this nontraditional group, only former South Bend, Indiana, mayor Buttigieg emerged as a leading candidate.

In a field that diverse, with so many and varied candidates, it was hard for any of them to stand out from each other in the way Obama did as the only African American in the race in 2008 and Hillary Clinton did as the only woman contender in 2016. By late summer, after the parties held their nominating conventions, the general election ballot offered the country its first opportunity to elect a Black and Indian American woman, Senator Kamala Harris of California, as vice president. (None of the forty-eight individuals who served as vice president before her were either women or persons of color.) As for age, the sum of the two major party nominees for president in 2020 was the greatest in history: 151. (Trump was seventy-four and Biden was seventy-seven.) This guaranteed that on January 20, 2021, the United States would inaugurate its oldest president in history.

Although Democrats had not nominated a white male for president since they chose Senator John Kerry of Massachusetts in 2004, to critics the choice between Trump and Biden—two straight, married, Christian, elderly white men, the former the incumbent president and the latter a recent vice president—came as both a surprise and a disappointment, considering the diversity of the field of candidates who sought the office. But no matter who won, neither Trump, ending his second and final term, nor perhaps Biden, considering his age, was ever likely to be on the ballot again, clearing the field in both parties for a range of other candidates to be nominated by their parties in 2024. In that sense, the diverse field in 2020 may have planted the seed for more diverse outcomes in the future.

To demonstrate just how remarkable the 2020 election was in the breadth and variety of its pool of candidates, I review the record of the previous 230 years of presidential elections to see what answers history provided to the question of who can be president—that is, what kinds of people have any realistic chance of being elected to the office. I also describe and analyze how that record was transformed by the events of recent elections, including the elections of 2020. Finally, I assess the ways in which the broadening of the presidential talent pool contributes to and detracts from the presidential election process.

Who Can Be President? The Constitutional Answer

The first answer to the question of who can be president is in the Constitution, which was written in 1787, ratified in 1788, and implemented in 1789. Article II, section 1, paragraph 5 states, "No person except a natural born Citizen, or a Citizen of the United States, at the time of the Adoption of this Constitution, shall be eligible to the Office of President; neither shall any Person be eligible to that Office who shall not have attained to the Age of thirty five Years, and been fourteen Years a Resident within the United States."

Why the framers chose to include this list of qualifications—thirty-five years or older, natural-born citizen, and at least fourteen years of residency—is far from obvious.[2] The recorded debates on presidential qualifications at the Constitutional Convention of 1787 are meager. Even so, the delegates' actions throughout the convention manifested a consistent principle: a constitution that states qualifications for those who fill an office need not state qualifications for the office itself, but a constitution that states no qualifications for those who select must do so for the one who is selected. In the case of Congress, the need for a qualifications clause for members was agreed on from the beginning. Conversely, in the case of judges, department heads, and other public officials mentioned in the Constitution, no qualifications ever were stated. None were needed, the delegates seemed to assume, because these individuals would be selected by constitutional officials for whom qualifications had been established.

The presidency received more varied but no less principled treatment from the delegates. During most of the convention they remained wedded to the idea that the president should be chosen by Congress. Because age, citizenship, and residency requirements were included for members of Congress, the delegates saw no need to establish any for the president. They believed that constitutionally qualified legislators could be counted on to select a qualified president.

By midsummer, however, the tide of opinion at the convention clearly had turned against election of the president by Congress. Although it took until September for the framers to agree that presidents would be chosen by the Electoral College, one thing was certain: however the president was chosen, it would not be by an electorate for which the Constitution stated qualifications. Hence, the convention's willingness to adopt a presidential qualifications clause without controversy.

Such qualifications would have to be high, in the delegates' minds, because of a second principle they deemed relevant: the greater the powers of an office, the higher the qualifications for holding that office must be. Just as senators had to satisfy stiffer age, residency, and citizenship requirements than did House members, so would the president have to be more qualified in these ways than senators. Regarding the requirement that the president be a natural-born citizen, it was not only steeper than the unadorned citizenship requirement for legislators, but it also helped to solve a political problem that the delegates anticipated as they considered how to persuade states to ratify the Constitution.

The framers realized that the presidency they were creating was the closest thing in the new constitution to a king. During the summer, rumors spread across the country that the delegates were plotting to import a foreign prince—perhaps Frederick, Duke of York, the second son of King George III, or Prince Henry of Prussia, the younger brother of Frederick the Great—to rule the United States. So vexing was this rumor that the delegates momentarily lifted the convention's veil of secrecy with a statement to the *Pennsylvania Journal*: "[August 22] We are informed that many letters have been written to the members of the Federal Convention from different quarters, respecting the reports idly circulating that it is intended to establish a monarchical government, to send for [Frederick] &c. &c.—to which it has been uniformly answered, 'though we cannot, affirmatively, tell you what we are doing, we can, negatively, tell you what we are not doing—we never once thought of a king.'"[3]

However effective the delegates' squelching of this rumor may have been, they knew that the mere presence of an independent, one-person executive in the Constitution would prompt further attacks on its latent monarchical tendencies during the ratification process. If nothing else, they could at least defuse the foreign-king issue by requiring that the president be a natural-born citizen.

The final reason for setting a natural-born citizenship requirement for the president was the office's power as commander in chief. With troops at the president's disposal, it was feared that a foreign subversive in the office would seize tyrannical power or lay down American arms before an invading army. John Jay of New York sent a letter to this effect to George Washington, the president of the convention, on July 25: "Permit me to hint, whether it would not be wise and reasonable to provide a strong check on the admission of foreigners into the administration of our National Government, and to declare expressly that the commander in chief of the American Army shall not be given to, nor devolve upon, any but a natural born citizen."[4]

One cannot be certain when Washington read Jay's letter or what effect it had. The record shows, however, that on September 2 Washington replied to Jay, "I thank you for the hints contained in your letter."[5] Two days later, the convention's Committee on Postponed Matters recommended that the president be "a natural born citizen or a citizen of the US at the time of the adoption of this Constitution."

How does the Constitution's presidential qualifications clause affect the nation's choice of its president? Chiefly by eliminating (in the 2020s) about 60 percent of the population from eligibility: the approximately 150 million people who are younger than thirty-five, the 11 million or so who are undocumented immigrants, and the roughly 30 million who are either naturalized citizens or legal immigrants eligible for citizenship.[6] Partly, too, by muddying the waters of presidential eligibility. "Natural-born citizen" is an especially murky term. At the time the Constitution was written, two meanings could be found in the English common law from which the term was borrowed: *jus sanguinis*, which held that anyone whose parents were citizens was a natural-born citizen, and *jus soli*, which held that one had to be born on the nation's soil to gain this status. Subsequently enacted American laws brought more clarity. The Naturalization Act of 1790 provided that "the children of the United States that may be born beyond the sea, or out of the limits of the United States, shall be considered as natural-born citizens." As for children of noncitizens born on American soil, the Fourteenth Amendment, which was added to the Constitution in

1868, made clear that "all persons born or naturalized in the United States . . . are citizens of the United States."

Thanks to Trump, the effects of the qualifications clause were felt in the 2012, 2016, and 2020 elections. Trump rose to national political notoriety in 2011 by challenging Obama's status as a natural-born citizen and demanding to see his birth certificate, fueling the so-called birther controversy. After Obama found and released the document, Trump tweeted that "an 'extremely credible source' has called my office and told me that @BarackObama's birth certificate is a fraud."[7] Trump claimed he had dropped the issue by 2016, but when CNN's Wolf Blitzer asked him in January where he thought Obama was born, he said, "Who knows?"[8] In a YouGov poll released that month, 53 percent of Republicans answered "not" when asked whether "Obama was born in the United States, or not?"[9]

Trump raised questions during the 2016 Republican nomination campaign about Senator Cruz's eligibility to be president. Although anyone born to a U.S. citizen is automatically a citizen by birth, Trump argued that because Cruz was born in Canada and only his mother was a U.S. citizen, Cruz's eligibility was "very precarious."[10] Legal scholars found this argument to be "specious," the term used by former solicitors general Neal Katyal and Paul Clement in a *Harvard Law Review* article on the subject.[11]

In 2020, while seeking a second term, Trump reacted to Biden's August 12 announcement of Harris's selection as his vice presidential running mate by questioning her status as a constitutionally eligible natural-born citizen, which under the Twelfth Amendment the vice president must also be. "I heard it today that she doesn't meet the requirements," Trump said the day after her selection, echoing a spurious Facebook post and an online guest column in *Newsweek*, both of which were disavowed by their platforms.[12] Harris's parents, a father from Jamaica and a mother from India, were working in California when she was born in 1964, several years after their arrival in the United States. Once again, constitutional scholars found no validity in Trump's insinuation, which as in previous elections appeared to reflect his desire to rouse animus toward immigrants and people of color more than any serious legal understanding.[13]

Who Can Be President? Career Background

The Constitution's answer to the question of who can be president is not very useful. About 150 million Americans were constitutionally qualified for the presidency in 2020, according to the most recent census estimates.

Far more important historically was an unwritten career requirement that included recent, prominent service in government. Nearly everyone elected or even nominated by a major political party for president since the founding has been a current or former senator, governor, vice president, general, or cabinet member.[14] Unlike the constitutional qualifications, this requirement emerged over time in the habits and preferences of the voters.

These habits and preferences were modified in 2016 among Republican voters, who rejected multiple senators and governors and nominated the celebrity businessman Trump. As a candidate, Trump actively disdained the value of governmental experience, claiming repeatedly that his time in business was better suited to the presidency. "I'm not controlled . . . by the lobbyists," Trump asserted. "I'm not using the donors. I don't care. I'm really rich." He added, "Do you want someone who gets to be president and that's literally the highest-paying job he's ever had?" Referring to his 1987 best-selling book, Trump bragged: "We need a leader that wrote *The Art of the Deal.* . . . I deal with killers that blow these [politicians] away. It's not even the same category. This [governing] is a category that's like nineteen levels lower."[15]

As the party most supportive of government, Democrats showed little inclination to nominate candidates for president or vice president who lacked extensive experience in office. Even so, Trump's defeat of the uber-credentialed Clinton in 2016 caused some to ask if the party should at least consider choosing a well-known Democratic businessman in 2020, such as Dallas Mavericks owner Mark Cuban, Disney CEO Bob Iger, or Facebook founder Mark Zuckerberg. Although hedge-fund billionaire Tom Steyer and New Age spiritualist Marianne Williamson did jump into the 2020 race, neither got very far, despite Steyer's massive spending and Williamson's celebrity status. Democrats instead chose Biden, who after thirty-six years in the Senate and eight years as vice president was by far the most experienced presidential nominee in history. With the exception of Buttigieg, all of Biden's leading rivals for the nomination—Sanders, Warren, Klobuchar, Harris, and Booker—had Senate experience as well.

The political value of each of the traditional career background credentials to would-be presidents has varied over the years in response to changing public expectations. In the early nineteenth century, secretary of state was the leading stepping-stone to the Executive Mansion. Starting with Thomas Jefferson, four consecutive presidents held this office between 1801 and 1829. From then until 2012, however, only three secretaries of state were even nominated by a major party, none of them serving at the time and none at all since 1884.[16] Indeed, the only cabinet members of any kind to be nominated for president in the twentieth century were chosen about a century ago: Secretary of War William Howard Taft in 1908 and Secretary of Commerce Herbert Hoover in 1928. Democratic nominee Hillary Clinton's experience as Obama's first-term secretary of state ended well before the 2016 election and, like that of Jefferson and the other early occupants of that position, was preceded by several years in elected office, in her case as a twice-elected senator from New York.

Military general was another much-valued credential for candidates seeking the presidency before the twentieth century. Washington, Andrew Jackson, William Henry Harrison, Zachary Taylor, and Ulysses S. Grant all earned national fame as generals. After that, only World War II Supreme Allied Commander Dwight D. Eisenhower successfully used his army service as a presidential springboard. General Wesley Clark sought the Democratic nomination in 2004 and General David Petraeus was a much-discussed potential Republican candidate in 2016. But Clark's bid foundered in the primaries and Petraeus's prospects were undone by scandal.

What modern cabinet members and generals have in common is that they are unelected officials, most of them inexperienced and often uninterested in political campaigning. This was not a barrier in the eighteenth and nineteenth centuries, when party leaders controlled the presidential nominating process and nominees did not campaign publicly to get elected. Subsequently, the rise of primaries, joined to new public expectations that candidates run rather than stand for office, placed cabinet members and generals at a disadvantage. Even former general Colin Powell, who was enormously popular in 1996, chose not to undergo the ordeal of a modern presidential campaign. "I never woke up a single morning saying, 'Gee, I want to go to Iowa,'" Powell told an interviewer.[17] Clinton, in contrast, was an experienced vote seeker, having campaigned for Bill Clinton, her husband, in more than a half dozen elections in Arkansas and two for president of the United States, as well as for herself in two successful Senate elections and a nearly successful campaign for the Democratic presidential nomination in 2008.

Except for Taft, Hoover, and Eisenhower, every president elected from 1876 to 2012 was a current or former senator, governor, or vice president. Each of these offices allows candidates to make a distinctive claim about their qualifications for the presidency. Governors, like presidents, have been chief executives. Senators, like presidents, have dealt with national and international issues. Vice presidents, although lacking independent responsibilities, have stood first in the line of presidential succession and, in most cases, were senators or governors before they became vice president.

Over the years, the persuasiveness of the competing claims by senators, governors, and vice presidents has waxed and waned. Governors dominated presidential elections in two periods: 1900–1932, when four of seven presidents were governors, and 1976–2004, when four of five presidents were. Compared with state governments, the government in Washington was relatively unimportant during the first period, which preceded the federal government's rise to prominence after the New Deal, and was unpopular during the second, in the aftermath of the Vietnam War and Watergate crisis. Senators, in contrast, dominated the post–New Deal, post–World War II era. In the twelve-year stretch from 1960 to 1972, all eight major party nominees for president were either senators or vice presidents who had served in the Senate. In 2008, a time of wars in Afghanistan and Iraq as well as against terrorists around the globe, both major parties nominated senators for president: Democrat Barack Obama of Illinois and Republican John McCain of Arizona. In 2020 Biden not only proclaimed his deep Washington experience but featured it in his campaign. Governors fared poorly in the 2020 Democratic nominating contest. Of the six who ran, none won even a single delegate.

The vice presidency became a leading stepping-stone to a presidential nomination when the Twenty-Second Amendment was added to the Constitution. By imposing a two-term limit on presidents, the amendment freed second-term vice presidents to campaign actively for president themselves. Richard Nixon in 1960, George Bush in 1988, and Al Gore in 2000 each won his party's presidential nomination at the end of his second term as vice president. That pattern was interrupted when George W. Bush and Barack Obama chose vice presidents whose presidential ambitions were thought to be in the past and who therefore could serve them free from political distraction. "When you're getting advice from somebody . . . ," said Bush, explaining his choice of Vice President Richard B. Cheney, "if you think deep down part of the advice is to advance a personal agenda, . . . you discount that advice."[18] Obama told Biden that he wanted him to view the vice presidency "as the capstone of your career."[19]

In preparation for the 2016 election, Biden surprised Obama by saying that he wanted to seek the Democratic nomination a third time. (His previous efforts in 1988 and 2008 were conspicuous failures.) But Biden badly trailed Clinton and Sanders in fall 2015 polls and was actively discouraged from entering the race by most party leaders, including Obama.[20] When

Biden was slow to take the hint, Obama sent campaign aide David Plouffe to tell the vice president he did not want to see his career "end in some hotel room in Iowa with you finishing third behind [Clinton] and Bernie Sanders." Soon after Biden announced that he would not run.

Clinton's defeat in 2016 opened the door to another Biden candidacy four years later. His long record in the Senate proved an occasional obstacle in his campaign, especially for his party's nomination. Although Biden's opposition to busing students to achieve school integration in the 1970s and his votes in favor of measures such as the 1994 crime bill, the 1996 welfare reform act, and the 2003 Iraq war were popular at the time, even among many Democrats, the party's primary electorate had recently become much more liberal. In 1994, 25 percent of Democrats identified as liberals, the same percentage who said they were conservatives. By 2018, the liberals' share had doubled to 51 percent and the conservatives' share had dwindled to 13 percent.[21] The party's leftward movement and critical stance toward items in Biden's voting record were even more pronounced among grassroots party activists.[22] Still, his Senate career, which lasted from 1973 to 2009, won him the respect and affection of several generations of congressional Democrats and other party leaders around the country.

Working entirely in Biden's favor in 2020 were his two terms as vice president. They allowed him to identify with the popular Obama in a way no other candidate could. Biden often spoke of his service in the "Obama-Biden administration" and proclaimed himself an "Obama-Biden Democrat." He pledged that he would "pick a woman to be vice president" and also "make sure there's a black woman on the Supreme Court."[23] But nothing did more to solidify Biden's popularity among African Americans and other Obama supporters than his close personal and professional association with the first Black president. After Biden suffered humiliating defeats in the overwhelmingly white Iowa caucuses and New Hampshire primary, African American voters propelled him to a landslide victory in the majority-Black South Carolina primary and, three days later, to a near sweep of the mostly southern Super Tuesday primaries on March 3. Having established a commanding lead against his rivals, Biden cruised to the nomination after nearly all of his opponents dropped out of the race and endorsed him.

The vice presidency also made Biden a nationally known figure among the broader electorate, which stood him in good stead entering the general election campaign. Voters were long familiar with him and so were his defeated Democratic rivals, which made the task of uniting the party behind his candidacy much easier than it might have been for another candidate. In ways consistent with the inclusive style of coalition building that Biden cultivated during his long career in Washington, he invited the far more liberal Sanders to work with him on a number of issue-oriented task forces to bridge their differences. "Personal relationships mean a lot," said Sanders, implicitly contrasting his respect and affection for Biden with his attitude toward Clinton, whom he battled nearly until the end in 2016.[24] Klobuchar, Warren, Harris, and Gillibrand also rallied behind Biden in hopes that the woman he chose for vice president would be one of them. His advanced age made the second slot on the ticket especially attractive in the event that he was not on the ballot again in 2024.

Historically, presidential candidates from outside government made only an occasional appearance on the national scene. In 1940, seeking to thwart Franklin D. Roosevelt's quest for a third term, the Republicans nominated business executive Wendell Willkie. In both 1984 and 1988, civil rights leader and ordained minister Jesse Jackson made a determined run for the Democratic nomination. In 1992 and 1996, another well-known business leader, Ross Perot, ran strongly as an independent candidate. None were elected, but a certain *Mr. Smith Goes to Washington*–style romance seemed to attach to the idea of finding a president outside the usual political channels.

In 2016, the Democrats followed the traditional pattern, limiting their choice to two high-ranking government officials: Clinton and Sanders. The GOP went in an entirely different direction. None of the nine former or current governors in the race—including those who held the position in major states such as Texas, Florida, New York, and Ohio—gained much traction for their candidacies. Of the five current or former senators who ran, only Cruz remained in the contest as late as March 16. None of these high-ranking officials led in polls of Republican voters at any point during the twelve months preceding the GOP convention.[25] In fact, the only candidates who ever did hold the lead in this period were surgeon Ben Carson in the summer of 2015 and Trump from that point on.

Trump's candidacy was initially regarded as a "sideshow" by mainstream media outlets. The *Huffington Post*, for example, refused for months to "report on Trump's campaign as part of [our] political coverage. Instead we will cover his campaign as part of our entertainment section."[26] Yet Trump's attractiveness as a candidate in 2016 stood squarely at the confluence of two roaring political streams: the mood at his party's grassroots, which was intensely antigovernment, and his iconoclastic, celebrity-based personal appeal. As someone who had never held public office, Trump (and briefly Carson) could appeal to GOP primary voters as a complete outsider committed to cleaning up "the mess in Washington." Trump was already well known as a best-selling author of braggadocious business books, a frequent talk show guest, and the host of the popular NBC television series *The Apprentice*. As for his rivals, former Florida governor Jeb Bush and Hillary Clinton are "controlled by those people," declared Trump, referring to wealthy individuals and interest groups. "Trump has none of those people. I'm not controlled. I do what's right for the people."[27] On the eve of the campaign, 58 percent of Republicans in a September 2015 *Washington Post* / ABC News poll said they would prefer "someone from outside the existing political establishment" to "someone with experience in how the political system works."[28]

Trump's inexperience as a candidate who had not been vetted in previous campaigns was tested in the general election when the electorate included Democrats and Independents as well as Republicans. Only 23 percent of Democratic voters and 40 percent of independent voters said they preferred "outside" status to governing "experience." But despite losing the national popular vote to Clinton by a 2.9 million margin, Trump won the election with a solid 304–227 majority in the Electoral College. Remarkably, Trump maintained his outsider demeanor while serving as president. He did so by refusing to conform to most long-standing norms of appropriate presidential conduct and by continuing to portray himself as someone whose main purpose in Washington was to "drain the swamp," which he saw as infested with hostile members of Congress, bureaucrats, lobbyists, and reporters.[29]

In 2020 voters faced an unusual choice when considering the career backgrounds of the two major party candidates. Although Trump had been president for nearly four years, Biden had considerably more experience in government—forty-four years as senator and, in the White House, as vice president—and knew much more about its programs and processes. In a year marked by pandemic and economic decline, a clear majority preferred Biden's experience to Trump's.

Who Can Be President? Social Characteristics

Among potential presidential candidates with the requisite career background to be taken seriously by voters, a further set of criteria has long defined the field of eligible contenders: the social characteristics traditionally associated with presidents.

From the first presidential election in 1788 to the fifty-fifth presidential election in 2004, every president—indeed, every major party nominee for president—was white. In addition, all were men and at least nominally Christian. All were older than forty and younger than seventy at the time of their inauguration. None identified as gay. Taken together, barriers of race, gender, age, religion, and sexual identity prevented well over half of the adult population and a large share of its political leaders from being genuinely considered for the presidency.

Not every lesson from this long history was limiting, however. Starting in the latter half of the twentieth century, a host of other long-standing social barriers to the presidency fell. In a book published on the eve of the 1960 presidential campaign, political scientist Clinton Rossiter offered a then-accurate catalog of historically grounded "oughts" and "almost certainly musts" for would-be presidents that included "northerner or westerner," "lawyer," "more than forty-five years old," "less than sixty-five years old," "Protestant," "a small-town boy," and "a self-made man."[30]

None of these barriers remained standing by year's end. In November 1960 forty-three-year-old (not forty-five) John F. Kennedy, a rich (not self-made), urban (not small-town), Roman Catholic (not Protestant) candidate with no law degree, was elected president. Subsequently, from 1964 to 2016 southerners Lyndon B. Johnson, Jimmy Carter, George Bush, Bill Clinton, and George W. Bush won seven of fourteen presidential elections. Six of the ten presidents in this era—Johnson, Carter, Reagan, both Bushes, and Trump—were not lawyers. Reagan was divorced ("an ought not to be" on Rossiter's list of the country's unwritten rules). As for the class backgrounds of these presidents, they could not have been more varied. The Bushes and Trump were born into wealth; Johnson, Carter, and Gerald R. Ford grew up in middle-class families; and Nixon, Reagan, Clinton, and Obama were sons of the working class. Obama was African American. Two women, Democratic representative Geraldine Ferraro of New York in 1984 and Republican governor Sarah Palin of Alaska in 2008, were nominated by their parties for vice president in this period, and one, Hillary Clinton, won the Democratic presidential nomination in 2016.

During the six decades since 1960 social barriers to the presidency typically have fallen in one of four ways: vice presidential succession, changing public attitudes, positive bias, and facing the issues. Of these four, the change in attitudes was most prominent in 2020, resulting in the Democrats nominating the oldest candidate in history for president and the first Black and Indian American woman for vice president.

Vice Presidential Succession

Although Trump declared that for Kamala Harris to succeed to the presidency "is no way for a woman to become the first president" because "that would rip the country apart," historically vice presidential succession to the presidency has been one means of toppling social barriers to the presidency.[31] After Whig Party nominee Zachary Taylor of Louisiana was elected in 1848, no southerner was nominated for president by a major party for more than a century. Intense opposition among southern whites to the civil rights movement of the 1950s and 1960s made it seem even less likely that either party would nominate a southerner any time soon. The vice presidency, however, was a different matter. Kennedy of Massachusetts added Johnson of Texas to the ticket in 1960 to help carry the South. Three years later Johnson succeeded to the presidency when Kennedy was assassinated. Defying regional stereotype, the new president became an ardent champion of civil rights. By the time Johnson ran for a full term in 1964, anti-southern prejudice had nearly vanished from the electorate. Johnson, Jimmy Carter of Georgia, Bill Clinton of Arkansas, and the two Bushes of Texas won seven of the eleven presidential elections between 1964 and 2004.

Since Johnson, no vice president has succeeded to the presidency as the result of a presidential death—a remarkable record considering that from 1841 to 1963 presidents died in office an average of once every fifteen years. On October 28, 2015, the previous record for the longest period in American history without a presidential death—fifty-one years, eleven months, and five days, set during the founding era—was broken.[32]

What accounts for the current era of presidential longevity? The ever-tighter security that surrounds modern presidents renders assassinations close to impossible. Regarding natural death, the marathon nature of the modern election process all but guarantees that whoever wins is in good health. During the 2020 Democratic nomination campaign, some of Biden's minor rivals tried and failed to bring him down for allegedly being forgetful, in decline, or generationally in the way of younger aspirants.[33] ("Pass the torch," said thirty-eight-year-old Rep. Eric Swalwell to Biden in a debate, with little effect.)[34] Equally futile during the general election campaign were Trump's far-fetched efforts to brand Biden as "Sleepy Joe" and convince voters that he was "a tired, exhausted man," as well as Democrat-spread rumors that Trump suffered a series of ministrokes in 2019 and showed debilitating weakness when lifting a water glass and descending a short stairway at the June 2020 West Point graduation ceremony.[35] Despite the charges and countercharges—"He's shaky, weak, trouble speaking, trouble walking," intoned an anti-Trump ad; "Joe Biden is slipping . . . is clearly diminished," rejoined the Trump campaign—the voters of each party seemed to regard their candidate as an exception to the rule that advanced age is a political liability.[36]

CHANGING PUBLIC ATTITUDES

The second way social barriers have fallen is through growing public acceptance. As with being a southerner, being divorced was long considered a disqualifier for the presidency. In the 1950s, when Illinois governor Adlai Stevenson, the twice-defeated Democratic nominee, and the 1960s, when Governor Nelson Rockefeller of New York unsuccessfully sought the Republican nomination two times, divorce proved an insuperable political obstacle. In 1980, however, Reagan was elected president with scarcely a whisper that his divorce from actress Jane Wyman should be held against him. Society's tolerance for divorce had grown so great during the 1970s that it was no longer a political barrier by the time Reagan ran. Trump's path to the White House in 2016 was unobstructed by his two divorces and multiple much-publicized affairs.

Concerning religion as a social barrier, in 2000 Democratic presidential candidate Al Gore chose Senator Joseph Lieberman of Connecticut as the first non-Christian nominee for vice president. In Election Day exit polls, 72 percent of voters said they thought Lieberman's Jewish religion would make him neither a better nor a worse vice president, and of the remaining 28 percent, twice as many thought it would make him a better one.[37] In February 2007, only 7 percent of respondents to a Gallup Poll said that they would not vote for "a generally well-qualified person for president who happened to be Jewish." But more than half—53 percent—said they would not vote for an atheist.[38] Eight years later the resistance to a Jewish president remained at 7 percent and the share opposed to voting for an atheist fell to 40 percent, with 76 percent of younger voters and 64 percent of Democrats (but only 45 percent of Republicans) willing to support a nonbeliever.[39] Those numbers remained nearly constant in 2019.[40]

In 2016 Sanders became the first Jewish candidate ever to win a presidential primary or caucus by sweeping to victory in New Hampshire and going on to prevail in twenty-two more contests, finishing a strong second in the battle for the Democratic nomination. Sanders's Jewishness proved no obstacle either then or in 2020, when he again finished second in the nominating contest. Nor did Sanders's expressed decision to be "not actively involved in organized religion" in any form as an adult.[41] This did not pose a major problem for Sanders among white Democrats, who increasingly claim little or no religious affiliation but are different in this way from most Black and Latino Democrats.[42] In a 2018 survey, for example, only 49 percent of white Democrats said that religion was "very important" or "somewhat important" in their lives, compared with 85 percent of Black Democrats and 67 percent of Hispanic Democrats.[43] In a general election that also included independent and Republican voters less indifferent to the religious beliefs of their presidents than many white Democrats professed to be, however, Sanders's self-identification as a strongly secular person may have cost him substantially more votes than his Jewish upbringing.

In 2020 Sanders was far from alone in downplaying any claim to a religious identity. Of the more than two dozen candidates who sought the Democratic nomination, only Buttigieg, an Episcopalian; Booker, a Baptist; Warren, a Methodist; and Biden, a Roman Catholic who said that faith is the "bedrock foundation of my life," talked much about their religious beliefs.[44] For Buttigieg, this was part of a broader effort to show that although he was a highly nontraditional candidate in terms of career background, youth, and sexual identity, he was also highly traditional in his religion, wartime military service, and marital status. As for Biden's bidding to become only the second Catholic president in history (and the first seriously observant one), this historic aspect of his candidacy was barely mentioned by him or anyone else.

By 2020 additional historical barriers to a major party nomination for president appeared to be cracking in the face of changing social attitudes. In a 2019 survey, 76 percent of Americans (up from 74 percent in 2011 and 26 percent as recently as 1978) said they were willing to vote for a "gay or lesbian" candidate for president. Among Democrats the proportion was even higher: 82 percent; among Republicans it was 61 percent.[45] As a result of the 2018 midterm election, two openly LGBT senators and eight representatives were serving in Congress—all of them Democrats. Oregon elected the nation's first gay governor, Democrat Kate Brown, in 2014, and Colorado elected the second, Jared Polis, in 2018.

Buttigieg was the least traditional candidate for the 2020 Democratic nomination in several ways. His most recent office was mayor of a small city; no president in history had waged a credible campaign from even a large city. At age thirty-seven, just two years above the constitutional minimum of thirty-five, he was bidding to be the youngest elected president in history by a margin of six years. And he was openly gay, the first-ever LGBTQ contender for a major party nomination. Buttigieg even suggested that "we've probably had excellent presidents who were gay—we just didn't know which ones."[46]

In the face of these challenges to traditional norms of presidential social and career background, Buttigieg rose from obscurity to finish at or near the top in the Iowa caucuses and the New Hampshire primary. "Washington experience is not the only experience that matters," he said at one debate. "There's more than one hundred years of Washington experience on this stage, and where are we right now as a country?"[47] Once the primary calendar moved south, however, concerns among southern Black Christians about Buttigieg's sexual identity contributed to a series of crushing defeats in the South Carolina and Super Tuesday Democratic contests.[48] When Buttigieg told Black audiences that he too had "the experience of sometimes feeling like a stranger in my own country, turning on the news and seeing my own rights come up for debate," they rejected the argument.[49] Although he faced hurdles because he was gay, many Black voters felt that Buttigieg was privileged in every other way as a white man, educated at Harvard and Oxford universities, and able to decide when to reveal his identity.

In 2015, 60 percent of respondents said they would be willing to vote for a Muslim for president, a share that rose to 66 percent four years later. That still left 34 percent of all voters (and 62 percent of Republicans) who said they would not.[50] Three Muslims, all of them House Democrats, were elected to the 116th Congress. One might reasonably forecast that if present trends continue (always a dangerous assumption), at some point in the future, as younger cohorts replace older ones in the electorate and more members of these historically disfavored groups win prominent elective office, the nation will regard without prejudice its first atheist, LGBT, and Muslim candidates for president.

Facing the Issue

Facing public prejudices squarely was the strategy Kennedy employed to overcome widespread prejudice against Roman Catholics in 1960. Although adherence to Protestant Christianity was a requirement for office in several states at the time of the nation's founding, the Constitutional Convention voted unanimously that "no religious Test shall ever be required as a Qualification to any Office or public Trust under the United States." In practice, however, all thirty-four presidents from Washington to Eisenhower were Protestants.

Kennedy's strategy, unusual in an era when competing in presidential primaries was generally regarded as a sign of political weakness, was to enter several in order to convince the leaders of his party (many of them Catholics themselves) that a Catholic could win. In the midst of his crucial primary campaign in overwhelmingly Protestant West Virginia, Kennedy told a television audience: "When any man stands on the steps of the Capitol and takes the oath of office as President, he is swearing to support the separation of church and state."[51] In September, again with cameras rolling, he addressed the Greater Houston Ministerial Association, declaring: "I do not speak for my church on public matters; and the church does not speak for me."[52] In 1958, 24 percent of Americans said they would not vote for any presidential candidate "who happened to be Catholic." Soon after Kennedy was elected that number fell to 13 percent and, by 1969, to 8 percent. By 2019 it was a negligible 5 percent.[53] Still, liberal objections to Supreme Court nominee Amy Coney Barrett's "dogma [that] lives loudly within you" in 2020 showed that anti-Catholic prejudice was not entirely extinct.[54]

The candidate who faced the most difficult religious challenge after Kennedy was former Republican governor Mitt Romney of Massachusetts, who first sought his party's nomination in 2008 and won it in 2012. In a 2007 Gallup poll, 24 percent said they would not vote for a Mormon.[55] Kennedy's mission as a Catholic in 1960 had been to convince voters that his religion did not matter. Romney's challenge was different: to persuade white evangelical Christians, who expect candidates to speak freely about their faith and who constitute a large share of the Republican primary electorate, that he was one of them. In a much-publicized speech in December 2007, Romney declared, "I believe that Jesus Christ is the Son of God and the Savior of mankind." Still, Romney lost all of the Republican primaries in the heavily Christian South in 2008 and, although he prevailed in the region against the Democrat Obama in the 2012 general election, again lost most of that year's southern primaries in which he faced credible opponents.

Age was another unwritten barrier to the presidency, less so for younger candidates than for older ones. In 1973 Biden was sworn in as a senator from Delaware at the minimum constitutional age of thirty after defeating the sixty-three-year-old incumbent J. Caleb Boggs in a campaign that branded him as too old. The Constitution includes a minimum age requirement for the presidency but places no limit on how old a president can be. The voters were different. An August 2007 Gallup poll offered a national sample of Americans a long and varied list of social and career characteristics of potential presidential candidates and asked if each "would be a desirable characteristic for the next president to have, an undesirable characteristic, or if it wouldn't matter much to you either way." Of the twenty characteristics on the list, a majority of voters identified only two as undesirable. One was employment as a "government lobbyist." The other was being "70 years of age or older."[56]

Commentators felt comfortable raising doubts about candidates' age.
Some branded Ronald Reagan as too old both in 1968, when he was fifty-
seven, and in 1980 (he was sixty-nine). In 2008 "McCain's Age Is a Legitimate
Issue" was the headline of one typical article about the seventy-two-year-old
senator's candidacy; another was titled "Is McCain Too Old to Be President?"[57] Pundits trotted out actuarial tables attempting to prove that men of
McCain's age with his medical history were likely to deteriorate or die during
the four to eight years that he would serve as president.[58]

Reagan and McCain worked hard to overcome, through words and
actions, the political stigma of age. Reagan jokingly claimed to remember a
time when newspaper editors shouted "Stop the chisels!" instead of "Stop
the presses!"[59] McCain's campaign days were long and vigorous, and he
asked voters to regard age as a proxy for experience. "My friends, I'm not
the youngest candidate," he told a Wisconsin primary crowd, "but I am
the most experienced."[60] In the end, Reagan overcame enough of the concerns about his age to be elected and, at age seventy-three, reelected as
president. Although McCain lost the general election, he won the Republican nomination. In exit polls in 2008, 39 percent of voters said that age was
a factor in their decisions, and 66 percent of them voted for Obama,
McCain's forty-seven-year-old opponent.

In 2016 both Trump (seventy) and Clinton (sixty-nine) were older than
any previous newly elected president. Clinton avoided the topic, allowing
Trump to make an issue of it. Clinton, Trump claimed, lacked the "stamina" to be president, repeating the charge in four consecutive sentences
during their first televised debate and then, days before their third debate,
insisting that both candidates "take a drug test," the implication being that
Clinton was relying on performance-enhancing drugs to overcome her supposed lack of vitality.[61] Tweeting that stamina is "one of my greatest assets"
and claiming in an interview that he saw "a person who is thirty-five years
old" when he looked in the mirror, Trump persisted in charging that
Clinton was too frail to be president and implying that she was too old.[62]

By 2019 public attitudes concerning the appropriate age of presidents
were little changed. Sixty-three percent of voters said they would be open
to voting for a candidate over the age of seventy, a remarkably low figure
considering that the leading contenders for both parties' 2020 nominations at the time were all in their seventies: Trump for the GOP and Biden

and Sanders for the Democrats.[63] Former president Jimmy Carter, who turned ninety-five in 2019, said, "If I were just eighty years old, if I was fifteen years younger, I don't believe I could undertake the duties I experienced when I was president."[64] Interestingly, 71 percent of voters said they were willing to vote for a candidate under the age of forty. Even so, candidates who fell on either side of the traditional forty-to-seventy age range faced a significant share of the electorate that regarded them as either too old or too young to be president.[65]

Unwilling to make Clinton's mistake of brushing off the age issue, Buttigieg, Sanders, Biden, and Trump addressed it in varying ways. Buttigieg hung a lantern on his youth. "7 Times Pete Buttigieg Highlighted His Age at the Democratic Debate" was the headline of one typical news story. During the course of the July 30, 2019, encounter, Buttigieg pointed out that other countries were turning to "a new generation of leaders" and that only he was young enough to understand the war in Afghanistan, having fought in it, or to remember what it was like to be a student when mass school shootings occurred. "I don't care how old you are," he said. "I care about your vision."[66] Sanders, who suffered a minor heart attack in October 2019, came back more energetically than before after stents were inserted into a previously blocked artery. As in 2016, he emerged as the most popular candidate among younger Democratic voters. "I am old," declared Sanders. "But there are advantages to being old. The ideas that I am fighting for now didn't come to me yesterday."[67]

As for Biden, "Watch me," he said as he jogged from one side of the street to the other when marching in parades. In a bit of overreach, he even challenged skeptics to push-ups and IQ contests and wrestling matches while claiming more seriously that "with experience, hopefully, comes judgment and a little bit of wisdom."[68] Facing charges from Trump that Biden was taking performance-enhancing drugs and from the Biden campaign showing Trump struggling to walk down a ramp, both candidates lay the age-related insinuations to rest by engaging actively in their two ninety-minute presidential debates. Nevertheless, Biden described himself as a "transition candidate" to "newer, younger people" in the Democratic Party, which some interpreted to mean he would not seek a second term in 2024 at age eighty-two.[69]

Concerning race, after two centuries of being closed to African Americans and in uncanny fulfillment of the late Senator Robert F. Kennedy's 1968 prediction that "a Negro could be president in forty years," the doors of the White House at last were ready to be opened when Obama announced his candidacy for president in February 2007.[70] Americans had grown accustomed, at least notionally, to the idea of a Black president. "Colin Powell's flirtation with a presidential run [in 1996] was a critical turning point in this shift in white attitude," noted sociologist Orlando Patterson, "effectively priming the nation for the possibility of a black candidate."[71] Increasing numbers of constituencies with white majorities had elected African Americans to office, including Illinois, which sent Obama to the Senate with 70 percent of the vote in 2004.[72] In a February 2007 Gallup poll, 94 percent of voters said they were willing to support a "generally well-qualified" Black for president, a number that had risen sharply since 1937, when only 33 percent said they would.[73]

Most political experts assumed that Obama's main challenge in seeking the Democratic nomination would be to win votes from whites. Yet his candidacy initially was greeted with greatest skepticism in the African American community. Black voters initially favored Clinton by 46 to 37 percent in a November 2007 *Wall Street Journal* / NBC News poll.[74] Like many older Black political leaders, they doubted that Obama could win enough white votes to be elected.[75] Consequently, Obama approached the January 2008 Iowa caucuses knowing that he needed a victory to demonstrate that whites would vote for a Black man for president. He succeeded by focusing his appeal on issues that transcended race, such as expanded health care and his early opposition to the war in Iraq, as well as by downplaying issues that white voters tended to associate with Black political leaders, including poverty and affirmative action. After finishing first in Iowa by a healthy margin, Obama won nearly 80 percent of the Black vote in the crucial January 26 South Carolina primary, setting the stage for his nomination. In the November election, Obama won 44 percent of the white vote, considerably better than the average of 39 percent that white Democratic nominees won in the ten elections from 1968 to 2004.[76] Added to the overwhelming support he received from voters of color, Obama won the election by a comfortable margin.

By 2020 openness to Blacks and other candidates of color had grown even more. Ninety-six percent of voters professed their willingness to vote for a Black candidate for president, and 95 percent for a Latino candidate.[77] The field of Democratic contenders featured two well-funded and well-organized African Americans (Booker and Harris) and two less well-resourced Black candidates (Governor Deval Patrick of Massachusetts and Miramar, Florida, mayor Wayne Messam). It also included Julian Castro, a Mexican American, and Asian Americans Gabbard and Yang. Still, by January 2020 none of these candidates had the required number of donors and support in the polls to qualify for the year's first debate. Surveys showed that majorities of Black and Latino voters said they would not be more enthusiastic about nominating a candidate of their race or ethnicity than about nominating a white candidate.[78]

As was the case with Clinton, voters of color in 2020 had a long and positive history with Biden and were unwilling to throw their support to a Black, Latino, or Asian candidate unless they demonstrated an ability to win enough white votes to mount a successful campaign. But failure to catch on in the months leading up to the Iowa and New Hampshire contests led Messam to drop out in November 2019, Harris to drop out in December 2019, and Castro and Booker to drop out in January 2020. Yang, Patrick, and Gabbard exited the race after they failed to gain traction in the first two contests or any of those that followed. Harris in particular hoped that by ending her candidacy early, she would have ample time to make herself attractive as a vice presidential candidate with whoever won the nomination. As the only Black woman holding the office of senator or governor, she was the logical choice: a conventional running mate in terms of career background and a pathbreaking one in terms of social characteristics.

Positive Bias

A fourth historical barrier-buster in presidential elections has been positive bias. Although Kennedy's religion cost him some votes among anti-Catholics, it also won him support among Catholics proud to see one of their own contending for the presidency. In general, anti-Catholic voting hurt Kennedy in the South, and pro-Catholic voting helped him in the much larger and more populous North.[79] Similarly, Romney benefited in some ways from his Mormonism: he won strong support from Republican voters who are Mormon and raised substantial contributions from Mormon donors.

As the first African American major party nominee for president in 2008, Obama secured 95 percent of the Black vote, up from Senator John F. Kerry's 88 percent share in 2004. This prize turned out to be all the more valuable because Black turnout surged from 11 percent of the electorate in 2004 to 13 percent in 2008. Obama also won 66 percent of Latino votes, a 13-point improvement over Kerry's 53 percent showing. The pattern was repeated when Obama sought reelection in 2012 and won 93 percent of the Black vote and 71 percent of Latinos.[80]

Hillary Clinton's campaigns for her party's presidential nomination—nearly successful in 2008 and entirely successful in 2016—were distinctive because she is a woman. In surveys taken from 1937 to 2007, the Gallup Poll found that Americans had become increasingly willing to vote for a "generally well-qualified" woman for president. In 1937 and 1945 only 33 percent said they would consider doing so, but that number rose to 52 percent in 1955, 66 percent in 1971, 73 percent in 1975, 80 percent in 1983, and 88 percent in 2007.[81] About 8 percent of voters in 2015 still said they would not vote for a woman, but their numbers were offset by the many women and some men who were eager to elect the first woman president. In part, this was because the ranks of women meeting the public's career background criteria for president had grown. As recently as 1976, no women served in the Senate and only one was a governor. By 2008 there were nine woman governors and sixteen woman senators, including Clinton, whom New Yorkers elected to the Senate in 2000 and reelected in 2006. By 2015, twenty-seven states had been led by a woman governor and twenty senators were women.[82]

Feminists, however, argued that Clinton confronted unfairly high hurdles when seeking her party's nomination in 2008 because of her gender. Clinton herself protested against "the incredible vitriol that has been engendered" against her "by people who are nothing but misogynists."[83] Her gender-grounded strategy was to claim leadership qualities traditionally associated with men, especially strength. It was enough to bring her close to the nomination but not to win it. In her second bid for the presidency in 2016 Clinton decided to emphasize rather than downplay her gender, telling *Time* magazine, "This really comes down to whether I can encourage and mobilize women to vote for the first woman president."[84] In campaign speeches, she argued, "One of my merits is I'm a woman," weaving women's issues into most elements of her policy agenda, including paid leave for new mothers and equal pay for women.[85]

Clinton faced obstacles related to her gender in both the nomination contest and the general election. Younger women who supported Sanders as their party's 2016 nominee, wrote *Washington Post* digital producer Molly Roberts, "see it as inevitable that one day a woman will occupy the [office] that is oval-shaped. So the necessity of having that occupant be Hillary Clinton, or of having that moment occur in 2017, feels less urgent."[86] But older women solidly supported Clinton in the primaries, enabling her to run more strongly overall among women than men against Sanders in every primary by an average of 11 percentage points.[87]

Many younger women rallied to Clinton in the general election, in large part because of Trump's sexist rhetoric and behavior. "Donald thinks belittling women makes him bigger," Clinton said in their final debate. "He goes after their dignity, their self-worth, and I don't think there is a woman anywhere who doesn't know what that feels like." "Such a nasty woman," Trump replied.[88] In the end, exit polls showed that 54 percent of women voted for Clinton, even as 53 percent of men voted for Trump. This earned her a plurality over Trump in the national popular vote but only a minority of electoral votes.

As was the case with all the other categories of nontraditional candidates, voters in 2020 were more open to the possibility of electing a woman as president than at any time in history: 94 percent. The 6 percent who dissented were more than outnumbered by the 10 percent who said it was "very important" that the Democrats nominate a woman.[89] Nonincumbent women candidates for the House, Senate, and other offices in 2018 actually won at a higher rate than did nonincumbent men. The ranks of women in Congress rose to 127 as a result of that year's midterm elections.[90] Only 17 percent of them were Republicans, however, which prompted GOP recruiting efforts in 2020 that more than doubled the party's female representation in Congress from thirteen to twenty-eight.[91] Still, with six women (four of them senators) seeking the 2020 Democratic presidential nomination, it was hard for any of them to become, as Clinton did in 2016, the party's consensus woman candidate. Klobuchar and Warren ran the strongest campaigns, but neither yielded to the other before both withdrew in early March. Warren stressed that she was "running for president because that's what girls do," and Klobuchar argued that if a woman were as inexperienced in office as Buttigieg, her candidacy would never have gotten as far as his did.[92] In the end, however, Warren centered her campaign on liberal economic issues, and Klobuchar offered herself as the centrist Democrat who could win back the industrial Midwest from Trump.

Not just gender but also sexual and ethnic identity spurred positive as well as negative bias in 2020. When it came to fundraising, Harris scored heavily among Indian Americans, with whom she shared ethnicity on her mother's side, and Buttigieg did the same among LGBT Democrats.[93] Still, even though 86 percent of Democratic voters said they were open to electing a gay president, only 40 percent thought the country was.[94]

Conclusion

Joe Biden's election as the oldest president in history and Kamala Harris's election as the first woman and the first Black and Indian American vice president in 2020 were historic. Like the election of the first Catholic president in 1960, the first African American president in 2008, the first southern president in more than a century in 1964, and the first major party nomination of a woman for president in 2016, they represent an altogether sensible broadening of the talent pool from which the United States draws its chief executives. So does growing public receptivity, as measured by public opinion polls and by nominations and elections to other prominent political offices, to the possibility of choosing future presidents without regard to their religion, age (as opposed to health), race and ethnicity, and sexual identity. Historically, these and other artificial barriers excluded large numbers of potentially excellent presidents from consideration on the basis of social characteristics unrelated to their ability to do the job. Vice presidential succession, changing public attitudes, positive bias, and facing the issue—sometimes in combination—seem likely to be the vehicles of change in the future, just as they have been in the past.

To be sure, this remains a journey in progress. No woman, Latino, Asian, Jewish, Muslim, younger, or LGBTQ person has ever been elected president, although Sanders and Bloomberg (Jewish), Buttigieg (gay, young), and Klobuchar and Warren (women) ran strong races in 2020 and Harris's election as vice president makes her a strong contender for president—perhaps even the presumptive Democratic nominee—in 2024 if Biden retires or 2028 if he doesn't. Polls that ask people if "their neighbors" would be as comfortable as they are with various nontraditional kinds of candidates find lower numbers of support, which may indicate a shallower openness than indicated by the more direct questions.[95] So do polls that allow respondents to say they "have some reservations" about various candidate categories rather than limiting them to a purely negative response.[96] Yet not one of the seven leading candidates for the party's 2020 nomination fits squarely within the white-male-married-straight-Christian-forty-to-seventy template that marked all forty-three eighteenth-, nineteenth-, and twentieth-century presidents and all forty-five of their major party opponents in the presidential election.

The recent broadening of the presidential talent pool to include candidates lacking in governing experience is more worrisome. Virtually without precedent in American history, the public's growing openness to political novices in the presidency originated in the late twentieth century, when frustration with government led many voters first to devalue service in Washington and then to look askance at any experience in governing at all. Reforms of the political parties that devolved control of nominations from party leaders to primary and caucus voters accelerated this process.

Trump's candidacy for the Republican nomination in 2016 came less than a quarter century after the independent campaigns launched in the 1990s by another celebrity business leader, Ross Perot. Perot, like Trump, led in the polls for a period of time. Like Trump, Perot's candidacy caught fire with his appealing performances in a debate setting. Trump was elected, but the shallowness of his understanding of the challenges a president must address was all too apparent in 2016 and, even after four years in office, in 2020.

President of the United States, the most powerful office in the world, is not an entry-level job. Trump's presidency was flawed by many things, but among them was his complete lack of experience in or understanding of the office and its constitutional setting. A candidacy grounded in appeals such as "I'm not part of that mess," "My success in business (or academe or the media or some other realm) proves that I can lead the government," or "I'll pay for my own campaign" may sound good but is ungrounded in the realities of governing a complex country in a complex world.

Presidents need certain skills if they are to lead effectively.[97] Skills of political rhetoric and bargaining seem to be developed best by running for office and serving in government for a period of years. Deals with a Congress whose existence and influence are mandated by the Constitution are different from deals with contractors or developers who can readily be replaced. The same can be said of the subtle but vital capacity to sense the broader public's willingness to be led in different directions at different paces at different times, as opposed to inhabiting an echo chamber of supportive news outlets and social media within an established base of devoted supporters. The challenges of administrative management in government are different from those in the corporate world, much less in the small-scale private companies Trump led without having even to share power with a board of directors or shareholders. Success in the private sector may speak well of a person and usually requires some of these skills. But only politics and government require all of them.[98]

Notes

1. Bill Scher, "How Does a Straight White Male Democrat Run for President?," *Politico*, February 17, 2019; and Jocelyn Kiley and Shiva Maniam, "Lesbian, Gay and Bisexual Voters Remain a Solidly Democratic Bloc," Pew Research Center, October 25, 2016, https://www.pewresearch.org/fact-tank/2016/10/25/lesbian-gay-and-bisexual-voters-remain-a-solidly-democratic-bloc/.

2. A fuller account of the argument that follows is found in Michael Nelson, "Constitutional Qualifications for President," in *Inventing the Presidency*, ed. Thomas E. Cronin (Lawrence: University Press of Kansas, 1989), 1–32.

3. Quoted in Cyril C. Means Jr., "Is Presidency Barred to Americans Born Abroad?," *U.S. News & World Report*, December 23, 1955, 26–30.
4. Quoted in Charles C. Thach Jr., *The Creation of the Presidency* (Baltimore: Johns Hopkins University Press, 1969), 137.
5. Quoted in Means, "Is Presidency Barred to Americans Born Abroad?"
6. U.S. Census Bureau, *Statistical Abstract of the United States 2012* (Lanham, MD: Rowman & Littlefield, 2011), 11; and Jens Manuel Krogstead, Jeffrey S. Passel, and D'Vera Cohn, "Five Facts about Illegal Immigration in the U.S.," Pew Research Center, September 20, 2016, http://www.pewresearch .org/fact-tank/2016/09/20/5-facts-about-illegal-immigration-in-the-u-s/.
7. "Trump's Reversal on Obama Birthplace Conspiracy Stokes More Controversy," *Chicago Tribune*, September 16, 2016.
8. Nick Gass, "Trump Concedes Obama Was Born in the US," *Politico*, September 15, 2016.
9. Charles M. Blow, "Trump: Grand Wizard of Birtherism," *New York Times*, September 19, 2016.
10. Robert Costa and Philip Rucker, "Trump Says Cruz's Canadian Birth Could Be 'Very Precarious' for GOP," *Washington Post*, January 5, 2015.
11. Neal Katyal and Paul Clement, "On the Meaning of 'Natural Born Citizen,'" *Harvard Law Review Forum*, March 11, 2015, http://cdn.harvard lawreview.org/wp-content/uploads/2015/03/vol128_ClementKatyal.pdf.
12. Katie Rogers, "Trump Encourages Racist Conspiracy Theory about Kamala Harris," *New York Times*, August 13, 2020.
13. See, for example, Jack Maskell, *Qualifications for President and the "Natural Born" Citizenship Eligibility Requirement* (Washington, DC: Congressional Research Service, 2011). Reportedly, Biden eliminated Senator Tammy Duckworth of Illinois from consideration as vice president in part because he feared similar legally ungrounded challenges based on her birth in Bangkok to an American military veteran and a Thai mother. Alexander Burns, Jonathan Martin, and Katie Glueck, "How Biden Chose Harris," *New York Times*, August 13, 2020.
14. The exception was Abraham Lincoln, whose previous political experience consisted of several terms in the Illinois legislature and one term in Congress.
15. Michael Nelson, *Trump: The First Two Years* (Charlottesville: University of Virginia Press, 2019), 14, 146–47.
16. They were Martin Van Buren, James Buchanan, and James Blaine.
17. Quoted in David Remnick, "The Joshua Generation," *New Yorker*, November 17, 2008.
18. Stephen F. Hayes, *Cheney: The Untold Story of America's Most Powerful and Controversial Vice President* (New York: HarperCollins, 2007), 307.
19. Matt Flegenheimer, "Joe Biden's Time in Sarah Palin's Shadow," *New York Times*, May 11, 2020.

20. Janet Hook and Colleen McCain Nelson, "WSJ Poll: Hillary Clinton Widens Lead in Primary Race," *Wall Street Journal*, October 20, 2015; and Glenn Thrush, "Party of Two," *Politico Magazine*, July/August 2016.

21. Janie Valencia, "Most Democrats Now Identify as 'Liberal,'" FiveThirtyEight, January 11, 2019, https://fivethirtyeight.com/features/most-democrats-now-identify-as-liberal/.

22. Alan I. Abramowitz, *The Disappearing Center: Engaged Citizens, Polarization, and American Democracy* (New Haven, CT: Yale University Press, 2010), chap. 3.

23. Annie Linskey, "Biden's Promise to Choose a Woman Veep Reignites Hopes of a Female President," *Washington Post*, March 16, 2020; Harper Neidig, "Biden Pledges to Nominate Black Woman to Supreme Court," The Hill, February 25, 2020, https://thehill.com/regulation/court-battles/484656-biden-pledges-to-nominate-black-woman-to-supreme-court.

24. Sydney Ember and Katie Glueck, "Bernie Sanders Endorses Joe Biden for President," *New York Times*, April 13, 2020.

25. "2016 Republican Presidential Nomination," Real Clear Politics, http://www.realclearpolitics.com/epolls/2016/president/us/2016_republican_presidential_nomination-3823.html?utm_source=hootsuite. Accessed 2/3/21.

26. Ryan Grim and Danny Shea, "A Note about Our Coverage of Donald Trump's 'Campaign,'" *Huffington Post*, July 17, 2015, http://www.huffingtonpost.com/entry/a-note-about-our-coverage-of-donald-trumps-campaign_us_55a8fc9ce4b0896514d0fd66.

27. Thomas B. Edsall, "Hurricane Trump," *New York Times*, September 23, 2015.

28. "Rise of the Anti-establishment Presidential Candidates," *Washington Post*, September 14, 2015.

29. Nelson, *Trump: The First Two Years*.

30. Clinton Rossiter, *The American Presidency*, rev. ed. (New York: New American Library, 1960), 193–94.

31. Matthew Choi, "Trump Says a Harris Presidency Is 'No Way for a Woman' to Become President," *Politico*, September 17, 2020.

32. Michael Nelson, "A New Record for Presidential Longevity," Cook Political Report, October 22, 2016, http://cookpolitical.com/story/8954. Accessed 2/3/21.

33. Catherine Lucey and Ken Thomas, "Trump Campaign Boosts Emphasis on Biden's Age, Fitness," *Wall Street Journal*, May 13, 2020; and Joshua Jamerson, "Democratic Rivals Differ on Whether It's Fair to Attack Biden's Fitness for Office," *Wall Street Journal*, September 13, 2019.

34. Amber Phillips, "Who Is Eric Swalwell? And Why Did He Just Tell Joe Biden to 'Pass the Torch,'" *Washington Post*, June 27, 2019.

35. Peter Baker, "As He Questions His Opponent's Health, Trump Finds His Own under Scrutiny," *New York Times*, September 2, 2020.
36. Ashley Parker and Josh Dawsey, "Trump Is Increasingly Preoccupied with Defending His Physical and Mental Health," *Washington Post*, June 22, 2020.
37. Michael Nelson, "The Election: Ordinary Politics, Extraordinary Outcome," in *The Elections of 2000*, ed. Michael Nelson (Washington, DC: CQ Press, 2001), 75.
38. Jeffrey M. Jones, "Some Americans Reluctant to Vote for Mormon, 72-Year-Old Presidential Candidates," Gallup, February 20, 2007, www.gallup.com/poll/26611/Some-Americans-Reluctant-Vote-Mormon-72YearOld-Presidential-Candidates.aspx.
39. Justin McCarthy, "In U.S., Socialist Presidential Candidates Least Appealing," Gallup, June 22, 2015, http://www.gallup.com/poll/183713/socialist-presidential-candidates-least-appealing.aspx.
40. Justin McCarthy, "Less Than Half in U.S. Would Vote for a Socialist for President," Gallup, May 9, 2019, https://news.gallup.com/poll/254120/less-half-vote-socialist-president.aspx?version=print. Those numbers represented dramatic improvements from the time voters were first asked these questions. In 1937 only 46 percent said they were willing to vote for a Jew, and in 1958 only 18 percent said they would consider voting for an atheist.
41. Aaron Blake, "Bernie Sanders: Our First Non-religious President?," *Washington Post*, January 27, 2016.
42. "In Changing U.S. Electorate, Race and Education Remain Stark Dividing Lines," Pew Research Center, June 2, 2020, https://www.pewresearch.org/politics/2020/06/02/in-changing-u-s-electorate-race-and-education-remain-stark-dividing-lines/.
43. Amelia Thomson-DeVeaux, "Why Democrats Struggle to Mobilize a Religious Left," FiveThirtyEight, May 29, 2019, https://fivethirtyeight.com/features/why-democrats-struggle-to-mobilize-a-religious-left/.
44. E. J. Dionne, "Joe Biden Can't 'Hurt God.' He Can End the Catch-22 around Religion," *Washington Post*, August 9, 2020.
45. McCarthy, "Less Than Half in U.S. Would Vote for a Socialist for President."
46. Caitlin O'Kane, "Pete Buttigieg Says 'It's Almost Certain' He Wouldn't Be First Gay President," CBS News, June 17, 2019.
47. "Full Transcript: Ninth Democratic Debate in Las Vegas," NBC News, February 19, 2020, https://www.nbcnews.com/politics/2020-election/full-transcript-ninth-democratic-debate-las-vegas-n1139546.
48. In a 2019 *Politico* / Morning Consult poll, white voters said they were ready to vote for a gay or lesbian candidate by a 1-point majority, but a 4-point

majority of Black voters said they were not. Nathaniel Rakich, "What Happens If Buttigieg Wins Iowa?," FiveThirtyEight, November 18, 2019, https://fivethirtyeight.com/features/what-happens-if-buttigieg-wins-iowa/.

49. Frank Bruni, "Mayor Pete's Gay Reckoning," *New York Times*, February 1, 2020.

50. McCarthy, "Less Than Half in U.S. Would Vote for a Socialist for President."

51. Quoted in Theodore H. White, *The Making of the President, 1960* (New York: Pocket Books, 1961), 128–29.

52. John F. Kennedy, "Address to the Greater Houston Ministerial Association," September 12, 1960, www.americanrhetoric.com/speeches/jfk houstonministers.html.

53. George H. Gallup, *The Gallup Poll: Public Opinion, 1935–1971*, vol. 3 (New York: Random House, 1971), 1605, 1735, 2190; Jones, "Some Americans Reluctant to Vote for Mormon, 72-Year-Old Presidential Candidates"; Lydia Saad, "In U.S., 22% Are Hesitant to Support a Mormon in 2012," Gallup, June 20, 2011, http://www.gallup.com/poll/148100/hesitant-support-mormon-2012.aspx; and McCarthy, "Less Than Half in U.S. Would Vote for a Socialist for President."

54. The charge made by Senator Dianne Feinstein when Barrett was nominated for an appellate court judgeship in 2017.

55. Jones, "Some Americans Are Reluctant to Vote for Mormon, 72-Year-Old Presidential Candidates."

56. Joseph Carroll, "Which Characteristics Are Most Desirable in the Next President?," Gallup, September 17, 2007, www.gallup.com/poll/28693/Which-Characteristics-Most-Desirable-Next-President.aspx.

57. Bud Jackson, "McCain's Age Is a Legitimate Issue," *Politico*, May 22, 2008; and Steve Chapman, "Is McCain Too Old to Be President?," RealClearPolitics, September 9, 2007, www.realclearpolitics.com/articles/2007/09/is_mccain_too_old_to_be_presid.html.

58. Alexander Burns, "McCain and the Politics of Mortality," *Politico*, September 4, 2008.

59. Rick Pearlstein, *Reaganland: America's Right Turn, 1976–1980* (New York: Simon and Schuster, 2020), 369.

60. Burns, "McCain and the Politics of Mortality."

61. "The First Trump-Clinton Presidential Debate Transcript, Annotated," *Washington Post*, September 26, 2016; and Nick Corasanitti, "'We Should Take a Drug Test' before Debate, Donald Trump Says," *New York Times*, October 15, 2016.

62. Adam Edelman, "Donald Trump, 70, Tells Dr. Oz He Feels 'the Same Age' as 39-Year-Old QB Tom Brady," *New York Daily News*, September 15, 2016; and "First Trump-Clinton Presidential Debate Transcript."

63. Rakich, "What Happens If Buttigieg Wins Iowa?"

64. John Wagner, "'I Hope There's an Age Limit': Jimmy Carter Questions Whether He Could Have Handled the Presidency at 80," *Washington Post*, September 18, 2019.

65. McCarthy, "Less Than Half in U.S. Would Vote for a Socialist for President."

66. Andrew Romano, "7 Times Pete Buttigieg Highlighted His Age at the Democratic Debate," Yahoo! News, July 30, 2019, https://news.yahoo.com /7-times-pete-buttigieg-highlighted-his-age-at-the-democratic-debate -032344564.html.

67. Sean Sullivan, "Bernie Sanders, 78, Declares His Age Is an Asset," *Washington Post*, October 25, 2019.

68. Matt Viser and Cleve R. Wootson Jr., "Joe Biden Is a 'Healthy, Vigorous' 77-Year-Old, His Doctor Declares," *Washington Post*, December 17, 2019; and Frank Bruni, "Give Joe Biden His Due," *New York Times*, December 20, 2019.

69. Evan Osnos, *Joe Biden: The Life, the Run, and What Matters Now* (New York: Scribner, 2020), 18.

70. Ronald Goldfarb, "RFK, the Prophet," The Hill, October 31, 2008, https:// thehill.com/blogs/pundits-blog/civil-rights/31853-rfk-the-prophet.

71. Orlando Patterson, "An Eternal Revolution," *New York Times*, November 7, 2008.

72. Rachel L. Swarns, "Quiet Political Shifts as More Blacks Are Elected," *New York Times*, October 14, 2008.

73. Jones, "Some Americans Reluctant to Vote for Mormon, 72-Year-Old Presidential Candidates"; and Linda Feldman, "In 2008, Many Presidential 'Firsts' Are Possible," *Christian Science Monitor*, February 16, 2007.

74. Jonathan Kaufman, "Whites' Great Hope?," *Wall Street Journal*, November 10, 2007.

75. See, for example, Perry Bacon Jr., "Can Obama Count on the Black Vote?," *Time*, January 23, 2007.

76. All 2008 exit poll results are from "President: National Exit Poll," CNN, www.cnn.com/ELECTION/2008/results/polls/#USP00p1. Accessed 2/3/21.

77. McCarthy, "Less Than Half in U.S. Would Vote for a Socialist for President."

78. Jennifer Medina, "Why Voters Don't Seem Interested in Barrier-Breaking Candidates," *New York Times*, November 14, 2019.

79. Philip E. Converse et al., "Stability and Change in 1960: A Reinstating Election," in *Elections and the Political Order*, ed. Angus Campbell et al. (New York: John Wiley and Sons, 1966).

80. "President: Full Results," CNN Politics, https://www.cnn.com/election /2012/results/race/president/#exit-polls.

81. Jones, "Some Americans Reluctant to Vote for Mormon, 72-Year-Old Presidential Candidates."

82. Kate Zernike, "Both Sides Seeking to Be What Women Want," *New York Times*, September 15, 2008.

83. Lois Romano, "Clinton Puts Up a New Fight," *Washington Post*, May 20, 2008.

84. Quoted in Nicholas Kristof, "Clinton, Trump and Sexism," *New York Times*, January 23, 2016.

85. Peter Nicholas, "Clinton Steps Up Efforts to Woo Women Voters," *Wall Street Journal*, September 11, 2015.

86. Molly Roberts, "Why Millennials Are Yawning at the Likely First Female Major-Party Nominee for President," *Washington Post*, June 7, 2016.

87. Barbara Norrander, "Women Vote at Higher Rates Than Men. That Might Help Clinton in November," *Washington Post*, June 27, 2016.

88. "Full Transcript: Third 2016 Presidential Debate," *Politico*, October 20, 2016.

89. McCarthy, "Less Than Half in U.S. Would Vote for a Socialist for President."

90. The number rose still further in 2020, with the number of Republican women in Congress nearly doubling from 2018 while still being only about one-third the number of Democratic women.

91. Michele L. Swers, "More Republican Women Than Before Will Serve in This Congress. Here's Why," *Washington Post*, January 5, 2021.

92. Erin Corbett, "Elizabeth Warren on Being a Woman Running for President: 'That's What Girls Do,'" *Fortune*, April 23, 2019; and Maggie Astor, "'Women Are Held to a Higher Standard,' Klobuchar Says at Debate," *New York Times*, November 20, 2019.

93. Peter Hamby, "Gay Money, Democratic Secret Weapon, Comes out for Buttigieg," *Vanity Fair*, April 25, 2019.

94. Harry Enten, "A Gay President? The Majority of Americans Believe the Country Isn't Ready," CNN Politics, May 4, 2019, https://www.cnn.com/2019/05/04/politics/poll-of-the-week-gay-president/index.html.

95. See, for example, Ledyard King, Sarah Elbeshbishi, and Marco della Carva, "Elizabeth Warren's Latest Hurdle to the Presidency," *USA Today*, September 10, 2019.

96. NBC / Wall Street Journal Survey 19062, February 2019, https://www.wsj.com/public/resources/documents/19062NBCWSJFebruary2019Poll.pdf.

97. Erwin C. Hargrove and Michael Nelson, *Presidents, Politics, and Policy* (Baltimore: Johns Hopkins University Press, 1984), chap. 4.

98. Michael Nelson, "Who Vies for President?," in *Presidential Selection*, ed. Alexander Heard and Michael Nelson (Durham, NC: Duke University Press, 1987), 120–54.

The Presidential Nominations

William G. Mayer

The presidential nomination process was one of the few major aspects of the 2020 elections that was not significantly affected by the COVID-19 pandemic. A number of presidential primaries had to be rescheduled, but by that time the Democratic nomination race had clearly been settled. The Republican nomination was never seriously contested. From a historical perspective, the more noteworthy characteristic of the 2020 nominations was the readiness with which the Democrats rallied around a candidate who hadn't shown much appeal in the supposedly critical Iowa caucuses and New Hampshire primary.

The Democratic Race Takes Shape

The most conspicuous feature of the 2020 Democratic candidate field was its size. There is no simple, universally agreed upon standard for determining who is and who is not a serious candidate for the presidency. Table 1, which lists 26 candidates, is based on previous governmental service, participation in the debates, and performance in polls and the primaries and caucuses. A number of sources list a few more names.[1] Whatever criteria one uses, it was a very large field—far larger than any other set of declared aspirants for either party's nomination in the modern era.

Also worthy of note is how early most candidates officially launched their campaigns. Table 1 shows that by February 19, 2019, there were already eleven announced candidates. By mid-April, six more candidates had entered the race. By way of comparison, of the very large number of Republicans who ran for that party's presidential nomination in 2016, the earliest entrant was Texas senator Ted Cruz, who didn't announce his candidacy until March 23, 2015. On the Democratic side, the first candidate in was Hillary Clinton, who officially started her campaign on April 12, 2015.[2]

The large and early field of Democratic candidates is probably attributable to a number of factors. Many Democrats, of course, believed that

TABLE 1. 2020 Democratic presidential candidates and some basic information about their campaigns

Candidate	Announcement date	Date of filing FEC statement of candidacy	Participated in at least one debate?	Withdrawal date	Amount of money candidate contributed to his or her own campaign
John Delaney	July 28, 2017	August 10, 2017	Yes	January 31, 2020	$1,079,077[e]
Andrew Yang	February 2, 2018	November 6, 2017	Yes	February 11, 2020	$6,000
Tulsi Gabbard	January 11, 2019	January 11, 2019	Yes	March 19, 2020	$75
Julian Castro	January 12, 2019	January 23, 2019[a]	Yes	January 2, 2020	$0
Kirsten Gillibrand	January 15, 2019	March 17, 2019[b]	Yes	August 28, 2019	$78
Kamala Harris	January 21, 2019	January 21, 2019	Yes	December 3, 2019	$0
Marianne Williamson	January 28, 2019	February 4, 2019	Yes	January 10, 2020	$0
Cory Booker	February 1, 2019	February 1, 2019	Yes	January 13, 2020	$0
Elizabeth Warren	February 9, 2019	February 9, 2019[c]	Yes	March 5, 2020	$5,778
Amy Klobuchar	February 10, 2019	February 11, 2019	Yes	March 2, 2020	$0
Bernie Sanders	February 19, 2019	February 19, 2019	Yes	April 8, 2020	$0
Jay Inslee	March 1, 2019	March 1, 2019	Yes	August 21, 2019	$0
John Hickenlooper	March 4, 2019	March 4, 2019	Yes	August 15, 2019	$32,800
Beto O'Rourke	March 14, 2019	March 14, 2019	Yes	November 1, 2019	$0
Tim Ryan	April 4, 2019	April 11, 2019	Yes	October 24, 2019	$0
Eric Swalwell	April 8, 2019	April 8, 2019	Yes	July 8, 2019	$0
Pete Buttigieg	April 14, 2019	April 13, 2019[d]	Yes	March 1, 2020	$0
Seth Moulton	April 22, 2019	May 7, 2019	No	August 23, 2019	$0
Joe Biden	April 25, 2019	April 25, 2019	Yes	None	$0
Michael Bennet	May 2, 2019	May 5, 2019	Yes	February 11, 2020	$2,800

Steve Bullock	May 14, 2019	May 14, 2019	Yes	December 2, 2019	$0
Bill de Blasio	May 16, 2019	May 16, 2019	Yes	September 20, 2019	$0
Joe Sestak	June 23, 2019	July 1, 2019	No	December 1, 2019	$2,800
Tom Steyer	July 9, 2019	July 9, 2019	Yes	February 29, 2020	$315,694,976[f]
Deval Patrick	November 14, 2019	November 14, 2019	No	February 12, 2020	$0
Michael Bloomberg	November 24, 2019	November 21, 2019	Yes	March 4, 2020	$1,075,954,120[g]

Source: Statement of candidacy filing date and candidate contribution data come from the reports filed by the campaigns, available at Federal Election Commission (FEC), fec.gov. All other information is taken from contemporary news reports.

[a]Castro formed an exploratory committee on December 19, 2018.

[b]Gillibrand formed an exploratory committee on January 15, 2019.

[c]Warren formed an exploratory committee on December 31, 2018.

[d]Buttigieg formed an exploratory committee on February 22, 2019.

[e]Figure shown is Delaney's personal contribution through February 29, 2020.

[f]Figure shown is Steyer's personal contribution through March 31, 2020.

[g]Figure shown is Bloomberg's personal contribution through April 30, 2020.

Donald Trump would be highly vulnerable in 2020, making the Democratic nomination an even more valuable prize than usual. Trump's victory in 2016 affected the Democratic race in a second way, by seeming to rewrite the rules of presidential availability. No longer was it necessary to have a substantial record of previous governmental experience. Of the candidates in table 1, three—Andrew Yang, Marianne Williamson, and Tom Steyer—had never held public office. Six others had never served in any office higher than the U.S. House of Representatives, a position that has almost never served as a launching pad for a successful presidential nomination bid.[3] With the exception of Tim Ryan, moreover, none of the representatives who ran had served in the House for more than four terms, nor were any regarded as prominent leaders of their party's congressional delegation. Still, many of these candidates may have said to themselves, If Trump could do it, why not me?

Finally, the large field of Democratic presidential candidates in 2020—and the larger-than-usual number of Republican candidates in 2016—is due to one other noteworthy characteristic of contemporary American politics: even if a candidate is unsuccessful, running for president has lots of advantages and virtually no downside. On the plus side, a presidential candidacy gives the candidate a good platform for talking about pet issues and raising their national profiles. (Of the twenty-six candidates listed in table 1, all but three participated in at least one nationally televised debate.) Andrew Yang, for example, never finished higher than sixth place in any of the Democratic primaries or caucuses, but he was able to gain considerable attention for his favorite policy proposal: a "universal basic income" plan that would give every American adult $1,000 every month, regardless of whether they were working or even seeking work.

Running for president is, of course, a very expensive undertaking. But except for a few extremely wealthy individuals, very little of the money comes from the candidates themselves. Of the twenty-six candidates listed in table 1, sixteen did not contribute a cent to their own campaigns. Six other candidates gave their campaigns $6,000 or less. At the other end of the spectrum, Tom Steyer spent $315 million from his own pocket, and Michael Bloomberg's four-month-long presidential odyssey cost him more than $1 billion—but such spending was clearly exceptional and came from candidates who were so wealthy that it imposed no great hardship on them.

There was a time when running for president may have required a person to give up his or her current office or forgo the opportunity to run for a different office. But as much of the nomination race now takes place in the year before the election, that is no longer the case. Of the seven sitting senators who entered the Democratic race, only one was up for reelection in 2020: Cory Booker, who dropped out in mid-January 2020 and promptly announced that he was running for another term in the Senate (he was easily reelected). And even if Booker had stayed in 'til the bitter end, a New Jersey law allowed him to run for the Senate and the presidency at the same time. Three of the four sitting representatives also ran for reelection after withdrawing from the presidential contest; and Jay Inslee was able to run for another term as governor of Washington after his presidential campaign was over. Having gained no traction in their quests for a presidential nomination, both Steve Bullock and John Hickenlooper then ran for the U.S. Senate.

Table 2 shows the national preference polls of Democratic identifiers conducted by two survey organizations that did regular polls throughout 2019: the Monmouth University Polling Institute and the Quinnipiac University Poll. Both polls show that Joe Biden was generally at the top of the heap, with Vermont senator Bernie Sanders in second place. Compared with candidates like Al Gore in 2000 or Hillary Clinton in 2016, however, Biden was a fairly weak front-runner. Through the second half of 2019 and the first month of 2020, Biden was generally supported by less than 30 percent of the nation's Democrats.

At the end of the invisible primary—the period of presidential campaigning that runs from shortly after the preceding midterm election to the start of the delegate selection season—Biden and Sanders were still one-two in the national polls of Democrats, but two other candidates briefly threatened to dislodge one or both of them from their positions.

The first such contender was California senator Kamala Harris. When Harris announced her candidacy in January 2019, many commentators saw her as one of the Democratic Party's strongest potential challengers against Donald Trump, someone who could increase Black turnout and thus reassemble the coalition that had worked so well for Barack Obama. The high point for her campaign came in late June. On June 19, as part of a plea for "civility" and getting things done in Washington, Biden had talked about his ability to work with Senators James Eastland of Mississippi and Herman Talmadge of Georgia, two ardent segregationists.[4] Eight days later, in the first Democratic debate, Harris said she had found Biden's comments about the southern senators "hurtful" and also criticized him because he had "worked with them to oppose busing." Biden responded by defending his overall record on civil rights, pointedly mentioning his service as Barack Obama's vice president, and saying that he had only

TABLE 2. Presidential nomination preferences of national Democratic identifiers during the 2020 invisible primary (in percentages)

	Biden	Sanders	Warren	Harris	O'Rourke	Buttigieg	Bloomberg	Klobuchar	Yang
MONMOUTH									
January 25–27, 2019	29	16	8	11	7	0	4	2	1
March 1–4, 2019	28	25	8	10	6	*	2	3	1
April 11–15, 2019	27	20	6	8	4	8	n/a	1	*
May 16–20, 2019	33	15	10	11	4	6	n/a	3	1
June 12–17, 2019	32	14	15	8	3	5	n/a	1	2
August 16–20, 2019	19	20	20	8	2	4	n/a	1	3
September 23–29, 2019	25	15	28	5	1	5	n/a	1	2
Oct. 30–Nov. 3, 2019	23	20	23	5	n/a	9	n/a	2	3
December 4–8, 2019	26	21	17	n/a	n/a	8	5	4	3
January 16–20, 2020	30	23	14	n/a	n/a	6	9	5	3
QUINNIPIAC									
March 21–25, 2019	29	19	4	8	12	4	n/a	2	*
April 26–29, 2019	38	11	12	8	5	10	n/a	1	1
May 16–20, 2019	35	16	13	8	5	5	n/a	2	1
June 6–10, 2019	30	19	15	7	3	8	n/a	1	1
June 28–July 1, 2019	22	13	14	20	1	4	n/a	1	1

July 25–28, 2019	34	11	15	12	2	6	n/a	1	2
August 1–5, 2019	32	14	21	7	2	5	n/a	1	1
August 21–26, 2019	32	15	19	7	1	5	n/a	1	3
September 19–23, 2019	25	16	27	3	2	7	n/a	2	2
October 4–7, 2019	26	16	29	3	1	4	n/a	2	3
October 11–13, 2019	27	11	30	4	2	8	n/a	2	2
October 17–21, 2019	21	15	28	5	1	10	n/a	3	1
November 21–25, 2019	24	13	14	3	n/a	16	3	3	2
December 4–9, 2019	29	17	15	n/a	n/a	9	5	3	4
December 11–15, 2019	30	16	17	n/a	n/a	9	7	3	3
January 8–12, 2020	25	19	16	n/a	n/a	8	6	4	5
January 22–27, 2020	26	21	15	n/a	n/a	6	8	7	3

Source: Monmouth University Polls are taken from www.monmouth.edu/polling-institute/reports/ (accessed October 1, 2020).
Quinnipiac University Polls are taken from www.poll.qu.edu (accessed October 1, 2020).

Note: Results are shown only for candidates who received at least 5 percent of the vote in at least one poll. Most polls included a number of other candidates. "N/a" indicates that the candidate was not included in the list read to survey respondents, either because the candidate had not announced yet or because the candidate had withdrawn from the race.

*indicates the candidate received less than 0.5 percent of the vote.

opposed "busing ordered by the Department of Education."[5] The whole exchange lasted only about four minutes, but it was widely featured in media coverage of the debate. A later news story would say that Harris had "landed perhaps the hardest and clearest punch of the early primary debate cycle."[6] The result, according to the Quinnipiac Poll, was that the number of people who said they intended to vote for Harris in the primaries almost tripled, from 7 percent in early June to 20 percent in a poll that was conducted in the four days immediately after the debate (June 28–July 1).

But Harris was unable to sustain the momentum. By the end of July, her support had fallen to 12 percent, then fell further to 7 percent in early August and 3 percent in mid-September. Part of the problem was her inability to find a consistent, compelling message. "What doomed her candidacy," said one Democratic pollster, "is there just wasn't any clear rationale. She didn't give the voters . . . a clear sense of 'why am I doing this.'"[7] Before being elected to the Senate in 2016, Harris had spent thirteen years as a prosecutor, and in a more normal year would probably have placed great emphasis on this experience. In 2020, however, with the Black Lives Matter movement a pervasive force, claiming to be the person who put lots of criminals in jail, especially minority criminals, was not likely to be a winning theme in the Democratic Party. She also couldn't decide whether to target the far-left wing of the party or to position herself as a more moderate alternative to candidates like Bernie Sanders. On several occasions, for example, Harris endorsed a Medicare for All health-care plan that would have eliminated private insurance, then claimed later that she wanted to retain a role for private insurance.[8]

The campaign's inability to resolve such issues was made more difficult by what numerous accounts suggest was a very flawed and chaotic campaign, with "competing power centers" that made it "unclear who, exactly, is in charge."[9] To make matters worse, none of her top campaign people had ever worked in a national campaign before. As is often the case with struggling presidential campaigns, it was money troubles that finally drove her out of the race. She announced her withdrawal on December 3, saying that her campaign "simply doesn't have the financial resources we need to continue."[10]

The campaign of Massachusetts senator Elizabeth Warren appeared to offer a considerably more potent challenge to the two front-runners. In an earlier era, when presidential nominations were settled by negotiations among a relatively small number of party leaders, Warren might have made an ideal candidate, a nice compromise between the Biden and Sanders forces. As a prominent critic of Wall Street and the banking industry and a major force behind the creation of the Consumer Financial Protection Bureau, she had unassailable progressive credentials, especially on economic issues, but without being a declared socialist and all the other baggage that made Sanders look like an almost certain loser in a general election. Unfortunately, as many analysts of the nomination process have lamented, nothing in the modern, plebiscitary system takes second choices into account.[11] Primaries allow voters to indicate only their first choice among the candidates. Caucuses permit a certain amount of switching, but mostly by the followers of the non-front-runners.[12]

Warren's principal strategy for increasing her support was to impress the voters as a candidate who went well beyond the general rhetoric and vague promises that often pass for policy discussion in a presidential campaign. From early in her candidacy, she released a blizzard of policy papers, detailing her plans concerning a long list of issues including taxes, health care, student debt, child care, corporate governance, corruption, climate change, the opioid crisis, and gun control. Her higher education plan, for example, promised that on the first day of her presidency, she would take advantage of a little-used provision in the Higher Education Act to cancel student loan debt entirely for 75 percent of Americans who had such debt and to provide at least some relief for 95 percent.[13] That done, she would seek legislation to eliminate the cost of tuition and fees at all public two- and four-year colleges and provide sizable increases in both Pell grants and aid to historically Black colleges.[14] As this example illustrates, Warren's plans were rarely of the sort that could be described as timid or halfway, merely tinkering around the edges of existing policy. "Big structural change" is the phrase that recurs like a mantra in almost all of her position papers. "Our country is in a time of crisis," she told the California Democratic Convention. "The time for small ideas is over."[15]

Regardless of what one thinks of her various proposals, one has to give Warren credit for specificity and vision. A report in May 2019 concluded, "Elizabeth Warren leads the Democratic 'ideas primary.' . . . Her unofficial campaign slogan has become: 'I have a plan for that.'"[16] In June, the *New York Times* observed, "By pushing out so many proposals so early, Ms. Warren has framed much of the debate in the Democratic primary race. . . . Now, other Democratic campaigns are being measured against Ms. Warren's policy benchmarks."[17] And in the short term, her approach seemed to be working. Four different Quinnipiac polls conducted between mid-September and mid-October 2019 showed her in first place, narrowly ahead of Biden and substantially ahead of Sanders (see table 2).

As the polls also show, however, in late October and early November Warren's numbers declined significantly, nationally as well as in Iowa and New Hampshire. The timing suggests that Warren's candidacy was undone by two principal factors. The first was the impressive resilience of the Sanders campaign. Whatever his other weaknesses, Sanders had gained great credit with many on the left for the campaign he ran against Hillary Clinton in 2016. The chair of one progressive group observed, "Bernie Sanders ran—in 2016—an incredible campaign that won 23 contests, changed the narrative in this country about what is possible for progressives, and even moved the entire Democratic Party to the left."[18] For those on the left who were undecided, the Sanders campaign received a major boost in mid-October when three members of the "Squad"—a high-profile group of far-left Democratic House members—endorsed the Vermont senator: Ilhan Omar on October 15, Alexandria Ocasio-Cortez on October 19, and Rashida Tlaib on October 29.[19] Although their endorsements were primarily based on Sanders's policies, they also reflected the fact that when the Squad members were attacked during the Trump presidency, Sanders was one of the few politicians who quickly, regularly came to their defense.[20] The Squad members' backing came at a critical time in the campaign: on October 4, the Sanders campaign revealed that the candidate had had a heart attack several days earlier, raising serious questions about whether the then-seventy-eight-year-old senator had the stamina to serve as president. With the Squad behind him, the leader of another major progressive group would later say, "You started to see dominoes fall after that."[21] In December, a number of important progressive groups that had been hesitating between Sanders and Warren came out in favor of Sanders.

At almost the same time, Warren started to learn what many other campaigns have also found: that being specific has disadvantages as well as advantages. Few policies bring unalloyed good while imposing substantial costs on no one. And the more specific a candidate is, the more those costs become apparent. As Warren released her plans for a Green New Deal, Medicare for All, universal child care, student-debt forgiveness, affordable housing, and free college, it gradually became clear that she was calling for a huge increase in federal spending; and while she insisted that she could pay for all her promises solely through increased taxes on corporations and the wealthy, even many Democratic economists were skeptical.[22] Health care proved to be a particular stumbling block. Like many other Democratic candidates, especially on the left, Warren was a supporter of Medicare for All. Yet her health-care policy paper had one conspicuous blank space, especially noticeable precisely because her other plans were so much more specific: there was no indication as to how she intended to pay for it. In the fourth Democratic debate, held on October 15, a number of the other candidates confronted Warren on this issue.

The critical segment of that debate began when moderator Mark Lacey of the *New York Times* noted that Warren had "proposed some sweeping plans . . . but you have not specified how you're going to pay for the most expensive plan, Medicare for all. Will you raise taxes on the middle class to pay for it, yes or no?" Warren's answer was evasive: she said that "costs will go up for the wealthy and for big corporations, and for hard-working middle-class families, costs will go down," but never addressed the tax question. Lacey pressed her further: "Senator Sanders acknowledges he's going to raise taxes on the middle-class to pay for Medicare for All. You've endorsed his plan. Should you acknowledge it, too?" Again, Warren ducked the question.

South Bend, Indiana, mayor Pete Buttigieg jumped on her response: "We heard it tonight, a yes or no question that didn't get a yes or no answer. Look, this is why people here in the Midwest are so frustrated with Washington in general and Capitol Hill in particular. Your signature, Senator, is to have a plan for everything. Except this. No plan has been laid out to explain how a multi-trillion-dollar hole in this Medicare for all plan . . . is supposed to get filled." Another candidate, Senator Amy Klobuchar, attacked Warren on the same grounds: "At least Bernie's being honest here and saying how he's going to pay for this and that taxes are going to go up. And I'm sorry, Elizabeth, but you have not said that, and I think we owe it to the American people to tell them where we're going to send the invoice."[23]

In the first two weeks of November, Warren tried to answer her critics. She first released a financing plan that claimed it was possible to finance a Medicare for All program without increasing middle-class taxes "by one penny."[24] Though sufficiently detailed and backed up by an assortment of expert authorities, the plan was widely criticized for relying on overly optimistic assumptions about costs and savings. For example, the most widely cited cost estimate of Medicare for All, produced by a left-leaning think tank called the Urban Institute, stated that the program would require $34 trillion in new federal spending in its first ten years. In contrast, Warren claimed that it would only require another $20.5 trillion. Then, on November 15, Warren announced that in her first two years as president, she would adopt a more incremental approach, seeking only to reduce health-care costs and add a so-called public option to the existing system.

Not until year three would she try to pass legislation that would "complete the transition to Medicare for All."[25]

Warren's new plan seemed to please no one. Supporters of the more moderate candidates still insisted that her plan was too radical. Of her financing scheme, the Biden campaign commented, "The mathematical gymnastics in this plan are all geared toward hiding a simple truth from voters: It's impossible to pay for Medicare for All without middle class tax increases. To accomplish this sleight of hand, her proposal dramatically understates its cost, overstates its savings, inflates the revenue, and pretends that an employer payroll tax increase is something else."[26] Her proposal to stretch out the transition period was described by an adviser to Pete Buttigieg as "a transparently political attempt to paper over a very serious policy problem, which is that she wants to force 150 million people off their private insurance—whether they like it or not."[27]

Many on the left were equally unhappy. In their eyes, Warren had waffled on a previous commitment; unlike Sanders, she was no longer an unalloyed champion of one of their favorite policies. Said the copresident of a national nurses union: "We know that there are ample opportunities for politicians to compromise on Medicare for All, and we know, having worked with Senator Sanders before, that he won't compromise when people's health is at stake." The president of Physicians for a National Health Program opined, "Doing this [Medicare for All] in stages creates a political danger and an opening for opponents to prevent further progress. The longer the rollout, the more political risk."[28] On the day Warren ended her campaign, a report in the New York Times noted that the Medicare episode "captured a fundamental pain point for her candidacy: She was too much of an insider for those demanding revolution, and too much of an outsider for those who wanted to tinker with the system and focus on beating Mr. Trump."[29]

Democrats: The Delegate Selection Season

The Democratic delegate selection process began, as it has in every election cycle since 1976, with the Iowa caucuses, which were held on February 3. Iowa may find its preeminence challenged in 2024, however, because the biggest story out of the 2020 caucuses was the mess that ensued in the state party's effort to count the votes. For several days, the campaigns of both Bernie Sanders and Pete Buttigieg were able to plausibly declare victory, with most of the other campaigns insisting that they too had done very well.[30] The caucuses eventually produced three different measures of candidate support.[31] Sanders led in the initial and final expressions of preferences, and Buttigieg narrowly won the most state delegate equivalents. Warren came in third by all three measures. (For results of all Democratic primaries and caucuses, see table 3.)

Next on the calendar was the New Hampshire primary, on February 11. This, too, turned out to be a close battle between Sanders and Buttigieg, though this time there was no confusion in the counting. In the end, Sanders won by a bit more than 1 percentage point, 25.6 percent to 24.3 percent. Amy Klobuchar finished third, with 19.7 percent, thus allowing her to claim that she had exceeded expectations and had momentum for the ensuing contests. Though New Hampshire has traditionally shown a pronounced favoritism for candidates from the other New England states, Elizabeth Warren slumped to a distant fourth, with 9.2 percent of the vote.

In an effort to ensure that a diverse set of states would each have a moment in the spotlight and, thus, a chance to evaluate the candidates and register its preferences, Democratic Party rules dictated that the next delegate selection event would take place in Nevada. Like Iowa, Nevada chose its delegates through a caucus-convention system, a method that has traditionally favored candidates with fervent, though sometimes narrow, followings, such as Jesse Jackson, Pat Robertson—and Bernie Sanders.[32] True to form, Nevada gave Sanders his first solid victory of the 2020 season. Sanders won 47 percent of the county delegates, versus 20 percent for Joe Biden and 14 percent for Pete Buttigieg.

Along with the results from Iowa and New Hampshire, Sanders's Nevada victory led many major news organizations—including the *New York Times*, NBC News, National Public Radio, *60 Minutes*, the BBC, and FiveThirtyEight—to declare that he was now the "front-runner" for the Democratic nomination.[33] Though media pundits are notoriously quick to render such judgments, in this case their pronouncements were supported by a good deal of survey evidence. According to the realclearpolitics.com website, which collects polling results from a large number of survey organizations, Sanders was the leading candidate in twenty-two distinct polls of the nation's Democrats conducted between February 4 and February 28. (Biden led in one poll during this period; another had the two candidates tied.) Eleven of these surveys showed Sanders with a double-digit lead over the rest of the field.

For some time, the Biden campaign had viewed the South Carolina primary, on February 29, as its ace in the hole, the "firewall" that would save the former vice president in case of poor showings in some of the earlier

TABLE 3. 2020 Democratic presidential primary and caucus results (in percentages)

Date	State	Biden	Sanders	Warren	Bloomberg
PRIMARIES					
February 11	New Hampshire	8.4	25.6	9.2	1.6[a]
February 29	South Carolina	48.6	19.8	7.1	—
March 3	Alabama	63.3	16.5	5.7	11.7
March 3	Arkansas	40.6	22.4	10.0	16.7
March 3	California	27.9	36.0	13.2	12.1
March 3	Colorado	24.6	37.0	17.6	18.5
March 3	Maine	33.4	32.4	15.6	11.8
March 3	Massachusetts	33.4	26.6	21.4	11.7
March 3	Minnesota	38.6	29.9	15.4	8.3
March 3	North Carolina	43.0	24.2	10.5	13.0
March 3	Oklahoma	38.7	25.4	13.4	13.9
March 3	Tennessee	41.7	25.0	10.4	15.7
March 3	Texas	34.6	29.9	11.4	14.4
March 3	Utah	18.4	36.1	16.2	15.4
March 3	Vermont	21.9	50.6	12.5	9.4
March 3	Virginia	53.3	23.2	10.8	9.7
March 10	Idaho	48.9	42.4	2.6	2.4
March 10	Michigan	52.9	36.3	1.6	4.6
March 10	Mississippi	81.0	14.8	0.6	2.5
March 10	Missouri	60.1	34.6	1.2	1.5
March 10	Washington	37.9	36.6	9.2	7.9
March 17	Arizona	50.0	37.4	6.6	—
March 17	Florida	62.0	22.8	1.9	8.4
March 17	Illinois	58.9	36.2	1.5	1.5
April 7	Wisconsin	62.9	31.7	1.5	1.0
April 10	Alaska	55.3	44.7	—	—
April 28	Ohio	72.4	16.7	3.5	3.2
May 2	Kansas	76.8	23.2	—	—
May 12	Nebraska	76.8	14.1	6.3	—
May 19	Oregon	66.0	20.6	9.6	—
May 22	Hawaii	55.9	30.8	4.8	1.3
June 2	Dist. of Columbia	76.0	10.4	12.8	—
June 2	Indiana	76.5	13.6	2.9	1.0
June 2	Maryland	83.7	7.8	2.6	0.6
June 2	Montana	74.5	14.7	8.0	—
June 2	New Mexico	73.3	15.1	5.9	—

(continued)

TABLE 3 *(continued)*

Date	State	Biden	Sanders	Warren	Bloomberg
June 2	Pennsylvania	79.3	18.0	—	—
June 2	Rhode Island	76.7	14.9	4.3	—
June 2	South Dakota	77.5	22.5	—	—
June 9	Georgia	84.9	9.4	2.0	0.7
June 9	West Virginia	65.4	12.2	3.1	2.0
June 23	Kentucky	67.9	12.1	2.8	—
June 23	New York	64.6	16.2	4.7	2.2
July 7	Delaware	89.4	7.5	3.1	—
July 7	New Jersey	84.9	14.6	—	—
July 11	Louisiana	79.5	7.4	2.4	1.6
August 11	Connecticut	84.9	11.5	—	—
CAUCUSES					
February 3	Iowa	15.8	26.2	18.1	*
February 22	Nevada	20.2	46.8	9.7	—
March 10	North Dakota	39.5	52.8	2.5	0.8
April 17	Wyoming	72.2	27.8	—	—

Source: thegreenpapers.com (accessed November 15, 2020).

— indicates that a candidate was not listed on that state's ballot.

*indicates that a candidate received less than 0.5 percent of the vote.

aBloomberg's votes in New Hampshire were write-ins.

states. The campaign probably did not anticipate, however, that its candidate would perform quite so badly in the three previous events. Biden came in fourth in Iowa, fifth in New Hampshire. He did finish second in Nevada, but lagged 27 points behind Sanders.

But South Carolina played to Biden's strengths—and accentuated some of Sanders's key weaknesses. Most importantly, South Carolina was the first delegate selection event that featured a significant number of Black voters. Polls had long shown Biden doing disproportionately well among Blacks, presumably because of his record as Barack Obama's vice president. Sanders, by contrast, had shown conspicuously little appeal to Black voters in his 2016 presidential nomination race. Perhaps because his previous campaigns had taken place in lily-white Vermont, or perhaps because as a socialist he tended to emphasize economic as opposed to racial issues, Blacks had never responded to Sanders as fervently as many whites had. In 2016, Sanders split the white vote evenly with Clinton, 49 percent to 49 percent. But Clinton trounced Sanders among Black voters, 79 percent to 20 percent.[34] If some South Carolina Black voters were starting to waver in their support for Biden, they were probably reassured when, just three days before Election Day, Biden was endorsed by Representative Jim Clyburn (D-SC), the highest-ranking African American in the House and an especially influential figure among South Carolina Democrats.

Less well known was that Sanders also had trouble winning support from southern whites. In 2016, Sanders won the non-southern white vote, 52 percent to 46 percent, while losing the southern white vote to Clinton, 43 percent to 55 percent. In addition, though Biden's second-place finish in Nevada was hardly impressive, the other non-Sanders candidates had done even worse. Anyone who had hoped that Buttigieg, Klobuchar, or Warren might emerge as a serious rival to Sanders and Biden had to have second thoughts after the Nevada voters weighed in.

Finally, with Sanders's new front-runner status came increased scrutiny from the press—and increased criticism from the other candidates. Just one day after his victory in Nevada, Sanders provided a golden opportunity to his opponents when he offered partial praise for Cuban dictator Fidel Castro in an interview on the CBS News program *60 Minutes*: "We're very opposed to the authoritarian nature of Cuba but you know, it's unfair to simply say everything is bad. You know? When Fidel Castro came into office, you know what he did? He had a massive literacy program. Is that a bad thing? Even though Fidel Castro did it?"[35] The other candidates were quick to pounce on his comment. Former New York City mayor Michael Bloomberg tweeted, "Fidel Castro left a dark legacy of forced labor camps, religious repression, widespread poverty, firing squads, and the murder of thousands of his own people. But sure, Bernie, let's talk about his literacy program." Pete Buttigieg wrote, "After four years of looking on in horror as Trump cozied up to dictators, we need a president who will be extremely clear in standing against regimes that violate human rights abroad. We can't risk nominating someone who doesn't recognize this."[36]

The result, in the final week before the South Carolina primary, was a remarkable coalescing of the Democratic electorate around the candidacy of Joe Biden. As shown in table 4, on February 21, the day before the Nevada caucuses, Biden had only a narrow lead over Sanders in the South Carolina polls, 24 percent to 21 percent. Seven days later, Biden's lead had grown to 13 percentage points. In the actual voting, Biden scored a decisive triumph, winning 49 percent of the vote to just 20 percent for Sanders and 11 percent for Tom Steyer. According to the National Election Pool exit

TABLE 4. How pro-Biden momentum transformed the Democratic nomination race just before and after the South Carolina primary (in percentages)

THE SOUTH CAROLINA PRIMARY

	Polls as of February 21	Polls as of February 28	Actual vote (February 29)	Gain (+) or loss (−)
Biden	24	37	49	+25
Sanders	21	24	20	−1
Steyer	16	13	11	−5
Buttigieg	10	11	8	−2
Warren	8	8	7	−1
Klobuchar	7	5	3	−4

SUPER TUESDAY PRIMARIES

	Final pre–South Carolina polls	Actual vote	Gain (+) or loss (−)
CALIFORNIA			
Biden	12	28	+16
Sanders	32	36	+4
Warren	15	13	−2
Bloomberg	11	12	+1
TEXAS			
Biden	20	35	+15
Sanders	26	30	+4
Warren	13	11	−2
Bloomberg	19	14	−5
NORTH CAROLINA			
Biden	25	43	+18
Sanders	20	23	+3
Warren	11	10	−1
Bloomberg	16	13	−3
VIRGINIA			
Biden	19	53	+34
Sanders	28	23	−5
Warren	17	11	−6
Bloomberg	17	10	−7

(continued)

TABLE 4 *(continued)*

SUPER TUESDAY PRIMARIES

	Final pre–South Carolina polls	Actual vote	Gain (+) or loss (−)
MASSACHUSETTS			
Biden	9	33	+24
Sanders	25	27	+2
Warren	17	21	+4
Bloomberg	13	12	−1
COLORADO			
Biden	10	25	+15
Sanders	30	37	+7
Warren	18	18	0
Bloomberg	12	18	+6

Source: Poll numbers for South Carolina are the realclearpolitics.com polling average on the days indicated. Figures for California, Texas, and North Carolina are also the realclearpolitics.com average as of the day before the South Carolina primary (February 28). Numbers for Virginia are taken from the Data for Progress survey of February 23–25, 2020. Figures for Massachusetts are from the WBUR/MassINC survey of February 23–26. Colorado numbers are an average of the Magellan survey of February 24–25 and Data for Progress survey of February 23–25.

poll, 56 percent of the South Carolina primary electorate was Black, and Biden whipped Sanders among such voters, 61 percent to 17 percent. But Biden also beat Sanders among white voters, albeit more narrowly, 33 percent to 29 percent. Actually, Biden won a plurality of almost every major group in the Palmetto State: men and women; liberals, moderates, and conservatives; Democrats and independents; voters who said their most important issue was race relations, health care, climate change, or income inequality; those who most wanted a candidate who agreed with them on the issues and those whose principal concern was to beat Trump. The only groups who stuck with Sanders were young voters (who constituted just 11 percent of the electorate) and those who said they never attended religious services (17 percent).

The 2020 version of Super Tuesday took place on March 3, when fourteen states and American Samoa held their primaries. In the scant four days between the South Carolina primary and Super Tuesday, the nation's

Democrats rallied solidly behind Biden. On March 1, just one day after South Carolina, Pete Buttigieg, his strong showings in Iowa and New Hampshire notwithstanding, ended his candidacy. One day after that, he endorsed Biden. On March 2, Amy Klobuchar withdrew from the race; in her withdrawal speech, she too endorsed Biden. Table 4 compares the polls in six major Super Tuesday states on the eve of the South Carolina primary and the final vote in each of these states. In every instance, Biden gained at least 15 percent of the vote in the final four days before the voting.

Super Tuesday was also noteworthy for being the first time when another major candidate, multibillionaire Michael Bloomberg, was listed on the ballots. On March 5, 2019, Bloomberg had announced that he would not be a candidate for the 2020 Democratic presidential nomination. But over time, he seemed to have grown progressively more dissatisfied with the Democratic field and more optimistic about his own prospects. On November 24, Bloomberg threw his hat in the ring. By that time, it was no longer possible to mount a serious campaign in the first four states, so he set Super Tuesday as the date of his initial encounter with the Democratic primary electorate.

Besides his late entrance, Bloomberg's candidacy was noteworthy for the furious pace at which he spent from his considerable fortune, putting such previous big spenders as Ross Perot, Steve Forbes, Jon Corzine, and Meg Whitman to shame. According to a report filed with the Federal Election Commission, Bloomberg spent $1.051 billion between the launching of his campaign in late November and the end of March 2020.[37] And at one point, it seemed to be paying off. As of mid-February, various polls showed Bloomberg with about 20 percent of the vote in such key, delegate-rich states as California, Texas, North Carolina, and Virginia.

Unfortunately for Bloomberg, his first appearance in a candidate debate, on February 19, was a disaster. Attacked on a variety on counts, Bloomberg seemed strikingly unprepared to answer the charges. Just a few minutes into the debate, Elizabeth Warren delivered a particularly harsh denunciation: "So I'd like to talk about who we're running against, a billionaire who calls women 'fat broads' and 'horse-faced lesbians.' And, no, I'm not talking about Donald Trump. I'm talking about Mayor Bloomberg. Democrats are not going to win if we have a nominee who has a history of hiding his tax returns, of harassing women, and of supporting racist [policies] like redlining and stop and frisk. . . . Democrats take a huge risk if we just substitute one arrogant billionaire for another."[38] In the end, Bloomberg averaged just 13 percent of the vote in the fourteen Super Tuesday states. His only victory that day was in American Samoa.

Biden won ten of the fourteen state primaries on Super Tuesday, with Sanders winning the other four, including California. Like Bloomberg, Warren came up empty, even coming in third in her home state of Massachusetts. This reduced the candidate field still further. On March 4, Bloomberg exited the race and endorsed Biden. Warren dropped out on March 5, though to avoid angering her far-left constituency, she declined to endorse Biden until April 15, by which time Sanders had ended his candidacy. A number of the earlier withdrawers from the race also endorsed Biden in early March: Beto O'Rourke on March 2, Kamala Harris on March 8, Cory Booker on March 9, and Andrew Yang on March 10.

On paper, the Sanders campaign was by no means finished after Super Tuesday. When all the March 3 votes were tallied, Sanders's victory in the California primary meant that Biden had a comparatively small lead in the delegate count: 714 for the former vice president to 605 for Sanders.[39] But never again would the race be that close. Biden won all five of the state primaries on March 10 and swept the three major primaries held on March 17, including Florida and Illinois. Outside of the Washington state primary on March 10, none of these elections was even close. Sanders's only victories during this period came in the North Dakota caucuses, the Northern Marianas Islands convention, and the Democrats Abroad primary.

It was only after Biden's victory was reasonably secure that the COVID pandemic began to disrupt the Democratic primaries. The Ohio primary, originally scheduled to take place on March 17, was pushed back to April 28. Over the next several months, thirteen primaries and one state caucus were moved to a later date in the (futile) hope that the pandemic would abate by then. Six states held their primaries after the June 9 date that had been established as the end of the "window" in which Democratic national rules required all primaries and caucuses to take place. (All were granted a waiver by the Democratic National Committee's Rules and Bylaws Committee.) Connecticut didn't hold its primary until August 11, six days before the start of the national convention.

Fortunately for the Democrats, the party's presidential nomination race had been effectively resolved before the COVID lockdown began, so that even the perennially suspicious Sanders supporters couldn't complain that their candidate had been done in by the altered calendar. Sanders made one last stand against Biden in the Wisconsin primary, a state in which he had handily beaten Hillary Clinton four years earlier. This time, Biden beat Sanders by almost 2–1. One day later, on April 8, Sanders formally ended his candidacy.

Table 5 shows some of the major demographic and attitudinal factors that affected the Biden and Sanders votes in the Democratic primaries, based on the combined results of the National Election Pool exit polls in twenty-one primaries. Biden ran better among Blacks, older voters, Democrats, and moderates. Sanders won a plurality of the votes cast by Hispanics, younger voters, independents, and the very liberal. Sanders voters were more concerned to find a candidate who agreed with them on the issues; Biden voters placed greater priority on beating Trump. Biden fared better among voters who thought race relations was the most important issue; Sanders's best issue was income inequality.

Why Biden Won

How did the Democrats, long regarded as the more fractious of the two American parties, manage to achieve such striking unity around a candidate who had, up until South Carolina, never seemed to have much appeal to the party's electorate?[40] A number of factors helped set the Biden bandwagon in motion in 2020. Most important was that, by the time the votes were tallied in Nevada, the Democratic race appeared to have narrowed to two real possibilities: Biden and Sanders. And whatever his other weaknesses, Biden seemed like a far stronger candidate in the general election. Finding an electable nominee is, of course, a significant concern in every presidential nomination contest, but it was particularly important to the Democrats in 2020, given their hatred of Trump. As we will see when we look at Trump's approval ratings, the incumbent president had virtually no support at all among the nation's Democrats. Indeed, sizable numbers considered him to be "the worst president America has ever had."[41] The result is vividly shown by the fifth item in table 5, which asked Democrats whether the party should nominate a candidate who "agrees with you on the issues" or one who could "beat Trump." Sixty-three percent of the exit poll respondents gave higher priority to beating Trump, while just 34 percent cared more about agreement on the issues. However much their hearts may have been with Sanders, many Democrats clearly worried that his leftist policy positions made him unelectable, that America just wasn't ready for a socialist president.

Questions of electability aside, many of the other candidates were plainly irritated by the behavior of Sanders's supporters and what they felt was Sanders's failure to restrain them more energetically. Warren articulated the complaint most explicitly, in an interview with MSNBC host Rachel Maddow on the day after her withdrawal.

TABLE 5. Who voted for whom in the 2020 Democratic presidential primaries

	Percentage of the primary electorate	Percentage voting for Biden	Percentage voting for Sanders
All voters		41	31
Gender			
Men	43	38	36
Women	57	44	28
Race			
White	63	39	30
Black	17	65	18
Hispanic	15	28	46
Asian	3	n/a	n/a
Other	3	n/a	n/a
Age			
18–29	13	16	62
30–44	21	26	47
45–64	37	47	23
65 and older	29	55	14
Party identification			
Democratic	70	45	28
Independent	27	30	40
Republican	3	n/a	n/a
Ideology			
Very liberal	25	24	51
Somewhat liberal	36	40	31
Moderate	31	55	18
Conservative	8	n/a	n/a
Should Democrats nominate someone who . . .			
Agrees with you on the issues	34	30	44
Can beat Trump	63	46	24
Which issue mattered most?			
Race relations	9	49	24
Health care	41	44	31
Climate change	21	37	32
Income inequality	22	32	38

Source: Entries represent the percentage of the primary vote received in twenty-one Democratic primaries held from February 11 to March 17, weighted by state turnout. "N/a" indicates that there were so few respondents in the given category that the results were not reported in most exit polls. Results for individual state exit polls are from CNN.com.

MADDOW: There have been some really untoward attacks by Senator Sanders' supporters, not by him. . . . His supporters have called you a snake. . . . They've called you a traitor.

WARREN: You know, it's not just about me. I think there's a real problem with this online bullying and sort of organized nastiness, and I'm not just talking about who said mean things. I'm talking about some really ugly stuff that went on.

Out in Nevada, when the UNITE HERE [a union whose membership includes many workers in the hotel and gaming industries] had put out an analysis of the different candidates and their views on health care and other issues, and some of the Bernie supporters online took exception to it and they didn't just take exception that we disagree, you know, which anybody can do. . . . They actually published the phone numbers and home addresses of the two women, the executive director and the communications director, women of color, immigrant women, and really put them in fear for their families. . . .

MADDOW: And it's particularly—it's a particular problem with Sanders' supporters.

WARREN: It is. I mean, it just is. Just a factual question, and it is.[42]

Three reporters for CNN found that Warren's sentiments were widely shared:

More than a dozen social media users spoke to CNN about their experiences with bullying by Sanders supporters. They described threats against family members, the creation of imposter accounts that resembled their own and what some described as being "swarmed," where barrages of vitriol filled their Twitter feeds and inboxes for days after they posted something critical of Sanders. . . . Two other targets . . . said Sanders supporters exposed their addresses, shared their personal photos and spread information about their relatives and work colleagues. . . . Ben Decker, who runs the digital investigations consultancy Memetica, says he has observed higher levels of online harassment among Sanders' followers relative to those of his Democratic rivals.[43]

One must also credit many of the losing candidates, who behaved in a much more responsible way than many of the Republican candidates had in 2016. Buttigieg and Klobuchar decided not to prolong the agony: they got out of the race immediately after South Carolina and then endorsed Biden. Michael Bloomberg and Elizabeth Warren exited right after Super Tuesday.

By contrast, a number of the 2016 Republican candidates stuck around long after it was clear that they had no realistic prospect of winning their party's nomination. Particularly egregious was the conduct of Ohio governor John Kasich. Though Kasich would emerge as a prominent Trump critic in 2020—even speaking in behalf of Biden at the Democratic National Convention—in 2016, when it probably would have mattered more, he acted in a way that seemed almost deliberately designed to advance Trump's fortunes. During the invisible primary season, Kasich had largely ignored Iowa and targeted New Hampshire, holding more than one hundred town meetings in the Granite State. As a result, Kasich finished second in the New Hampshire primary, but he received a paltry 16 percent of the vote, almost 20 points behind Donald Trump. Over the next several weeks, Kasich received 4 percent of the vote in the Nevada caucuses and 8 percent in the South Carolina primary. Yet he insisted on staying in the race until early May, continuing to divide the anti-Trump vote in ways that did particular damage to the campaign of Marco Rubio.[44] Kasich also proved to be a disruptive presence in the Republican debates, refusing to criticize Trump and regularly changing the subject when other candidates tried to do so. A case could also be made that Jeb Bush stayed in the race well after it became clear that he had no real chance of winning; his Super PAC, meanwhile, spent far more money attacking Rubio and Cruz than the front-running Trump.

When the major Democratic candidates began dropping out of the 2020 race, moreover, they had, in Joe Biden, a natural person to unite behind. Especially after the South Carolina results were in, Biden and Sanders were the only candidates who seemed to have a realistic prospect of winning the party's nomination. Though Biden was somewhat more moderate than many of his leading rivals, his views were at least widely acceptable to his fellow partisans. Biden also seems to have a gift for getting along with other politicians (including Sanders), an underrated virtue in the current political climate. There is no indication, in any of the press coverage I have examined, that any of the other candidates were actively angry at Biden.

Here, too, the Republican predicament in 2016 provides a striking contrast with the Democrats' situation in 2020. Republicans who wanted above all else to prevent the nomination of Donald Trump did not have a single, clear alternative. The two non-Trump candidates who fared best in the early going were Ted Cruz and Marco Rubio, but until the 2016 Super Tuesday, on March 1, neither candidate had clearly outperformed the other. Cruz narrowly edged out Rubio in Iowa and New Hampshire, but Rubio had a slight advantage in Nevada and South Carolina. Cruz fared far better than Rubio on Super Tuesday, winning three states, including his native Texas, whereas

Rubio's only victory came in the Minnesota caucuses. Cruz also won substantially more delegates that day: 218 to just 96 for Rubio. But Cruz, unlike Biden, was widely disliked by other Republicans. (As South Carolina senator Lindsey Graham famously joked, "If you killed Ted Cruz on the floor of the Senate, and the trial was in the Senate, nobody would convict you.")[45] Jeb Bush dropped out of the race on February 20 but didn't endorse Cruz for more than a month, on March 23.

The Republican Nomination

The story of the 2020 Republican presidential nomination can be told more briefly. Donald Trump was renominated without any significant opposition.

As is well known, President Trump provoked vehement opposition among large segments of the American population. Yet he also had a core of strong, very loyal supporters and admirers. Most important for present purposes, those supporters dominated the Republican Party.

The presidential approval data in table 6, taken from the Gallup poll, summarize quite nicely Trump's standing with the American public. Most Americans consistently disapproved of how Trump was handling his job responsibilities. Only for a brief period from about February to May 2020 did the president's approval rating exceed his disapproval numbers. Even more than his three predecessors—each a polarizing figure in his own right—Trump's ratings varied sharply by party. While the president's approval rating among Democrats was consistently below 10 percent, his rating among Republicans was just as undeviatingly above 80 percent, and above 90 percent during most of 2020. Independents, not surprisingly, fell between the two parties, though significantly closer to the Democrats.

Obviously, this profile augured poorly for the general election. In a presidential nomination contest, however, a president's popularity among his own partisans is far more important than his standing with the general public. In past election cycles, about two-thirds of the electorate in Republican presidential primaries have been self-identified Republicans; most of the remainder were independents.[46] Among his fellow partisans, Trump was as popular as Ronald Reagan had been in early 1984 and somewhat more popular than Bill Clinton in 1996 or George W. Bush in 2004.

Technically, Trump was not entirely unopposed in his quest for renomination. Former Massachusetts governor Bill Weld, former South Carolina governor Mark Sanford, and Joe Walsh, a one-term House member from Illinois, each filed a statement of candidacy with the Federal Election

TABLE 6. Donald Trump's approval ratings at six points during his presidency (in percentages)

Sampling date	American adult population	Republicans	Independents	Democrats
July 2017	38	84	33	8
January 2018	38	85	33	6
July 2018	42	88	36	9
January 2019	37	88	32	6
July 2019	43	89	38	6
January 2020	46	91	40	8

Source: Based on data from "Presidential Approval Ratings—Donald Trump," Gallup, accessed November 11, 2020, https://news.gallup.com/poll/203198 /presidential-approval-ratings-donald-trump.aspx. Respondents were asked: "Do you approve or disapprove of the way Donald Trump is handling his job as president?"

Commission. Weld and Walsh got their names onto a handful of state ballots. But none of them had the slightest chance of beating or even inconveniencing the Trump campaign. In the end, Trump won 94 percent of the Republican primary vote, as compared with 2.4 percent for Weld and 0.9 percent for Walsh.

The National Conventions

With Joe Biden having formally clinched the Democratic nomination on June 5, the one significant matter still to be decided was the selection of his running mate. Having pledged during a mid-March debate that he would pick a woman vice presidential candidate, Biden came under increasing pressure during a summer marked by Black Lives Matter protests to select a woman of color. On August 11, he announced his choice: California senator Kamala Harris, who had both Black and South Asian ancestry.

The 2020 national conventions will go down in history as the first in which the delegates never actually assembled. Other than that, they were pretty much business as usual: four-day efforts to sell each party's wares to a national television audience.

The Democratic National Convention (if that word is appropriate for something that never actually convened) was originally supposed to take place in Milwaukee, Wisconsin, from July 13 to July 16, but with the coronavirus pandemic still raging, it was postponed until August 17–20. Even then,

Milwaukee was used only as a kind of production center, with most of the content actually taking place in other locations around the country. Both Kamala Harris and Joe Biden delivered their acceptance speeches from Wilmington, Delaware. In addition to the usual assortment of party potentates and failed presidential candidates, the Democrats made a special effort to give speaking slots to disaffected Republicans, including Kasich, former New Jersey governor Christine Todd Whitman, former California gubernatorial nominee Meg Whitman, former New York representative Susan Molinari, and former secretary of state Colin Powell.

Planning for the Republican convention was made considerably more chaotic by Donald Trump's repeated attempts to hold a traditional, in-person convention without masks or social distancing in spite of all the public health warnings to the contrary. The convention was originally set for Charlotte, North Carolina, but when the state government refused to agree to Trump's conditions, it was moved to Jacksonville, Florida, which also became increasingly skittish about what Trump wanted to do. In the end, 336 Republican delegates (out of an original cast of 2,550) assembled in Charlotte on August 24 and quickly renominated both Trump and Vice President Mike Pence. Most of the speeches that took place over the next four nights, August 24–27, were delivered at the Andrew W. Mellon Auditorium in Washington, DC. Pence gave his acceptance speech at Fort McHenry in Baltimore. Trump's acceptance speech was held on the South Lawn of the White House, despite substantial criticism that this was a violation of federal law.

The Process in Retrospect

Almost every recent presidential nomination race has ended with a spate of recriminations—mostly from the losers in the general election, but sometimes from both sides—about the process that gave us such an awful candidate (or two such awful candidates). In the case of 2020, however, it is not obvious that either party has much to complain about.

Some Republicans might reasonably find fault with a system that allowed Donald Trump to win the nomination in 2016, though as I have argued elsewhere, it is not clear that any plausible set of rules changes would have produced a different outcome.[47] But by 2020, Trump was clearly the favorite candidate of most Republicans. Though his personal conduct set new lows for presidential behavior, his policies were, in most respects, a very faithful implementation of long-standing Republican policies: cutting taxes, appointing conservative judges, opposing abortion and gun control, deregulating business, seeking to reduce the level of illegal immigration, and defending religious freedom. In some respects, indeed, this recent convert to Republicanism adhered more closely to long-standing party doctrine than did lifetime member George W. Bush. Although the various November exit polls differ on some matters, all show Trump winning more than 90 percent of the votes cast by self-identified Republicans. Sometimes, democracy means letting the people nominate or elect the person they want, even though many others find that choice despicable.

Democrats have even less cause for complaint. Whether Joe Biden will turn out to be an effective president is yet to be seen. In the short term, however, a strong case can be made that he was the most electable of the major Democratic candidates, perhaps the only one who could have beaten Donald Trump. Assessing who among a set of presidential aspirants would have made the strongest general election candidate is not, it should be said, a question that can be answered in any simple or rigorous way. In particular, polls conducted during the nomination season are often highly misleading. During the first five months of 2016, for example, Bernie Sanders had a substantially higher favorability rating than either Hillary Clinton or Donald Trump.[48] But would Sanders have made a stronger general election candidate than Clinton? This seems highly unlikely. Sanders had a high favorability rating in 2016 because virtually no one was attacking him. Clinton by and large gave him a free pass because she never seriously believed he could beat her and she knew she would need his supporters' help in the general election. The Republicans also had no incentive to attack Sanders: to have done so would only have helped Clinton. But in the unlikely event that Sanders had won the 2016 nomination, the Republicans would have delightedly savaged him on a whole raft of issues.

By all the criteria that voters traditionally value, however, Biden seems to have been in a far stronger position than any of his partisan rivals. On the one hand, he was clearly the most experienced of the Democratic contenders, especially on matters of foreign policy. He had also mostly resisted the tendency to which all-too-many presidential aspirants succumb: to take positions so far to the left (for Democrats) or so far to the right (in the case of Republicans) as to undermine their appeal in the general election. He opposed fracking (to what extent was a subject of some dispute), but he did not endorse Medicare for All; he expressed sympathy with the Green New Deal's goals but equivocated as to its specific provisions; the press graciously allowed him not to say whether he favored expanding the number of Supreme Court justices; he claimed to support tax increases only for the wealthy. Though many on the far left would disagree, Biden was almost certainly more electable than Bernie Sanders. Even running against Donald Trump, it is hard to imagine that a plurality of Americans would have voted for a self-described socialist, especially one with a pronounced sympathy for Communist dictators.

Finally, it is time to take note of a major new colossus in the American presidential nomination process: the South Carolina primary. Though New Hampshire denizens have long boasted that their state holds the most important primary in the nation (and scholars and pundits have mostly agreed), in recent years South Carolina has more frequently been the make-or-break, determining step on the road to a presidential nomination. The South Carolina primary was the key event in the nominations of Bob Dole in 1996, George W. Bush in 2000, Barack Obama in 2008, Hillary Clinton in 2016, and now Joe Biden in 2020. All of these candidates lost the New Hampshire primary but rebounded by winning South Carolina. New Hampshire played the decisive role for Al Gore in 2000, John McCain in 2008 (though one could also make a case for South Carolina), and Donald Trump in 2016.

What is particularly remarkable about the influence of recent South Carolina primaries is that this is one "reform" in the presidential nomination process that actually worked the way it was supposed to work. Past efforts to restructure the nomination process have frequently been haunted by the recurrence of "unanticipated consequences." When the Democrats rewrote their delegate selection rules in the wake of the 1968 convention, there was no evidence that the rules writers wanted to increase the number of presidential primaries, dramatically lengthen the nomination campaign, further reduce the role of the national convention, front-load the nomination calendar, increase the number of declared candidates, or prematurely end most candidates' campaigns. Yet there is clear evidence that the new rules brought about each of these results.[49] In the lead-up to the 1976 nominations, many Democrats supported greater use of proportional representation rules for delegate allocation on the grounds that such rules would return power and decision-making authority to the national convention. In fact, such rules helped Jimmy Carter secure that year's nomination before the convention, by allowing him to win sizable numbers of delegates in primaries that were won by other candidates.

It was against this background that, after a string of nomination races in which Iowa and New Hampshire alone were entrusted with the job of "winnowing" the field, southerners complained that those two states generally advanced the fortunes of candidates who were too liberal to compete effectively in the South during the general election. Minorities also objected that the Democratic nomination gave such power to two states that were overwhelmingly white. So beginning in 2008, the Democratic Party's delegate selection rules, which had already carved out a privileged position for Iowa and New Hampshire, now specified that two other states could hold their delegate selection events in advance of everyone else: Nevada and South Carolina.

And it actually worked. In 2016 and especially 2020, the South Carolina primary substantially derailed the candidacy of Bernie Sanders, in both years plainly the more extreme of the two major Democratic candidates. And in both years, and in 2008, it was the Black vote that turned what might otherwise have been a close, indecisive event into a rout.

I still believe that the works of Edmund Burke should be required reading for all would-be party reformers, but as Burke also said, "A state without the means of some change is without the means of its conservation."[50]

Notes

1. A *New York Times* web page lists twenty-eight candidates, the twenty-six shown in table 1 and two additional people I had never heard of until seeing their names on the *Times*'s list: Wayne Messam, the mayor of Miramar, Florida, and Richard Ojeda, a former West Virginia state senator. See Alexander Burns, Matt Flegenheimer, Jasmine C. Lee, Lisa Lerer, and Jonathan Martin, "Who's Running for President in 2020?", *New York Times*, April 8, 2020, https://www.nytimes.com/interactive/2019/us/politics/2020-presidential-candidates.html (accessed November 21, 2020).

2. For a list of the 2016 Republican and Democratic presidential candidates and their announcement dates, see William G. Mayer, "The Nominations: The Road to a Much-Disliked General Election," in *The Elections of 2016*, ed. Michael Nelson (Thousand Oaks, CA: Sage, CQ Press, 2018), table 2.1, p. 31.

3. The only sitting member of the House of Representatives to be elected president was James Garfield in 1880. Before being nominated by the Democratic Party in 1896, 1900, and 1908, but losing in all three cases, William Jennings Bryan's only government service had been two terms in the House.

4. See Isaac Stanley-Becker, "'We Got Things Done': Biden Recalls 'Civility' with Segregationist Senators," *Washington Post*, June 19, 2019.

5. All quotations are taken from Jeremia Kimelman, "Full Transcript: 2019 Democratic Debate Night Two," NBC News, June 28, 2019, https://www.nbcnews.com/politics/2020-election/full-transcript-2019-democratic-debate-night-two-sortable-topic-n1023601.

6. Kevin Breuninger and Brian Schwartz, "Kamala Harris Drops Out of Presidential Race after Plummeting from Top Tier of Democratic Candidates," CNBC, December 3, 2019, https://www.cnbc.com/2019/12/03/kamala-harris-drops-out-of-2020-presidential-race.html.

7. Paul Maslin, as quoted in Chelsea James, "Harris Faces Uphill Climb amid Questions about Who She Is," *Washington Post*, November 28, 2019.

8. See Margot Sanger-Katz, "Where Is Kamala Harris on Medicare for All vs. Private Insurance?," *New York Times*, June 28, 2019.

9. Two particularly good accounts of the disarray in the Harris campaign are James, "Harris Faces Uphill Climb"; and Jonathan Martin, Astead W. Herndon, and Alexander Burns, "How Kamala Harris's Campaign Unraveled," *New York Times*, November 29, 2019.

10. As quoted in Breuninger and Schwartz, "Kamala Harris Drops Out."

11. See, for example, Nelson W. Polsby, *Consequences of Party Reform* (New York: Oxford University Press, 1983), 163–67.

12. Caucusers who initially expressed a preference for Biden or Sanders would later have the opportunity to switch to another candidate; but unless the Biden or Sanders group fell below the 15 percent threshold, why would they?

13. For a good explanation of how Warren proposed to do this, see Cory Turner, "Canceling Student Debt Is Easier Than It Sounds," National Public Radio, January 14, 2020, https://www.npr.org/2020/01/14/796329598/canceling-student-debt-is-easier-than-it-sounds.

14. For further details, see Elizabeth Warren, "My Plan to Cancel Student Loan Debt on Day One of My Presidency" and "Affordable Higher Education for All," both at https://elizabethwarren.com/plans (accessed November 27, 2020).

15. As quoted in Deborah D'Souza, "Elizabeth Warren's Economic Plan: Break Things That Are Fixed," Investopedia, November 6, 2019, https://www.investopedia.com/elizabeth-warren-s-economic-plan-explained-4706529.

16. Lauren Gambino, "'I Have a Plan for That': Elizabeth Warren Leads the Democratic 'Ideas Primary,'" *Guardian*, May 11, 2019.

17. Thomas Kaplan and Jim Tankersley, "Elizabeth Warren Has Lots of Plans. Together, They Would Remake the Economy," *New York Times*, June 10, 2019.

18. Charles Chamberlain, chair of Democracy for America, as quoted in Asma Khalid, "Why Progressives Chose Bernie Sanders over Elizabeth Warren," National Public Radio, March 7, 2020, https://www.npr.org/2020/03/07/812903782/why-progressives-chose-bernie-sanders-over-elizabeth-warren.

19. Ayanna Pressley, the fourth member of the Squad, endorsed Elizabeth Warren on November 6, but since Pressley was from Massachusetts, her endorsement probably had less impact.

20. See Eliza Relman, "Bernie Sanders Won Key Endorsements from Alexandria Ocasio-Cortez, Ilhan Omar, and Rashida Tlaib by Defending

Them When Few Others Would," *Business Insider,* October 28, 2019, https://www.businessinsider.com/the-squad-endorsed-bernie-sanders -after-he-defended-them-2019-10.

21. George Goehl, director of People's Action, as quoted in Khalid, "Why Progressives Chose Bernie Sanders."

22. For a quick listing of most of Warren's big-ticket spending promises, see Mish [Mike Shedlock], "Elizabeth Warren Has a Bad Plan for Everything," The Street, accessed November 27, 2020, https://thestreet.com/mish/talk /economics/elizabeth-warren-has-a-bad-plan-for-everything.

23. All quotations are from "The October Democratic Debate Transcript," *Washington Post,* accessed November 26, 2020, washingtonpost.com /politics/2019/10/15/October-democratic-debate-transcript/.

24. For explanation and analysis of Warren's financing plan, see Margot Sanger-Katz and Sarah Kliff, "Elizabeth Warren's 'Medicare for All' Math," *New York Times,* November 1, 2019; Danielle Kurtzleben, "Here's How Warren Finds $20.5 Trillion to Pay for 'Medicare for All,'" National Public Radio, November 1, 2019, https://www.npr.org/2019/11/01/775339519 /heres-how-warren-finds-20-5-trillion-to-pay-for-medicare-for-all; and especially Glenn Kessler, "Warren's Plan to Pay for Medicare-for-All: Does It Add Up?," *Washington Post,* November 5, 2019.

25. See Abby Goodnough, Thomas Kaplan, and Margot Sanger-Katz, "Elizabeth Warren Vows to Expand Health Coverage in First 100 Days," *New York Times,* November 15, 2019; and Paige Winfield Cunningham, "Elizabeth Warren Is No Longer a Medicare-for-All Purist," *Washington Post,* November 18, 2019.

26. As quoted in Tami Luhby, Gregory Krieg, MJ Lee, and Leyla Santiago, "Elizabeth Warren Releases Plan to Fund Medicare for All, Pledges No Middle Class Tax Hike," CNN, November 7, 2019, https://www.cnn.com /2019/11/01/politics/elizabeth-warren-medicare-for-all-financing-plan /index.html.

27. Liz Smith, as quoted in Goodnough, Kaplan, and Sanger-Katz, "Elizabeth Warren Vows."

28. Both are quoted in Cunningham, "Elizabeth Warren Is No Longer a Medicare-for-All Purist."

29. Shane Goldmacher and Astead W. Herndon, "Elizabeth Warren, Once a Front-Runner, Drops Out of Presidential Race," *New York Times,* March 5, 2020.

30. For a good account of the post-caucus chaos, see Quint Forgey, "Bernie and Buttigieg Elbow Each Other with Claims of Leads in Iowa," *Politico,* February 3, 2020.

31. The three measures are due to the way that most caucuses work. After the participants have assembled and their eligibility has been verified, the caucuses record an *initial expression of candidate preferences.* According to

national party rules, any candidate who is supported by less than 15 percent of the caucusers is not eligible to win any delegates to the next set of meetings (in Iowa's case, the county conventions). So time is allowed for those who support one of the candidates with less than 15 percent to either attract more supporters or join one of the candidate groups with more than 15 percent. When all such switches have taken place, a *final expression of candidate preferences* is recorded. And on that basis, *delegates to the county conventions* are allocated among the candidates. For further details and a worked-out example, see William G. Mayer, "Caucuses: How They Work, What Difference They Make," in *In Pursuit of the White House: How We Choose Our Presidential Nominees*, ed. William G. Mayer (Chatham, NJ: Chatham House, 1996), 108–16. Because of complaints from past Iowa candidates, in 2020 the state Democratic Party agreed to report all three measures to the media.

32. For data on Jackson and Robertson, see Mayer, "Caucuses," 140–45. On Sanders's performance in the 2016 caucuses, see Mayer, "Nominations," 40–43.

33. See, respectively, Jonathan Martin and Alexander Burns, "Bernie Sanders Wins Nevada Caucuses, Strengthening His Primary Lead," *New York Times*, February 22, 2020; Chuck Todd, Mark Murray, and Carrie Dunn, "Six Reasons Why Bernie Sanders Became the Front-Runner," NBC News, February 25, 2020, https://www.nbcnews.com /politics/meet-the-press/six-reasons-why-bernie-sanders-became -democratic-front-runner-n1142371; Domenico Montanaro, "After Nevada Caucuses, Bernie Sanders Emerges as Democratic Front-Runner," National Public Radio, February 24, 2020, https://www.npr.org/2020 /02/24/808995251/after-nevada-caucuses-bernie-sanders-emerges-as -democratic-front-runner; "Bernie Sanders on Being the Democratic Front-Runner," *60 Minutes*, February 24, 2020, cbsnews.com/news /bernie-sanders-democratic-presidential-front-runner-anderson -cooper-60-minutes; "Bernie Sanders Cements Front-Runner Status with Nevada Caucuses Win," BBC, February 23, 2020, https://www.bbc .com/news/world-us-canada-51601813; and Sarah Frostenson, "Bernie Sanders Is the Front-Runner," FiveThirtyEight, February 23, 2020, https://fivethirtyeight.com/features/bernie-sanders-is-the-front -runner.

34. See the summary data from the 2016 exit polls in Mayer, "Nominations," table 2.6, pp. 44–45.

35. *60 Minutes*, "Bernie Sanders on Being the Democratic Front-Runner." Sanders's comment on *60 Minutes* was merely one episode in a long history of saying positive things about various Communist regimes. See, for example, Aaron Blake, "Bernie Sanders Greets His New Front-Runner Status with One of His Greatest Hits: Praising Fidel Castro," *Washington*

Post, February 24, 2020; and Griff Witte, "In Cold War Travels, Bernie Sanders Found Much to Admire behind Enemy Lines," *Washington Post*, February 24, 2020.

36. Both are quoted in Patricia Mazzel, "Sanders's Comments on Fidel Castro Provoke Anger in Florida," *New York Times*, February 24, 2020.

37. This figure is taken from the amended April 2020 report the Bloomberg campaign filed with the Federal Election Commission on June 19, 2020, available at fec.gov.

38. The quotation is from "Full Transcript: Ninth Democratic Debate in Las Vegas," NBC News, February 20, 2020, nbcnews.com/politics/2020-election/full-transcript-ninth-democratic-debate-las-vegas-n1139546.

39. This is my own calculation, based on the delegate numbers reported at thegreenpapers.com (accessed November 16, 2020).

40. For evidence that the Democratic Party was more ideologically divided than the Republican Party, at least in the years between 1968 and 1990, see William G. Mayer, *The Divided Democrats: Ideological Unity, Party Reform, and Presidential Elections* (Boulder, CO: Westview Press, 1996), especially chap. 4.

41. The quotation is from Joe Biden in "September 29, 2020 Debate Transcript," Commission on Presidential Debates, accessed November 16, 2020, https://www.debates.org/voter-education/debate-transcripts/september-29-2020-debate-transcript/. But as anyone can verify by googling the words "trump worst president ever," many other people made the same claim. See, for example, "Is Trump the Worst President in American History?," Robert Reich, March 29, 2018, https://robertreich.org/post/172379557905/; "Environmental and Public Health Advocates Agree: Trump Is the Worst President for Our Environment in History," Earthjustice, February 4, 2020, defenders.org.newsroom/environmental-and-public-health-advocates-agree-trump-worst-president-our-environment; David Rothkopf, "'The Most Ignorant and Unfit': What Made America's Worst Ever Leader?," *New York Review of Books*, July 3, 2020, nybooks.com/daily/2020/07/03/the-most-ignorant-and-unfit-what-made-americas-worst-ever-leader/; Richard Striner, "Is Trump the Worst President in History?," History News Network, July 28, 2019, https://historynewsnetwork.org/articles/172612; Bill McCann, "Commentary: Seven Reasons Why Trump Is the Worst President Ever," *Austin American-Statesman*, May 30, 2019, https://www.statesman.com/news/20190530/commentary-seven-reasons-why-trump-is-worst-president-ever; and Michael D'Antonio, "Trump May Reach a New Milestone by Election Day," CNN, September 9, 2020, cnn.com/2020/09/08/opinions/trump-worst-president-ever-opinion-dantonio/index/html.

42. "Elizabeth Warren Interview Transcript: 3/5/20, The Rachel Maddow Show," MSNBC, March 5, 2020, msnbc.com/transcripts/rachel-maddow

-show/2020-03-05-msna1338256. Joe Biden also criticized the behavior of Sanders's supporters in Nevada and urged Sanders "to accept greater accountability" for such tactics. See Mike Memoli, "Biden Calls on Sanders to Take Accountability for Supporters' Threats," NBC News, February 15, 2020, https://www.nbcnews.com/politics/2020-election/biden-calls -sanders-take-accountability-supporters-threats-n1137466?cid=sm_npd _nn_tw_mtp.

43. Curt Devine, Drew Griffin, and Scott Bronstein, "The 'Swarm': How a Subset of Sanders Supporters Use Hostile Tactics to Drown Out Critics," CNN, February 9, 2020, cnn.com/2020/02/07/politics/bernie-sanders -social-media-attacks-invs/index.html.

44. See David Wasserman, "Kasich May Have Cut Off Rubio's Path to the Nomination," FiveThirtyEight, March 4, 2016, https://fivethirtyeight.com /features/what-would-happen-if-marco-rubio-and-john-kasich-were -one-candidate/.

45. As quoted in Catherine Treyz, "Lindsey Graham Jokes about How to Get Away with Murdering Ted Cruz," CNN, February 26, 2016, https://www .cnn.com/2016/02/26/politics/lindsey-graham-ted-cruz-dinner/index .html.

46. See the data in William G. Mayer, "Voting in Presidential Primaries: What We Can Learn from Three Decades of Exit Polling," in *The Making of the Presidential Candidates 2008*, ed. William G. Mayer (Lanham, MD: Rowman & Littlefield, 2008), table 7.9, p. 184.

47. See William G. Mayer, "Was the Process to Blame? Why Hillary Clinton and Donald Trump Won Their Parties' Presidential Nominations," *New York University Law Review* 93 (October 2018): 759–85.

48. In four polls conducted by the Quinnipiac University Polling Institute between January 1 and May 30, 2016, 47 percent of the public, on average, said they had a favorable opinion of Bernie Sanders, versus a 38 percent average for Hillary Clinton and 34 percent for Donald Trump. See Quinnipiac surveys of February 2–4, February 10–15, March 16–21, and May 24–30, 2016.

49. See especially Michael G. Hagen and William G. Mayer, "The Modern Politics of Presidential Selection: How Changing the Rules Really Did Change the Game," in *In Pursuit of the White House 2000: How We Choose Our Presidential Nominees*, ed. William G. Mayer (New York: Chatham House, 2000), 1–55.

50. Edmund Burke, *Reflections on the Revolution in France* (1790; Baltimore: Penguin, 1976), 106.

The Election

THE MORE THINGS CHANGE . . .

Marc J. Hetherington

PEOPLE COMMONLY MISUSE the term "unprecedented." It means that, more than being rare, some event or eventuality has never occurred before. By that standard the election of 2020 was, indeed, unprecedented in several respects. Never before had a presidential election been contested during a global pandemic. In the months leading up to the election, COVID-19 claimed 223,000 American lives. Despite the potential physical dangers, over 150 million voters cast ballots, an unprecedented number. Garnering more than 81 million of them, Joe Biden won more votes than any candidate in history. And with over 74 million, Donald Trump won the second-most votes ever. That is because the election featured the highest percentage of voting-eligible participants in over one hundred years. At 67 percent, voter turnout smashed the modern standard of 63 percent set in 1960 when John F. Kennedy defeated Richard Nixon.[1]

The central reason for the explosion in voter turnout is the unprecedented level of partisan polarization that exists in the electorate. The sad fact is that most Republicans hate the Democratic Party and most Democrats hate the Republican Party. And no president in the history of American politics has ever generated reactions as polarized as those generated by Donald Trump. Because of his effort to "make America great again," his Republican supporters came to love him, while those same efforts caused his Democratic detractors to loathe him. One way to illustrate Trump's unique ability to polarize is to examine his approval ratings. On average, 89 percent of Republicans approved of his performance during the year before he ran for reelection, while only 5 percent of Democrats did. That is the widest partisan gap in the history of polling.[2] But it is important to note that polarized approval numbers are not unique to Trump. His are a continuation and intensification of a trend. Barack Obama's and

George W. Bush's approval numbers are the second and third most polarized in history.

Polarization almost always generates high voter turnout because the emotions connected to it are action emotions: enthusiasm on one end, anger on the other. The negative emotions are the more powerful motivators. If you are choosing between Tweedledum and Tweedledee, you can be excused for sitting out the election. But when voters perceive the contest as between a devil and a savior, much more is on the line. In addition, many states rendered excuse-making more difficult in 2020. To protect public safety during the pandemic, they made it easier for citizens to cast ballots by mail and to vote early in person. Being too busy on Election Day or being scared off by long lines would not cut it as excuses in 2020. Indeed, 101 million of the more than 150 million votes cast in the election were early votes—cast either by mail (65 million) or in person before Election Day (36 million).[3]

In the contest itself, Joe Biden emerged the winner and Trump the (sore) loser. But it was not the kind of sweeping repudiation that Democrats had hoped for. When the incumbent party loses the presidency, it almost always loses seats in Congress, often a lot of them. In 2020, however, Republicans actually picked up more than a dozen seats in the House of Representatives, although the Democrats maintained a slim majority. In the Senate, Democrats picked up three seats, which evened the count at 50–50 in the chamber. With Vice President Kamala Harris' tiebreaking vote, the Democrats have majority status. After Election Day itself, however, it seemed a long shot that Democrats would find themselves in such an advantageous position. A one-seat pickup seemed the most likely result. That was the number the Democrats added on Election Day itself, with two races still undecided.

Those two undecided races were in Georgia, which has election laws that are a vestige of a long-past party system. For nearly a century after the Civil War, the Republican Party barely existed in much of the South, so the only real competition in elections was among Democratic candidates. Under these election laws, a candidate who wins a majority of the vote on Election Day is declared the winner. But, if no candidate reaches 50 percent, a runoff election between the top two vote getters in the first round of voting occurs a couple months later. In the first round of voting in Georgia, the two Republican candidates both outperformed the two Democratic candidates, but neither secured the required majority to win the seat outright. In the runoff on January 5, the two Democrats, Raphael Warnock and Jon Ossoff, turned the tables, winning razor-thin victories to deliver their party Senate control.

With historically small majorities in both the House and Senate, the likely result is more of the same bruising partisan gridlock that has characterized politics since the mid-1990s even with Democrats in control of both houses of congress and the presidency. The politics of today has only one parallel in American history: the late 1800s. That is probably not good news for decisive leadership. Even remembering the names of the political leaders of that time—Rutherford B. Hayes, James Garfield, Chester Arthur, Grover Cleveland, Benjamin Harrison—is not easy. Their list of accomplishments is even harder to recall.

The aftermath of the 2020 election was also unprecedented. Never before has a losing presidential candidate challenged an election outcome with no evidence of wrongdoing. Yet Donald Trump hurled baseless charges of widespread voter fraud for weeks while presenting no evidence of it. Indeed, when his lawyers went to court to argue cases suggesting that irregularities occurred, they explicitly stated to judges that they had no evidence of actual voter fraud.[4] Eventually what became known by Trump's critics as "The Big Lie" fueled an invasion of the Capitol Building by Trump supporters the day Congress met to certify the Electoral College vote. Several died in the attack, including a Capitol Police officer. Haunted by the attack, two other Capitol Police died by suicide in the weeks after. The House of Representatives impeached Trump for inciting the violence, making him the only president ever to be impeached twice.

The damage to democracy itself caused by the end of the Trump presidency may be profound. One thing that allows democracies to function is that losers acknowledge their defeat. Even in the most controversial of circumstances—Richard Nixon in 1960 and Al Gore in 2000—that is what the vanquished have always done in America. Trying to overturn the outcome of a free and fair election is the most serious of challenges to democratic practice. If losers believe they can overturn an outcome they do not like, elections cease to matter. Donald Trump has been unconventional in many ways, so perhaps it should not be surprising that his departure from the White House would be as well, with an unfortunate but predictable range of tragic consequences.

The General Election

In analyzing the general election before the primary election, it may seem I am putting the cart before the horse. How can we understand the general election without first understanding the primaries? Why I have done so will become clear below.

Table 1 shows the state-by-state results from the fifty states plus the District of Columbia, arrayed by how close state outcomes were. As has been characteristic of most of the past six elections, the national electoral vote was close, but very few states' popular votes were. In 2020, only eight (Arizona, Florida, Georgia, Michigan, Nevada, North Carolina, Pennsylvania, and Wisconsin) were decided by 5 percentage points or less, of which Biden won six. These states represent his path to victory.

TABLE 1. 2020 presidential election results

State	EV	Biden (%)	Trump (%)	Margin (%)	State	EV	Biden (%)	Trump (%)	Margin (%)
Georgia	16	49.5	49.3	0.2	Mississippi	6	41.1	57.6	16.5
Arizona	11	49.4	49.1	0.3	Illinois	20	57.6	40.5	17.1
Wisconsin	10	49.6	48.9	0.7	Louisiana	8	39.9	58.5	18.6
Pennsylvania	20	50.0	48.8	1.2	Delaware	3	58.8	39.8	19.0
North Carolina	15	48.7	50.0	1.3	Nebraska	2	39.4	58.5	19.1
Nevada	6	50.1	47.7	2.4	Washington	12	58.4	39.0	19.4
Michigan	16	50.6	47.9	2.7	Connecticut	7	59.3	39.2	20.1
Florida	29	47.9	51.2	3.3	Utah	6	37.7	58.2	20.5
Texas	38	46.5	52.1	5.6	Rhode Island	4	59.7	38.8	20.9
Minnesota	10	52.6	45.4	7.2	New York	29	60.6	38.0	22.6
New Hampshire	4	52.9	45.5	7.4	Tennessee	11	37.5	60.7	23.2
Ohio	18	45.3	53.3	8.0	Alabama	9	36.7	62.2	25.5
Iowa	6	45.0	53.2	8.2	Kentucky	8	36.2	62.1	25.9
Maine	2	53.1	44.0	9.1	South Dakota	3	35.6	61.8	26.2
Alaska	3	43.0	53.1	10.1	Arkansas	6	34.8	62.4	27.6
Virginia	13	54.4	44.2	10.2	California	55	63.5	34.3	29.2
New Mexico	5	54.3	43.5	10.8	Hawaii	4	63.7	34.3	29.4
South Carolina	9	43.4	55.1	11.7	Idaho	4	33.1	63.9	30.8
Colorado	9	55.4	41.9	13.5	Oklahoma	7	32.3	65.4	33.1
Kansas	6	41.3	56.5	15.2	Maryland	10	65.8	32.4	33.4
Missouri	10	41.4	56.8	15.4	Massachusetts	11	65.9	32.3	33.6
New Jersey	14	57.3	41.4	15.9	North Dakota	3	31.9	65.5	33.6
Indiana	11	41.0	57.1	16.1	Vermont	3	66.4	30.8	35.6
Oregon	7	56.9	40.7	16.2	West Virginia	5	29.7	68.6	38.9
Montana	3	40.6	56.9	16.3	Wyoming	3	26.7	70.4	43.7
					DC	3	93.0	5.5	87.5

Source: https://www.cnn.com/election/2020/results/president

Five of these states—Pennsylvania, Michigan, Wisconsin, Georgia, and Arizona—switched from Republican red to Democratic blue compared with 2016. This produced an exact mirror image of the electoral college vote between the two years. Trump defeated Hillary Clinton by 306 to 232 in 2016 and was defeated by Joe Biden by the exact same score in 2020.[5] The real story, however, is the overall continuity of the Electoral College map. The last time the presidency moved from one party to the other with fewer than five states changing hands was in 1888.[6] When the president's party loses reelection, it usually indicates a sharp change from the status quo, as when Ronald Reagan drubbed Jimmy Carter in 1980 or Franklin Roosevelt destroyed Herbert Hoover in 1932. But not this time.

Importantly, it is not just that the 2016 and 2020 Electoral College maps are so similar. Perhaps even more remarkable is the continuity of the Electoral College map over each of the six elections that have occurred in this century. With the exception of the 2008 election, which occurred during the worst financial crisis since the Great Depression in 1932 and was something of a blowout for Obama and the Democrats, every contest has been basically the same. In the five competitive elections between 2000 and 2020, thirty-seven states voted for the same party each time, and ten voted for the same party four of five times.[7] Again, the late nineteenth century was the last time such continuity in state-by-state outcomes existed, with the elections stretching from the 1870s to the 1890s much like the present century's.

To illustrate the modern-day stagnation, in the 2000 election, which pitted George W. Bush against Al Gore in one of the closest presidential contests in history, the Democrats dominated New England and the Middle Atlantic states, as they have in every election since. Republicans racked up victories in the South. In the middle of the country, Republicans did well in the Great Plains and the Mountain West, while Democrats won most of the industrial Midwest east of the Great Plains. On the Pacific coast, Democrats prevailed by huge margins.

Three geographic areas require further exploration because they are evolving. The first is the Southwest, which is among the fastest-growing parts of the country. This cluster of states—Nevada, Utah, Colorado, New Mexico, and Arizona—accounted for a total of thirty electoral votes in 2000, all but five of which went to Bush. Only New Mexico voted for Gore, and its margin was razor thin. In 2020, however, these five states, which accounted for thirty-seven electoral votes due to population gains in the region, favored Joe Biden. He won all but Utah's six electoral votes. This represents a shift from a Republican advantage of twenty-five electoral votes in 2000 to a Democratic advantage of thirty-one electoral votes in

2020. The transformation of this region has produced a swing of fifty-six electoral votes toward the Democrats.

The beginning of the Southwest's partisan evolution can be traced to the first Obama election in 2008, which started a run of four elections and counting in which Colorado, Nevada, and New Mexico voted for the Democratic presidential candidate. Arizona joined that group of states in 2020, voting for a Democrat for the first time since 1996. A formerly Republican stronghold is now an emerging Democratic one.

A closer look at the South is also warranted. The eleven states of the former Confederacy have been a bulwark of Republican support for decades, but at least some change may be afoot in this region as well. Comparing the 2000 and 2020 Electoral College maps reveals that both Virginia and Georgia voted Republican in 2000 but backed Biden in 2020. Like several of the states in the Southwest, Virginia has actually gone for the Democrat in every election since 2008, and it is hardly even considered a swing state any longer. But Biden's narrow win in Georgia was surprising. It is also noteworthy that Biden lost North Carolina by only 1.2 percentage points, suggesting it too is no longer safely Republican. The rest of the region remains mostly dark red. Indeed Trump's average margin of victory in the other eight states of the former Confederacy (South Carolina, Florida, Alabama, Mississippi, Louisiana, Texas, Arkansas, and Tennessee) was nearly 20 points. Importantly, the population in several of these solid Republican states is growing. In 2000, they accounted for a total of 107 electoral votes, all won by Bush. In 2020, those same states registered 116 electoral votes for Trump. Based on population projections, the number will reach 120 in 2024 after the next decennial census is accounted for.[8]

The bulk of the population growth in the South has occurred in Florida and Texas, arguably the two most competitive states in the region and two of the three biggest electoral vote and U.S. House prizes in the country. Florida remains the swing state it has been for the past twenty years. In 2000, Bush famously won it by a mere 537 votes, which made him the Electoral College winner. However, in his two victories in 2008 and 2012, Barack Obama pulled Florida into the Democratic column both times. It returned to the Republicans with Trump's 2016 victory and remained there in 2020. But in each of the past six elections, the largest margin of victory in the Sunshine State was 5 points, and it is usually less than 3. The other electoral vote jackpot in the region is Texas. Republicans have traditionally won the state by double digits, but the margin has been narrowing as the state has become more racially and ethnically diverse. In 2020, Trump won by 5.5 points.

Finally, the Rust Belt, a strip of industrial states running from Pennsylvania in the east to Minnesota in the west, is crucial to understand. Although these states are often called the "blue wall," because of the Democrats' consistent wins there over the past thirty years, the margins are ordinarily close. If anything, the Rust Belt appears to be moving in a Republican direction. For example, Ohio and Iowa were once Republican-leaning swing states, but both the 2016 and 2020 elections suggest they are no longer especially competitive. Both went for Trump by 8 or more points.

The Democratic-leaning swing states that were competitive in the past have grown even more so. Gore won Pennsylvania, Michigan, and Wisconsin by 4, 5, and 0.2 points, respectively; Biden won them by even narrower margins of 1, 3, and 0.7 points. Although all these states have lost significant population over time, they still account for forty-six electoral votes, giving them outsize importance. When Trump won all three in 2016, it provided him his Electoral College majority even as he lost the national popular vote by 3 million votes. That made these states the battleground of all battlegrounds in 2020. By adding their 46 electoral votes to the 232 won by Hillary Clinton in 2016, Biden would have accrued an Electoral College majority of 278. Adding the 28 electoral votes from his narrow victories in Arizona and Georgia along with the Omaha congressional district in Nebraska provided some cushion.

The Nomination of Joe Biden

Although the nomination process comes before the general election, one cannot understand why Biden became the Democratic nominee without understanding the Electoral College map that convinced the party's establishment wing that Biden might be the only candidate in the field capable of defeating Donald Trump. The need to win back the Rust Belt was central to their thinking. Hillary Clinton lost because she failed to win Pennsylvania, Michigan, and Wisconsin, but Trump's combined margin of victory in those states was only 70,000 votes. The easiest path back to the White House for Democrats was to reclaim these three states. Nominating a candidate who could do that was job one.

Joe Biden's background, especially in contrast to most of his competition for the 2020 nomination, made him the safest and, in retrospect, perhaps only choice to accomplish that task. He is much more like what the Democratic Party traditionally has been, less like what its future is likely to be. Importantly, the key Rust Belt states represent the Democrats' past more than their future. Biden is older, white, male, and from working-class roots, and all these groups are disproportionately well represented in the Rust Belt, making his personal characteristics especially advantageous.

None of the other top-tier candidates for the Democratic nomination was well suited to arresting the party's losses with these traditional New Deal Democratic groups. The "progressive" lane was occupied by Bernie Sanders and Elizabeth Warren, two New Englanders and the two most liberal members of the U.S. Senate. Hillary Clinton was not nearly as far to the left as either of them and yet perceptions of how liberal she was made her toxic to the white working class in 2016, especially men. As such, neither Sanders nor Warren was likely to outperform Clinton, and the risk was high that they would significantly underperform her. Progressives argued that either Sanders or Warren could win without much support from older, white voters because they could generate higher voter turnout among younger and more liberal voters. Although that is possible, it is hard to imagine voter turnout could have been higher in 2020 than it actually was.

Biden shared the more "centrist" lane in the primaries with South Bend, Indiana, mayor Pete Buttigieg and Minnesota senator Amy Klobuchar. A compelling campaigner, Buttigieg generated great enthusiasm early on, despite his thin résumé. No mayor has ever been elected president, much less one from a relatively small city. Beyond concerns about experience, the fact that he is a gay man would almost certainly undermine his appeal with some working-class whites in the Rust Belt. From working-class roots herself, Klobuchar might have had more success with this group than the progressives and Buttigieg, but she was not especially well known. In addition, being a woman did not help Hillary Clinton with these more traditional voting groups in the Rust Belt, and there is little reason to think Klobuchar would have done significantly better.

Given the field of candidates vying for the Democratic nomination, February 26 emerges as perhaps the most important day of the election year. That was the day that James Clyburn, the House majority whip from South Carolina and the most influential Democrat in his state, endorsed Joe Biden for president. The endorsement came just three days before the South Carolina primary. An African American himself, Clyburn had especially high credibility with African American voters, a group that makes up 56 percent of the state's Democratic primary electorate. On February 29, Biden won in a landslide and saved what were, at the time, his fading hopes for the nomination.

That Biden needed so desperately to win the South Carolina primary illustrates just how poorly things had gone for the centrist wing of the party before that contest. The Palmetto State is the fourth of four nomination contests that kick off the Democratic race. The three earlier contests—Iowa, New Hampshire, and Nevada—had all gone badly for Biden, who came in fifth place twice and second place once. The Democratic socialist senator from Vermont, Bernie Sanders, swept the first three contests and seemed poised to win the nomination. None of those states, however, featured many African American voters, the most loyal group in the party's coalition and one that is central to its establishment wing.

Clyburn's endorsement and Biden's huge win in South Carolina set in motion the breathtaking chain of events that catapulted the former vice president to victory. After South Carolina and just days before Super Tuesday, his two centrist competitors—Klobuchar and Buttigieg—suddenly dropped out of the race and endorsed Biden, leaving him the only centrist in the race. Elizabeth Warren, however, stayed in the race, which meant she would continue to split votes with Sanders among the party's progressive wing. While Biden could now consolidate support in the party's ideological middle, Sanders could not do the same with progressives. This symphony was orchestrated by Democratic Party leaders. Sensing how important it was for Biden to win the nomination, they encouraged Buttigieg and Klobuchar to drop out in his favor. They also encouraged Warren to stay in.[9]

With fifteen states holding contests on Super Tuesday, March 3, Biden found himself in an advantageous position. He was alone in the center while Sanders and Warren were splitting votes on the left. Biden won eleven of the Super Tuesday states while Sanders won only four. Warren dropped out days later. Riding his momentum, Biden won six of the seven primaries held the following week in what amounted to a head-to-head matchup with Sanders. These states included Michigan, a state where Sanders had pulled a big upset over Hillary Clinton four years earlier, and Washington, part of Sanders's stronghold in the Pacific Northwest. Realizing his path to victory was blocked, Sanders exited the race in mid-March. The nomination was Biden's.

Sanders again finished second in his quest for the Democratic nomination, but this time was different. In 2016, he battled Clinton through the entire primary schedule into June, and he never fully embraced her general election candidacy. In 2020, however, he dropped out early and strongly endorsed Biden. Especially important was his impassioned speech on Biden's behalf at the Democratic National Convention in September. Sanders sent a clear message to his progressive supporters. Although he understood their disappointment, he encouraged them to get behind the former vice president because Donald Trump posed a much greater threat to progressive interests than centrist Democrats. Considering how close the outcome was in Pennsylvania, Wisconsin, Georgia, and Arizona—each decided by less than 2 percentage points—it's reasonable to conclude that without a unified Democratic Party, President Trump likely would have won reelection. That process of unification, which started with Clyburn's endorsement in February, created the conditions that allowed for a Democratic victory.

The Group Basis of the 2020 Presidential Vote

Parties and their candidates attempt to knit together coalitions of different groups. In large measure, both parties rely on the same groups year in and year out. Racial minorities, women, and young people, for example, are key to the Democratic coalition just as whites, men, and older people are to the Republican coalition. Especially because the margins between Republicans and Democrats today are so tight, doing just a little bit better or worse with one or two groups can change the outcome. For example, Trump did somewhat better than Republicans typically do with the white working class in rural areas and small towns, which made him the winner in 2016. Doing better, however, doesn't necessarily mean winning a majority of votes from a group. For example, George W. Bush won just under 40 percent of the Latino vote in 2000, but that was about 5 points better than Republicans typically did. Simply minimizing damage with a group your party usually loses can produce a win, as it did for Bush in 2000.

Ordinarily, analysts can judge what changed and what stayed the same in the voting behavior of different groups by using exit poll data. A conglomerate of media organizations pool their resources to collect a sample of well over 10,000 voters who are interviewed as they depart the polling station. That way, pollsters know they are interviewing voters rather than people who just claim they will vote. Unfortunately, questions about the reliability of the 2020 exit poll abound. Because so many people voted early, either by mail or in person, exit polls couldn't simply rely on interviewing voters as they left polling stations on Election Day. They needed to sample by phone as well. Complicating matters further, early voters and Election Day voters differed fundamentally. Concerned that high turnout would hurt his electoral chances, President Trump worked to undermine confidence in voting by mail and discouraged Republicans from doing so. As a result, Republicans were much more likely to vote on Election Day than Democrats were. Exit pollsters had an impossibly difficult job.

Whatever steps the pollsters took to ensure a representative sample, they appear not to have been entirely successful. As I analyze these data, I will add caveats to my interpretation when appropriate. In defense of the

2020 exit polls, traditional preelection polls had a miserable record, too, with many highly reputable organizations predicting a much bigger win for Biden than his 4.5-point victory in the actual event. Pollsters tended to do even worse in the state polls. Nate Silver's FiveThirtyEight website, the most well-known and respected aggregator of national and state polls, predicted an 8-point Biden win nationally and 351 electoral votes for Biden, including narrow wins in Florida and North Carolina. These polls also showed Trump with leads of less than 2 points in Texas, Ohio, and Iowa.[10] Obviously many of these forecasts were far off.

National Exit Poll Data

With these qualifications in mind, consider the exit poll results in table 2. They suggest that the 2020 election was almost certainly the most partisan affair in the history of public opinion surveys. Of course, elections are always partisan, but not this partisan. Both Democrats and Republicans gave 94 percent of their votes to their party's standard bearer. Usually the winner gets about 90 percent from their party and the loser gets somewhere in the mid-80s. In this election, however, nineteen in twenty partisans stuck with their party's nominee. This is the clearest manifestation of party polarization in the electorate. It is nearly impossible for a partisan to consider voting for the other party these days, no matter how dissatisfied they might be with their own party's candidate.

This record level of partisan loyalty is especially remarkable in the context of the 2020 election. Both candidates had obvious flaws. It is hard to believe that 94 percent of Republicans were enamored of Donald Trump. After all, more than 200,000 had died from COVID in the eight months leading up to the election, and Trump's performance on the issue was panned by a substantial number of Republicans.[11] In addition, many Republicans surely found his sometimes profane and erratic personal behavior troubling; his more than 22,000 false or misleading statements as president couldn't have been a source of pride either.[12] Among Democrats, Biden was far from everyone's first choice. Before party leaders took unprecedented steps to clear the nomination field for him, he won only one primary and his standing in national polls typically showed his support among Democratic primary voters in the teens. To key constituencies, he was the past, not the future. Yet both Trump and Biden got all but 6 percent of their party's votes, which suggests that, when you hate the other party, anyone from your party is acceptable.

The exit poll results relative to ideology must have been gratifying to establishment Democrats who argued that Biden's centrism made him the

TABLE 2. 2020 presidential election exit polls (in percentages)

Demographic	Biden	Trump	Margin	Demographic	Biden	Trump	Margin
Democrat	94	5	89	Latino men	59	36	23
Republican	6	94	88	Latino women	69	30	39
Independent	54	41	13	Urban	60	38	22
Liberal	89	10	79	Suburban	50	48	2
Moderate	64	34	30	Rural	42	57	15
Conservative	14	85	71	White voters, no degree	32	67	35
Age: 18–29	60	36	24	White women, college graduate	54	45	9
Age: 30–44	52	46	6	White women, no degree	36	63	27
Age: 45–64	49	50	1	White men, college graduate	48	51	3
Age: 65 or older	47	52	5	White men, no degree	28	70	42
White	41	58	17	Bachelor's degree	51	47	4
Black	87	12	75	Advanced degree	62	37	25
Latino	65	32	33	Never attended college	46	54	8
Asian	61	34	27	Some college	51	47	4
Male	45	53	8	Income: Less than $30,000	54	46	8
Female	57	42	15	Income: $30,000–$49,999	56	43	13
White men	38	61	23	Income: $50,000–$99,999	57	42	15
White women	44	55	11	Income: $100,000–$199,999	41	58	17
Black men	79	19	60	Income: $200,000 or more	44	44	0
Black women	90	9	81				

Source: https://www.nytimes.com/interactive/2020/11/03/us/elections/exit-polls
-president.html

right candidate to defeat Trump. Among self-identified liberals, Biden won 89 percent of the vote, a number that either Sanders or Warren would have struggled to improve on. Crucially, Biden cleaned up among self-identified moderates, the group his candidacy was designed to attract. Usually, these voters split pretty evenly between the parties, albeit with a slight

Democratic lean. In 2020, Biden won the group by a decisive 30 points. Finally, as expected, Trump was a dominant force among those who call themselves conservative, winning them by 85 percent to Biden's 14 percent.

As usual, voting differed fundamentally by racial and ethnic group. When considering race, analysts typically focus on the behavior of minority groups. But whites, the nation's majority racial group, have become increasingly distinctive in recent elections. The exit polls in 2020 indicate that white voters favored Trump by 17 points, 58–41. Nonwhite voters favored Biden by even larger percentages: 87–12 among African Americans, 65–32 among Latinos, and 61–34 among Asian Americans. That said, the exit poll's sampling of voters by race has been the source of much controversy. Indeed, the racial composition of the electorate according to the exit polls—with only 67 percent of voters identifying as white—appears wrong when placed in recent historical context. In 2016, 73 percent of voters identified as white; a 6 percentage point decrease in such a short period of time is unrealistic. Thus, making too many judgments about racial and ethnic groups in 2020 is somewhat risky.

Gender differences were also large. In the exit poll, men favored Trump by a 53–45 margin, while women favored Biden by a 57–42 margin, an 11-point gender gap. Although preelection polls suggested the possibility of an even larger gulf, this difference is comparable to that found in previous elections. Because both women and people of color are mostly Democrats, the size of the gender gap is driven by women of color. Among white women, Trump actually bested Biden by 11 points. Among African American women, in contrast, Biden walloped Trump by 90–9. The same basic pattern holds for Latino women. They chose Biden by 69–30. Especially among whites, education interacts with gender to provide more insight on the gender gap. White women with a college degree actually favored Biden over Trump by 9 points (54–45), but those with less than a college degree voted overwhelmingly for Trump by 27 points (63–36). For white men, the differences by education are similar. College-educated men gave Trump a slight 51–48 advantage, while less educated men favored Trump by much more, 70–28.

These results foreshadow one of the major changes in voting behavior over the past couple of decades. When it comes to socioeconomic status, education has replaced income as the major dividing line. In fact, voters making over $200,000 per year split evenly (44–44) between the candidates, something that would have been unthinkable twenty years ago. For education, the difference is the reverse of the old income divide. High-education voters favored the Democrat, whereas high-income voters traditionally favored the Republican in decades past. In 2020, Biden won voters with a college degree by 55–43. Lower-education voters, in contrast, favored the Republican Trump by 50–48. The old blue collar–white collar divide has been supplanted by something new.

Much has also rightly been made in election studies of the politics of place. Analysts typically focus on red states and blue states, but it is more accurate to focus on red and blue areas within states. That is because population density is now so important to voting behavior. Those who live in cities vote strongly Democratic, whereas those who live in more rural areas vote even more strongly Republican. For the most part, that is why states are either red or blue. Most blue states have one or more large population centers—think Boston, New York, Chicago, and Los Angeles. Most red states have giant swathes of undeveloped land—think the Great Plains, the mid-South, and Mountain West. Swing states tend to have both big cities and significant rural populations—think how Philadelphia and Pittsburgh, Pennsylvania, and Milwaukee, Wisconsin, offset small towns and farms throughout the rest of these states. This pattern again held in 2020. Urban voters went 60–38 for Biden, while rural voters went 57–42 for Trump. Suburban voters split evenly between them.

Age also affected vote choice, but in subtly different ways than in 2016. Young people went overwhelmingly for the Democratic nominee, as is typical. Voters under thirty cast their ballots 60–36 for Biden, a measurable increase over the 19-point advantage they gave Hillary Clinton. Older Americans supported Trump more than Biden, as also expected. However, Trump's advantage with voters forty-five and older shrunk relative to 2016. He enjoyed an 8-point edge when he was first elected but only a 3-point edge in his reelection bid. One possible explanation is that some older voters who felt vulnerable to COVID punished Trump for what they perceived as his lackluster handling of the pandemic. If true, that may have had a bearing on the election's outcome. Pennsylvania, Michigan, and Wisconsin are all among the fifteen-oldest states in the country, and all three flipped from Trump to Biden in 2020.

A Closer Look at Group Voting Behavior in Individual States

In gathering the exit poll data, interviewers oversampled voters in most of the swing states. That provides an opportunity to look more closely at why some of them changed hands while others stayed the same. The analysis below focuses on the voting behavior of several social groups. It carries a surprising theme. The conventional wisdom in American politics these days is that campaigns should try to maximize support among groups that are most likely to support your candidate. Democrats, then, should focus on young people and racial minorities. Republicans should focus on men and white people. My swing state analysis, however, would seem to suggest that doing less badly with groups their party usually loses was key to why Trump held Florida and Texas despite their increasing diversity and why Biden was able to flip Arizona, Georgia, and Pennsylvania. Trump did less badly with voters of color, while Biden did less badly with whites, especially white men.

One puzzle that is important to solve is the effect that increased racial and ethnic diversity has on a state's voting. Some analysts have long assumed that as the percentage of Latino voters increases in a state, the likelihood that Democrats will win also increases.[13] And, in some states, increasing Latino populations have led to Democratic gains. This has been especially true in the Southwest. But Electoral College jackpots Florida and Texas are also becoming more diverse while continuing to vote Republican. Although the margin in Texas narrowed significantly in 2020 relative to past elections, some heavily Latino areas actually voted more Republican than they did in 2016. Trump's fortunes also improved in south Florida, which is also home to a large concentration of Latino voters. Why does increasing ethnic diversity cause change in some states but not others?

Part of the answer is that analysts should not assume Latinos will vote Democratic just because they are part of a minority group. In Florida, Trump appears to have actually made big inroads with Latino voters. In 2016 he lost this group by 62–35, but he narrowed the gap to 53–46 in 2020, a 10-point improvement. Although we must be careful not to make too much of the 2020 exit polls given their flaws, county-level voting seems to corroborate the exit poll data. Clinton won heavily Latino Miami-Dade county in 2016 by 290,000 votes. Biden's margin was only 85,000 votes. In fact, Trump's 200,000 vote improvement in this county alone accounts for more than half of his 375,000 vote margin of victory in Florida.

At least in Florida, specific campaign themes may have been influential in the state's Latino community. Cuban Americans, specifically, are the dominant group in the southern part of the state, and those of Cuban descent have especially negative feelings toward the communist Castro regime, which has ruled Cuba since the late 1950s. Many were forced to flee Cuba for Florida for fear for their lives. An emerging conventional wisdom suggests that the Trump campaign successfully tagged Democrats as socialists, which, given this history, had an especially big effect on the

Cuban American community, not to mention smaller but equally anti-Marxist people of Venezuelan, Nicaraguan, and Colombian descent.[14] In addition, the Trump campaign invested heavily in door-to-door canvassing, taking its message to voters' front doors. Democrats, in contrast, decided that COVID made such outreach efforts too dangerous. It is possible that the voter contact advantage had a disproportionately strong impact on Latino voters as well.

But that can't be the whole story as it relates to Trump's apparent gains among Latino voters. After all, few if any Cuban Americans live in Texas. Mexican American voters, in addition to some of Central American descent, dominate the Lone Star state. Because the president's harshest anti-immigrant rhetoric has been directed at Mexicans and Central Americans, specifically, many analysts expected that Latino areas of the state would grow even more Democratic in 2020. Yet the story appears much the same as in Florida. The exit polls reveal that Biden won only 58 percent of the Latino vote in Texas. That is 3 points less than Clinton in 2016 and nearly 10 points below the support Biden received from Latinos in the rest of the country. Much like in Miami-Dade, the normally dark blue, heavily Latino counties that run along the Mexican border provided Trump more support in 2020 than they did in 2016.[15] This dashed any hopes of Democrats winning Texas despite historically high turnout in the state's largest cities.

Arizona may potentially hold some answers concerning the effects of increasing ethnic diversity. As in Florida and Texas, about 20 percent of the Arizona electorate identified as Latino in 2020. Unlike those two states, it surged into the Democratic column. Indeed, a major reason Democrats have flipped almost the entire desert southwest region over the past twenty years is the increase in the percentage of Latino voters. However, if Arizona's journey from red state in 2016 to blue state in 2020 is any indication, the story is more complicated. In both 2016 and 2020, exit polls indicate that the Democratic candidate won 61 percent of Arizona's Latino vote. Although Biden didn't do better than Clinton did, the percentage of voters who identified as Latino increased from 15 percent in 2016 to 20 percent in 2020. Still, that increase alone wasn't enough to flip the state.

An underappreciated part of the story is the voting behavior of whites in these increasingly diverse states. Specifically, a deep divide exists between how whites vote in the South and how they vote in the non-South. In Texas, a state that was part of the Confederacy, whites favored Trump by a staggering 66–33 percent advantage, much higher than in the country as a whole. The same is true in Florida, where exit polls reveal that Trump won

62 percent of the white vote. In Arizona, however, his margin among whites was only 52–46. Moreover, Biden narrowed Trump's advantage among white voters considerably compared with Clinton's 2016 showing. Biden lost whites only by 6, while Clinton lost them by 14.

This is not only true in Arizona. Whites who live in increasingly diverse southwestern states vote much differently than whites in increasingly diverse southern states. In Colorado, another southwestern state where Democrats now win regularly, Biden actually won a majority of white voters. In Nevada, Trump won 56 percent of whites, not as high a share as he won nationally. The states of the former Confederacy are different. Trump won 66 percent of the white vote in North Carolina, the same percentage that he won in Texas. He did even better in Georgia, where he won 69 percent of the white vote.

Consider the following. In southern states, whites are actually far more pro-Republican in their voting behavior than Latinos are pro-Democratic. Taken together, then, it appears that accounting for whites' voting behavior in increasingly diverse states is as important as accounting for the increasing number of minority voters.

This analysis prompts an important question: How could Biden have won Georgia when nearly seven in ten whites, a group that made up 61 percent of the 2020 electorate in the Peach State, voted for Trump? To repeat, election-to-election comparisons of the exit polls are not without risk given the irregularities that existed in 2020's polling. But to the extent that they can be trusted, they tell an interesting tale. Georgia's story is not Arizona's. There was no marked increase in the percentage of nonwhite voters there. In fact, the racial composition of the Georgia electorate was about the same in both 2016 and 2020. And the percentage of African Americans voting for the Democratic candidate was also about the same.

When it comes to race, what appears to have changed the most was the voting behavior of whites. When Trump won Georgia by 5.1 points in 2016, 75 percent of whites voted for him. In 2020, however, that percentage dropped to 69 percent. Many have posited that Trump's rhetoric may have alienated white women in the Atlanta suburbs, and that seems to be true. Clinton won 26 percent of white women's votes in Georgia in 2016, while Biden won 32 percent in 2020. But it is not the whole story. More surprisingly, Biden's gains among white men in Georgia appear larger than his gains among white women. Whereas Clinton won only 16 percent among white men in 2016, Biden won 27 percent in 2020.

The mix of urban, suburban, and rural voters in Georgia appears to have changed substantially between 2016 and 2020, which may also help explain the change in whites' voting behavior. Recall that Republicans dominate rural areas. The exit polls suggest that the percentage of voters in Georgia who hailed from rural areas plummeted from 23 percent of the electorate in 2016 to 14 percent in 2020, while the percentage of the electorate from urban areas—a highly Democratic group—increased by 5 percentage points. The suburbs' share of the vote increased by 4 points. It is not that rural Georgia voters stayed home. The numbers of votes cast in rural counties actually increased between 2016 and 2020, reflecting the overall surge in turnout nationwide. But the numbers of votes cast in more-Democratic-friendly urban and suburban areas increased by a lot more. Put another way, Democrats appear to have mobilized more new voters than the Republicans did. It seems plausible that the increase in Democratic support among whites is because more of those white voters lived in cities and suburbs than in rural areas.

Stacey Abrams is probably more responsible for these mobilization efforts than anyone else. In 2018, Abrams lost a very close race for governor of Georgia to Brian Kemp. Kemp, the Republican secretary of state in Georgia before he ran for governor, engineered a purge of 560,000 names from the active voter rolls a year before his gubernatorial election against Abrams. According to American Public Media, 107,000 of these names belonged to people who met national eligibility requirements. A small handful of states, including Georgia, allow names to be removed from the rolls if those individuals have not voted recently. A disproportionate share of these newly ineligible voters were Democrats, which worked to the Republican Kemp's advantage.[16] After her defeat, Abrams pledged that she would work to register more new voters for the 2020 election than were purged in 2018. Her group, the New Georgia Project, and other allied groups managed to register more than 800,000 new voters in Georgia before the 2020 election. Of course, not all of them were Democrats, but the majority were, which was decisive in turning blue a state that had voted Republican in every presidential election since 1992.

Joe Biden's Pennsylvania roots were a key source of his appeal in that state as a general election candidate. Because Trump won Pennsylvania in 2016 by only 45,000 votes, Biden didn't need to do much to win back the state for the Democrats. Winning by about 80,000 votes, he did little more than what was required. As in Georgia, Pennsylvania's racial composition didn't change between 2016 and 2020. However, the composition of the electorate by population density changed in a direction disadvantageous to the Democrats. Whereas the percentage of voters from Georgia's Republican rural areas dropped, the percentage of the vote from Democratic urban areas in Pennsylvania dropped by 5 points. The percentage of the vote from the suburbs and rural areas actually increased.

The exit poll results suggest that Biden won the Keystone State because he did substantially less poorly with rural and suburban voters than Clinton did four years earlier. Whereas Clinton lost suburbia by 8 points, Biden lost by only 3. His 4-point improvement in the heavily populated Philadelphia suburbs, specifically, was critical. In addition, Biden competed somewhat better than Clinton did in rural Pennsylvania. Clinton lost these areas by 45 points, but Biden lost them by "only" 39 points. As in Georgia, it appears that white men, in particular, were central to understanding these changes. In 2016, Clinton lost them by 32 points (64–32). Biden stanched the bleeding a bit, losing by only 25 points (62–37). Democratic Party leaders had hoped a white man from Pennsylvania would make a difference, and it appears to have made just enough of one. Given that turnout in overwhelmingly Democratic Philadelphia increased at a slower rate than it did in the rest of the state, Biden's "regular Joe" persona outside the big city apparently paid off.

Because of the issues with the exit poll data, it is reassuring that this analysis is consistent with county-level voting results in Pennsylvania. They reveal that, of the sixty-seven counties in the state, Philadelphia County was actually the one that moved the most toward Trump in 2020 relative to 2016. Whereas Biden got 3 percent more votes from the state's biggest city, Trump increased his share by 22 percent.[17] Clinton's vote margin was 475,000, while Biden's was only 455,000. With turnout skyrocketing across the state, a smaller margin in Philadelphia might have doomed the Democrats. Consistent with the exit poll data, the four collar counties around Philadelphia helped bail Biden out. He increased the Democratic margin here by over 100,000 votes, more than his overall margin of victory. In addition, the rural counties were less of a disaster than they might have been had another candidate been running. Indeed, there were forty-five mostly rural counties that voted for Trump, usually overwhelmingly, in both 2016 and 2020, but where Biden narrowed the gap, ever so slightly. In contrast, only nine counties voted for Trump both years and increased his share of the vote in 2020 relative to 2016.[18]

The Aftermath: A Threat to Democracy

Among the unsung norms that make democracy work is the willingness of losing candidates to acknowledge their own defeat. It is such a routine part of American life that most never even consider it, at least not until this year. When election losers concede defeat, they confer legitimacy on the outcome and on the next administration. That subtle bit of splendor that allows for representative democracy to operate did not happen in the wake of the 2020 presidential election. Always the self-proclaimed fighter, President Trump refused to acknowledge the obvious in the days and weeks after his defeat. Despite losing the popular vote by more than 5 million and the electoral vote by exactly the same margin he won it in 2016, he said the election was rigged, stolen by fraud, rather than admitting defeat. On November 4, the day after the election, he began to exhort his supporters to "stop the steal."

The basis for Trump's often-wild charges evolved over time. He claimed the millions of ballots cast by mail were fraudulent. This was not true. He insinuated that tens of thousands of fraudulent ballots were illegally introduced into polling stations in big cities like Philadelphia and Detroit while Republican poll observers were not allowed in the room. This was not true. He claimed that voting machines had been programmed to add tens of thousands of his votes to Joe Biden's overall tally. This was not true. Indeed, his own attorney general William Barr and the Justice Department concluded that there was no evidence of voter fraud on a scale that could have affected the election's outcome.[19] Yet, Trump continued to level these charges.

In addition to tweeting that he had won the election easily, Trump attempted to persuade state and county election canvassers not to certify vote totals in their jurisdictions. If the votes were not certified by election officials, Trump's legal team believed it could potentially provide state legislatures the leeway to choose Republican electors instead of the Democratic electors who actually won their states. In the end, neither election officials nor state legislatures went along with the gambit even though many were Republicans themselves.

The last step in certifying the election's outcome is for Congress to count the Electoral College votes, which is a pro forma process because electors across the country have already cast their votes in accordance with the election outcome in their states. As this ceremonial act was taking place in the US House chamber, the seemingly unimaginable happened, the last and worst unprecedented occurrence of the election season. On January 6, Donald Trump led a rally less than two miles from the Capitol Building. He repeated lies that the election had been stolen and told his supporters to march to the Capitol. Within minutes, they violently overwhelmed police at the Capitol and invaded the building for the first time since the British set fire to it in 1814. Five died in the ensuing riot. Soon after, the House voted to impeach Trump for the second time, this time for incitement of an insurrection to overturn the outcome of the 2020 election.

The nation's electoral institutions ultimately held. Joe Biden was inaugurated as scheduled. But the costs appear high. Even after the carnage on January 6, 75 percent of Republicans still reported in a CNN poll that they didn't believe Joe Biden won the 2020 election legitimately.[20] It is not clear how sincere or deeply held these attitudes about the election were. Perhaps Republicans were just cheerleading for their side. But it is not far-fetched to think that most of these cynical attitudes remain real because they echo what their party leader, Donald Trump, has told them is true. This could have negative implications for future leaders, especially Joe Biden, and will doubtlessly continue to fuel the party polarization that has plagued the country for years to come.

Notes

1. http://www.electproject.org/home/voter-turnout/voter-turnout-data.
2. https://news.gallup.com/poll/248135/subgroup-differences-trump-approval-mostly-party-based.aspx.
3. https://www.usatoday.com/story/news/politics/elections/2020/11/03/voter-turnout-2020-early-voting-tops-100-million/6133004002/.
4. https://www.washingtonpost.com/politics/2020/11/19/trumps-own-lawyers-keep-undermining-his-voter-fraud-claims/.
5. Several faithless electors did not follow the will of the voters of their states, producing a somewhat different final number. But 306–232 was the score based on the states won by the two candidates both years.
6. This observation is based on Lee Drutman's analysis, which he posted on Twitter on November 19, 2020.
7. Only Iowa, Nevada, and Virginia have voted three times for one party and two times for the other.
8. I relied on the presidential election website 270towin.com for this projection.
9. Billionaire former New York City mayor Michael Bloomberg also joined the fray during this time. His candidacy demonstrated how hard it is to run for president. Although he spent over $900 million of his own money, the only nomination contest he won was in America Samoa. He collected barely fifty delegates before exiting the race.
10. See Silver's final forecast here: https://projects.fivethirtyeight.com/2020-election-forecast/.
11. An AP-NORC poll taken in mid-October showed that barely half of Republicans approved of Trump's handling of COVID. https://apnews

.com/article/election-2020-virus-outbreak-donald-trump-pandemics-elec
tions-6e638bcaaebe4b5e83721440203b7511.

12. https://www.washingtonpost.com/politics/2020/10/22/president-trump-is
    -averaging-more-than-50-false-or-misleading-claims-day/.

13. John Judis and Ruy Teixeira, *The Emerging Democratic Majority*.

14. See, for example, https://www.nbcnews.com/news/latino/trump-cultiva
    ted-latino-vote-florida-it-paid-n1246226.

15. See, for example, https://www.nytimes.com/interactive/2020/11/05/us/texas
    -election-results.html.

16. https://www.apmreports.org/story/2019/10/29/georgia-voting-registration
    -records-removed.

17. https://www.inquirer.com/politics/election/pennsylvania-2020-election
    -biden-trump-20201129.html.

18. Ibid.

19. https://www.washingtonpost.com/national-security/barr-no-evidence
    -election-fraud/2020/12/01/5f4dcaa8-340a-11eb-8d38-6aea1adb3839_story
    .html.

20. https://www.politico.com/news/2020/11/09/republicans-free-fair-elec
    tions-435488.

Voting

STABILIZING DEMOCRACY–AND REHEARSING A REALIGNMENT?

Nicole Mellow and Candis Watts Smith

When a president runs for reelection, the contest is a referendum on the job done in the previous four years.[1] This was true in 2020 for President Donald Trump, just as it has been in every previous election featuring an incumbent. Yet unlike other reelection battles, 2020 was also a referendum on the health of American democracy after four years of a president whose authoritarian inclinations led him to ignore long-standing norms and conventions of presidential leadership. Given the unprecedented nature of the election, was the electorate that refused President Trump a second term standing up for democracy, merely dissatisfied with his accomplishments, or something else altogether?

During the president's term, many noted the ostensible upsides of the administration's early years: a booming stock market, low unemployment rates, tax cuts especially benefiting corporations and wealthy Americans, regulatory rollbacks, and the president's efforts to maintain his foreign policy promise to put "America first." Others balked at the downsides that Trump brought to the White House: a government run like a family business, a revolving door of key administrative posts, an obsessive focus on his perceived adversaries (whether previous political opponents, the media, or members of his own party and administration), policy decree by Twitter, sporadic attention to national problems and policy reversals, promulgation of white supremacist sentiments, and denunciations of long-standing international alliances. The president's norm-busting tendencies, willingness to utter falsehoods, and promotion of conspiracy theories bred in the fringes of the internet produced a daily media firestorm. Trump's actions led in 2017 to the appointment of a special prosecutor to investigate his role in Russian interference in the 2016 election and, for a different set of offenses, in 2019 to impeachment (though not conviction) for abuse of power and obstruction of Congress. In 2020, Trump became the first president to run for reelection having lost the popular vote in his election and having been impeached while in office, a dubious honor.

Responding to the president's chaotic leadership and his effort to rebrand the Republican Party as a vehicle for right-wing nationalism—what some referred to as "Trumpism"—more than twenty Democrats announced their presidential candidacies as early as January 2019. The most diverse set of candidates in history included six women, a member of the LGBT community, Blacks, Latinos, and Asian Americans. Together, they represented generational cohorts from millennials to the silent generation and varied in religious faiths and ideological stances from former Republican moderates to Democratic socialists. Despite their diversity, all of the candidates argued that Trump was singularly unfit for office. Out of this varied field, an elder statesman representing the moderate wing of the party, former vice president Joseph Biden, gained the nomination. While Biden's general election campaign was quickly constrained by the springtime eruption of COVID-19, the Trump administration's delayed and fumbling response to the pandemic—which cost roughly 240,000 American lives by Election Day—provided Biden and his vice presidential running mate, Kamala Harris, with a stark way of illustrating the president's unfitness for office that they exploited on their road to victory.

Biden's win was ultimately a comfortable one. In an election that produced a turnout unparalleled in the modern era, the Democrat won a majority of the popular vote, 51.3 to 46.8 percent, over 7 million more votes than the Republican. By contrast, Hillary Clinton, the 2016 Democratic candidate, secured nearly 3 million more votes than Trump but failed to capture a majority. Biden's popular vote triumph was matched by his improvement over Clinton in electoral votes. Whereas Clinton failed to capture the necessary 270 votes in 2016, Biden netted 306, a clear majority.

In her victory speech, Vice President-Elect Harris told Americans that the country's "very democracy," indeed the "soul of America," had been at stake in the election.[2] At a fundamental level, in 2020, Americans overcame hurdles to the ballot box to stabilize democracy against an unprecedented assault. Yet although many pollsters thought a landslide repudiation of the unorthodox president was a distinct possibility, this did not happen.[3] Trump earned more than 74 million Americans' votes—11 million more than in 2016—raising questions about how to understand voters' decisions in this historically significant moment.

Analyzing the 2020 election will be the project of many years. Early assessment is difficult, not just because of the unprecedented circumstances of the election. A consensus about the quality of the exit poll data we rely on most after the election has yet to emerge. Already cautious after polling miscues in 2016 led many to expect a Clinton victory, pollsters in 2020 faced two distinct but related challenges in polling. First, polling outfits relied on their prior but outdated expectations of the American voter. For instance, Gallup's "traditional model" of "likely voters" is determined by a combination of voters' previous behavior coupled with their stated intention to vote, but "unlikely voters" turned out at unexpected rates in 2020.[4] Additionally, pollsters have yet to successfully find the balance between making generalizations about voting blocs and producing nuanced assessments of diverse groups. For example, many pollsters who sought to predict "the" Latino vote failed to capture the variation within this historically hard-to-define group, one better understood as pan-ethnic and varied in geography, identity, and most importantly, policy preferences.[5]

Another difficulty with polling data is that the polls themselves have become politicized. Researchers have noted that people who respond to polls are different from those who refuse. Some suggest that people who answer pollsters' questions are more likely to have high levels of social trust, and these people tend to be Democrats. The corrections that data scientists have traditionally made in their numbers failed in 2020 to compensate for such high degrees of asymmetry in partisan response.[6] Additionally, the pandemic itself influenced exit polls because the means by which Americans cast their ballots in 2020 hinged on partisan identity, with Democrats more likely than Republicans to vote absentee or by mail.[7] These challenges complicate pollsters' efforts to render their data more representative of the American electorate.

With those caveats, this chapter is an early effort to make sense of the 2020 election. If not a widespread repudiation of President Trump, then what was it? Does the election portend a coming realignment of the two major political parties, or did it simply shine a brighter light on partisan cleavages that have existed for years? What was this election about for voters? What role do voters' economic fortunes play in their vote choice, and how has growing income inequality affected the parties? To what degree is the Republican Party a vehicle for white "identity politics" and racial resentment, and will it become a home for white nationalism? Did the multiracial Obama coalition come out in full force to support the Biden-Harris ticket, the first in American history to feature a woman of color?

Are the country's demographic dynamics shaping the political destinies of the parties?

In the following sections, we show how the 2020 results fit with some of the more significant patterns of voter behavior in recent decades, including new voter mobilization as well as geographic and demographic shifts in Republican and Democratic support. Although still too early to tell, trends in party support suggest that the country may be witnessing not just further polarization but also a redefinition of the parties' core identities and commitments. Whether this is a deviation in response to the polarizing figure of Donald Trump or the early stage of a long-term realignment of the parties remains to be seen.

Still a Partisan Affair

The ideas and policies that the two major parties stood for in 2020 were not always clear. Republicans declined to update their party platform from four years prior even though the country faced dramatic new problems. Despite his anti-immigrant and anti-Black rhetoric, Trump repeatedly appealed to these typically Democratic groups with messaging to Black male voters on issues of criminal justice and community uplift and with spectacles, like staging a naturalization ceremony during the Republican National Convention, aimed at immigrants. For their part, Democrats incorporated planks in their platform favored by their most progressive supporters while also highlighting the endorsements of establishment Republicans and the support of organizations like the Lincoln Project, a group of anti-Trump former Republican operatives. In the end, both parties' efforts to convert voters were largely unpersuasive. In 2020, 94 percent of Democrats supported Biden, just as 94 percent of Republicans supported Trump.[8]

Of the many ways to assess voter behavior, party affiliation remains, far and away, the best predictor of vote choice. As evident in figure 1, partisans in the electorate stayed loyal to their party's candidate in 2020 at rates largely consistent with recent elections and, in fact, at an all-time high in the modern era. This accounts for most of the votes that were cast. Nearly three of four voters identify with one of the two major parties, with the division between them essentially even. The remainder claim to be "independent or something else," and in a reversal from how they voted in 2016, they broke for the Democratic nominee in 2020: 54 percent supported Biden, compared with 42 percent for Clinton in 2016. Although independents helped tip the election to Biden, major party voters stuck nearly universally by their candidate.

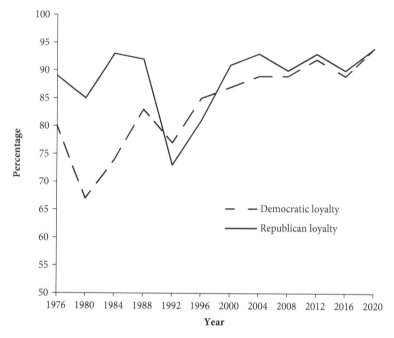

Fig. 1. Party loyalty in presidential elections, 1976–2020
Source: Roper Center National Election Pool (NEP) data (1976–2004); New York Times
NEP data (2008–20).

With the exception of 1992, when billionaire Ross Perot was on the ballot
as an independent, Republican voters have been consistently loyal supporters of their party's presidential candidate. More interesting is the
steady increase, since 1980, in Democratic loyalty. This development partly
reflects the ideological realignment of voters in the two-party system
in response to clearer divisions among party elites. Democratic and
Republican lawmakers, especially in Congress, have sharply divided
over economic, social justice, and foreign policy issues since the 1980s,
but the process by which voters have sorted themselves into the party best
corresponding to their own beliefs has taken longer to unfold. Conservative Democratic voters, who often supported the Republican presidential
candidate in the 1970s and 1980s, have slowly migrated out of the Democratic Party. Liberal Republicans have shifted to the Democratic Party. The
result, by the 2000s, is greater partisan loyalty in both parties and across
all levels of the party system.[9]

Many observers lament partisanship and its more severe cousin polarization, claiming that the extreme views of party elites do not represent the views of American voters.[10] Yet evidence is building that the electorate is becoming more polarized, leading some to claim a worrisome new level of "tribalism." On this view, voters' partisan attachments have become, in essence, super-identities, often aligning with their social identities. Republicans have become a more homogenous group of white Christians, and Democrats a heterogeneous group of nonwhite citizens of varying faiths, including no religion. Importantly, for scholars who hold this view, identity more than ideology or policy preference drives voters' partisan attachment now, and with an "us versus them" mindset, winning and losing elections is more about identity affirmation than policy achievement.[11]

The view that issues do not matter as much as identity may help explain the continuity of voters' party loyalty despite significant policy and issue changes that have occurred within the parties. As the Democratic nominating contest made evident in 2020, clear policy differences divide progressive candidates like Bernie Sanders and Elizabeth Warren and more centrist candidates like Biden, Amy Klobuchar, and Pete Buttigieg. Similar factionalism is on display in Congress, where Speaker Nancy Pelosi has struggled to keep her caucus together in the face of resistance from young progressives, such as Alexandria Ocasio-Cortez and Ilhan Omar. In 2020, although only 42 percent of those who identify as Democrat or lean Democrat expressed satisfaction with Biden as the party's nominee—the lowest percentage since Bill Clinton headed the ticket in 1992—these voters nonetheless stayed overwhelmingly loyal, turning out in record numbers despite their reservations.[12]

A greater percentage of Republican and Republican-leaning voters, 59 percent, reported satisfaction with Trump as their party's candidate, nearing the level of support former president George W. Bush received in 2000 and 2004. This is especially noteworthy because Trump represented a significant departure from both mainstream and conservative Republican politicians, including recent presidential candidates about whom Republican voters expressed less satisfaction but nonetheless supported.[13] He rejected long-standing Republican positions in several policy domains and advanced a more explicit and vitriolic white nationalism than previous Republican presidents or presidential candidates.[14] Additionally, Trump frankly dismissed what is perhaps the most fundamental conservative position: respect for institutions and traditions. Yet his new combination of positions generated just as much loyalty from his party's voters as other recent but more conventional Republicans.

Another indication of voters' deep identification with their parties is that their partisanship correlated nearly perfectly with their answers to a range of questions about the personal qualities of the candidates. Consistent with research on voters' motivated reasoning and confirmation bias, which shows that partisans respond to new information selectively and in ways that reinforce their prior beliefs, Republicans consistently approved of Trump and disapproved of Biden (vice versa for Democratic voters), regardless of the question—be it about temperament, mental and physical health, job done, or ability to handle the country's problems.[15] Trump's voters supported him even while acknowledging his unprecedented lies, behaviors, and character flaws—in fact, partly because of those norm-busting attributes.[16] Their devotion might be separate from generic party loyalty, and Trump's presence at the top of the ticket may have helped strengthen Republican loyalty. If true, the Republican Party going forward may remold itself around a nationalist populist agenda and a leadership style similar to Trump's in an effort to retain his voters.[17]

Scholars have long argued that clear differences between the parties function as useful information shortcuts, engaging voters and helping them make sense of electoral choices.[18] The clarity of the ideological distinctions between the parties predates Trump but is still a relatively recent development. From the 1930s to the 1960s, America was generally described as having a politics of consensus, with nonideological parties and frequent demonstrations of bipartisanship among lawmakers. This was the height of the New Deal era, when Democratic ideas about national government activism defined the terms of normal politics. Keynesian fiscal policy, the welfare state, a social contract between labor and capital, and containment of Soviet communism were regularly reauthorized by a broad majority of Americans. The one Republican president of the era, Dwight D. Eisenhower, was a moderate whose governance was more in step with the New Deal than with conservatives in his own party.

By the 1970s, Democratic dominance was gone and bipartisanship soon left with it. Disruptions in the 1960s from civil rights and feminist movements, dissension over the Vietnam War, and economic uncertainty upended the political order. To many people, Democratic solutions appeared obsolete. Richard Nixon was the first Republican to capitalize on this weakness, and by 1980, with Ronald Reagan's election, the country seemed poised to embrace a new governing philosophy. Reagan summed up this new philosophy in his 1981 inaugural address, saying, "Government is not the solution to our problem; government is the problem."

Although skepticism of national government power has existed since the founding, Reagan's 1980 victory restored the idea to public prominence. Republican philosophy combined military strength with limited government, stressing the benefits that would accrue from tax cuts, deregulation, and privatization. When the effects of this approach appeared inconsistent, conservative social values became Republicans' new ballast. Churning economic and social change, they argued, was best answered with the stability and security of traditional values.[19] Republicans joined neoliberal economic policies and devolution of power to the states with an emphasis on race-neutral individual rights, a resurrection of traditional "family" values, and support for law and order. When Reagan's election was followed by a resounding reelection in 1984 and then the election, in 1988, of his vice president, George H. W. Bush, the string of Republican presidential victories seemed, at last, to represent a full-scale repudiation of the New Deal. Indeed, recent works of political history characterize the late twentieth century as a conservative Republican era that began with Reagan, or possibly Nixon.[20]

But unlike the New Deal and earlier party eras, voters reacted with ambivalence to the new Republican regime. Except for the Senate from 1981 to 1987, Congress stayed under Democratic control throughout the 1970s and 1980s. Even after Republicans finally won control of both the House and Senate in 1994, Democrat Bill Clinton remained in the White House and was reelected two years later. Indeed, divided party government has become the norm in Washington, with the same party ruling both houses of Congress and the presidency for just fourteen of the past fifty-two years. No president since Reagan has been able to claim a significant electoral mandate. Pluralities prevailed in the elections won by Clinton in 1992 and 1996. George W. Bush in 2000 and Donald Trump in 2016 were elected despite losing the national popular vote. Recent presidents who have won a popular vote majority have typically done so by a slim margin. President Bush earned just 51 percent in 2004, similar to President Obama's reelection showing in 2012. In keeping with recent elections, Biden won with 51 percent of the popular vote.

The election of 2020 was different from these others in an important regard, however. In a jump from previous elections, a record number of voters—over 159 million—turned out to cast ballots, despite the pandemic and other challenges to voting. This number represents an estimated 66.7 percent of the voting-eligible population, making 2020 the highest-turnout election since 1900.[21]

Historically, high turnout and substantial voter concerns, both on display in 2020, signal the potential for a realignment of the parties.

Realignment has a complex, even technical, definition, yet the general form involves significant political change that is electorally driven, substantive, and durable. Scholars have documented, and disagreed about, a number of such moments of change, including the elections of Andrew Jackson (1828), Abraham Lincoln (1860), William McKinley (1896), and Franklin D. Roosevelt (1932). What is of signal importance, though, is that realignments represent a lasting shift in voter behavior and the emergence, often dramatic, of a new majority. By definition, realignments can only be confirmed in hindsight, yet the rise of new cross-cutting issues along with the conversion of, or increase in new, voter support for the parties alerts scholars to the prospect of a developing realignment.[22]

Despite some signs of realigning activity—increased voter turnout and the rise of new, highly salient, and polarizing issues—the party loyalty that also marked 2020 suggests that there was no massive shift of voters from one party to the other, to either embrace or repudiate Trump. Both parties turned out large numbers of angry voters, old and new, for their causes, and although Biden prevailed, so did many Republicans in down-ballot races. The question remains: What was the cause for which voters turned out? Was the election merely a reaction to the polarizing figure of Donald Trump, one unlikely to be repeated in 2024, or is the country in the early stages of a party realignment along a new axis of conflict and identity?

A Majority Blue Nation?

When election night and the days that followed brought no clear victor, voters turned their attention to the electoral map, following regular media updates of the vote tallies in counties such as Maricopa (AZ), Clayton (GA), Wayne (MI), and Allegheny (PA)—places that seemed to hold the key to which candidate would get each state's electoral votes and be declared the next president. With Trump denouncing counts that seemed to favor Biden, state and local election workers were routinely in the national news defending the integrity of their processes and in at least one case providing a livestream of vote counting in Philadelphia. With so much at stake, seldom was democracy more suspenseful. Even after Pennsylvania was called for Biden, putting him over the 270 electoral vote threshold needed to win, attention did not flag, merely shifting to the still-unresolved states of North Carolina, Georgia, Nevada, and Arizona. Biden eventually captured the latter three to push his final electoral vote count to 306.

In response to polls predicting a Biden win, Trump had asserted that his loss would signal an unfair election and he would challenge the results.

Consequently, the number of states Biden won and their margins of victory were important in underscoring the legitimacy of the outcome and determining whether he had a mandate to govern.[23] Yet for party strategists, another reason to focus on states like Arizona and Georgia was that they were not part of the traditional Democratic base in the Northeast, Midwest, and Pacific coast. In recent decades, Nevada had trended Democratic, voting blue in five of the previous seven elections, but Democrats had prevailed only once in Arizona (1996), North Carolina (2008), and Georgia (1992). As Democrats' hopes for a nationwide repudiation of Trump fizzled on election night, these four states, along with Colorado and New Mexico—two states Biden, as well as previous Democrats, won comfortably—offered perhaps the best hope for building a new and enduring geographic majority for the party.

Arizona, Nevada, North Carolina, and Georgia were among the true "battlegrounds" in 2020, competitive states that ultimately were won by less than 3 percentage points. The other three similarly competitive states were Pennsylvania, Wisconsin, and Michigan—midwestern states that, although traditionally Democratic, had voted for Trump in 2016. Of these seven competitive states, Biden ultimately won six. He succeeded in rebuilding his party's "blue wall" in the Midwest and gained ground outside traditional Democratic regions.

Elections with only a small number of competitive states, fewer than ten, have been the norm since 1980. Having few states in play has become routine because the parties dominate different areas of the country, thereby contributing to the recent intensity of partisan standoffs. In 1972, Richard Nixon won every state but Massachusetts. In 1980, Ronald Reagan won all but five states, and these five were distributed around the country. In 1984, he won every state but Minnesota. Landslide presidential victories that were national in scope were the norm for much of the twentieth century. But since the 1990s, the parties have represented different regions of the country. By 2000, the media had labeled this geographic division the "red state/blue state" divide. In that election, George W. Bush captured "red" states that were largely in the South and interior West, while the "blue" states captured by Al Gore were concentrated in the Northeast, the Midwest, and the Pacific coast. This basic division of red and blue states has been largely sustained in every election since then. As the maps in figure 2 show, 2020 generally followed this pattern. Biden won northeastern, midwestern, and Pacific coast states that have voted Democratic in recent decades, while Trump captured states in the Republican South and West. The regional exceptions of Virginia, Colorado, Nevada, and New Mexico

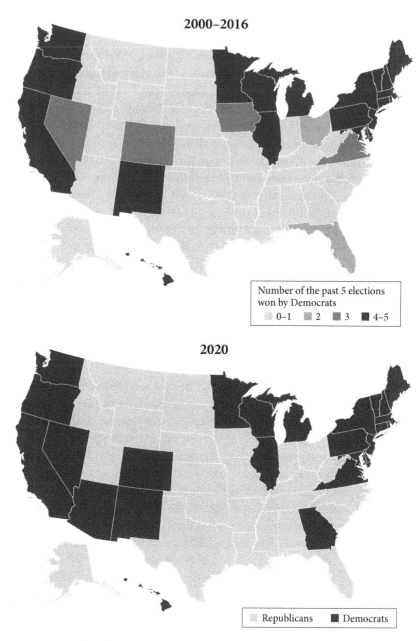

FIG. 2. Geography of presidential election results, 2000–2016 and 2020
Source: Compiled by authors.

had voted Democratic in at least the previous three elections, and they did so again in 2020. Ohio and Florida, often described as battleground states, have voted Democratic only twice in the past five elections, and Trump won both easily. Arizona and Georgia were new pickups for the Democratic Party.

The existing regional organization of the party system has its origins in the 1960s, when New Deal Democrats still dominated national elections. The party's electoral strength since the 1930s had derived from an accord brokered between its regional wings in the urban North and rural South. The basis of this accord was that national policy would be tailored to accommodate the dominant interests in each region: organized labor and manufacturers in the North, and agriculture and labor-intensive industries in the all-white electorate that still prevailed in the South. The party suppressed issues that defied regional tailoring, such as civil rights for Black Americans. By the late 1960s, this accord was in jeopardy. Republican leaders were quick to exploit emerging fissures in the New Deal coalition—most obviously, but not entirely, in the area of civil rights. Republicans gained an advantage at this time by appealing to white southern Democrats, not just on racial issues but also on other social issues (for example, abortion), economic issues (such as welfare policies), and foreign affairs (including Vietnam).

The regional discord that marked the late New Deal era led to a realignment of the geographic basis of the party system. The most obvious outcome of Republican efforts to destabilize Democrats' geographic base was an acceleration of the GOP's capture of the South. But Republicans concentrated their attention on the West as well, a region that, like the South, contained states with fast-growing economies and populations. Also, as in the South, the farming, ranching, and mining states of the West had a political history of antagonism toward their perceived domination by northern financial and political elites. These economic, social, and symbolic resentments were fodder for a growing Republican Party in the region.[24]

With the regional crack-up of the Democratic Party, the New Deal coalition was revealed to be an ultimately unstable sectional fusion. Two new versions of the Republican and Democratic Parties replaced the New Deal party system in the 1970s. One was an "emerging Republican majority" centered in the fast-growing suburbs, small towns, and rural areas of the South and the West.[25] The other was a refashioned Democratic Party, with enhanced electoral muscle in the historically urbanized, densely populated, and commercially developed states of the North and the Pacific coast. Just as Republicans displaced Democrats in some regions, such as the South,

Democrats, in turn, displaced Republicans in other regions, especially New England, where the GOP had historically reigned.

As the demands made by the South and the West on the national government began to clash with those of the North and the Pacific coast, the parties responded. For example, in the 1970s, as northern lawmakers came to dominate the Democratic Party, they abandoned that party's long-held commitment to free trade in the face of deindustrialization in their strongest region. As Republicans simultaneously shifted south and westward into the trade-dependent regions of the rising Sunbelt, the two parties came into increasing conflict with one another over trade policy.[26] On trade, as on a range of foreign and domestic policy issues, red versus blue partisan conflict intensified as the parties' geographic bases shifted.

Instead of a national realignment that elevated one or the other party to majority status, the current party system has been one of stalemate between two regionally centered parties. The parties' different geographic footprints are also why, no matter how big a president's win in recent elections, a substantial partisan opposition has remained in government and a significant swath of the country has felt betrayed by election outcomes. Because of the geographic sorting between the parties, voters often live in communities alongside others who share, and amplify, their partisan identity and worldview. That those who disagree with them live elsewhere makes their different choice in elections even more incomprehensible.[27]

In 2008 and 2012, Obama appeared to partially disrupt the prevailing geographic pattern. He won traditionally blue states in the Pacific coast and the North but also picked up a number of red states, notably Virginia, Colorado, and Nevada, thanks to urban and suburban growth in those states. These states stayed in the Democratic column in 2016 and 2020. Democrats' sustained success may be a harbinger of a future party realignment. Although Trump improved his standing and turned out voters in much of rural and small-town America, Biden did the same in urban areas and also in suburbs—where most Americans now live. In 2020, as in the 2018 congressional elections, Democrats scored important victories in suburbs, and it was the strength of multiracial suburban support in states like Pennsylvania, Arizona, and Georgia that helped swing the election.[28]

Coalition Renovation: All Hands on Deck

What is the will of the people? What is our mandate? I believe it's this: America has called upon us to marshal the forces of decency, the forces of fairness. To marshal the forces of science and the forces of hope in the great battles of our time. The battle to control the virus, the battle to build prosperity, the battle to secure your family's health care. The battle to achieve racial justice and root out systemic racism in this country. And the battle to save our planet by getting climate change under control.

—President-Elect Joseph R. Biden, November 7, 2020

By the start of primary voting in early 2020, Americans already had plenty of controversial presidential politics to consider. In addition to impeachment, Americans had watched two controversial confirmations of conservative Supreme Court justices; children being separated from their parents at the nation's southern border; and the president's embrace of conspiracy theories, foreign dictators long opposed by the national security establishment, and white nationalist groups labeled the "most persistent and lethal" domestic terrorist threat by his own Department of Homeland Security.[29]

One asset the president had going for him was a strong economy. The downward trend in unemployment rates that began during the Obama administration continued under Trump. He also touted massive stock market gains, produced in part by the passage of major tax cuts early in his tenure. Although many Americans in both parties did not approve of the president's conduct in office, they approved of his economy. But just as election season got under way, the global outbreak of the COVID-19 pandemic sent the economy into a tailspin and illuminated vast inequalities that had festered unaddressed for decades. Economic and especially racial inequalities were underscored when a nearly nine-minute video of the killing of George Floyd, a Black American, by police in May 2020 went viral, throwing additional light onto the persistence of structural racism and pushing people into the streets to protest. Sitting at home under statewide quarantines, Americans had few distractions from the news of the country's health, economic, and social crises.

As Biden suggested in his victory speech, Democrats saw the election as about much more than the economy, which has traditionally been voters' central concern in determining whether incumbents should keep their job.[30] Instead, several matters were at the forefront of Americans' considerations as they cast ballots. Although the economy remained the top issue for Republicans, Democrats were much more likely to say that health care, COVID, and racial and ethnic inequality were "very important" to their electoral decision. Indeed, the partisan gap concerning whether these other issues were priorities ranged from 36 points on health care to 52 points on matters of racial equity.[31] This variation makes it difficult to extract a single message about voters' concerns in 2020—the election was not all about the economy, or the pandemic, or racial injustice—but demographic group behaviors in 2020 largely reinforce and help explain the previously discussed developments in the geographical basis of partisanship.

TO WHOM DO VOTERS TURN IN UNCERTAIN ECONOMIC TIMES?

In 2016, Trump promised working- and middle-class voters in America's "heartland" that as president he would bring back manufacturing jobs and help farmers and small business owners. He claimed that Democrats were willing to sacrifice these groups' economic well-being for a greener economy and cleaner environment. To uphold his promise, President Trump adopted some traditional Republican policy commitments, signing into law a major tax cut, withdrawing from the Paris Climate Accord, and letting states decide how to respond to the pandemic. Trump also deployed executive actions to disavow several core conservative economic principles—starting a trade war with China and withdrawing from the Trans-Pacific Partnership, for example. The major implications of his mixed ideological bag of policies were that deficits soared; the nation's wealth was redistributed upward; the administration was forced to bail out farmers hurt by its actions on trade; and the pandemic-produced recession further aggravated a trade-war-induced manufacturing slump.

How did voters respond to these policies in 2020? Typically, voters who think the economy is in poor shape punish the incumbent.[32] Indeed, those who were pessimistic about the well-being of future generations were much more likely to support Biden, as were those who made less than $100,000 annually. Biden's support from low-income and working-class voters— those making less than $50,000 annually—is consistent with Democrats' historical strength among these voters, who since the New Deal have valued the party's efforts to provide a social safety net. Biden also improved Democrats' standing with middle-income voters, those making $50,000 to $100,000, from recent elections.

Shifts in the economic and education bases of the parties in recent years, however, may be eroding the traditional relationship between income and party support. In particular, while poor and working-class voters were the mainstay of the New Deal Democratic Party throughout the mid-twentieth century, in recent decades the party has improved its standing with educated white voters, regardless of income, while Republicans have made gains with less educated and less affluent white voters. This development was part of what led Democratic strategists in the early years of the first decade of the twenty-first century to anticipate an "emerging Democratic majority" grounded in the highly educated, affluent, and diverse metropolitan "ideopolises" of the new technology-driven economy.[33] Obama's successes in 2008 and 2012 seemed to validate the thesis that a Democratic coalition that included educated whites and people of color would keep the party in power.[34] Between 2016 and 2020, differences between red and blue counties in education levels, household incomes, and projected long-term job growth widened further.[35] And in keeping with the emerging Democratic majority thesis, whites with college degrees gave slightly more of their votes to Biden than Trump.

Adding more complexity to the relationship between income and party support, research shows that voters' perceptions of the economy are influenced as much by their partisan identity as their place in that economy.[36] Voters' partisan dispositions affect how they judge economic conditions and candidate performance, often leading Democrats and Republicans to fundamentally different assessments of how the economy is doing. For example, Republican voters in 2020 living in areas with greater economic downturns were more likely to say that Trump was better suited to handle the economy than Biden. Trump also grew his support in counties where more jobs are at risk for automation. They also tended to view the effects of the pandemic on the economy as "more like an act of God than a product of policy choices."[37] Clearly no simple correlation marks the relationship between economic standing and party identity.

The Obama Coalition Strikes Back?

Donald Trump began his 2016 presidential bid with a speech denigrating Mexican immigrants. For many white Americans, his "Make America Great Again" rhetoric evoked memories of a 1950s' manufacturing-based economy and a pre-civil-rights era of white supremacy. His victory was made possible, in part, by his dipping into an existing, deep reservoir of white racial resentment.[38] As president, Trump's characterization of a deadly attack by white supremacists in Charlottesville in 2017 was a bland equivocation; he asserted that the "egregious display of hatred, bigotry, and violence on many sides" was to blame. Toward the end of his term, he employed the U.S. Park Police and National Guard to use pepper spray on Black Lives Matters protesters so that he could engage in a Bible-wielding photo-op in front of a church near the White House. Some observers predicted that the combination of Trump's racist vitriol, demographic shifts in the American electorate, and the Democrats' nomination of a woman of multiracial ancestry for vice president would produce a landslide for the Biden-Harris ticket. Although this did not happen, with turnout at historically high levels, 2020 was nonetheless in part a referendum on the explicit white nationalism of Trumpism.

Since the 1960s, the racial divide in party support has been the most pronounced demographic division in the electorate, with Democratic candidates receiving overwhelming support from Black Americans and strong support from Latinos and other people of color. This trend continued in 2020. Most Black, Latino, Asian American, and Native American citizens gave their votes to Biden, while white voters largely supported Trump. This divide was sustained across gender lines, with women of color giving their votes to Democrats at a higher rate than their male counterparts, and white women's support for Republicans only slightly lagging that of white men. Yet although a majority of white voters supported Trump in 2020, their level of support declined by about 3 percentage points. In comparison, the historically high gap in Black support for Democrats over Republicans shrunk to 75 points in 2020, a level not seen since 2004. Latino and Asian American margins in favor of Democrats also decreased somewhat from 2016 to 2020.

Some analysts view these small shifts as evidence of a narrowing racial gap.[39] Others note that "these shifts do not apply to all states, and are not applicable to most battleground states where voters of color were crucial to Biden's win."[40] For example, the long-term, multiracial registration and get-out-the-vote campaigns led by Stacey Abrams helped turn Georgia blue for the first time since 1992.[41] In Arizona, grassroots organizations helped Native American and Latino citizens overcome voting barriers and flip the state to the Democrats as well.

If there is a new party system on the horizon that pits a largely white Trump coalition against a multiracial Obama coalition, then how new voters behave may well determine which will prevail. Although converting partisans can be important in a realignment, mobilizing new voters is even more consequential. The 2020 election saw record turnout from new and previously registered voters. Capturing the support of newly eligible voters, especially when their first vote is cast in turbulent times, can produce lifelong partisans.[42] From 2016 to 2020, an additional 1 million eligible Latino voters entered the electorate. Meanwhile, younger cohorts, which include most first-time voters, are more racially diverse than their elders, and in recent years young people have tended to lean liberal. Additionally, millions of disengaged voters are available to be mobilized by either party. In 2020, experienced voters split evenly between the parties, but first-time voters—14 percent of the 2020 electorate, up from 10 percent in 2016—voted 64 percent for Biden.

In early 2020, many young voters were initially energized by candidates like Bernie Sanders and Andrew Yang, who focused on issues of importance to them: racial equity, capitalism's failures, and climate change. Despite Biden's moderation, these young voters nevertheless voted for him in the general election and did so in historic numbers. Pollsters noted a significant increase in turnout among young voters: an estimated 52–55 percent of eighteen-to-twenty-nine-year-old eligible voters turned out to vote, up from 42–44 percent in 2016. They gave a majority of their votes to Biden, which was especially important in Michigan, Georgia, Arizona, and Pennsylvania. Nonetheless, as with older Americans, there were notable cleavages by race, gender, and level of education.[43] Youth of color overwhelmingly supported Biden, while white youth were more evenly split. This is a promising development for the future of the Democrats, but whether the party keeps their loyalty may depend in part on how willing it is to take their concerns seriously.

A New America

I'm proud of the coalition we put together, the broadest and most diverse coalition in history. Democrats, Republicans, independents, progressives, moderates, conservatives, young, old, urban, suburban, rural, gay, straight, transgender, white, Latino, Asian, Native American.

—President-Elect Joseph Biden, November 7, 2020

The future of the [Republican] party is based on a multiethnic, multiracial, working-class coalition.

—Republican senator Marco Rubio, November 11, 2020

In a country as large, diverse, and dynamic as the United States, electoral change is constant. Historically, when changes become too much for the status quo two-party system to absorb, politicians have responded by either adapting or losing.[44] The country is currently in the midst of profound change: in the new, technologically driven economy, inequality has reached heights not seen in a century, and in decades to come, no one racial group will form a majority. To secure electoral dominance, both parties must try to be relevant to a majority of voters in a changing electorate.

Appealing to a multiracial, multiethnic economically struggling majority is not the only way to political power, though. The election of 2016 made that evident. As Senator Mitch McConnell and other Republican leaders said in 2020, turning out voters has not always benefited their party, and so strategies to repress the democratic vote, whether through more restrictive voting laws, gerrymandered districts, or intimidation, have been sought to, in effect, choose the voters that will sustain the party's power.[45] These tactics reached new heights in 2020 with the Trump administration's efforts at post-hoc voter disenfranchisement through allegations of fraud. But this is a difficult strategy with which to succeed over the long run. Massive voter disenfranchisement goes against the country's purported commitment to democratic norms, and each such effort must survive challenges in the courts.

Republican demobilization of likely Democratic supporters in recent years has been made more potent by Trump's successful mobilization of a dwindling, but still significant, voter base of white Americans, especially those who are economically precarious or threatened by economic marginalization. But it is not clear that another Republican at the top of the ticket will be able to mobilize these voters to the extent that Trump's charismatic leadership did, because charismatic authority is not easily transferred.[46] Other right-wing populists, like George Wallace and Pat Buchanan, have tried but failed to make a similar impact on the national electorate. And although the presidential primary system allows an outsider like Trump to commandeer the party, this is by no means an easy task.

An alternative, more democratically defensible strategy would be for Republicans to try to realize Rubio's ambition, building on the small successes it had in 2020 with Latinos, Black men, and working-class whites who have been left behind by the globalized economy. Doing so successfully could also produce a realignment of the parties, this time dividing them along more conventional axes of economic and social values, but with a twist: it would require a shift in Republican elites' current economic positions to more closely align with some of Trump's populist promises—positions that the party's governing elite has generally shunned. It would also require a more forthright repudiation of not just Trumpism but the racialized politics of the party's recent past.

Democrats have been more successful at building for tomorrow's electorate. The party's message of economic and social justice is generally more consonant with the concerns of the changing, increasingly diverse electorate, and the new states that Biden picked up in 2020 only add to Obama's coalition of multiracial urban and suburban voters. Yet a sustained

Democratic majority is by no means ensured. Tensions within the party between youthful progressives and multigenerational centrists are not easily resolvable. The remarkable diversity of the Biden coalition may have been united solely by displacing Trump. Going forward, Republicans' structural advantages and their gerrymandering successes mean Democrats have to mobilize in an outsize fashion just to gain power. Biden will need to be a transformational president in order to consolidate and strengthen the Democratic majority. In 2020, voters stabilized American democracy. What they do with that democracy next remains to be seen.

Notes

1. V. O. Key, *The Responsible Electorate* (Cambridge, MA: Harvard University Press, 1966). The theory of retrospective voting suggests that with limited political knowledge, voters nevertheless vote rationally based on whether they are "better off than they were four years ago." There is debate about the extent to which voters employ even this minimal amount of rationality.

2. "Transcript of Kamala Harris's Victory Speech in Wilmington, Del.," *Washington Post*, November 7, 2020.

3. Nate Silver, "Biden's Favored in Our Final Presidential Forecast, but It's a Fine Line between a Landslide and a Nail-Biter," FiveThirtyEight, November 3, 2020, https://fivethirtyeight.com/features/final-2020-presidential -election-forecast/. Also see Margaret Renkl, "71 Million People for Trump. They're Not Going Anywhere," *New York Times*, November 9, 2020.

4. "Understanding Gallup's Likely Voter Procedures for Presidential Elections," Gallup, https://news.gallup.com/poll/111268/How-Gallups-likely -voter-models-work.aspx. Accessed on February 6, 2021.

5. Geraldo Cadava, Lisa Garcia Bedolla, and Jack Herrera, "Trump Didn't Win the Latino Vote in Texas. He Won the Tejano Vote," *Politico*, November 17, 2020.

6. Dylan Matthew, "One Pollster's Explanation for Why the Polls Got It Wrong," *Vox*, November 20, 2020, https://www.vox.com/policy-and-poli tics/2020/11/10/21551766/election-polls-results-wrong-david-shor.

7. Mackenzie Lockhart, Seth J. Hill, Jennifer Merolla, Mindy Romero, and Thad Kousser, "America's Electorate Is Increasingly Polarized along Partisan Lines about Voting by Mail during the Covid-19 Crisis," *Proceedings of the National Academy of Sciences* 117, no. 40 (2020): 24640–42.

8. Unless otherwise noted, data are from National Election Pool exit polls, provided by the *New York Times*, updated as of November 20, 2020, https://www.nytimes.com/interactive/2020/11/03/us/elections/exit-polls -president.html.

9. Matthew Levendusky, *The Partisan Sort: How Liberals Became Democrats and Conservatives Became Republicans* (Chicago: University of Chicago Press, 2009).

10. Morris Fiorina, with Samuel J. Abrams and Jeremy Pope, *Culture War? The Myth of a Polarized America* (New York: Pearson Longman, 2005).

11. Liliana Mason, *Uncivil Agreement: How Politics Became Our Identity* (Chicago: University of Chicago Press, 2018); Larry Bartels and Christopher Achen, *Democracy for Realists: Why Elections Do Not Produce Responsive Government* (Princeton, NJ: Princeton University Press, 2017); Jonathan Ladd, "Negative Partisanship May Be the Most Toxic Form of Polarization," *Vox*, June 2, 2017, https://www.vox.com/mischiefs-of-faction/2017/6/2/15730524/negative-partisanship-toxic-polarization.

12. "Election 2020: Voters Are Highly Engaged but Nearly Half Expect to Have Difficulty Voting," Pew Research Center, August 13, 2020, https://www.pewresearch.org/politics/2020/08/13/perceptions-of-trump-and-biden/.

13. "Election 2020: Voters Are Highly Engaged."

14. In *Let Them Eat Tweets: How the Right Rules in an Age of Extreme Inequality* (New York: Liveright Publishing, 2020), Jacob Hacker and Paul Pierson argue that Republican elites promote right-wing populism precisely to appeal to their base and distract from their unpopular economic agenda, which serves corporations and affluent Americans.

15. Also see John Sides, Michael Tesler, and Lynn Vavreck, *Identity Crisis: The 2016 Presidential Campaign and the Battle for the Meaning of America* (Princeton, NJ: Princeton University Press, 2018).

16. Oliver Hahl, Minjae Kim, and Ezra Zuckerman Savan, "The Authentic Appeal of the Lying Demagogue," *American Sociological Review* 83, no. 1 (2018): 1–33.

17. Republican establishment support of Trump's assault on the legitimacy of the 2020 election suggests that this is a fear of party elites. Nicholas Fandos, "Republicans in Congress Stay Largely in Line behind Trump," *New York Times*, November 20, 2020. Also see Jonathan Last, "Trump Is Forever," The Bulwark, December 17, 2019, https://thebulwark.com/trump-is-forever/; Jan Werner Mueller, "Democracy for Losers," Boston Review, August 6, 2020, http://bostonreview.net/politics/jan-werner-m%C3%BCller-democracy-losers.

18. Alan Abramowitz, *The Disappearing Center: Engaged Citizens, Polarization, and American Democracy* (New Haven, CT: Yale University Press, 2010).

19. Similar impulses have been observed in reactions against industrial modernization at the turn of the twentieth century. See Richard Hofstadter, *The Age of Reform: From Bryan to F.D.R.* (New York: Knopf, 1955).

20. Donald Critchlow, *The Conservative Ascendancy: How the Republican Right Rose to Power in Modern America* (Lawrence: University Press of Kansas, 2011); Bruce J. Schulman, *The Seventies: The Great Shift in American Culture, Society, and Politics* (New York: Free Press, 2001); and Stephen Skowronek, *The Politics Presidents Make: Leadership from John Adams to George Bush* (Cambridge, MA: Harvard University Press, 1993).

21. Michael McDonald, "2020 November General Election Turnout Rates," United States Election Project, November 16, 2020, http://www.electproject.org/2020g.

22. For classic statements, see Walter Dean Burnham, "The Changing Shape of the American Political Universe," *American Political Science Review* 59, no. 1 (1965): 7–28; Vladimir O. Key Jr., "A Theory of Critical Elections," *Journal of Politics* 17, no. 1 (1955): 3–18; James L. Sundquist, *Dynamics of the Party System: Alignment and Realignment of Political Parties in the United States*, 2nd ed. (Washington, DC: Brookings Institution Press, 1983).

23. Though see Julia Azari's insights on the relationship between a president's mandate claims and the size of the victory. Julia Azari, *Delivering the People's Message: The Changing Politics of the Presidential Mandate* (Ithaca, NY: Cornell University Press, 2014).

24. Nicole Mellow, *The State of Disunion: Regional Sources of Modern American Partisanship* (Baltimore: Johns Hopkins University Press, 2008).

25. The phrase "emerging Republican majority" was coined by Republican strategist Kevin Phillips, *The Emerging Republican Majority* (New Rochelle, NY: Arlington House, 1969).

26. Mellow, *State of Disunion*, chap. 3.

27. Bill Bishop, *The Big Sort: Why the Clustering of Like-Minded America Is Tearing Us Apart* (New York: Mariner Books, 2009).

28. Domenico Montanaro and Connie Hanzhang Jin, "How Biden Won: Ramping Up the Base and Expanding Margins in the Suburbs," NPR, November 18, 2020, https://www.npr.org/2020/11/18/935730100/how-biden-won-ramping-up-the-base-and-expanding-margins-in-the-suburbs.

29. Zolan Kanna-Youngs, "Delayed Homeland Security Report Warns of 'Lethal' White Supremacy," *New York Times*, October 6, 2020.

30. Lynn Vavreck, *The Message Matters: The Economy and Presidential Campaigns* (Princeton, NJ: Princeton University Press, 2009).

31. "Election 2020: Voters Are Highly Engaged, but Nearly Half Expect to Have Difficulties Voting," Pew Research Center, August 13, 2020, https://www.pewresearch.org/politics/2020/08/13/election-2020-voters-are-highly-engaged-but-nearly-half-expect-to-have-difficulties-voting/.

32. Alan I. Abramowitz. "Will Time for Change Mean Time for Trump?," *PS: Political Science & Politics* 49, no. 4 (2016): 659–60.

33. John B. Judis and Ruy Teixeira, *The Emerging Democratic Majority* (New York: Simon and Schuster, 2004).

34. Nicole Mellow, "Voting Behavior: How the Democrats Rejuvenated Their Coalition," in *The Elections of 2012*, ed. Michael Nelson (Washington, DC: CQ Press, 2013), 73–95.

35. Jed Kolko, "Election Showed a Wider Red-Blue Economic Divide," *New York Times*, November 15, 2020.

36. Sides, Tesler, and Vavreck, *Identity Crisis*.

37. Annie Lowrey, "Why the Election Wasn't a Biden Landslide," *Atlantic*, November 6, 2020.

38. Christopher D. DeSante and Candis Watts Smith, *Racial Stasis: The Millennial Generation and Stagnation of Racial Attitudes in American Politics* (Chicago: University of Chicago Press, 2020); Juliet Hooker, "How Can the Democratic Party Confront Racist Backlash? White Grievance in Hemispheric Perspective," *Polity* 53, no. 3 (Summer 2020): 355–69; Sides, Tesler, and Vavreck, *Identity Crisis*.

39. Nate Cohn, "The Election's Big Twist: The Racial Gap Is Shrinking," *New York Times*, October 28, 2020.

40. William H. Frey, "Exit Polls Show Both Familiar and New Voting Blocs Sealed Biden's Win," Brookings Institution, November 12, 2020, https://www.brookings.edu/research/2020-exit-polls-show-a-scrambling-of-democrats-and-republicans-traditional-bases/.

41. Nate Cohn, Matthew Conlen, and Charlie Smart, "Detailed Turnout Data Shows How Georgia Turned Blue," *New York Times*, November 17, 2020.

42. Angus Campbell, Phillip Converse, Warren Miller, and Donald Stokes, *The American Voter* (1960; Chicago: University of Chicago Press, 1976).

43. "Election Week 2020: When and How Young People Voted," CIRCLE, November 25, 2020, https://circle.tufts.edu/latest-research/election-week-2020#issues:-the-top-concerns-that-drove-youth-to-the-polls. CIRCLE reports that 51 percent of young white voters supported Biden, while NEP estimates 53 percent.

44. Sundquist, *Dynamics of the Party System*.

45. David Frum, "The Raw Desperation of the Republican Party," *Atlantic*, October 29, 2020.

46. Seth Abrutyn, (@seth_abrutyn), "Seeing sociologists struggle with Trump makes me want to reassign Weber's entire corpus on charisma. We are accustomed to what I call "bottled" charisma, or charisma that is restrained by the possessor's traditional or legal-rational authority. Clinton or Kennedy had charisma." Twitter.com, November 4, 2020, 10:18 a.m., https://twitter.com/seth_abrutyn/status/1324008142452129792. Also see Paul Joose, "Expanding Moral Panic to Include the Agency of Charismatic Entrepreneurs," *British Journal of Criminology* 58 (2018): 993–1012.

Campaign Finance

TRENDS AND DEVELOPMENTS

Charles R. Hunt

Amid the highest-stakes election in recent memory, candidates, parties, and interest groups made every effort to raise and spend as much money as possible in 2020, only to find in many cases that it was the Beatles who had the top-notch campaign analysis—namely, that for many candidates, "money can't buy [them] love." The 2020 election, at both the presidential and congressional levels, showcased two simultaneous but conflicting realities about money in politics. Parties, outside groups, and of course the candidates themselves raised and spent record amounts of cash in what all participants agreed was an enormously important election; and yet, much of this cash was wasted on races that did not end up being particularly competitive. These two realities illustrate that money—and lots of it—continues to be a crucial component in elections of all sorts at the federal level, but that directing those funds to the right places remains a challenge for parties and their allies.

These trends also raise anew the question of where and for which types of races money can determine the outcome. Although Democrats made some headway in traditionally Republican areas thanks to longer-term demographic shifts and significant public disapproval of President Donald Trump, no amount of money could help them break through many areas' partisan fundamentals that favored Republicans.

Assessing the impact of contributions and spending on election outcomes is notoriously difficult, as many scholars have shown.[1] This chapter will not attempt a new methodology with the aim of cracking this particular code, but rather will use specific evidence from 2020's federal races in conjunction with existing theories to help explain why the 2020 election was the most expensive in history; which types of races and candidates accounted for its record-shattering totals; and what the "money chase" of the 2016 and 2020 elections might portend for federal elections in the years ahead.

This is a significant enough task, but no analysis of the 2020 election—and particularly of how candidates navigated a tricky electoral terrain—is complete without accounting for the public health, economic, and political catastrophes resulting from the onset of the COVID-19 pandemic. COVID was settling into America's consciousness just as the 2020 Democratic nominating contest was beginning to wrap up. On March 10, 2020, former vice president Joe Biden delivered decisive primary victories over Vermont senator Bernie Sanders in Michigan, Missouri, Washington, and Mississippi, a string of "commanding victories" that the *New York Times* assessed would amount to a "short, orderly primary."[2] The very next day, March 11, the NBA suspended the remainder of its season after a number of players tested positive for the coronavirus,[3] and beloved actor Tom Hanks announced that he and his wife, Rita Wilson, had also contracted the virus.[4] Democrats breathed a sigh of relief that subsequent primary elections would not be decisive, as Biden continued his clear path to the nomination. But epidemiologists, other health experts, and soon just about every American understood not only that the COVID-19 outbreak was here to stay but that it was likely to affect politics—especially the crucial set of elections being held that fall—in ways we couldn't yet foresee. That the pandemic threw the 2020 campaign, at both the presidential and congressional levels, into flux is a significant understatement. What we do not yet know is exactly how the pandemic may have affected the nuts and bolts of campaigns. In comparing the 2020 campaign spending practices of congressional candidates with those of 2016, this chapter offers a very preliminary set of potential answers to this question.

The goals of this chapter are, first, to renew our descriptive understanding of how economic status, party, and gender play crucial roles in how money is raised and spent in federal elections; second, to offer updated theory and evidence concerning the long-term questions in the political science literature about the broader role of money in such elections; and to incorporate new transaction-level spending data to begin to answer lingering questions about COVID-19 and its effects on the presidential and congressional campaigns.

General Trends: Money, Partisanship, Gender in 2020

The most obvious place to begin is with what can only be called the staggering cost of the 2020 elections, even by modern standards. As table 1 indicates, not only did 2020 shatter every previous record for combined congressional and presidential costs, but it clocked in at just below

TABLE 1. Total cost of elections (billions/2020 dollars)

	Total cost	Congressional	Presidential
1998	2.6	2.6	n/a
2000	4.6	2.5	2.1
2002	3.1	3.1	n/a
2004	5.7	3.1	2.6
2006	3.6	3.6	n/a
2008	6.3	2.9	3.3
2010	4.3	4.3	n/a
2012	7.1	4.1	3.0
2014	4.2	4.2	n/a
2016	7.0	4.5	2.6
2018	5.9	5.9	n/a
2020	14.4	8.7	5.7

Source: Federal Election Commission / Center for Responsive Politics.

$14 billion—nearly double the previous record set in the 2012 elections. Totals doubled for presidential campaign spending from the previous record in 2008, and also increased by more than $1 billion in congressional races compared with 2018, a historically high-stakes set of midterm contests.

Where exactly did all of these billions of dollars come from, and why? A good chunk of it came from the candidates, who spent record amounts on both the presidential contest and on a number of competitive (and a number of not so competitive) contests for the House and Senate. A larger portion of the money than usual came from small donors—that is, individual contributions of less than $200. In all, small donors made up around 22 percent of 2020 fundraising, up from 15 percent in 2016. The Center for Responsive Politics and other organizations have attributed this increase to digital outreach efforts on behalf of both parties through ActBlue (Democrats) and WinRed (Republicans) that made it easier than ever to donate small amounts to chosen candidates, parties, or affiliated groups.[5] At the presidential level, Donald Trump in particular continued his (perhaps unexpected) dominance in 2016 in the area of small donors, despite his continued talk of self-funding his own campaign. Finally, donors who gave more than $200 but did not "max out" their donations (call them smallish donors) made up a much more significant portion of the donor base than usual: 3.6 million Americans (or a little over 1 percent of the population) made donations of this middling size, compared with only 1.6 million (about 0.5 percent of the population) in 2016.[6]

TRENDS IN OUTSIDE SPENDING

One important trend worth discussing in more detail is the ongoing balance—or perhaps imbalance—between candidate spending and spending by outside groups and the political parties. Outside groups accounted for about $2.6 billion of the total spending in 2020, far outstripping these groups' previous totals of $1.4 billion in 2016 and $1 billion in 2012.[7] One area of fascinating decline over the past several election cycles is in the spending of "dark money." Dark money is raised by 501(c)4 nonprofit organizations in unlimited amounts and spent without needing to legally disclose who donated the money. Groups can then spend enormous sums of this money on items like so-called issue ads, so long as such ads do not include express advocacy for or against a particular candidate. On the surface, it appears that the amount of dark money spent in 2020 is the lowest it's been since before the 2008 election. From its high watermark of $313 million in 2012, just a little over $100 million was spent using this untraceable cash in 2020.[8]

Many critics of dark money argue that rather than declining, dark money groups are simply investing elsewhere—or at another time. This is because dark money groups must report to the Federal Election Commission (FEC) only money spent on issue ads and other political organizing within sixty days of an election. This means that any money from dark money organizations that was spent (or donated to affiliated super political action committees [PACs]) before September 3, 2020, isn't on FEC's books, making the money even darker—what the Brennan Center's Ciara Torres-Spelliscy calls "black hole money."[9] Considering how difficult it is to trace such money to its sources, it is likely impossible to know whether early dark money spending accounts for the recent decline in reported spending. The logic is that super PACs will hold off on their own spending, while their affiliated dark money groups can spend with impunity before the official "general election season." Super PACs did indeed spend around $2 billion in 2020, nearly doubling the amount they spent in 2016.[10]

PARTISAN SPENDING AND VOTER ENTHUSIASM

With politics at the federal level defined by partisanship as much as it has been in modern memory, how did Democrats and Republicans match up against each other financially in the 2020 election? At first glance, it appears to be not so much a squaring up as a beating down. Republican

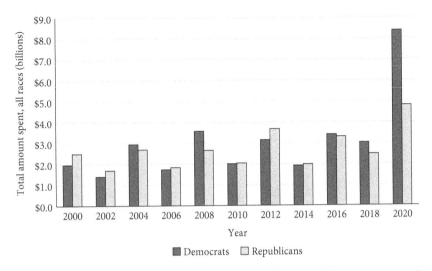

FIG. 1. Total amount spent by Democratic and Republican candidates, parties, and affiliated organizations, 2000–2020
Source: Center for Responsive Politics.

candidates, associated PACs, supportive outside spenders, and the party itself spent a combined $4.8 billion on federal elections. This is an impressive number, particularly considering that the previous party record was the $3.8 billion Republicans spent in 2012. And yet it was chump change compared with the amount that Democrats and their allies spent in 2020: $8.4 billion, according to projections from the Center for Responsive Politics. Figure 1 depicts the financial massacre that ensued compared with previous years. Democrats in 2020 spent at least 75 percent more than Republicans, shattering any previous partisan gap in modern history. For reference, Democrats spent 21.9 percent more in advance of the 2018 "blue wave," and Republicans spent 17 percent more in 2012 in their efforts to unseat President Obama.

What explains this unprecedented, and perhaps surprising, advantage on the part of the Democrats? Two answers immediately jump out: Michael Bloomberg and Tom Steyer. The two billionaires ran self-funded campaigns for the Democratic presidential nomination, spending a combined $1.4 billion of their own money, as well as hundreds of millions of additional money they spent in support of other candidates. And yet even after taking this massive sum into account, Democrats still outspent Republicans by more than $2 billion. It is also true that Democrats held a primary in which multiple candidates spent over $100 million, whereas the Republicans held more of a coronation for the incumbent president. Yet these imbalances were the same in 2012 and 2004, when incumbent presidents Barack Obama and George W. Bush, respectively, won uncontested renominations but the partisan differences in spending were not quite so stark.

The more likely explanation of Democrats' campaign finance dominance in 2020 relative to their rival party is the presence of Donald Trump on the ballot, and the Democrats' unbridled enthusiasm, pent up over the course of four years, for getting him out of the White House. Since 2000, Gallup has polled whether voters are more or less enthusiastic in each new presidential election than in previous ones. Table 2 shows that the 2016 election was a recent low for both parties, likely attributable to the historic unpopularity of both the Democratic and Republican nominees for president. But analyzing the high points for both parties reveals an important truth about American politics that likely helps explain the partisan spending gap in the 2020 elections. Democrats in 2004 and 2008, Republicans in 2012, and the Democrats in 2020 were all responding "enthusiastically" about how ready they were to be rid of the ruling party in the presidency. These four instances represent the only points in table 2 where enthusiasm reached 70 percent or higher. They also represent four points in figure 1 in which the more enthusiastic party outspent the less enthusiastic one. This overall trend in campaign finance is as good a piece of evidence as any of what Alan Abramowitz and Steven Webster called "negative partisanship."[11] Voters—and in this case, donors and spenders—were motivated to act not so much out of inspiration to support their chosen party or candidate but by the opportunity to oust the opposition.

TABLE 2. Percentage of voters feeling "more enthusiastic" than usual about voting

	All voters	Democrats	Republicans
2000	38	35	45
2004	67	70	68
2008	68	76	61
2012	64	61	73
2016	50	50	53
2020	69	75	66

Source: Gallup polling.

Gender Dynamics and Campaign Contributions

One final important trend over the past decade involves the intersection of campaign finance and gender. There is a well-known "gender gap" in modern American politics, in which female voters are more likely to support Democratic candidates at all levels of government, while male voters are more likely to support Republicans.[12] This voting gap persists in partisan campaign donations. In 2020, women were more one-sided in their donations than in any modern election, hitting an all-time high in the proportion of their donations to Democrats (69 percent) as opposed to Republicans (31 percent). This may spell long-term trouble for Republicans, particularly given their recent downward spiral among suburban (and financially well off) women. However, it does run counter to some expectations considering some of the inroads Republicans made in recruiting successful female congressional candidates in 2020 after a disastrous midterm in 2018.[13]

Men also donated more heavily to Democrats in 2020 (57 percent), and the gap between the male and female proportions donating to Democrats (12 percentage points) was actually smaller than the gender donation gaps recorded in 2012 (13 points), 2016 (16 points), and 2018 (16 points). This gender gap in campaign contributions will need to be watched in subsequent federal elections, particularly ones in which Donald Trump—with his well-documented history of misogynistic behavior and dozens of sexual assault allegations[14]—is neither on the ballot nor a major factor in the election.

The Presidential Election

In 2016, political commentators, analysts, and political scientists alike faced the unenviable task of explaining how a political neophyte like Donald Trump, who was outspent by orders of magnitude by his well-established Democratic opponent Hillary Clinton, managed to squeak out a presidential victory. How did a political amateur with no major connections within the Republican Party apparatus manage to defeat a Democratic former first lady, U.S. senator, and secretary of state who enjoyed the backing of a relatively popular incumbent president, while spending half as much money on his election?

Attempting to answer this question (again) is not the object of this chapter, but these facts serve as a crucial backdrop to the high-stakes 2020 presidential election in which the Democrats, perhaps more than any party in modern history, were hell-bent on unseating the incumbent no matter the monetary or political costs. This phenomenon of negative partisanship motivates much of the discussion that follows, at both the presidential and congressional levels. For the Democrats, this is also a complicated tale of billionaire presidential aspirants (Michael Bloomberg and Tom Steyer) and those who sought to stifle their candidacies (Bernie Sanders and Elizabeth Warren). From a monetary perspective, these four candidates dominated the Democratic primary without ever garnering close to enough support to win.

During a time of such dizzying change, complication, and tragedy, how did money play a role in the pursuit of the highest office in the land? How did Joe Biden coast to a primary victory with a depleted war chest, while winning in the general election with what ended up as a tremendous financial advantage? What explains the deep chasm between his primary and general election fundraising?

Enthusiasm and Electability and the 2020 Democratic Primary

Following the shock of defeat in 2016, Democratic voters were more than ready to begin the search for the candidate who would rid them of President Donald Trump in four years. They had no shortage of options, and soon more than two dozen notable candidates were crisscrossing early primary states like Iowa, New Hampshire, and South Carolina in search of support. They were also in search of money. As it often does in presidential primaries, fundraising played a crucial role not just in terms of media coverage and perceived viability for the candidates before the actual contests began, but in the candidates' real-life viability on the debate stage.

In reaction to lingering charges of favoritism toward certain candidates in 2016, the Democratic National Committee (DNC) instituted a new set of viability thresholds candidates had to meet in order to appear in each successive primary debate. These included reaching certain polling thresholds, as well as proving one's mettle as a fundraiser, in order to be eligible. Candidates generally had to demonstrate fundraising prowess both in terms of total amounts raised and in terms of the breadth of their support. For example, for the debate on January 14, 2020—crucially, the final one before the Iowa caucuses—the DNC raised its thresholds such that each candidate needed donations from at least 225,000 individuals nationwide, with a minimum of 1,000 donors in each of at least twenty states.[15]

Despite the party's efforts to cull the field, Democratic voters' financial enthusiasm overpowered the DNC's initial expectations. By the time the primary was effectively over at the end of March, six different

Democratic primary candidates had raised more than $100 million (Biden, Sanders, Warren, Buttigieg, Steyer, and Bloomberg), and nine had raised more than $10 million. Six or seven candidates participated in every subsequent debate through Super Tuesday. Democrats produced by far the most expensive primary ever despite the race itself not being all that competitive. But did these vast sums of money end up translating into electoral success? The answer broadly appears to be no.

Polling averages in the 2020 primary tell a fairly simple story of the race that is not reflected by the candidates' fundraising receipts. Between the beginning of 2019 and the end of the primary in early April 2020, Joe Biden lost his lead only twice, and briefly: first to Massachusetts senator Elizabeth Warren in October 2019, and then more significantly to Vermont senator Bernie Sanders after Sanders's primary victories in Iowa and New Hampshire.[16] In retrospect, the former vice president was the front-runner all along, a status quite apparent when more racially diverse blocs of voters in states like South Carolina had their say. Yet while Biden ended up running away with the primary, one wouldn't know it by comparing his fundraising totals with those of his rivals.

Table 3 offers a clear delineation of candidate types. The table includes all Democratic primary candidates who raised over $10 million, drawing attention first to the mind-boggling total amount of money raised, which left 2016's primaries for both parties in the dust. But as alluded to earlier, the two far-and-away highest fundraising candidates, Bloomberg and Steyer, raised almost every last penny from their own wallets (low-polling former representative John Delaney also largely self-funded his campaign). Both Steyer and Bloomberg lasted longer than most Democratic candidates, and Bloomberg even won a couple dozen delegates. Steyer and Bloomberg were also two of the three biggest individual political contributors in 2020 (mostly to themselves), losing out only to GOP financier Sheldon Adelson.[17] Given the measly return on investment of their campaigns, debates will undoubtedly continue to rage within Democratic Party circles about whether these two candidates' campaigns could have found more effective ways to spend $1.4 billion, particularly in light of the Democrats' worse-than-expected electoral performance in state legislative and congressional races. It is worth noting, however, that even after subtracting Bloomberg's and Steyer's mammoth totals, Democratic primary candidates raised nearly as much as their 2008 counterparts, despite that year's contest dragging out months longer.

Other major candidates, including the only two who posed a serious challenge to Biden in the polls throughout the contest, pursued a much

TABLE 3. Democratic primary candidate fundraising and self-funding through March 31, 2020

Candidate	Total receipts	% self-funded	% small donors
Michael Bloomberg	$1,062,963,445	99	0
Tom Steyer	$347,533,363	98	1
Bernie Sanders	$214,770,176	0	53
Joe Biden	$134,790,836	0	39
Elizabeth Warren	$128,442,944	0	52
Pete Buttigieg	$102,739,747	0	43
Amy Klobuchar	$53,957,026	0	42
Andrew Yang	$41,148,908	0	49
Kamala Harris	$41,077,632	0	38
Cory Booker	$26,022,021	0	30
John Delaney	$23,292,723	82	2
Beto O'Rourke	$19,218,051	0	51
Kirsten Gillibrand	$15,951,202	0	12
Tulsi Gabbard	$15,101,213	0	48
Julián Castro	$10,302,020	0	65

Source: Federal Election Commission / Center for Responsive Politics.

different fiscal route. Both Bernie Sanders and Elizabeth Warren consistently outraised Biden throughout most of the contest, but primarily through networks of small donors. Sanders and Warren were among the only big-raising candidates to amass more than half of their totals from small donors (along with Texan also-rans Beto O'Rourke and Julián Castro), and both also shared wide-ranging admiration among the ideological left of the Democratic Party. Sanders in particular had spent much of the four years since running in 2016 developing his small-donor network through his nonprofit campaign spin-off organization Our Revolution.

It was not enough, however. Despite Biden's fundraising woes (at least compared with his rivals), he maintained his polling lead almost throughout, recapturing it even after losing to Sanders in the first two primary contests. Once Biden got his lead back after his dominant victory in South Carolina, renewed fundraising success followed. More than a third of Biden's total receipts came in March, the first month of the entire campaign in which he managed to outraise Sanders and Warren. Every candidate other than Biden, whether they self-funded or raised a grassroots army of donors and volunteers, was essentially eliminated from contention by the end of March. Other than Biden, only Sanders ever amassed a signifi-cant number of delegates, but the race was not close. Unavoidable is the simple truth that in the Democratic primary, campaign cash appears to have been of secondary importance, at best a following rather than a lead-ing indicator of success with the voters.

How, then, did Biden win the nomination? The likeliest answer to this question, as well as why this primary shattered overall financial records, lies in voters' motivations for why they voted the way they did. On the same primary election day that most analysts agree Biden gained his com-manding lead for the nomination, NBC News reported that according to exit polls, "a majority of Democratic voters . . . said choosing a candidate who they believe can [beat Donald Trump] is more important than choos-ing one who agrees with them on major issues."[18] Democratic primary vot-ers were quite literally desperate to get Donald Trump out of office; they reflected this in the sheer amount of money they dished out, as well as in their ultimate choice of Biden. It is beyond the scope of this chapter to assess why voters believed Biden was the most effective choice to unseat the incumbent (name recognition? prior experience? his age, race, or gender?). Whatever the reasons, they redounded to Biden's advantage despite his lackluster fundraising during the primaries and relative absence from the airwaves. Whatever won Biden the nomination, it was not the sheer amount of money he raised or spent compared with his primary rivals.

THE "TRUMP FACTOR" AND MONEY IN THE 2020 GENERAL ELECTION

While Democrats exchanged fire with each other in a sometimes-contentious primary, Donald Trump was building up an arsenal of cam-paign cash. By the time the Democratic primary was turning in Biden's favor in March 2020, Trump's campaign had nearly $100 million in cash on hand, compared with Biden's depleted $12 million. Behind the scenes, Democrats reportedly "shuddered" at Trump's fundraising apparatus, which by the end of 2019 had raised more than twice as much as President Barack Obama had raised in the year before his 2012 reelection.[19]

Trump's initial advantage going into 2020, particularly in light of his comparatively weak cash totals in 2016, may be explained by a number of factors. Incumbency, and Trump's status as the presumptive nominee with no serious competition in the primary, was paramount. Rather than engage with a mix of serious same-party contenders, Trump's team could lay low and quietly amass an enormous war chest, all while continually engaging their supporters, particularly on digital media. Second, Trump consolidated political support in his party in a way that he was unable to do even by the end of the 2016 campaign. The party itself, and its corresponding supportive groups, united fully behind Trump financially. And finally, all the polls indicated that the president's reelection chances were just about even. For the various reasons touted in the political science literature, the competitive election drove interest and turnout among the president's wide and dedicated base of supporters.

By May, Biden had settled into his role as the presumptive Democratic nominee and begun to kick up his fundraising totals. Still, there was reason to fear the Trump campaign's money advantage because of the number of ways it could attack. "For nearly three years we have been building a juggernaut campaign (Death Star)," Brad Parscale, Trump's campaign manager at the time, boasted on Twitter. "It is firing on all cylinders. Data, Digital, TV, Political, Surrogates, Coalitions, etc. In a few days we start pressing FIRE for the first time."[20]

Fire they did. At the beginning of the general election campaign, Trump's advertisements dominated all corners of the internet in particular. The campaign also—being notoriously unburdened by efforts to physically distance in the midst of a pandemic—held dozens of rallies and executed a significant door-knocking get-out-the-vote campaign.[21] But like the actual Death Star, the Trump campaign ended up facing an opponent that overmatched it in the end. Table 4 illustrates that in every single month but one after Biden clinched the nomination, he outraised the president by a significant amount. Most jaw-dropping were Biden's fundraising hauls in the last two months of the campaign: nearly half a billion dollars, well over three times as much as Trump raised during the same crucial period. Biden outstripped the president both in direct campaign contributions and in the amount raised by outside groups: Trump-affiliated super PAC juggernauts America First Action and the Preserve America PAC raised a combined $269 million, but their Biden counterparts included not just similarly large groups like the familiar Priorities USA Action (who had spent in support of Hillary Clinton in 2016) but also a vast array of smaller PACs like Unite the Country, Pacronym, and Republican Voters Against Trump, which combined for nearly half a billion dollars and placed high-profile viral campaign spots in all corners of the internet. Still, it is worth noting that, as in 2016, Trump maintained his dominance among small donors.

Biden's fundraising comeback was astonishing. But did it help him win the election? As usual, it's difficult to say. There is a good deal of evidence that throughout the general election campaign, Biden was able to use his

TABLE 4. Fundraising summary, 2020 presidential general election (millions of dollars)

	Biden (D)	Trump (R)
Monthly fundraising		
April 2020	47	14
May 2020	43	17
June 2020	37	24
July 2020	64	56
August 2020	49	72
September 2020	213	61
October 2020	281	82
Total fundraising summary		
Campaign committee	938	596
Outside groups	443	269
Combined total	1,380	865
% small donors	39%	45%

Source: Federal Election Commission.

campaign apparatus to improve his favorability ratings by a decent margin, particularly among Independents, suburban women, and seniors, all of whom were must-win groups for Trump. Biden reached Election Day near his peak, with an average net favorability rating of +6.2, while Trump continued to languish at −12.8.[22] In the end, however, it's not at all that clear that fundraising and spending totals mattered any more in the general election than they seemed to during the primaries. Biden's drawn-out victory was decisive in the national popular vote, but by no means a landslide in the Electoral College. About 100,000 votes across a few states would have flipped the election to Trump, and this chapter would likely be about how Trump—once again—won by a hair despite being outgunned financially, just as he was in 2016.

Congressional Elections

The outsize focus on President Trump from both the Left and the Right in the presidential election may have had the effect of diminishing the importance of federal races for Congress in both the House and the Senate. And yet, a number of factors—including the nationalization of congressional elections and the increased focus on winning and retaining party majorities in Congress—ensured not only that these races would not fly under the radar but also that they would be some of the most expensive of the 2020 election. In this section, I analyze the effects of partisan fundamentals, incumbency, and negative partisanship on campaign finance in these crucial elections, as well as what these patterns tell us about the state of congressional politics in a polarized era.

2020 FUNDAMENTALS AND THEIR CONSEQUENCES

In the 2018 midterm elections, Democrats made historic gains in the House of Representatives, taking back the chamber and putting a significant dampener on President Trump's policy agenda during the remaining two years of his term. A poor Senate map in 2018 prevented the Democrats from making similar gains in the upper chamber; four Democratic incumbents lost, three in heavily Republican states, and Democrats made only two pickups of their own. But the taste of victory in the House sent the party into 2020 focused not just on winning back the presidency from Donald Trump but on expanding that House majority and potentially even winning the Senate. No longer, Democrats said, would they take down-ballot races for granted. And while they had only limited success in the race for Congress, there is no denying that for the most part Democrats and affiliated organizations put their money where their mouth was.

The Senate map was much more favorable to Democrats in 2020, with Republican incumbents defending seven seats in battleground or Democratic-leaning states, as well as five in traditionally Republican areas that were seen as potentially competitive because of compelling Democratic candidates and because of the (in the end, misleading) polling. Although Democrats were always likely to lose incumbent senator Doug Jones's seat in Alabama, they only had to defend two other seats that ever seemed in danger (Minnesota and Michigan).[23] As a result, Democratic small donors, large donors, outside groups, and the party itself unleashed a flood of spending to win these Senate seats, as well as to retain and grow their House majority. In the end, Democrats outspent Republicans by about $100 million in House races and by nearly $300 million in Senate races.[24]

OUTSIDE SPENDING AND "INSECURE MAJORITIES" IN 2020

Much of the Democrats' and Republicans' spending in the battle for control of Congress came not from the candidates but from a record expansion of independent expenditures (IEs) by outside groups. Over $1 billion in IEs could be found in the eleven most expensive Senate races alone. And while noncandidate spenders likely had a number of interlocking motivations for pouring as much money as they did into these congressional races, the highest-spending groups in this sphere were focused with laser-like intensity on races where it was perceived to matter most: races that were likely to decide whether Democrats won back the majority in the U.S. Senate.

This ongoing, single-minded focus on securing and retaining majorities in the two chambers of Congress has been put into historical context by many scholars, including Frances Lee in her 2016 book *Insecure Majorities: Congress and the Perpetual Campaign*. In this work, Lee cites the increasing volatility of party majorities in Congress as a key determinant of congressional gridlock and polarization. Other authors since then have connected this majoritarian "insecurity" with independent spending in elections of all sorts. For example, Charles Hunt and colleagues found that at the state level, partisan competition—including the likelihood of shifts in state legislative majorities—had a much more consistent and substantial effect on the size and manner of independent spending than did the types of campaign finance laws on the books in those states. They theorize that owing in part to the extreme issue and ideological polarization that has arisen over the past several decades, IE groups were not simply motivated by narrow priorities and supportive only of candidates closest to their beliefs on those priorities, but rather that the largest (and growing) subsets of independent spending groups are partisan in nature if not in name, given both the significant governing capacity afforded to the winning party and the growing inability of the two parties to come together on major issues. As a result, even ostensibly narrowly focused issue groups are spending more money exclusively on one party or the other and are directing those dollars to the most competitive races—races that more often than not feature ideologically middling candidates rather than progressive or conservative champions.[25]

A significant number of high-profile groups displayed these motivations in 2020, continuing a trend from 2018. Perhaps most emblematic of this partisan shift was a group called Swing Left, which focused in both 2018 and 2020 on capturing millions in donations from enthusiastic Democratic voters early on in the election cycle and then funneling that money directly to the "eventual Democratic nominees" for key House and Senate races (as well as the presidency) regardless of who the nominee ended up being. Even more on the nose was Crooked Media, the podcasting empire founded by former Obama staffers in 2017. Crooked's "Get Mitch or Die Trying" fund was established to spread donations evenly among several key Senate races to help Democrats gain the majority. In the hour after news broke of the passing of Supreme Court justice Ruth Bader Ginsburg on September 17, 2020, the "Get Mitch" fund raised $1.5 million. By the next morning, it had raised $6.5 million. The Democrats' nonprofit fundraising outfit ActBlue reported that after Ginsburg's death was announced, the site began taking in $100,000 in donations per minute and raised tens of millions in that single evening.[26] Focusing events like Justice Ginsburg's death raised the stakes for winning back the Senate (the body responsible for the confirmation of presidential nominees to the Supreme Court) even higher than they already were, and Democratic donors did so via outside groups as well as the parties themselves. This trend toward majority-focused spending was most evident in the pair of Senate races in Georgia which, following the general election in November, left the Republicans' majority in the chamber hanging in the balance. The two races, which went to January runoffs, ended up securing the slimmest of majorities for Democrats in the Senate, and the money poured into them reflected this: when all was said and done, nearly a billion dollars was spent on these two races alone, making them the first and second most expensive races in the history of the Senate.[27]

Incumbency, Competition, and Negative Partisanship

These patterns demonstrate a key difference between most outside spenders and donors who gave directly to candidates. IEs from outside groups tend to correlate strongly with how competitive a race is. That is, these groups invest billions of dollars primarily in places where they believe they can have the most impact. Voters, on the other hand, who tend to donate directly to candidate campaigns, are driven by a more complicated blend of motivations. Like IEs, the amount individuals give is naturally conditional on socioeconomic facts: those with the time and money to participate in politics are the most likely to do so.[28] We also know that despite classical theories of voters making rational choices about their votes and their contributions,[29] many voters participate as an act of political expression.[30] More specifically, political scientists have found that Americans who are most likely to vote, contribute, or otherwise participate are motivated more and more by forces like negative partisanship and affective polarization,[31] trends made sharper in recent years because of social and partisan sorting in the electorate.[32]

    With these bedrock motivations in mind, the two countervailing trends in figure 2 are fascinating but perhaps not surprising. This figure displays aggregated spending totals for candidates' official campaigns and

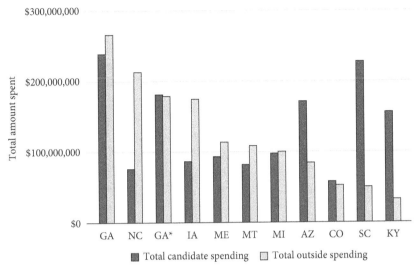

Fɪɢ. 2. Total candidate vs. outside spending in key Senate races, 2020
Source: Center for Responsive Politics.
* This was for the GA special election (Warnock v. Loeffler). The other GA was for the scheduled Senate election.

from outside groups (including parties) separately. The trend for outside spenders is relatively clear: parties and IE groups spend more significant amounts of money as the perceived closeness (and majoritarian importance) of the Senate race over the total course of the election cycle increases.[33] Although Senate races in South Carolina, Kansas, and Texas appeared to be comparatively close in 2020 (within the single digits in the polling), they did not turn out to be very close in reality. More importantly, they were races that if won by Democratic candidates almost assuredly would have meant that Democrats had already won their Senate majority in other, better-polling states like North Carolina, Maine, and Arizona. This made these races a comparatively low return on investment for outside spenders.

Spending on the part of the actual campaigns, however, followed an entirely different pattern. Although nearly all of these races saw unprecedented candidate spending of $50 million or more, the biggest spenders were in races not thought to be particularly close. The three races that jump out in total candidate spending were in South Carolina, Kentucky, and Arizona. South Carolina and Kentucky in particular featured perhaps Democratic voters' two most despised Republicans in the country after Donald Trump: Senators Lindsey Graham and Mitch McConnell. Arizona's incumbent Republican Martha McSally had also drawn significant ire from Democrats over the past two years because of her defiant advocacy for President Trump and his agenda. In Graham's and McConnell's races in particular, the story is clear: donors from around the country, polarized on a partisan basis, acted on the basis of negative partisanship and directed hundreds of millions of dollars in donations toward (mostly hopeless) efforts by Democratic challengers to unseat them. By the end of the campaign, fully 95 percent of the funds raised by Graham's challenger, Democrat Jamie Harrison, were from out of state,[34] as were 97 percent of donations to McConnell's challenger, former air force fighter pilot Amy McGrath.[35]

In short, it appears that while the Democratic Party and other IE groups were laser focused on races most crucial to winning a majority in the Senate, many of their supporters appear to have been motivated to a much greater extent by their affectively polarized opinions on well-known Republicans like McConnell and Graham. Hindsight is very literally 2020 in this case: it is impossible to know whether these excess funds in places like Kentucky and South Carolina could have made the difference in much closer Democratic losses like North Carolina, Maine, or Iowa. But surely the parties will be rethinking how to redirect candidates' campaign cash in more efficient ways in the future, particularly if the main effort of these elections remains holding or taking back the majority in congressional chambers.

A number of other trends emerged from funds spent by the candidates themselves. For the ten previous congressional elections since the turn of the century, incumbents consistently outspent challengers in the aggregate. The incumbency advantage—be it in the traditional form of name recognition, congressional office perks, and constituency service, or due to their increasingly safe partisan seats—appeared to reign supreme. Challengers flipped the script in 2020, outspending incumbents in the aggregate. And, as figure 3 illustrates, it wasn't particularly close. By the end of the campaign, House and Senate challengers spent a combined $766 million to incumbents' $627 million. To be sure, these totals are something of a mirage. High-flying but ill-fated red-state Democratic challengers like Jaime Harrison (SC) and Amy McGrath (KY) accounted for more than $250 million of this total. The average incumbent still outspent the average challenger by a 5:1 ratio. But this was the lowest such ratio since at least 2000. Whether through their individual campaign apparatus, the national party organization, or other independently spending organizations, it's clear that challengers are better funded than ever, particularly when a Senate majority is on the line.

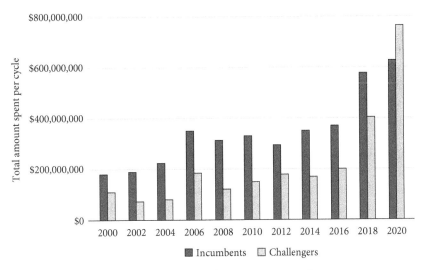

FIG. 3. Total incumbent vs. challenger spending in congressional races, 2000–2020
Source: Center for Responsive Politics / author data.

But that does not mean that the massive outraising of incumbents in many of these races actually led to victory. Quite the opposite: of the eleven Senate challengers in the highest-spending races found in figure 2, ten outspent their incumbent opponents; but only three came out ahead in November. Both were Democrats in states that Joe Biden also won (Colorado and Arizona). Drawing causal conclusions about the best and most efficient ways to spend money in congressional elections is notoriously a hotly debated subject. This chapter cannot and will not solve this particular conundrum. But it does offer another piece of evidence that, in many cases, no amount of money may be enough to overcome unfavorable partisan fundamentals.

The COVID Campaign

After Joe Kennedy III lost his primary bid for the Democratic Senate nomination in Massachusetts, it looked as though Congress would once again be without a Kennedy in its halls—that is, unless Amy Kennedy, the spouse of retired representative Patrick Kennedy, was able to prevail over party-switching congressman Jeff Van Drew (R-NJ). Just days before the election, Kennedy was forced to quarantine because of potential exposure to COVID-19 at a campaign event.[36] She lost to Van Drew by 6 points.

It is of course unknowable whether Kennedy might have managed to whip up enough additional support had she not been forced to quarantine to comply with New Jersey's state laws. What is abundantly clear, however, is that the onset of COVID-19—which came into the public's awareness most fully once it began to spread exponentially throughout the country in mid-March—had enormous implications for campaigns at both the presidential and congressional levels. Volumes can and likely will be written about the myriad ways the coronavirus affected multiple aspects of the 2020 elections: public opinion; partisan differences; and candidates' statements, behavior, and example-setting around the virus, to name just a few. Here, I theorize and provide some very preliminary evidence regarding the virus's influence on how congressional candidates conducted their campaigns based on how they spent their campaign dollars.

How might we expect the virus to affect how a political campaign spends its scarce resources? Some areas of campaign spending are unlikely to change. Especially in competitive campaigns, advertising of all sorts is the most expensive portion of a campaign budget. Spending on ads, which are already experienced virtually, should theoretically not be greatly affected by the pandemic. Other activities, however, almost certainly were. In particular, the pandemic significantly restricted travel, as well as the staging of large events. Even though travel and events are not usually the most expensive elements of campaigning,[37] active candidates run campaigns replete with both. Second, it seems likely that the significant job loss associated with stay-at-home orders similarly affected campaign staff, particularly those usually tasked with in-person responsibilities like getting out the vote and organizing events. Finally, it seems likely that because of the significant lockdowns and stay-at-home orders issued in many states, campaigns would spend comparatively less money on office space, supplies, utilities, and other physical infrastructure during the pandemic.

Using original data from the Congressional Campaign Spending Project (CCSP), I directly compared spending patterns in these particular categories in 2016 and 2020. The CCSP uses transaction-level campaign expenditure data from the FEC, coding each transaction into one of a number of categories—polling, administrative costs, and digital advertisements, to name just a few. I use these data to ascertain whether the pandemic caused reductions in total spending, as well as in four categories of spending: travel, campaign staff, events, and infrastructure. Specifically, I identify a cut point in which national awareness of the pandemic was triggered: March 11, 2020, the date on which the NBA decided to cancel the remainder of its season, and Tom Hanks received a positive test result.

Campaigns to this point had little public incentive to significantly alter their operations, but many, if not most, campaigns likely did afterward. I used the same date to split the transaction-level data from 2016, when March 11 had no intrinsic meaning. I compare total spending in each of the categories for the full span of the election before and after that date in 2016 and in 2020. By comparing these two differences, we can ascertain some initial descriptive evidence as to whether the onset of the pandemic caused spending on travel, events, and infrastructure to be reduced more than it normally would during this time period.

In an effort to obtain some validity in measuring these differences, I limited the sample only to candidates who ran for election in both 2016 and 2020. I also included only congressional candidates.[38] Table 5 summarizes the spending totals and percentage changes for the three categories of interest in 2016 and then in 2020, before and after the March 11 cutoff point. I also include changes in total dollars spent as a comparison point.

In 2016, total spending on events and infrastructure by the candidates increased by a small but significant amount: 7 percent and 15 percent, respectively. Spending on travel and staff increased by astronomical amounts: 677 and 1,099 percent respectively. Overall spending also saw a significant increase. This is to be expected. Most campaigns, particularly competitive ones, only significantly ramp up their spending in August, September, and October, unless they had to endure a hard-fought primary campaign as well (and even then, primaries in a vast majority of states are held later than March 11). In 2020, however, spending on events, infrastructure, and travel actually *decreased* by significant percentages during that same time period. In fact, these areas were the only categories of campaign spending that decreased in the post-COVID environment. And while spending on staff did increase post-COVID, the increase was minuscule (14 percent) compared to the massive campaign hiring increases during the same period in 2016.

TABLE 5. Spending differences on select categories, 2016 and 2020

	1/3/15 to 3/11/16	3/11/16 to 10/15/16	% change	1/3/20 to 3/11/20	3/11/20 to 10/15/20	% change
Total spending	$374,885,152	$627,366,272	67	$336,383,927	$749,788,348	123
Events	$13,123,654	$14,005,319	7	$18,757,992	$4,356,822	−77
Infrastructure	$28,781,578	$33,119,754	15	$27,281,866	$17,229,154	−37
Travel	$2,001,152	$15,558,600	677	$14,807,317	$5,226,321	−47

Source: Federal Election Commission / author data.

Relative decreases in areas like events, staff, infrastructure, and travel are indeed what we would expect to find given the well-documented job loss and decreases in consumer spending in those areas caused by widespread business closures, lockdowns, unemployment, and stay-at-home orders.[39] Crucially, these massive relative decreases all took place while overall spending—and spending in other categories like advertising, fundraising, and GOTV—increased at rates far greater than in 2016. The evidence offered in table 5 indicates that while COVID appears to have hit campaigns hard generally in 2020, the impact was disproportionate on budget items that are not conducive to the physical distancing and other public health practices that health experts recommended. While it may take some time to more fully understand the many ways COVID affected congressional campaigns, it is clear that candidates made strategic choices in how to spend their precious funds.

Conclusion

What can we learn from the mind-boggling sums of money that were spent in the federal elections of 2020? The findings from this chapter broadly indicate that, rather than a clear determinant of success, campaign cash is often a trailing indicator of other political conditions and events that have much more consistent grounding in political science. In the Democratic primary, no amount of money—either from the grassroots in the case of Sanders and Warren or from billionaires' checkbooks in the case of Bloomberg and Steyer—could overcome voters' single-minded goal of nominating the candidate most likely to defeat Donald Trump in the fall. In the general election campaign for the presidency, COVID raged, the partisan spending gap reversed itself in the closing months, and yet the polls remained shockingly steady throughout. In the race for Congress, Democrats dominated the money chase across the board but were not as dominant in garnering actual votes. More statistically advanced analyses can and should come next to more rigorously ascertain how the pandemic affected campaign finance in 2020, as well as to test many of the connections posited here between the campaign finance activity of candidates and voters alike, on the one hand, and various political science theories, on the other. I hope this chapter has provided a starting point for further research on the potential linkages between campaign finance and important phenomena like negative partisanship, affective polarization, and the discrepant motivations of highly energized partisan voters and deeply vested parties and IE groups.

Notes

1. Gary Jacobson, "Campaign Spending Effects in U.S. Senate Elections: Evidence from the National Annenberg Election Survey," *Electoral Studies* 25, no. 2 (2006): 195–226.
2. Matt Flegenheimer and Katie Gluek, "Joe Biden Is Poised to Deliver the Biggest Surprise of 2020: A Short, Orderly Primary," *New York Times*, March 10, 2020.
3. Tim Reynolds, "NBA Says Virus Hiatus Will Likely Last 'at Least' a Month," Associated Press, March 12, 2020.
4. Nicole Sperling, "Tom Hanks Says He Has Coronavirus," *New York Times*, March 11, 2020.
5. Ollie Gratzinger, "Small donors give big money in 2020 election cycle," *Center for Responsive Politics*, October 30, 2020. https://www.opensecrets .org/news/2020/10/small-donors-give-big-2020-thanks-to-technology/.
6. "Donor Demographics Overview, 2020 Election Cycle," *Center for Responsive Politics.* https://www.opensecrets.org/elections-overview/donor-demo graphics?cycle=2020&display=A. Accessed February 12, 2021.
7. "Outside Spending Overview, 2020 Election Cycle," Center for Responsive Politics: https://www.opensecrets.org/outsidespending/. Accessed February 12, 2021.
8. "Dark Money Basics," *Center for Responsive Politics*: https://www .opensecrets.org/dark-money/basics. Accessed February 12, 2021.
9. Ciara Torres-Spelliscy, "Dark Money in the 2020 Election," Brennan Center for Justice, November 20, 2020, https://www.brennancenter.org/our -work/analysis-opinion/dark-money-2020-election.
10. "Outside Spending Overview, 2020 Election Cycle," *Center for Responsive Politics*: https://www.opensecrets.org/outsidespending/index.php?type =Y&filter=S. Accessed February 12, 2021.
11. Alan Abramowitz and Steven Webster, "The Rise of Negative Partisanship and the Nationalization of US Elections in the 21st Century," *Electoral Studies* 41 (2016): 12–22.
12. "The Gender Gap: Voting Choices in Presidential Elections," *Rutgers University, Center for American Women in Politics*: https://cawp.rutgers.edu /sites/default/files/resources/ggpresvote.pdf. Accessed February 12, 2021.
13. "2020 House Potential Candidate Summary," *Rutgers University, Center for American Women in Politics*: https://cawp.rutgers.edu/potential -candidate-summary-2020#house. Accessed February 12, 2021.
14. Li Zhou, "Attention Has Faded on the More Than 20 Sexual Misconduct Allegations against Trump," *Vox*, November 3, 2020, https://www.vox.com /2020/11/3/21544482/trump-sexual-misconduct-allegations.
15. Zach Montellaro and Steven Shepard, "DNC Raises Thresholds Again for January Debate," *Politico*, December 20, 2019.

16. "2020 Democratic Presidential Nomination polling averages," *RealClear-Politics.* https://www.realclearpolitics.com/epolls/2020/president/us/2020_democratic_presidential_nomination-6730.html. Accessed February 12, 2021.

17. "Who Are The Biggest Donors?" *Center for Responsive Politics.* https://www.opensecrets.org/elections-overview/biggest-donors. Accessed February 12, 2021.

18. Ben Kamisar, "March 10 Exit Polls: Biden Rises with Broad Coalition, Desire to Defeat Trump," NBC News, March 10, 2020, https://www.nbcnews.com/politics/2020-election/march-10-exit-polls-majorities-democratic-primary-voters-prioritize-beating-n1154826.

19. David Siders, Maggie Severns, and Natasha Korecki, "'It's Too Much': Democrats Shudder at Trump's Money Machine," *Politico,* October 21, 2019.

20. Brad Parscale (@Parscale), "For nearly three years we have been building a juggernaut campaign (Death Star). It is firing on all cylinders. Data, Digital, TV, Political, Surrogates, Coalitions, etc. In a few days we start pressing FIRE for the first time." May 7, 2020, 7:30AM. "https://twitter.com/parscale/status/1258388669544759296?lang=en.

21. Alex Thompson, "Trump's Campaign Knocks on a Million Doors a Week. Biden's Knocks on Zero," *Politico,* August 4, 2020.

22. "Donald Trump and Joe Biden Favorability Ratings," *RealClearPolitics*: https://www.realclearpolitics.com/epolls/other/president/trumpbiden-favorability.html. Accessed February 12, 2021.

23. "2020 Senate Elections Polling Averages," *RealClearPolitics*: https://www.realclearpolitics.com/epolls/2020/senate/2020_elections_senate_map.html. Accessed February 12, 2021.

24. "2020 Elections Overview," *Center for Responsive Politics*: https://www.opensecrets.org/elections-overview?cycle=2020&display=T&type=G. Accessed February 12, 2021.

25. Charles R. Hunt, Jaclyn J. Kettler, Michael J. Malbin, Brendan Glavin, and Keith E. Hamm, "Assessing Group Incentives, Independent Spending, and Campaign Finance Law by Comparing the States," *Election Law Journal* 19, no. 3 (2020): 374–91.

26. Daniel Politi, "Donations to Democratic Groups Soar after Ruth Bader Ginsburg's Death," *Slate,* September 19, 2020, https://slate.com/news-and-politics/2020/09/donations-democratic-groups-soar-bader-ginsburgs-death.html.

27. Reid Wilson, "Georgia Senate Races Shatter Spending Records," *The Hill,* January 5, 2021. https://thehill.com/homenews/campaign/532749-georgia-senate-races-shatter-spending-records.

28. Sidney Verba, Kay Lehman Schlozman, and Henry E. Brady, *Voice and Equality: Civic Voluntarism in American Politics* (Cambridge, MA: Harvard University Press, 1995).

29. André Blais, *To Vote or Not to Vote? The Merits and Limits of Rational Choice Theory* (Pittsburgh, PA: University of Pittsburgh Press, 2000).

30. Leonie Huddy, Lilliana Mason, and Lene Aarøe, "Expressive Partisanship: Campaign Involvement, Political Emotion, and Partisan Identity," *American Political Science Review* 109, no. 1 (2015): 1–17.

31. Shanto Iyengar and Sean J. Westwood, "Fear and Loathing across Party Lines: New Evidence on Group Polarization," *American Journal of Political Science* 59, no. 3 (2015): 690–707.

32. Lilliana Mason and Julie Wronski, "One Tribe to Bind Them All: How Our Social Group Attachments Strengthen Partisanship," *Political Psychology* 39, no. S1 (2018): 257–277.

33. The perhaps surprising lack of outside spending in the Georgia Senate special election (starred) is most likely due to the widespread perception (which turned out to be true) that this race would go to a two-party runoff, leading outside spenders to save their money for when it mattered the most.

34. "South Carolina Senate 2020 Race," *Center for Responsive Politics*: https://www.opensecrets.org/races/geography?cycle=2020&id=SCS1&spec=N. Accessed February 12, 2021.

35. "Kentucky Senate 2020 Race," *Center for Responsive Politics*: https://www.opensecrets.org/races/geography?cycle=2020&id=KYS1&spec=N. Accessed February 12, 2021.

36. Dan Stamm, "NJ Congressional Hopeful Kennedy in Quarantine Due to Potential COVID-19 Exposure," NBC News 10 Philadelphia, November 3, 2020, https://www.nbcphiladelphia.com/news/politics/decision-2020/new-jersey-amy-kennedy-coronavirus-van-drew-race/2582238/.

37. Paul Herrnson, *Congressional Elections: Campaigning at Home and in Washington* (Washington, DC: CQ Press, 2019).

38. Analysis of how the presidential candidates spent their money is surely worth future research efforts, particularly in light of their polar-opposite approaches to messaging about the pandemic. But Donald Trump is the only consistent candidate, and his campaign was so vastly different as an incumbent than the upstart nature of his 2016 effort, making direct comparison at this juncture difficult.

39. Akrur Barua and David Levin, "What's Weighing on Consumer Spending: Fear of COVID-10 and Its Economic Impact," Deloitte Insights, August 27, 2020, https://www2.deloitte.com/us/en/insights/economy/spotlight/economics-insights-analysis-08-2020.html.

Media and the 2020 Presidential Campaign

Marjorie Randon Hershey

Life was bleak for journalists covering the 2020 presidential election. Because of changes in news consumption patterns, large numbers of reporters had already lost their jobs. Overall newsroom employment had fallen by 25 percent in a decade, and newspaper jobs in particular were down by more than half.[1] An NPR reporter described the previous year as a "media apocalypse": "Nearly 8,000 newsroom jobs disappeared this year in a flurry of layoffs, buyouts and mergers.... Legacy media giants like Gannett cut hundreds of positions after a merger, leaving huge swaths of the country with no local papers at all."[2] That meant fewer reporters to uncover the actions and missteps of public officials and candidates,[3] which in turn led to greater public reliance on the often skewed and unproven information on social media.[4]

As though that weren't enough of a challenge, the COVID-19 pandemic clobbered many revenue-starved news organizations during the height of the presidential nominating season. Newspapers suffered the most. Stores and services were closed for months during the economic shutdown, so they couldn't pay for ads. That cut deeply into newspaper revenues, and the increase in online readership didn't bring in enough money to offset the decline in paid print advertising. The only gainers were nightly network TV news and a few cable channels, such as Fox News.[5] Yet Americans were more desperate than ever for accurate information about the fast-spreading virus. So although Americans were hungry for news, many traditional news outlets were bleeding the funding they needed to stay alive.

Not that reporters weren't accustomed to hard times. By 2020 much of the American public had become highly suspicious of media coverage as a result of strong partisan and ideological polarization.[6] Since the mid-1900s, Republican conservatives have pressed their claim that the mainstream media—the so-called legacy television networks and newspapers such as NBC, CBS, the

New York Times, and the *Washington Post*—intentionally bias their coverage in favor of liberals and Democrats.[7] From the beginning of his 2016 presidential campaign, Donald Trump charged that mainstream media outlets, which he termed the "liberal media," were "fake news," even "enemies of the American people," and almost 40 percent of survey respondents said they agreed with him. This sizable group included more than 80 percent of Republicans and 82 percent of Fox News viewers.[8] The primary news source trusted by Republicans was Fox News, whereas Democrats in the survey said they trusted a wider range of news sources, none of which was Fox News. Thus, the two parties' supporters were getting their information from different media perspectives.[9]

That didn't mean that most Americans were exposed only to biased news. Although many media sites such as blogs and cable outlets clearly had a partisan slant, others held to the norm of journalistic impartiality—or at least to the practice of "both sides-ism," in which a news story includes information from a source opposed to those quoted in the rest of the article.[10] Social scientists looking for evidence of partisan bias in legacy media outlets' news reporting have usually failed to find it. One careful study, for example, asked journalists about their personal partisan leanings and then tested whether they were more likely to prefer covering a hypothetical candidate who was conservative or one who was progressive. The researchers found that "journalists weren't more likely to [choose to] cover a candidate of their own ideology."[11] And the wide range of viewpoints among the tens of thousands of media outlets, from Fox and conservative bloggers to MSNBC and liberal sites, should make it clear that "the media" in general cannot be characterized accurately as presenting only a single perspective.

How did journalists respond to these major challenges when covering the 2020 presidential campaign? Did they apply many of the lessons news organizations learned from covering Trump's campaign for the presidency in 2016?

Trump Dominated Media Coverage in 2020—Again

The 2020 election environment differed in many ways from that of 2016, yet journalists faced several of the same dilemmas. One was Trump's ability to push all other news off the front page. Coverage of the 2016 presidential campaign had been strikingly one-sided. From Trump's announcement of his candidacy in mid-2015 to the early 2016 Iowa caucuses, he was the subject of more than 60 percent of all mentions of the

Republican presidential candidates on national TV news. Sixteen other Republican candidates split the remaining 40 percent.[12] One expert estimated that Trump's free media coverage was worth almost $6 billion from July 2015 through October 2016—more than twice that of his Democratic opponent, Hillary Clinton.[13] Research also showed that the tone of Trump's coverage was more positive than Clinton's.[14] Even his negative coverage helped solidify his support among Republicans, whose contempt for what they regarded as the "fake news" was encouraged by the Trump campaign.

Trump also dominated media coverage of the 2020 campaign.[15] In elections in which voters need ample information about both major party candidates, how did Trump manage to own the coverage twice? He commanded an overwhelming share of media attention because, as a showman, he was skilled in drawing audiences. Trump knew that people look for the same characteristics in the news that draw their attention to entertainment programs, rather than the types of news more likely to help inform them about the health of a democratic system.[16] He provided reporters with a constant stream of controversy, drama, and conflict during both of his campaigns for president in the form of personal attacks, sensational charges, and claims that crossed the boundaries of political propriety.[17] Journalists could count on Trump to generate a good story in time for every news cycle. By doing so, he succeeded in setting the news agenda day after day.[18] As a columnist pointed out, media outlets "let Trump, the great distractor, hijack news coverage and play assignment editor. He became the shiny new toy that they couldn't take their eyes off."[19]

Trump's genius for attracting media coverage in 2020 was all the more impressive because he had no competition for the Republican nomination. The Democratic nomination contest was lively; more than two dozen Democrats vied for their party's presidential nomination. But the crowded Democratic field was never able to match the president's ability to command the news cycle.[20] Trump held massive and boisterous rallies in states immediately before their primaries or caucuses took place in order to keep the cameras focused on him rather than on the Democratic race. Democrat after Democrat fell out of the headlines during the winter of 2020, unable to compete with both their numerous intraparty rivals and the president's ability to eclipse other news stories.

In March, the spreading coronavirus pandemic put a hold on the president's massive rallies. Trump adapted by staging daily press conferences on the virus. The president provided journalists with dramatic and ever-changing pronouncements: on one day, the pandemic would magically disappear with the coming of warm weather; on another, it might kill as many as 2 million Americans.[21] He claimed that the economy must and would reopen by Easter, and at other times agreed with Pentagon officials that reopening was too risky.[22] He threatened to quarantine New York, then changed his mind.[23] He championed supposed "cures" for the virus that his own administration acknowledged didn't work.[24] He celebrated the high ratings his coronavirus updates were receiving, noting that they matched the ratings of the popular TV reality show *The Bachelor*.[25]

In contrast with 2016, however, the president's continuing domination of the news eventually began to wear. His disjointed musings at these news conferences (in which he once suggested that scientists research the possibility that ingesting disinfectants would cure the virus[26]) did little to benefit his public approval ratings.[27] Even Trump's big advantage in fundraising through July 2020 (see the chapter "Campaign Finance," this volume) did not raise his approval level, which remained very stable at a comparatively low level for a first-term president. Although his major Democratic rival, Joe Biden, was not as well known as Trump and therefore was more at risk from campaign attacks,[28] Biden began to gain ground in the polls.

Trump's staff carefully controlled his exposure to the media, as they had throughout his presidency. Presidential press conferences, infrequent during his first year in office, soon stopped altogether. By late summer 2020, fully 40 percent of Trump's interviews (excluding those with local news stations) were given to Fox News and Fox Business Network. Sympathetic interviewers on these networks often guided or reinterpreted the president's comments to protect him against criticism. For instance, in August 2020, the president expressed support for a Wisconsin police officer who shot an unarmed Black man seven times in the back. Trump compared the police officer's near-lethal action to a golfer becoming anxious and missing an easy three-foot putt. Fox host Laura Ingraham softened the inflammatory comparison by reminding the president on air, "You're not comparing to golf . . . because, of course, that's what the media would say. Yes. . . . People make—people panic."[29]

Another safe harbor for Trump in the media was Twitter. As in 2016, the president relied heavily on this platform to speak directly to tens of millions of people, thus avoiding the filter of the Washington press corps. Trump tweeted almost 6,000 times between June 2020 and Election Day; in September alone, he averaged 44 tweets per day, compared with Biden's 11. As in 2016, Trump used tweets not so much to claim credit for his own policies but to blame others for events that could be seen as his

failures.[30] He leveled much of the blame at the media, which he characterized in the harshest terms. Among the president's common descriptions of
journalists were not only "fake news" and "the enemy of the people" but also
"dishonest," "corrupt," "low life reporters," "bad people," "human
scum," and "some of the worst human beings you'll ever meet." For instance,
when the president was questioned by a CBS News reporter about his statements that the pandemic would have little effect on Americans, Trump's
response was to attack the reporter for raising the question: "You're so disgraceful. It's so disgraceful the way you say that. . . . You know you're a fake,
your whole network the way you cover it is fake."[31]

Presidents typically have an ambivalent relationship with reporters, but
Trump's constant barrage of attacks on the media was unprecedented
among recent chief executives.[32] His likely aim, as this chapter will later
show, was to undermine public confidence in news sources, one of the primary checks on the power of government. He was successful at least with
his base of loyal supporters. Polls just before the election found that
60 percent of Republicans (including 67 percent of those who strongly
approved of the president) agreed that a major reason mistakes make it
into news stories was reporters' desire to mislead.[33] Trump's attacks even
led some media executives to post armed guards outside their newsrooms
after some individuals threatened to assault reporters.[34]

In short, President Trump dominated media coverage in 2020 by using
many of the same techniques he used in 2016. Most journalists had not yet
found ways to reestablish balance in their coverage. As one columnist
wrote in 2020, "The press is still—mostly—covering [President Trump] on
the terms he dictates. . . . We've never quite figured out how to cover
Trump for the good of citizens. We've never really fully changed gears
despite Trump's constant, norm-busting behavior," resulting in a president
"who played the media like a puppet while deeply damaging the public's
trust in the press as a democratic institution."[35]

Covering Bernie Sanders in the Trump Era

President Trump wasn't the only presidential contender to complain about
media coverage.

Democratic candidate Senator Bernie Sanders was no Donald Trump.
Sanders's campaign for the Democratic nomination in 2016 attracted rela-
tively little coverage, even compared with that of his opponent, Hillary
Clinton. Many analysts did not consider Sanders a credible challenger to
Clinton, so they paid little attention to his candidacy.[36] This lack of media

attention came at a price: Sanders was not thoroughly vetted by the media. His background went largely unexamined, his issue positions were not extensively covered, and other politicians' assessments of his skills were rarely cited. But ironically, despite Sanders's slim coverage in 2016, he was "old news" when he reappeared as a serious candidate in the 2020 race and continued to receive limited coverage.

Many Sanders supporters preferred a more conspiratorial explanation for their candidate's failure to attract media attention. They claimed he was being silenced by media corporations because of his anticorporate stands.[37] Yet in many ways, the limited media attention to Sanders protected him from reports that he was objectively outside the norm for presidential contenders. He had long refused to run for office as a Democrat, taking the label Independent, though he caucused with Democrats in the Senate. He called himself a socialist or democratic socialist—terms viewed with suspicion by most Americans[38]—and had previously campaigned for the Socialist Workers Party. His unapologetic leftist stance, though attractive to left-wing Democrats who felt their aims had long been brushed aside by the party, diverged from the well-accepted explanation for why the Democratic Party did well in the 2018 midterm election results, when Democrats who beat Republicans were predominantly moderate on major issues.[39] Further, like Trump, Sanders refused to release his full health records, though he was treated for a heart attack months before the 2020 Iowa caucuses.

In a large field of primary candidates, the results of any one contest can be unpredictable, and in February 2020 Sanders edged out a win in the New Hampshire primary. That suddenly made him the apparent front-runner for the Democratic nomination. The party then found itself with a front-runner who had not yet been extensively scrutinized by the mainstream media. Almost immediately, news outlets scrambled to cover Sanders's partisan affiliations, his stands on issues, his personal history, and his health. Several party and elected officials quickly claimed on the record that to nominate a candidate with Sanders's issue positions would cost the party its chance of defeating Trump. As analyst Dan Balz put it, "Whether the collective attacks on Sanders will blunt his momentum won't be known immediately. But what's even more difficult to assess is what might have happened if the other candidates had taken Sanders more seriously earlier and subjected him to sustained cross-examination over a period of months. Sanders has escaped that kind of scrutiny."[40]

In short, just as Trump's dominance of media coverage affected the race, so did Sanders's ability to fly beneath the media radar for most of 2016 and 2020. Even with the huge expansion of media outlets that came with the internet, journalists' fascination with some candidates and under-coverage of others can make a difference in voters' opportunities to gather election information easily. Avoiding media coverage can help candidates at some times and hurt them at others, but it rarely benefits the public. In what was often described as a "stunning turnaround,"[41] Biden soon replaced Sanders as the party's front-runner in the Super Tuesday primaries and caucuses.

Covering Kamala Harris: A Candidate in a Double Bind

Journalists had little precedent for covering Biden's vice presidential running mate, California senator Kamala Harris. She was the first Black woman chosen by a major party as its vice presidential nominee. Four years earlier, reporters had trouble figuring out how to cover Hillary Clinton's campaign as well. Although Clinton was the first woman to be nominated for president by a major party in 228 years, only a tiny portion of Clinton's coverage mentioned the historic nature of her candidacy.[42] And stories about the fall 2016 campaign mentioned Clinton's dishonesty many times more often than they did her opponent's, despite Trump's extensive, documented record of lies by that time.[43]

Coverage of Harris was colored by both racial and gender stereotypes.[44] In a nation in which most elected leaders are white males, images of leadership are typically infused with traditionally masculine qualities such as assertiveness, even aggression, dominance, and power. If women candidates display traditionally feminine qualities such as nurturance and deference, they are less likely to be viewed as leaders. Yet if they show more traditionally masculine qualities, they risk being viewed as overbearing and unlikable.[45] The bind is even more acute for Black women because the trope of the "angry Black woman" is just as common, and just as antithetical to popular images of leadership as are the qualities of gentleness and femininity.[46]

In fact, Harris was often portrayed in a stereotyped way. The style she developed as a prosecutor led to characterizations of her as an "uppity black woman," "abrasive," "condescending,"[47] and aiming "above her station," as in claims that she would usurp Biden's role if they were elected. Several journalists quoted sources that attempted to sexualize and therefore belittle Harris. A false claim by a former California state legislator that Harris attained her positions through sexual favors was viewed more than 630,000 times on Twitter.[48] Black Americans are often perceived as political liberals,[49] and Trump's campaign referred to Harris as a "trojan horse for a radical leftist agenda,"[50] a "communist,"[51] and one who aimed to make the United States a "socialist hellhole."[52] Candidates and commentators who intentionally mispronounced her first name (including her Senate colleague David Perdue, who mocked her as "Kamalamalamala") drew a lot of reporting.[53] Coverage of Harris, then, often reflected the stereotypes that have long challenged Black women in politics and society.

Covering Lies and False Equivalents

In both 2016 and 2020, reporters and editors had to determine how to handle candidates' "misstatements." It is hardly news that candidates, like most other people, occasionally slant the truth. Yet the volume of clearly false statements by Trump in 2016 posed a dilemma for the reporters covering him: Should they flag his misstatements and correct them? If they did, would it reinforce the notion that journalists were biased against Trump, even though the frequency of his misstatements went far beyond that of other campaigners? Coverage in 2016 did not resolve this dilemma; only 2 percent of local news coverage of the 2016 race included any fact-checking of the candidates' claims,[54] and in national coverage, only the so-called elite press dared to identify any of Trump's statements as lies.

The need for fact-checking heightened once Trump became president. In a single month—October 2017—one fact-checking database reported 1,200 false or misleading statements issued by the president.[55] As a columnist pointed out, "It had always been normal to let a president have his say—to let his statements top the news while letting the fact checks follow. That has changed somewhat during the lie-ridden Trump administration, but not nearly enough. The reflexive media urge, deep in our DNA, is still to quote the president without offering an immediate challenge."[56] Even by 2020, most of the mainstream media remained reluctant to call out the president's misstatements. When *New York Times* executive editor Dean Baquet was asked what to do if a source is not factual, he responded, "In some cases, you engage in 'deep reporting.' . . . But you don't do 'labeling and cheap analysis.' You don't call it a lie. . . . Let somebody else call it a lie.'"[57]

No matter what journalists called them, Trump's misstatements increased every year. The *Washington Post* reported that Trump averaged 6 false claims a day in 2017, 16 per day in 2018, 22 in 2019, and 56 a day, on average, during August 2020, for a total of nearly 25,000 false claims by Election Day.[58] In fact, when Trump and his key allies were suspended from Twitter and some other social media sites in early 2021, research found that online misinformation about the election dropped by 73 percent, demonstrating that a great deal of the false information circulating online had come from Trump himself.[59] During the 2020 campaign, the *Post* and some other legacy newspapers followed the practice of calling out false statements in the body of their stories; for example, "Amid his frequent and false criticisms of mail-in voting . . ."[60]

However, many other traditional outlets refused to label Trump's misstatements as lies, or even as incorrect. "Both sidesism" was present even in coverage of the election result. Trump claimed victory in the election well before the vote counting was completed. Although most major media outlets pointed out that the count was ongoing, the *Atlanta Journal-Constitution*'s headline on the day after Election Day read "Trump: I Have Won. Biden: It's Not Over." A reporter compared that to announcing, "One marathon runner declared himself the winner after 20 miles. The other runners say marathons are 26.2 miles. We'll leave it up to you to decide."[61] The impact of false statements by the president probably declined over time as a result of their sheer abundance; yet only a few legacy outlets were willing or able to maintain an institutional counterbalance such as a fact-checking column.[62]

In addition to journalists' reluctance to spotlight the president's misstatements, their coverage also frequently failed to point out instances when Trump stumbled over his words in rallies, sounded incoherent, or showed other signs that might be considered worrisome in a seventy-four-year-old. Journalists worried that accurately labeling the president's instances of bizarre musings (for instance, a lengthy tirade at a Milwaukee rally about low-flow toilets needing to be flushed ten to fifteen times) would corroborate charges that the media were anti-Trump.[63] At least in the mainstream media, the abnormal qualities of the Trump administration seem to have been downplayed or normalized.

Coverage of Trump did benefit in some ways from journalists' added experience. At least in the national media, fact-checking was more frequent in 2020, and cable TV networks were less inclined to cover Trump rallies in their entirety. During election week, many reporters showed notable restraint in waiting to declare a winner, given that many more Democrats than Republicans had voted early and by mail, casting ballots that would not be counted until the Republican-leaning votes at the polls on Election Day were reported. After Biden was declared the winner, many journalists experienced a sudden surge of courage in reporting that President Trump's claims of massive voter fraud lacked evidence. Overall, however, even after years of experience, journalists were still struggling to deal with Trump's unique personal style and to balance the need for accuracy in the news columns with their respect for the presidency and their fear of being accused of bias.[64] The challenge continued after Trump left office, and as media outlets struggled with how to cover some Trump wannabes in the U.S. House and Senate.

Social Media: Political Disinformation Becomes More Sophisticated

Misinformation was much more frequent on social media than in print media. As in the Russian misinformation campaign to benefit Trump's election in 2016,[65] malicious falsehoods often went viral on social media platforms in 2018 and 2020. Russian actors and bots worked hard to spread the message that the big increase in voting by mail would lead to massive fraud, lost ballots, and untrustworthy results.[66] Lurid conspiracy theories circulated. Although Facebook, Twitter, and some other major social media platforms tried to police the posts they carried, these efforts were often insufficient. The platforms defended themselves on the ground that they did not want to interfere with free speech, but critics suggested that the platforms' reluctance had more to do with concern about lost profits.[67]

Media have always been vulnerable to the spread of false information. As Mark Twain is reputed to have said more than a century ago, it is hard to combat misinformation when a lie can travel around the world while the truth is still lacing up its boots—or, as one columnist put it, "A lie can spread just about as fast as a human finger can click 'retweet.'"[68] Lies that are constructed to misinform usually have a compelling narrative (they tell an interesting story), which is clear and easy to follow and conforms to the receiver's preexisting beliefs.[69] The truth, by comparison, is often more complicated and less fascinating. As a result, if the target of a lie tries to correct the record, the correction will probably get less attention, because the lie was more interesting. Perversely, the correction reminds people of the lie and, thus, increases its credibility.

The ability to target particular segments of the population—those thought to be especially vulnerable to misinformation—increases the danger. The national party organizations and other groups have compiled huge databases of personal information about social media users. Such collections of data permit more effective microtargeting: delivering bits of information to the types of people the targeter wants to influence, in a form that is most palatable to them.[70] A campaign eager to reduce the turnout of liberal college students, then, can direct a social media post to people between the ages of eighteen and twenty-three who live within a five-mile radius of a university and have "liked" Black Lives Matter, for the purpose of spreading the false claim that the liberal Senate candidate in their state is a slumlord who refused to rent to African American tenants. Such claims can be quickly disseminated by social media influencers, who systematically retweet misinformation that supports their cause.[71]

Campaigners and journalists tried several ways to solve the challenge of misinformation in 2020. Each solution had its shortcomings. One approach was to identify lies soon after they appeared on social media, before they went viral, and then persuade Twitter, Facebook, or other platforms to delete them. In May 2020 Twitter began to flag a small number of Trump's particularly inflammatory posts, delete parts of them, and indicate where correct information could be found. The platform focused especially on Trump's claims that the drug hydroxychloroquine could effectively treat COVID-19, without verified evidence,[72] and that voting by mail is inevitably a corrupt process. It didn't flag other provably false statements, however. Trump and other authors of flagged posts objected strenuously to what they considered the platform's bias against their views. As president, Trump could put some muscle behind his objections; after Twitter began to flag a few of his posts with correctives, Trump issued an executive order limiting social media platforms' protection from lawsuits.[73]

It took an enormous amount of time and effort for social media platforms and other outlets to identify and respond to such misinformation. Fact-checking groups such as Politifact, FactCheck.org, and Snopes fought to keep up with the 24/7/365 flow of misleading posts and to distinguish false statements from sarcasm or satire.[74] Their efforts were not always believed; for instance, a post on the satirical website TatersGonnaTate claiming that U.S. representative Alexandria Ocasio-Cortez said American soldiers were overpaid led to death threats against her, even after the claim was refuted.[75]

Another approach was more broadly educational: trying to help media audiences identify misinformation and conspiracy theories. Some websites offered clues as to how to spot fake news.[76] A few media outlets relied on the "truth sandwich," in which accurate information is presented first, then the false claim, and then the fact-check. Several major organizations distributed advice for journalists on how to respond to misinformation.[77]

But at a time when American party politics is highly polarized, many media viewers and readers are eager to find support for the conclusions they have already reached. Thus, it becomes even easier for conspiracy theorists and purveyors of misinformation to promote their deceptive explanations for stressful and ambiguous events.[78]

Twitter and Efforts to Delegitimize the Election Results

Perhaps the greatest challenge for journalists in covering the 2020 election involved active efforts to delegitimize the results. Democratic governments depend on a widespread sense of legitimacy—public acceptance that the rules and the leaders are functioning within fair and reasonable boundaries—to promote compliance with the leaders' decisions. When that public acceptance erodes (for instance, if a large proportion of the public concludes that elections are rigged), then a democracy becomes vulnerable.[79]

As early as the 2016 election, when asked if he would accept the election results if he lost, Trump astonished reporters by responding, "I will keep you in suspense."[80] Throughout his presidency, Trump complained that the media were working to undermine not only his own success but the interests of the American people.[81] These efforts to delegitimize two vital democratic institutions—elections and the free press—became an increasing source of concern as the 2020 election approached. Trump's claims were echoed by the Republican National Committee (RNC) and his campaign's surrogates.[82] Democrats feared that Trump, by attacking the legitimacy of the mass media and mail-in balloting (which increased dramatically in 2020 because of the pandemic), was laying the groundwork for a claim that if he lost the election, then its results should be overturned.

The president didn't stop at allegations. He called on supporters to show up at polling places on Election Day as members of "Trump's Army" and watch for people they judged to be committing voter fraud. This practice had often been used in past years to suppress the vote among minority populations.[83] In fact, after similar "ballot security" efforts in 1980, the RNC settled a lawsuit by agreeing to stop such tactics, but this consent decree expired in 2018.[84] Trump declined to censure white supremacist groups, who had been appearing, often armed, at Black Lives Matter protests and were expected to assemble at some polling places. And his new appointee as postmaster general instituted several changes in mid-2020 that slowed mail delivery in many communities. In spring and summer primary elections, in which the number of mailed ballots greatly increased, many voters' ballots were not delivered in time to be counted, and others never received their mail ballot.[85] Democrats termed the post office changes a partisan move. The RNC spent millions on lawsuits to prevent easier access to vote by mail, during a campaign in which many more Democrats said they planned to vote by mail than Republicans did.[86]

As the president's poll numbers dropped during the summer, he claimed more frequently that the election would be rigged. By late July, Trump had raised charges of election fraud in mail voting seventy times.[87] On June 22, for example, he tweeted, "RIGGED 2020 ELECTION: MILLIONS OF MAIL-IN BALLOTS WILL BE PRINTED BY FOREIGN COUNTRIES, AND OTHERS. IT WILL BE THE SCANDAL OF OUR TIMES!" In fact, research shows that documented instances of fraud in mail as well as in-person voting have been rarer than cases of people being struck by lightning.[88] But the president insisted that because of likely voter fraud, he could not promise to accept the results of the November election.[89] By mid-September, Trump had stated three times that unless he won, the outcome would be illegitimate, because there were no legitimate conditions in which he could lose a fair election.[90] He even proposed postponing the election until the pandemic subsided.[91]

Some commentators suggested that Trump's startling statements were simply aimed at distracting public attention from the pandemic and the bad economic news. Yet such statements threatened public support for a pillar upholding democratic institutions: losing candidates must accept the result of the election and step aside for the winners. To test the idea that Trump would lay the groundwork for a claim that the election results would be illegitimate, I coded tweets by both Trump (@RealDonaldTrump) and Biden (@JoeBiden) attacking various democratic institutions, from the media and election administration to state and local governments and law enforcement, during the last five months of the campaign.[92]

As Figure 1 shows, the contrast is stark; many more of Trump's tweets than Biden's could be classified as "delegitimizing." The greatest proportion of Trump's delegitimizing tweets attacked journalists and the media. Biden's few critical tweets instead targeted systemic racism and the pernicious effects of economic institutions on lower-income people. In contrast, Trump tweeted only twice about the unequal impact of economic institutions, and all but eight of his thirty-seven tweets about racism focused on "reverse racism"—his claim that racial sensitivity training was racist against whites.

Immediately after Election Day, Trump continued to attack the media, but the target of most of his tweets moved to election administration. In the two-week span from November 4 to November 17, he posted 237 tweets, averaging 17 per day, claiming that the election was rigged and the vote count false, including, "Most fraudulent Election in history!" Trump variously attacked the rules under which ballots were counted in the states he

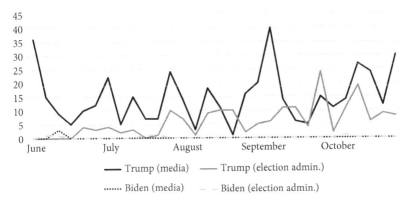

FIG. 1. Delegitimizing tweets by Biden and Trump, June 1–October 30, 2020
Source: Data collected and analyzed by the author.

lost, the corporation that produced the voting machines used in several of these states, what he termed "widespread voter fraud," and media reports of polls showing Biden's lead that Trump alleged were intended to suppress his vote. He frequently used such terms and phrases as "rigged and corrupt election," "stolen election," "dead people voting," "disenfranchise Trump voters," "massive scheme by Democrats," "votes were switched," "millions of Trump votes deleted," "massive ballot counting abuse," and "damage to the integrity of our system." By this time, however, Twitter had substantially increased its labeling of these tweets as "disputed" or "might be misleading."

Some analysts stated that this barrage of inaccurate claims weakened Americans' trust in elections.[93] By late September, large proportions of survey respondents (including 65 percent of Republicans) reported that they already lacked confidence in the election process.[94] In the 2000 election, which also involved charges that the presidential vote count may have been flawed, Democratic presidential candidate Al Gore won the popular vote, but Republican George W. Bush prevailed in the Electoral College following the Supreme Court's 5–4 decision that a contested vote count from Florida must be accepted. The process took thirty-five days to reach a conclusion. As soon as it did, Gore validated the court's decision, stating, "What remains of partisan rancor must now be put aside, and may God bless [Bush's] stewardship of this country."[95] Trump's choice to falsely claim victory a few hours after the polls closed, call for a halt to ballot counting when millions of votes remained to be counted, and file dozens of lawsuits to disallow votes cast in several battleground states, almost all of which were dismissed for lack of evidence, seems to have had a different aim.

Conclusion

The 2020 presidential election posed critical challenges for media coverage in a democracy. The COVID-19 pandemic restricted campaigns' ability to reach voters and gravely limited reporters' access to political events and sources. It unfolded at a time of such severe partisan and ideological polarization that even a deadly threat could not bring Americans together; Republicans and Democrats disagreed on almost everything, including whether the pandemic was a genuine threat or a hoax.[96] And protests against police killings of Black men intensified the racial tensions that had long afflicted American politics.

In this hyperpartisan environment, did media coverage of the election benefit American democracy? Many critics would claim that it didn't, because they perceived fake news or bias in the media. But bias in news sources is nothing new in the United States; some individual media outlets have been partisan since the beginning of the republic. The norm that journalism should be objective—should cover all sides without bias—was not dominant during the first century of the United States. Its influence began in the late 1800s and reached full flower only when a handful of broadcast networks dominated the airwaves in the mid to late 1900s.[97]

Yet even the presence of many individual news outlets with partisan leanings doesn't mean the media as a whole are biased or fake. Americans can currently choose among tens of thousands of individual media sources with differing perspectives, from the Far Right to the Far Left, as well as those that try to be objective. This remarkably diverse media environment is capable of fulfilling its vital function of holding government accountable. Even the notion that voters live in media bubbles, in which everything they choose to hear or read echoes their previously held opinions, seems to be overgeneralized. A recent Pew Research Center report found that only about a fifth of Republicans and Democrats get all of their political news in a given week from news outlets that, empirically, are used mainly by people who share their views.[98]

A greater danger to a democratic system is the manufacture of a "war on the media," intended to engender mistrust of well-established news outlets. When groups become convinced that a substantial portion of media outlets are lying to them to achieve some pernicious aims, they are more likely to call for censorship and repression. The risk increases when the attacks come from an incumbent president, who has the power to propose regulations of news outlets and thus to silence critics of his policies or administration. As a Fox News anchor stated, "I believe that President Trump is engaged in the most direct sustained assault on freedom of the press in our history. . . . He has done everything he can to undercut the media, to try and delegitimize us, and I think his purpose is clear: to raise doubts, when we report critically about him and his administration, that we can be trusted."[99] In an interview, Trump confirmed this aim, stating that "I do it to discredit you all [journalists] and demean you all so that when you write negative stories about me no one will believe you."[100]

This alarming threat to a democratic system was accompanied by a challenge at least as serious: the effort to undermine people's belief in the legitimacy of elections. Free elections are one of the defining characteristics of a representative government. But holding elections isn't enough; those who lose must be willing to accept the outcome, presuming that fair and effective rules have been followed to obtain it. The danger of Trump's efforts became even more apparent in early 2021, when his media campaign to subvert the election result led to an assault on the U.S. Capitol by Trump supporters trying to disrupt the certification of electoral votes.

Political scientists have long debated which does more to protect democracy in the United States: the institutions set up by the Constitution, including elections and a free press, or the political culture and values of citizens.[101] When leaders use their public platforms to cast doubt on the fundamental institutions of the political system, they encourage a disconnect between public opinion and the institutional protections of a democracy. The presence of significant amounts of antidemocratic sentiment can confound the effectiveness of the most carefully designed democratic institutions.[102]

Although the media have not been the originators of these threats to a democratic system, they can at least be a part of the solution. As has been true over time, some recent political actors have learned to exploit the traditional norms of the legacy media—the focus on the dramatic and the unexpected, deferral to official sources, a commitment to "both sidesism," and the limited resources devoted to fact-checking—to bolster their assault on majority rule. If they are to protect their vital role as a check on the power of government, traditional media outlets need to reevaluate these norms, to better understand the ways in which they contribute to their own vulnerability.

Notes

1. Elizabeth Grieco, "U.S. Newspapers Have Shed Half of Their Newsroom Employees since 2008," Pew Research Center, April 20, 2020, https://www.pewresearch.org/fact-tank/2020/04/20/u-s-newsroom-employment-has-dropped-by-a-quarter-since-2008/.

2. Lulu Garcia Navarro, quoted in David Folkenflik, "A Year of Bad News for the News Industry," NPR, December 29, 2019, https://www.npr.org/2019/12/29/792146686/a-year-of-bad-news-for-the-news-industry/.

3. Margaret Sullivan, "Goodbye to the Hometown Paper," *Washington Post* magazine, July 12, 2020, 1.

4. Amy Mitchell, Mark Jurkowitz, J. Baxter Oliphant, and Elisa Shearer, "Americans Who Mainly Get Their News on Social Media Are Less Engaged, Less Knowledgeable," Pew Research Center, July 30, 2020, https://www.journalism.org/2020/07/30/americans-who-mainly-get-their-news-on-social-media-are-less-engaged-less-knowledgeable/.

5. Michael Barthel, Katerina Eva Matsa, and Kirsten Worden, "Coronavirus-Driven Downturn Hits Newspapers Hard as TV News Thrives," Pew Research Center, October 29, 2020, https://www.journalism.org/2020/10/29/coronavirus-driven-downturn-hits-newspapers-hard-as-tv-news-thrives/.

6. See, for example, Nicole Asbury, "A Majority of Americans Believe the News' Role Is Vital but See an Increasing Level of Bias in Coverage, Poll Finds," Poynter, August 4, 2020, https://www.poynter.org/ethics-trust/2020/a-majority-of-americans-believe-the-news-role-is-vital-but-see-an-increasing-level-of-bias-in-coverage-poll-finds/.

7. David Domke, Mark D. Watts, Dhavan V. Shah, and David P. Fan, "The Politics of Conservative Elites and the 'Liberal Media' Argument," *Journal of Communication* 49 (December 1999): 35–58.

8. Philip Bump, "Half of Republicans Say the News Media Should Be Described as the Enemy of the American People," *Washington Post*, April 26, 2018.

9. Mark Jurkowitz, Amy Mitchell, Elisa Shearer, and Mason Walker, "U.S. Media Polarization and the 2020 Election," Pew Research Center, January 24, 2020, https://www.journalism.org/2020/01/24/u-s-media-polarization-and-the-2020-election-a-nation-divided/.

10. Marjorie Randon Hershey, "The Media: Covering Donald Trump," in *The Elections of 2016*, ed. Michael Nelson (Los Angeles: Sage, CQ Press, 2018), 113–135.

11. Hans Hassell, John Holbein, and Matthew Miles, "Journalists May Be Liberal, but This Doesn't Affect Which Candidates They Choose to Cover," *Washington Post*, April 10, 2020.

12. Kalev Leetaru, "Here's What the Rest of the World Is Saying about Donald Trump," *Washington Post*, December 18, 2015.

13. Niv M. Sultan, "Election 2016: Trump's Free Media Helped Keep Cost Down, but Fewer Donors Provided More of the Cash," OpenSecrets.org, Center for Responsive Politics, April 13, 2017, https://www.opensecrets.org /news/2017/04/election-2016-trump-fewer-donors-provided-more-of -the-cash/.

14. Hershey, "The Media," 126–30.

15. Linley Sanders, "Most Americans Heard a Lot about President Trump Last Week but Not Joe Biden," YouGov, March 30, 2020, https://today .yougov.com/topics/politics/articles-reports/2020/03/30/yahoo-news yougov-most-americans-heard-lot-about-pr.

16. See Doris A. Graber and Johanna L. Dunaway, *Mass Media and American Politics*, 9th ed. (Washington, DC: CQ Press, 2014), chaps. 4 and 5; and Diana C. Mutz, *In-Your-Face Politics* (Princeton, NJ: Princeton University Press, 2015).

17. Hershey, "The Media," 113–15.

18. Kyle Pope, "The One Way Sanders Is the New Trump," *Columbia Journalism Review*, February 27, 2020, https://www.cjr.org/first_person/one -way-sanders-is-the-new-trump.php.

19. Margaret Sullivan, "Five Ways the Media Can Avoid 2016 Errors," *Washington Post*, July 27, 2020, C1.

20. David Weigel, "The Trailer: Their Candidates Lost," *Washington Post*, January 9, 2020.

21. Dan Goldberg, "'It's Going to Disappear,'" *Politico*, March 17, 2020.

22. Andrew O'Reilly, "Trump Calls for Restarting Economy by Easter," Fox News, March 24, 2020, https://www.foxnews.com/politics/trump-during -fox-news-coronavirus-townhall-signals-desire-to-ease-guidelines-we -have-to-get-back-to-work.

23. Grace Segers, "Trump Reverses Earlier Call for Quarantine on New York Residents," CBS News, March 28, 2020, https://www.cbsnews.com/news /trump-says-he-is-considering-a-quarantine-of-the-new-york-metro -area/.

24. Ben Gittleson, Jordyn Phelps, and Libby Cathey, "Trump Doubles Down on Defense of Hydroxychloroquine to Treat COVID-19 Despite Efficacy Concerns," ABC News, July 28, 2020, https://abcnews.go.com/Politics /trump-doubles-defense-hydroxychloroquine-treat-covid-19-efficacy /story?id=72039824.

25. Jan Wolfe, "Trump Brags about High TV Viewership of Coronavirus Briefings," *U.S. News & World Report*, March 29, 2020.

26. Dan Evon, "Did Trump Suggest Injecting Disinfectants as COVID-19 Treatment?," Snopes.com, April 24, 2020, https://www.snopes.com/fact -check/trump-disinfectants-covid-19/.

27. Neal Rothschild, Sara Fischer, and Alexi McCammond, "Trump Show Dominates Pandemic While Biden's Voice Fades," Axios, April 18, 2020,

https://www.axios.com/trump-biden-attention-coronavirus-202c583e
-ecaf-46ef-8ce2-ec75df8105ae.html.

28. David E. Broockman and Joshua L. Kalla, "When and Why Are Campaigns' Persuasive Effects Small?," Working paper, OSF Preprints, June 8,
2020, https://osf.io/m7326/.

29. Quoted in Philip Bump, "And That's Why Trump Gives More Interviews
to Fox News Than Anyone Else," *Washington Post*, September 1, 2020.

30. Marjorie Randon Hershey, "The President and the Media," in *The Presidency and the Political System*, 12th ed., ed. Michael Nelson (Thousand
Oaks, CA: CQ Press, 2021), 314–15, 322.

31. Trump news conference, April 13, 2020.

32. "The Trump Administration and the Media," U.S. Press Freedom Tracker,
April 16, 2020, https://pressfreedomtracker.us/blog/trump-administration
-and-media/.

33. Jeffrey Gottfried, Mason Walker, and Amy Mitchell, "Americans See
Skepticism of News Media as Healthy," Pew Research Center, August 31,
2020, https://www.journalism.org/2020/08/31/americans-see-skepticism
-of-news-media-as-healthy-say-public-trust-in-the-institution-can
-improve/.

34. Manuel Roig-Franzia and Sarah Ellison, "A history of the Trump War on
Media," *Washington Post*, March 29, 2020.

35. Margaret Sullivan, "History Will Say Trump Coverage Was a Low Point,"
Washington Post, April 29, 2020, C1.

36. Nik DeCosta-Klipa, "This Harvard Study Both Confirms and Refutes Bernie Sanders's Complaints about the Media," Boston.com, June 14, 2016,
https://www.boston.com/news/politics/2016/06/14/harvard-study-con
firms-refutes-bernie-sanderss-complaints-media.

37. Paul Farhi and Jenna Johnson, "Bernie Sanders Criticizes MSNBC over
Coverage of His Campaign," *Washington Post*, February 26, 2020.

38. Frank Newport, "Public Opinion Review: Public Reactions to the Word
'Socialism,'" Gallup, March 6, 2020, https://news.gallup.com/opinion
/polling-matters/287459/public-opinion-review-americans-word-socia
lism.aspx.

39. Nate Cohn, "Moderate Democrats Fared Best in 2018," *New York Times*,
September 10, 2019.

40. Dan Balz, "Front-Runner Stays on Message amid Tumult," *Washington
Post*, February 26, 2020, A1.

41. For example, Stephen Collinson, "Biden's Surprise Win in Texas Caps
Historic Super Tuesday While Sanders Turns to California," CNN,
March 4, 2020, https://www.cnn.com/2020/03/30/politics/super-tuesday
-democratic-primary-2020/index.html.

42. Hershey, "The Media," 128.

43. Hershey, "The Media," 127–29.

44. Maggie Astor, "Kamala Harris and the 'Double Bind' of Racism and Sexism," *New York Times*, October 9, 2020.
45. Astor, "Kamala Harris."
46. Eugene Scott, "The Unique Pressures of Being Kamala Harris Come into Focus with Her in the Debate Spotlight," *Washington Post*, October 7, 2020.
47. Republican pollster Frank Luntz, on Fox News, October 8, 2020, https://www.foxnews.com/category/person/kamala-harris.
48. Karen Tumulty, Kate Woodsome, and Sergio Peçanha, "How Sexist, Racist Attacks on Kamala Harris Have Spread Online," *Washington Post*, October 7, 2020.
49. See Mark Peffley and Jon Hurwitz, "Whites' Stereotypes of Blacks," in *Perception and Prejudice*, ed. Jon Hurwitz and Mark Peffley (New Haven, CT: Yale University Press, 2008), 58–99.
50. Gabby Orr, "Trump Prepares a New Fall Offensive," *Politico*, September 6, 2020.
51. Phone interview on Fox Business, October 8, 2020.
52. Phone interview on Fox & Friends, October 20, 2020.
53. Donald Judd and Ryan Nobles, "Georgia Republican Senator Willfully Mispronounces Kamala Harris' Name at Trump Rally," CNN Politics, October 17, 2020, https://www.cnn.com/2020/10/16/politics/david-perdue -kamala-harris/.
54. Joshua Scacco and Natalie Jomini Stroud, "General Election News Coverage," American Press Institute Engaging News Project, April 6, 2017, https://www.engagingnewsproject.org.
55. Adam Gabbatt, "The 'Exhausting' Work of Factcheckers Who Track Trump's Barrage of Lies," *Guardian*, January 21, 2019.
56. Margaret Sullivan, "Pandemic of Lies Calls for a Truth Sandwich," *Washington Post*, March 2, 2020, C1.
57. Dan Froomkin, "Dean Baquet Interview Demonstrates Why Bothsideism Is Alive and Well at His New York Times," Press Watch, January 31, 2020, https://presswatchers.org/2020/01/dean-baquet-interview-demonstrates -why-bothsiderism-is-alive-and-well-at-his-new-york-times/.
58. Glenn Kessler, Salvador Rizzo, and Meg Kelly, "Trump Is Averaging More Than 50 False or Misleading Claims a Day," *Washington Post*, October 22, 2020.
59. Elizabeth Dwoskin and Craig Timber, "Dramatic Drop in Misinformation Online Amid Bans," *Washington Post*, January 17, 2021.
60. Scott Clement, Dan Balz, and Emily Guskin, "Post-ABC Poll," *Washington Post*, October 11, 2020, A1.
61. Quoted in Marisa Iati, "How Newspaper Front Pages Treated an Election Day with No Clear Winner," *Washington Post*, November 4, 2020.
62. Philip Bump, "The 2016 Campaign Inoculated the Public against Trump's 2020 Tactics," *Washington Post*, October 20, 2020.

63. Aaron Rupar, "NPR's Sanitizing of Trump's Milwaukee Rally Shows How He's Broken the Media," *Vox*, January 15, 2020, https://www.vox.com/2020 /1/15/21066935/trump-milwaukee-rally-media-sanitizing-npr.

64. See Robert M. Entman, *Scandal and Silence: Media Responses to Presidential Misconduct* (Cambridge: Polity Press, 2012).

65. "Inside the Mueller Report, a Sophisticated Russian Interference Campaign," PBS News Hour, June 3, 2019, https://www.pbs.org/newshour/show /inside-the-mueller-report-a-sophisticated-russian-interference-campaign.

66. Josh Margolin and Lucien Bruggeman, "Russia Is 'Amplifying' Claims of Mail-In Voter Fraud," ABC News, September 4, 2020, https://www.ksro .com/2020/09/03/russia-is-amplifying-claims-of-mail-in-voter-fraud -intel-bulletin-warns/.

67. Associated Press, "Facebook Moves to Target Misinformation Before U.S. Election," CBC, September 3, 2020, https://www.cbc.ca/news/world /facebook-misinformation-us-election-1.5710541.

68. Megan McArdle, "We Finally Know for Sure That Lies Spread Faster Than the Truth," *Washington Post*, March 14, 2018.

69. See Chris Meserole, "How Misinformation Spreads on Social Media," Brookings Institution, May 9, 2018, https://www.brookings.edu/blog /order-from-chaos/2018/05/09/how-misinformation-spreads-on-social -media-and-what-to-do-about-it/.

70. Ruth Igielnik, Scott Keeter, Courtney Kennedy, and Bradley Spahn, "Commercial Voter Files and the Study of U.S. Politics," Pew Research Center, February 15, 2018, https://www.pewresearch.org/methods/2018/02 /15/commercial-voter-files-and-the-study-of-u-s-politics/.

71. Yochai Benkler, Casey Tilton, Bruce Etling, Hal Roberts, Justin Clark, Robert Faris, Jonas Kaiser, and Carolyn Schmitt, "Mail-In Voter Fraud" (Berkman Center Research Publication No. 2020-6, Cambridge, MA,, October 2, 2020), https://papers.ssrn.com/sol3/papers.cfm?abstract_id=3703701.

72. Rachel Lerman, Katie Shepherd, and Taylor Telford, "Twitter Penalizes Donald Trump Jr. for Posting Hydroxychloroquine Misinformation amid Coronavirus Pandemic," *Washington Post*, July 28, 2020.

73. Chris Megerian, "Trump Signs Order Targeting Social Media," *Los Angeles Times*, May 28, 2020.

74. See https://www.politifact.com/, FactCheck.org, and https://www.snopes .com/.

75. Dan Evon and Jordan Liles, "Junk News, Real Consequences," Snopes, November 5, 2019, https://www.snopes.com/news/2019/11/05/junk-news -satire-consequences/.

76. Lauren Katz and Sean Rameswaram, "Next Time Someone Sends You Fake News, Share These Essential Tips," *Vox*, September 11, 2020, https://www .vox.com/21430923/fake-news-disinformation-misinformation-conspiracy -theory-coronavirus.

77. See Brian Friedberg, Emily Dreyfuss, Gabrielle Lim, and Joan Donovan, "A Blueprint for Documenting and Debunking Misinformation Campaigns," NiemanReports, October 20, 2020, https://niemanreports.org /articles/a-blueprint-for-documenting-and-debunking-misinformation -campaigns/.

78. See, for example, Eric Oliver and Thomas J. Wood, "Conspiracy Theories and the Paranoid Style(s) of Mass Opinion," *American Journal of Political Science* 58 (October 2014): 952–66; and Joanne M. Miller, Kyle L. Saunders, and Christina E. Farhart, "Conspiracy Endorsement as Motivated Reasoning," *American Journal of Political Science* 60 (October 2016): 824–44.

79. See, for example, Daniel Ziblatt and Steven Levitsky, *How Democracies Die* (New York: Broadway Books, 2019).

80. Cooper Allen, "Trump Slammed for Refusing to Say If He'd Accept Election Results," *USA Today*, October 19, 2016.

81. Hershey, "The President," 314–15.

82. Benkler et al., "Mail-In Voter Fraud."

83. Dan Evon, "Is This 'Trump Army' Fundraising Email Real?," Snopes, June 8, 2020, https://www.snopes.com/fact-check/trump-army-fund raising-email/.

84. Alison Durkee, "Here's Why Trump Telling Supporters to Watch the Polls Could Be an Even Bigger Threat This Year," *Forbes*, September 30, 2020.

85. Pam Fessler and Elena Moore, "Signed, Sealed, Undelivered," NPR, July 13, 2020, https://www.npr.org/2020/07/13/889751095/signed-sealed-undelivered -thousands-of-mail-in-ballots-rejected-for-tardiness.

86. Amber Phillips, "New Poll Confirms Republicans' Wariness of Voting by Mail," *Washington Post*, September 11, 2020.

87. Amy Gardner, Josh Dawsey, and John Wagner, "Trump Suggests Delaying Election," *Washington Post*, July 31, 2020, A1.

88. Wendy R. Weiser and Harold Ekeh, "The False Narrative of Vote-by-Mail Fraud," Brennan Center for Justice, April 20, 2020, https://www.brennan center.org/our-work/analysis-opinion/false-narrative-vote-mail-fraud.

89. Philip Rucker and Felicia Sonmez, "Trump Defends Actions on Virus," *Washington Post*, July 20, 2020, A1.

90. Quoted in Greg Sargent, "Trump Just Repeated His Ugliest Claim about the Election," *Washington Post*, September 15, 2020.

91. See, for example, Steve Peoples, "Trump Faces Rare Rebuke from GOP for Floating Election Delay," Associated Press, July 30, 2020, https:// apnews.com/08c1c9bb58ecb5392e2e59a4161233b1.

92. I did not include criticisms of the other party, which are to be expected in any democratic system, though the president did retweet in late May, surprisingly, that "the only good Democrat is a dead Democrat."

93. See Philip Bump, "Trump Has Achieved One of His Post-Election Goals," *Washington Post*, November 18, 2020.

94. Geoffrey Skelley, "Republicans Are Less Confident Than Democrats That the Election Will Be Conducted Fairly," FiveThirtyEight, October 2, 2020, https://fivethirtyeight.com/features/republicans-are-less-confident-than -democrats-that-the-election-will-be-conducted-fairly/.

95. Amy Gardner, "Barring a Landslide, What's Probably Not Coming on Nov. 3?," *Washington Post*, June 23, 2020, A1.

96. "Republicans, Democrats Move Even Further Apart in Coronavirus Concerns," Pew Research Center, June 25, 2020, https://www.pewresearch .org/politics/2020/06/25/republicans-democrats-move-even-further -apart-in-coronavirus-concerns/.

97. See Markus Prior, *Post-Broadcast Democracy* (New York: Cambridge University Press, 2007), chap. 1.

98. Mark Jurkowitz and Amy Mitchell, "About One-Fifth of Democrats and Republicans Get Political News in a Kind of Media Bubble," Pew Research Center, March 4, 2020, https://www.journalism.org/2020/03/04/about-one -fifth-of-democrats-and-republicans-get-political-news-in-a-kind-of -media-bubble/.

99. Chris Wallace, quoted in U.S. Press Freedom Tracker, "Trump Administration and the Media."

100. Dan Mangan, "President Trump Told Lesley Stahl He Bashes Press 'to Demean You and Discredit You So . . . No One Will Believe' Negative Stories about Him," CNBC, May 22, 2018, https://www.cnbc.com/2018/05/22 /trump-told-lesley-stahl-he-bashes-press-to-discredit-negative-stories .html.

101. See Robert A. Dahl, *A Preface to Democratic Theory* (Chicago: University of Chicago Press, 1963).

102. See Larry M. Bartels, "Ethnic Antagonism Erodes Republicans' Commitment to Democracy," *PNAS* 117 (September 2020): 22752–59.

The Presidency

RECOVERY, REFORM, AND JOE BIDEN

Paul J. Quirk

In the weeks leading up to his inauguration as the forty-sixth president of the United States, Joe Biden faced some of the most daunting challenges and precarious circumstances that have ever greeted an incoming president. Enacting a personal and partisan policy agenda (the typical goal of a new president) was only one of the tasks awaiting Biden. He also had to deal with the COVID-19 pandemic and the economic harm it produced—taken together, one of the worst crises in American history. Some of the most urgent concerns were to redress the damage that the Trump presidency had done to political norms, governmental capacity, democratic legitimacy, and the constitutional system and to erect protections against future efforts to undermine free and fair elections and the rule of law.[1] On top of all these challenges, Biden would have to work with a Congress prone to extraordinarily severe partisan gridlock. In the early stages, that work would be complicated by the bitterness, distrust, and distraction caused by Trump's desperate efforts to overturn his decisive defeat in the 2020 election, a violent January 6[t] attack on the Capitol that he largely provoked, and his second impeachment and Senate trial, on charges of inciting the attack.[2] At a later point, Biden may also have to deal with politically difficult issues and risk of distraction concerning several possible federal prosecutions of the former president.[3]

What are the prospects for the Biden presidency? To what extent will he be able to achieve significant action on his policy agenda? Looking beyond partisan or ideologically contested goals, will he be able to serve genuine national interests and enhance the well-being of Americans—beginning with helping to end the COVID-19 pandemic in the United States? In what aspects of his agenda, and the national agenda, will he succeed or fail?

I will approach these questions by examining three major topics: (1) the president and his team; (2) his resources, constraints, and venues for leadership; and (3) the challenges and strategies before him. The gist of this account is that the Biden presidency will have a distinctive profile of possibilities. There is little prospect of major new policy achievements, a common metric for assessing presidencies.[4] The Biden presidency, if successful, will be one of recovery and institutional reform. What will matter most about the Biden presidency, in the long run, will be its effect on the politics and policies that come after it.

Joe Biden, President

To assess the prospects for the Biden presidency, I begin with what Biden brings to the table: Biden himself, that is, his personal attributes; his positions and priorities; and his team—Vice President Kamala Harris and the administration's main senior aides, advisers, and appointees. Looking at these matters alone, one would see, on the whole, auspicious beginnings.

"THE PRESIDENTIAL DIFFERENCE"

There is no agreed-upon list of personal skills, attributes, or experiences that make for a good, great, or just satisfactory president. (The Constitution stipulates mainly that the president be at least thirty-five years old—probably a good idea—and a citizen from birth—a more dubious one.) By some credible criteria, however, Joe Biden has both notable strengths and some specific weaknesses.

The most influential recent work on the president's personal qualities is the late distinguished political scientist Fred I. Greenstein's engaging book *The Presidential Difference*.[5] Recognizing the vast variety of behavior that can affect a president's success or failure, or cause a president to serve constructively or do harm, Greenstein presents a list of six attributes that make up "the presidential difference"—that is, the features of the president as an individual that matter. In reality, each of them is a fairly broad category of related traits or behaviors. Presidents differ, first, according to Greenstein, in their effectiveness as a public communicator. This primarily involves persuasiveness in giving major speeches. He mentions the celebrated performances of presidents Franklin Roosevelt, John Kennedy, Ronald Reagan, and Bill Clinton. And he points out that effective communication is in large part a learned skill. Second, presidents differ in organizational capacity. This includes being willing to listen to aides who bear bad news or offer unwelcome advice; maintaining effective organizational structures and practices for decision-making and implementation; and ensuring an appropriate diversity of views among his or her advisers.

Greenstein contrasts the orderly, comprehensive advisory processes that President Dwight Eisenhower employed with the chaotic processes of the early Clinton presidency and the biased and prejudged deliberations that led to President Lyndon Johnson's disastrous escalation of the Vietnam War.[6]

A third presidential attribute is political skill, which includes matters ranging from assertiveness, determination, and willingness to employ rewards and punishments in exercising interpersonal influence to sophistication in calculating political support and opposition and flexibility and creativity in negotiating agreements. A fourth attribute, vision, is more of a grab bag—including attention to the content of policies, careful assessment of feasibility, and consistency in pursuit of a set of overarching goals. Greenstein was impressed by the rhetorical advantage that Reagan had in being able to invoke the same broad values (especially freedom from government) to explain his policies in most areas. He contrasts this with the labored explanations offered by presidents Jimmy Carter and George H. W. Bush, who defined their objectives in terms of multiple distinct policies, with different problems and different needs for improvement. In my view, this supposed advantage in offering a simple, consistent policy direction will generally be outweighed, under today's conditions, by the adverse effects of overlooking the genuine complexities of contemporary policy issues.

Greenstein's fifth category of the presidential difference is cognitive style. He makes some subtle distinctions, suggesting that Jimmy Carter sought to break major issues into separate parts, while Richard Nixon was better able to get to the heart of a complex situation; Nixon, well before his successful 1968 presidential campaign, had already conceived a grand strategy of negotiating an end to the Vietnam War, reaching a détente with the Soviet Union, and opening up diplomatic relations with China. Greenstein also noted the dangers of intellectual laziness and sheer ignorance—deficits that undermined Ronald Reagan and George W. Bush in some areas. Although Greenstein did not write about President Trump, he would have regarded Trump's ongoing war against science and expertise; refusal to receive intelligence briefings; reliance on Fox News commentators for information and advice; attacks on mainstream news organizations; and constant, delusional lying as unprecedented, profound defects of cognitive style.

The final attribute, somewhat misleadingly named, is emotional intelligence. Greenstein uses this term to refer to a president's ability to manage his or her emotions and thus avoid any destructive emotional influence on their conduct—noting, for example, how Nixon's persecution complex and deep-seated anger led to the constitutional transgressions that ended his presidency, and how Bill Clinton's reckless sexual relationship with a White House intern, followed by a desperate effort to cover it up, nearly ended his presidency.

I would argue that Greenstein's polite language here—pointing to intelligence about, and management of, emotions—deflects attention from the seriousness of the personality or mental-health problems that presidents sometimes bring to the office. Judging from presidential history, an adequate conception of this aspect of the presidential difference will include the absence of serious personality disorders or mental illness. In various ways, commentators have found such conditions at the root of critical mistakes and failures by several twentieth- and twenty-first-century presidents, in particular, Theodore Roosevelt, Woodrow Wilson, Lyndon Johnson, Richard Nixon, Bill Clinton, and Donald Trump—six of the twenty presidents since 1901.[7] These interpretations are often debatable, partly because most mental health professionals decline to diagnose a public official in the absence of an authorized, in-office examination.[8] It should not be surprising, however, if it turns out that people who can do what it takes over many years to become president will, with significant frequency, be driven by unhealthy forms of motivation.

Greenstein does not suggest that, to be successful, a president has to score high on every one of the six attributes, let alone on the multiple facets of each attribute. Any attribute, positive or negative, may or may not become critically important, depending on events and circumstances. In his profiles of individual presidents, Greenstein shows how their particular strengths and weaknesses shaped outcomes at critical junctures. For example, one president may get away with an emotional weakness that sinks another president, facing different challenges.

Unfortunately, presidential campaigns may not lead to discriminating judgments by voters about the candidates' suitability for the office.[9] Most voters have little awareness of the kinds of cognitive or intellectual performance or interpersonal skills involved in political leadership. Indeed, voters encounter little discussion of presidential candidates' personal qualifications, apart from issues that become highly noticeable in their public appearances or that the candidates or their opponents choose to emphasize. The case of Donald Trump is instructive.[10] By an early stage of the 2016 primaries, some journalists had discussed evidence that Trump had a serious personality disorder, generally identified as "malignant narcissistic personality," and that he was extraordinarily uninformed about government and public policy for a candidate for public office. His business career had repeatedly featured consumer frauds, refusal to pay vendors, loan defaults, and other disreputable or dubious activities. In an infamous audio recording, he had bragged about committing serial sexual assault. Most of these matters received little direct attention in the 2016 campaign, and Republican voters overlooked or forgave them.

In his 2020 campaign, and throughout his long political career, Biden demonstrated many of Greenstein's positive attributes.[11] He had shown effectiveness in public communication in generally well-reviewed speeches, town halls, press conferences, and debate performances over many years. A weakness was that he has been considered "gaffe prone," likely to make an occasional impolitic or embarrassing off-the-cuff remark.[12] He has given evidence of superior organizational capacity, having served as a leading adviser to President Obama during his eight years as vice president. Direct experience in White House decision-making is probably the ideal training for those tasks. Biden also had managed a well-regarded vice presidential staff, with responsibility for coordinating the federal response to potential epidemics, among other topics.

Biden's political skill had enabled him to win election to the Senate at age twenty-nine, and to win reelection six times. He was generally liked and respected on both sides of the aisle in the Senate, where he was a productive chair of the Judiciary and Foreign Relations Committees. As for cognitive style, Biden's press conferences and debate performances, and his advisory role in the Obama White House, demonstrate a robust command of policy issues and respect for science and expertise.

Biden has an unusual profile, for a political leader, with respect to Greenstein's category of emotional intelligence. His conduct in professional roles and relationships has been well regarded, resulting in a wide range of friendships in the Senate and a close working relationship with the president that endured through the full eight years of the Obama presidency. One deficiency of his emotional awareness has been a tendency, often in public settings (for example, in posing for a group photograph), to place his hands on a woman or young girl's back or shoulders in what he has considered a friendly gesture.[13] Although these actions did not have manifest sexual intent—and Biden has never been accused of sexual harassment—they were in some cases, by contemporary standards, inappropriate.

Biden's campaign and media coverage drew considerable attention to one notable aspect of his emotional makeup: strong, spontaneous, and obviously sincere empathy.[14] Supporters usually explained this empathy, and sought to magnify it, by pointing to Biden's oft-recounted experiences of loss and grief: the deaths of his first wife and a daughter in a car accident, and the death of an adult son from cancer. It is not self-evident that loss promotes empathy, but whatever the source, Biden was able to convey it—for example, for those who had lost loved ones to COVID-19—with compelling sincerity in public remarks. In addition, his campaign and supporters promoted videos, obviously unstaged, in which he went out of his way to provide comfort and assistance to an individual suffering from a handicap or some misfortune.[15] His campaign emphasized the contrast with Trump, who notoriously was without detectable compassion and rarely expressed concern for COVID victims, health-care workers, fallen soldiers, or others, even in scripted remarks.

In my view, outsize empathy is hardly a requirement for the presidency and is not necessarily beneficial, on balance.[16] Presidents need, for example, to be able to send troops into combat, support punishment for wrongdoing, and impose painful budget cuts. A balance of compassion and toughness is probably ideal. Whether Biden's unusually strong empathetic responses will serve him well on balance during his presidency is an open question.

Biden's primary defect with respect to personal qualifications for the presidency is undoubtedly his age. At seventy-eight on Inauguration Day, Biden is the oldest man ever elected president of the United States. He is almost twenty-five years older than the average head of government in the member countries of the Organization for Economic Co-operation and Development (OECD).[17] As research on aging shows, healthy older people, like Biden, will typically have, if anything, superior judgment in many practical matters, the benefit of many years of experience.[18] On the other hand, they take more time to process information and solve problems, and may be prone to rigidity. At his age, especially among males, there is a greatly increased risk of serious health problems—especially heart attack, stroke, or cancer—and of death. Appropriately, therefore, Biden has stressed that Vice President Kamala Harris is well qualified by disposition and experience to step in as president. Nevertheless, Biden's age poses a significant risk—mainly, that he will acquire some serious disability that is not immediately apparent or that he himself fails to recognize, and that affects his conduct in critical situations.

These risks do not necessarily preclude Biden's seeking and winning reelection in 2024, and potentially serving as president to the age of eighty-six. The risks of disability or compromised performance would of course increase in a second term. Although many expect Biden to forgo seeking reelection and instead step aside for Harris or another Democratic succes-sor, he has been noncommittal on the matter.[19]

PRIORITIES AND COMMITMENTS

Presidents define their priorities and make commitments through various stages—from the primary campaigns, to the general election campaign, the postelection transition, and their term in office. Contrary to a popular myth, presidents usually keep, or at least attempt to keep, most of their campaign promises.[20] But their campaign commitments can cause diffi-culty if they prove unexpectedly infeasible, overly divisive, or substantively unsound. In one well-known case, George H. W. Bush, in his successful 1988 campaign, vowed to tell congressional Democrats, "Read my lips. No new taxes." When he eventually agreed to tax increases as part of a bipartisan deficit-reduction agreement, he suffered a costly loss of cred-ibility. In his campaign and transition, Biden set some goals that will die at the hand of congressional Republicans. But, as the starting point for his presidency, his priorities and commitments appear to be highly serviceable.

Biden entered the Democratic nomination contest as the early front-runner among an eventual total of twenty-nine candidates. Associated with the Obama presidency, popular with the party's crucial Black con-stituency, and ideologically moderate, he proclaimed himself the most electable. In a campaign that included several prominent "progressives" (the term appropriated by the left wing of the Democratic Party)—especially Bernie Sanders and Elizabeth Warren—Biden had a strong stra-tegic rationale for standing firm with a moderate stance. After he sewed up the nomination in the late spring, Biden had a complex, mutually ambiva-lent relationship with the progressives.[21] Their willingness to support him, in the end, was bolstered by the overriding objective of defeating Trump, whose possible reelection Democrats and many nonpartisan commentators viewed as a mortal threat to American democracy.

For the most part, Biden managed to avoid becoming identified with con-troversial progressive positions that many strategists believed could under-mine his support among swing voters or help mobilize Republican voters.[22] His major focus was on the COVID-19 pandemic and the economic suffering it had produced. Because a large majority of the public disapproved of the Trump administration's response to the pandemic (or lack thereof), Biden was able to distinguish himself from Trump by promising to take science seriously, mobilize resources for testing and contact tracing, promote social distancing and wearing of masks, support health-care systems, open schools and economic activities cautiously, and make proven vaccines available as soon as possible—essentially the steps that any competent, responsible government would have taken. He also called for more generous and better-targeted economic relief and offered various, mostly plausible, measures to go beyond economic recovery and "Build Back Better"—with more jobs, reduced economic inequality, clean energy, and innovation. At the same time, Biden kept his distance from the most ambitious progressive proposals.[23] He rejected Medicare for All, the strategically apt label for proposals to establish a Canadian-style, single-payer health-care system. He declined to sign on to the Green New Deal, a set of large-scale measures intended to wean the economy rapidly from reliance on fossil fuels and massively subsidize clean energy.[24] Whatever the substantive merits of the progressive proposals, they called for a dramatic expansion of the federal government and were attacked by conservatives as "socialism." Biden announced and defended his own quite detailed plans, generally consistent with mainstream Democratic approaches, for health care, climate change, and other subjects. He promised to end the child-separation policy—widely criticized as a human-rights violation—used by the Trump administration to punish migrants at the Mexican border.

In responding to the nationwide wave of protests that followed the May 2020 killing of George Floyd by Minneapolis police officers, Biden endorsed the Black Lives Matter (BLM) movement, condemned racially biased police violence, and declared overcoming systemic racism an urgent priority. He also opposed the movement's confusing and inflammatory slogan, "Defund the Police," and condemned the rioting, looting, and destruction of property that often supplanted the peaceful protests.[25] Neither BLM nor Black political leaders had coalesced around an agenda of proposed federal policies. Nor did Biden put forward a set of immediate steps for addressing the challenges of racism and racial disadvantage.

Considering the bitterness of the presidential campaign, and the Democrats' hopes of winning unified control of the House, Senate, and presidency, Biden made notably emphatic promises that he would work to bridge the divide between Democrats and Republicans, achieve bipartisan solutions, and bring the country together.[26] The realism of these promises appeared increasingly dubious in the weeks after the election, however, as nearly all elected Republicans refused even to recognize Biden's victory, and mostly supported Trump's increasingly desperate battle to overturn the election by any means possible.

In sum, Biden's policy agenda was well adapted to the political circumstances of his presidency. It took advantage of the Trump administration's widely recognized failures in responding to the pandemic, and the Republicans' resistance to vast spending on economic relief, to identify generally popular positions. Beyond those easy choices, his agenda built on mainstream Democratic policy ideas. Biden did not make any major "read my lips"-type strategic mistakes.

THE TEAM

A newly elected president faces a major challenge in assembling an effective team of senior advisers and officials in time to take over the reins of government on Inauguration Day.[27] Mistakes are common, resulting in reversals, as when an intended nominee is not properly vetted and must be abandoned, slights to politically important groups, or senior officials who fail at their jobs. The central difficulty is the need to find, assess, and appoint—and in many cases, plan for Senate confirmation of—more than 200 high-level White House aides and senior officials in the departments and agencies.

In managing the transition, Biden labored under one unprecedented handicap: Trump's refusal to acknowledge Biden's victory in the election and a resulting two-week delay in the executive branch providing the normal meetings and briefings for the incoming administration. But Biden also had two important advantages. First, with a well-funded election campaign and high expectations of winning from an early point, Biden had devoted time and resources to transition planning during the campaign—an important contribution to a successful transition that presidential campaigns, completely focused on winning the election, often fail to make.[28] Second, and more important, Biden had played a central role in the two-term Obama presidency, which had ended only four years earlier. Biden and his advisers already knew, and had worked with, many of the people that they needed to recruit. After only four years out of office, many of them were available for a return to government service.

For White House chief of staff, Biden tapped Ron Klain, who had served Biden as chief of his vice presidential staff. He proceeded to name a series of additional senior officials with notable characteristics.[29] Biden's early senior personnel selections were marked by high, often genuinely exceptional competence (including, where relevant, scientific expertise); racial, ethnic, and gender diversity; policy views in the mainstream of the Democratic Party; and, often, prior working relationships from service in the Obama administration. His top national security appointees were, as secretary of state, Tony Blinken, a respected professional who had worked for Biden both on the Foreign Relations Committee staff and in the vice president's office; as director of national intelligence, Avril Haines, who had served as both deputy national security advisor and deputy director of the Central Intelligence Agency in the Obama administration; and as secretary of defense, Lloyd Austin, a recently retired Black army general who had served as head of U.S. forces in Iraq. Biden chose Janet Yellen, a distinguished economist and former chair of the Federal Reserve, to be the first woman secretary of the Treasury. He picked Anthony Fauci—the long-serving director of the National Institute of Allergy and Infectious Diseases, whom Trump had sidelined and publicly disparaged for his candid, science-based advice about COVID-19—to head the new administration's pandemic response. For attorney general—the official who would be most responsible for rebuilding a damaged Justice Department and for making major decisions on whether to indict Trump on various federal charges—Biden chose Merrick Garland, the federal judge whose nomination to a Supreme Court vacancy by President Obama had been blocked by Senate Republicans in the last year of Obama's presidency. Although such an experience might sometimes engender partisan animus inappropriate for an attorney general, Garland was a widely respected judicial moderate who earlier had enjoyed strong support among Republicans.

One appointment elicited serious criticism from many of Biden's supporters. The appointment of Austin as secretary of defense would require a congressional waiver to set aside a statutory requirement that the secretary not be a current or recent member of the armed services—a provision intended to ensure civilian control of the military.[30] Although some Democrats praised the selection of the first Black defense secretary, others objected strongly, arguing that the Trump administration's use of the same waiver, in appointing former general James Mattis, had left the expectation of a civilian secretary in need of reinforcement. Some observers also puzzled over the selection of Susan Rice—a Black woman with undeniably imposing foreign-policy credentials—as Biden's top adviser for domestic policy. Pursuing his aspiration to enhance bipartisan comity, Biden named an appointee to a newly created White House office for outreach to conservatives.

From the time he chose the influential senator and former prosecutor Kamala Harris to join the ticket, Biden emphasized that, as vice president, she would be his most important adviser.[31] Their frequent meetings and joint travel during the transition supported that expectation.

Taken together, Biden's personality and skills, his policy agenda, and his team were generally well suited to the challenges of the presidency and to the political moment.

Venues, Constraints, and Opportunities

The political and institutional field of play for Biden's presidency was rife with resistance. His prospects for policy and political achievement were in some ways encouraging, but very complicated. To a great extent, his most important potential achievements seemed likely to take unusual forms.

CONGRESS AND LEGISLATION

A new president's aspirations for accomplishment usually center on a successful legislative program, especially one or more major measures that, if enacted, will represent signature achievements. President Obama worked to enact a major health-care reform, financial- and automobile-industry rescue packages, and financial reform. President Trump struck out in efforts to repeal Obama's health-care program, build a border wall, and renew infrastructure but succeeded in passing a major tax cut. In Biden's case, the opportunities for signature legislative achievements will be very limited. Razor-thin margins of Democratic-Party control in the House and especially the Senate will severely constrain legislative action.

Biden has vowed that he will work with the Republicans to find common ground and overcome legislative gridlock. He is well suited to such an endeavor, having served in the Senate for six terms, presided over the Senate as vice president, and taken pride in working with members of both parties. He claims to have friendships with Republican senators and a relationship of mutual respect with Senate Republican leader Mitch McConnell (KY).

If having the appropriate legislative skills and experience, and making the needed personal efforts were the keys to presidential success in Congress, Biden arguably would be ideal for the tasks of legislative leadership in the current Congress. But as political scientists have repeatedly shown, the president's personal skill and efforts influence legislative outcomes in Congress primarily "at the margins."[32] A president can occasionally have an important effect on a particular bill—for example, by working with congressional leaders to put an advantageous measure on the agenda.[33] But for the most part, the president's success with Congress depends on the partisan and ideological balance of power in the House and Senate. In a word, it depends on how many members of each chamber happen to agree with the president's policy goals, for their own reasons, regardless of his efforts to persuade them.

From this point of view, the prospects for major Biden legislative achievements, reflecting his policy agenda, are quite limited. The Democrats control the House, after the 2020 elections, by the narrow margin of 222–211. Although Speaker Nancy Pelosi (D-CA) can control the chamber's agenda with that margin, the Democrats will need the votes of moderate party members, some of them representing mostly Republican districts—or, less likely, from moderate Republicans—to pass their bills.

The constraints in the Senate are even more severe. With the benefit of unexpected victories in January run-off elections for both Georgia Senate seats, the Democrats managed to eke out a 50–50 tie with the Republicans in control of Senate seats. Because Vice President Harris casts the deciding vote in the event of a tie, the result gave the Democrats control of the Senate. Chuck Schumer (D-NY) is now Majority Leader; Mitch McConnell (R-KY) is Minority Leader; the Democrats have majorities on every committee; and they control the Senate agenda. To assemble a bare majority, they will have to secure the votes of every Democratic senator—of whom the most difficult likely will be Joe Manchin, a moderate conservative from the Trump stronghold of West Virginia—or make up for any losses by picking up votes from Republican moderates such as Susan Collins (R-ME) or Lisa Murkowski (R-AK). Under Senate rules, a bare majority is sufficient for action on confirmation of appointments, passage of conference bills (which reconcile differences between House and Senate versions of legislation), and budget measures. Importantly, the budget measures may include at least one reconciliation bill per year, which can contain substantive legislation, provided that it directly (not merely "incidentally") affects taxing or spending.[34]

The requirements for support in the Senate are much more imposing, however, on matters subject to the filibuster—including most ordinary legislation. To overcome a filibuster, the Democrats need sixty votes—and thus, in the current lineup, ten or more Republican votes (depending on the degree of Democratic unity). If all fifty Democratic senators agreed (and had the vice president's support), they could abolish the filibuster, using a somewhat disreputable hardball procedure known informally as "the nuclear option." But Senate Democrats, like Republicans, have been reluctant to abolish it—at least partly because they expect their party to be in the minority again, relying on the filibuster to protect their interests, soon enough. Moderate Democrats have the additional rationale that Republican filibusters can protect them from having to cast tough votes on highly partisan legislation. For the most part, Biden's chances for legislative success will depend on obtaining support from at least ten Republican senators.

As political scientists have also shown, bipartisan legislation is far more common than typical commentary recognizes—even in recent Congresses, and even on important bills.[35] James Curry and Frances Lee point out that a large majority of major laws are enacted with substantial support from both parties. What this finding indicates, primarily, is quite simple: new developments in the society, economy, or international environment often require legislative action to serve interests that are not, or not entirely, ideologically controversial. Both parties will support action to cure a disease, repair bridges, save an industry, or support an allied nation, among other things. And in the American separation-of-powers setting, some degree of bipartisan support is usually required to enact legislation. In 2017, the Republicans, controlling the House, the Senate, and the presidency, and using budget procedures to bypass the filibuster, enacted one major law—the tax cut—without a single Democratic vote in either chamber. But such cases are rare.

What Biden can expect in dealings with Senate Republicans, however, is very limited cooperation and thus highly constrained opportunities for legislative success. As the two parties have become increasingly polarized, primarily through a rightward trend among Republicans, Congress has become less capable of action, at least in the absence of clear and unified party control.[36] Obama's last three Congresses, all under divided control, and Trump's two Congresses (one with unified control and one with divided) were all, in terms of the number of laws passed, the least productive in the modern era.[37] One cause of the lack of legislative productivity has probably been a strategic choice on the part of the Republican congressional leadership to elevate partisan electoral concerns over those of governing. Senator McConnell famously pronounced, during the 2010 midterm election campaign, that the Republicans' main goal was to ensure that Barack Obama was a one-term president.[38] Although the remark had a plausible innocent interpretation—that it referred only to election-related goals—McConnell did not seek to rebut the prevailing reaction, that Republicans would prioritize defeating Obama over passing laws that would benefit the country.

Insofar as possible, Senate Republicans will block Democratic initiatives on any ideologically divisive issue—abortion, climate change, health care, voting rights, and so on.[39] They will likely be open to bipartisan cooperation on legislative issues that are not ideologically divisive, but less open to it if a bipartisan measure would result in political credit for Biden. For observers, it will be difficult to determine how much Republican resistance to Biden's initiatives reflects partisan electoral strategy and how much genuine disagreement on the merits.[40]

In the end, Biden and the Democrats will face different kinds of constraints on legislative action, depending on the policies at stake. On issues that can be incorporated in a reconciliation bill, Democrats can act without Republican support in the House or Senate. The main political constraint will be the need for support from the moderate or center-right wing of their own party, especially Manchin. Such issues will include some of Biden's top priorities: resources for overcoming the COVID-19 pandemic; economic relief; taxation, including reversal of the 2017 upper-income and corporate tax cuts; and a limited expansion of access to health care, among others. (Some major policy initiatives to mitigate climate change, such as a carbon tax, would apparently qualify for inclusion under the rules but would probably not have unanimous support among Democrats.)

On issues that will not fit into a reconciliation bill, Biden and the Democrats will need to pass ordinary legislation, will face the threat of filibuster, and thus will need the support of at least ten Senate Republicans.[41] They will need to attract Republicans who are a good deal more conservative than Joe Manchin or any other Senate Democrat. Issues in this category will likely include regulatory approaches on climate change, immigration reform, police reform, racial equality and justice, anti-corruption and rule-of-law, and voting rights. If Biden and the Democrats decide to treat a single issue as a superordinate priority—most likely, voting rights— they might be able to induce Republican agreement not to block action on that issue in exchange for preserving the filibuster on most matters.

Executive and Administrative Action

The most promising means of accomplishing policy change for President Biden often will not be pushing legislation in Congress but rather relying on executive and administrative action that he or his appointees can take on their own authority. Such strategies will be attractive for Biden because they are largely immune to Republican opposition, and partly because they provide direct, efficient means of reversing policies that the Trump administration put in place in the same manner.[42]

Presidents issue executive orders on the basis of authority granted to them by Congress, in one or more statutes, or by the Constitution.[43] Departments and agencies issue a variety of regulations, policy statements, guidelines, and findings, on the basis of statutory authority.[44] Most agency actions are initiated by the agency itself. But some are associated with a particular presidential initiative, or carry out a direct instruction from the president. Individuals, businesses, or others that are harmed by these actions can challenge them in the federal courts.[45]

The ability of the Biden administration to achieve policy goals by executive or administrative action will vary sharply from one issue to the next.

Among other reasons, some statutes impose specific, detailed instructions and criteria while others grant broad discretion. What the administration seeks to do may comport with the intent of a statute, or may severely stretch its meaning. Two considerations suggest that Biden's effort to reverse many of Trump's executive and administrative actions will often succeed.[46] First, many of Trump's actions—for example, loosening environmental measures, weakening protection of workers' safety, and imposing harsh treatment of refugees—were presented as frontal attacks on the public-policy status quo. Second, the Trump administration often ignored procedural or evidentiary requirements for making administrative policy change.[47] On either substantive or procedural grounds, many of Trump's executive and administrative actions were defeated in the courts during his presidency. During the campaign, Biden declared that "on day one" of his presidency, he would immediately reverse multiple Trump decisions by issuing executive orders to rejoin the Paris Climate Accord, resume membership in the World Health Organization, cancel the ban on travel from certain Muslim-majority countries, and restore the DACA (Deferred Action for Childhood Arrivals) program that enabled people who had entered the country illegally, as children, to remain permanently.[48] In his first days and weeks in office, Biden hit the ground signing orders. With the benefit of extensive advance planning, he immediately issued orders reversing many of Trump's major policies. In the judgment of the *Economist*, his "current pace and the vigour of his appointees" suggested that "he may even achieve something like total de-Trumpification of federal policy."[49]

Election Prospects

Beyond the first two years of his presidency, Biden's prospects for policy achievements and political success turn largely on elections—both the 2022 midterm congressional elections and the presidential and congressional elections of 2024. Because of the limited opportunities for legislative policy change, many issues will be fought to a standstill during his first two years in office, to be resolved more definitively at a later date. Biden policies that are implemented by executive-branch action, without legislation, will be subject to reversal by the next president. Biden and the Democrats will have to succeed rather dramatically in at least one of those election years if Biden is to create an enduring legacy of policy change.

Although many events and circumstances as yet unknown will contribute to the congressional and presidential election outcomes, a few observations are especially pertinent. First, the president's party almost always loses seats in midterm elections.[50] It is thus highly likely that the Republicans will gain seats in both the House and Senate in the 2022 midterms, resulting in Republican control of both chambers during the last two years of Biden's term.[51] Second, however, first-term presidents usually win reelection for a second term, along with gains for the congressional party. If Biden declines to run in 2024, it is unclear how much of this incumbent advantage will transfer to another Democratic presidential candidate. But a plausibly optimistic scenario for the Democrats would give them unified control of the presidency and Congress in 2025. Third, the country's current miseries—the pandemic and severe economic downturn—probably bode well for the Democrats' prospects in 2024, and perhaps even in 2022. A party that begins a presidency during hard times usually benefits electorally from the return of prosperity.[52] By 2022, or at least by 2024, the country should be celebrating the end of the pandemic and enjoying the benefits of an economic recovery.[53] Fourth, and finally, Biden's enduring legacy may depend, even more than a typical president's, on his ability to strengthen his party's electoral coalition.

Challenges and Strategies

Biden's complex set of opportunities and constraints—especially the differences between the legislative and executive or administrative venues—has varying implications for different areas of policy, and for the corresponding challenges facing his presidency. In some areas, major successes are almost guaranteed. In other, very important areas, making any progress at all is a bit of a longshot.

THE PANDEMIC AND THE ECONOMY: RECOVERY

The Biden administration's top priority, for most of the first year or longer, will be to bring the catastrophic COVID-19 pandemic to an end. The approval of the first vaccines in mid-December 2020—a month before Biden's inauguration—appears to ensure the eventual success of the effort. But major challenges remain, with potential for significant conflict and resistance.[54]

Biden has declared many times that, unlike President Trump, he will put scientists at the controls of the federal response to the pandemic and will listen to their advice. The top appointees to his pandemic task force and related positions, such as director of the Centers for Disease Control and Prevention, are indeed distinguished scientists in epidemiology, virology, and allied fields—headlined by Dr. Anthony Fauci.

The most immediate task is one of extraordinary complexity: coordinating the acquisition, national distribution, promotion, and administration of the vaccines. A sensitive aspect of the task is to determine the sequence for various categories of people to receive the vaccine, over a period of several months (until all those who want it have received it). Many decisions and most of the work will be left to state and local governments, health-care providers, the vaccine manufacturers, and other businesses; but the federal government will provide coordination and set standards. Congressional Republicans will undoubtedly find fault with the administration's handling of the vaccines. Presumably, however, the main operations of the vaccine delivery program will not be politically controversial, and Congress, with Republican support, will provide the necessary resources and authority.

The administration will encounter more resistance in other areas of its pandemic response. In particular, it will promote mandatory mask wearing, social distancing, restrictions on gatherings, closures of certain businesses, and other measures intended to slow the spread of the virus until enough people have been vaccinated to provide herd immunity. As a result of Trump's efforts to deny the seriousness of pandemic, all of these measures have been highly politicized, and Republican governors, among others, may reject COVID-related advice from the Biden administration. It is unclear whether either the exponential growth in case numbers, hospitalizations, and deaths in late 2020 and early 2021 or Trump's departure from the presidency will produce conversions among COVID-denying Republican governors.

President Biden, House Democrats, and Senate Republicans will be the principal actors in predictably contentious negotiations over COVID-related economic relief, unemployment insurance, and stimulus spending.[55] In responding to the Democratic proposals, Republicans will insist on smaller spending packages, with more benefits for business and upper-income individuals—positions they took while Trump was in office and will hold even more firmly with a Democrat in the White House. In the first stages of legislative action on these issues, with a reconciliation bill as the expected vehicle, the administration discussed a possible bipartisan approach with a small group of relatively moderate Republican senators but soon pivoted to a much more ambitious $1.9 trillion proposal that likely would rely entirely on Democratic votes. In the end, both parties face strong constituency pressures to approve COVID relief, and at least a moderately sizable package is certain to pass. The economy, in any case, will recover, faster or more slowly, regardless of these policy conflicts.

Sooner or later, Biden should be in a position to declare victory over the coronavirus.

America in the World: Rebuilding Credibility

Biden's main priority in foreign policy will be restoring the United States to its long-standing position as the leader of the world's liberal democracies.[56] Trump eroded that position through a multitude of foreign-policy actions, reflecting some combination of an America-first nationalism; a friendly disposition toward dictators (especially Russian president Vladimir Putin); a hostile approach to international economic relationships; and a habit of taking consequential actions, without regard for qualified advice, on impulse. As a result, world leaders stopped taking the United States seriously as a constructive ally in economic and security relationships.[57]

As president, Biden can reverse most of Trump's ongoing foreign-policy positions—for example, by recommitting to the NATO alliance, dropping highly conflictual trade demands, working to restore international pressure on North Korea, and seeking to renew and rejoin the Iran nuclear deal—on his own authority. Because very few of Trump's important foreign-policy decisions were embodied in legislation, Biden does not need new legislation to overturn them.

Such reversals will not restore the pre-Trump status quo, however. Other countries will recognize that American policy has changed and that the United States is again ready to play a leading role in promoting international cooperation and underwriting mutual security arrangements. But they unavoidably will doubt the durability of the new policy direction, understanding that the next presidential election could produce yet another reversal. This uncertainty diminishes the value of all the alliances, agreements, and understandings that American policy consistently supported before the Trump presidency.

Domestic Policy: Increments and Postponements

In domestic policy, broadly defined, the constraint of Republican resistance in Congress, especially in the Senate, will play the central role in determining the prospects for the Biden administration. In every area high on Biden's list of priorities, major legislative achievements are highly unlikely, although administrative strategies will provide some compensation.

On health care, Biden wants to expand on Obamacare by adding a "public option" for the purchase of insurance coverage, increasing the availability of subsidized coverage, and restoring the individual mandate to obtain coverage.[58] A member of Biden's transition team explained to NBC News that to accomplish these changes Biden would use a series of executive orders and rely on his "longstanding history of getting stuff done in Congress to get legislation to build on the Affordable Care Act."[59] In light of the baked-in Republican opposition on these issues, it is a plan akin to pulling a rabbit out of a hat. Nevertheless, the Democrats may manage to obtain substantial gains in health care coverage through expanded subsidies for low-income families and enhanced incentives for state participation incorporated in the COVID relief bill.[60]

On climate change, the administration has rejoined the Paris Climate Accord, a nominal commitment with no direct policy effect. Importantly, it can reverse numerous Trump administration regulations that undermined many of the limited measures to reduce emissions that the federal government previously imposed, or sought to nullify measures adopted by climate-conscious states, such as California.[61] The Environmental Protection Agency (EPA) and other agencies, under Biden, can find additional administrative methods for discouraging fossil-fuel consumption and facilitating development of clean energy. But no federal agency can impose a national carbon tax, or other effective carbon-pricing policy, through creative interpretation of existing statutes. Without the ability to pass major new legislation, the Biden presidency cannot make decisive progress in mitigating climate change.

The situation is similar in other important areas of domestic policy, including abortion rights, job creation, economic inequality, racial justice, and immigration. Without major legislation, the Biden administration will not have the means to substantially advance policy goals in any of these areas.

The Constitution, Democracy, and the Authoritarian Threat

From any long-term, nonpartisan perspective, Biden's central and most urgent task is to restore and protect the institutions of American constitutional democracy. As a result of the Trump presidency, the United States has suffered a collapse of governmental competence; extensive corruption; loss of institutional integrity; undermining of the separation of powers; erosion of the rule of law; and efforts to interfere with, or overturn the results of, free and fair elections. Intimidated by Trump's unwavering support among most Republican voters, Republican Congress members, with a few exceptions, have failed to resist or condemn Trump's many violations of norms, laws, and constitutional principles.[62]

As even many conservative, Republican commentators point out, the country has had a brush with autocracy in the Trump presidency. In efforts to restore and protect democratic institutions, the Biden administration faces several distinct challenges, with differing requirements for bipartisan cooperation and prospects for success. It can begin to restore competence to those parts of the government that lost large numbers of highly qualified professionals by recruiting equally qualified professionals to replace those who were forced out or chose to leave during the Trump years.[63]

Biden will have to seek legislation, not merely take administrative action, to deal with issues of corruption, institutional integrity, and rule of law, because they all require controlling the president and his appointees.[64] The matters requiring attention include foreign "emoluments," presidential conflict of interest, enforcement of the Hatch Act, independence of inspectors general, the Special Counsel's Office, enforcement of congressional subpoenas, and timely judicial resolution of legislative-executive disputes, among others. Fortunately, Congress may be capable of bipartisan approaches to these issues. Although the issues arise from criticisms of Trump, the resolutions will arrive as means of controlling Biden.

Most of the issues involved in ensuring free and fair elections also appear tractable. The Department of Homeland Security, the FBI, and intelligence agencies can continue to prevent foreign hacking into election systems.[65] Most of the states strenuously protect their own systems. Federal legislation may be needed to ensure transparency and reliability in matters such as absentee and mail-in voting, signature verification, voting machines, ballot counting, election monitoring, vote certification, and—for presidential elections—the procedures of the Electoral College system. But here again, Democratic and Republican legislators, at both state and federal levels, may find common cause. After all, it was Democrats who worried about the integrity of election systems in 2016, and Republicans who did so in 2020.

The most difficult issues about elections concern efforts by Republican officials in many states to suppress voting in lower-income, minority, and mostly Democratic areas.[66] These efforts have become increasingly open, aggressive, and widespread in recent elections. As a matter of democratic theory, there is room for principled disagreement about how easy it should be to vote; an effortless vote may also be thoughtless. However, most Republican efforts to restrict voting have obvious, and often openly acknowledged, partisan motivation and racially discriminatory effect.

To block state efforts at voter suppression would require strong federal legislation—imposing standards for polling-place waiting times, early voting periods, identification requirements, and purges of registration rolls, among other matters. But such legislation will find little support among congressional Republicans. Indeed, in response to the 2020 controversies over voting procedures, Republican legislators and officials in numerous states have proposed dozens of new measures to restrict voting—mostly with the intention of suppressing Democratic-leaning black, Latino, or youth votes.[67] In the absence of some means for avoiding it, a Democratic voting-rights bill would meet inevitable and decisive defeat by Republican filibuster in the Senate. Advocates of voting-rights reform will urge Biden and Senate Democrats to draw a line in the sand— marking this bill as one whose defeat by filibuster they will not tolerate and will overcome through the nuclear option, if necessary.[68] Recognizing that all of their other policy accomplishments and aspirations depend on election successes in 2022, 2024, and beyond, they may take that advice.

The Biden Presidency: Reactive, Constrained—and Historic?

Far more than any previous presidency, the Joe Biden presidency will be largely occupied with attempting to undo many of the decisions of his immediate predecessor. He will likely not enact a substantial body of signature domestic legislation. As for the crucial national problems that he has inherited—climate change, economic inequality, racial injustice, and others—he may have to pass them on, mostly unchanged, to a successor. Yet, by his defeat of an incumbent president with undisguised authoritarian designs, along with important achievements in institutional restoration and reform, Biden may come to hold an exalted status in the reckoning of history—as the president who saved American democracy.

Notes

1. George Packer, "A Political Obituary for Donald Trump," *Atlantic*, December 9, 2020.
2. Jennie S. Gersen, "The Risks of Trump's Impeachment Trial," *New Yorker*, February 5, 2021.
3. George T. Conway, "Trump's New Reality: Ex-President, Private Citizen and, Perhaps, Criminal Defendant," *Washington Post*, January 22, 2021; Trump may also be exposed to potential state criminal charges: Richard Fausset and Danny Hakim, "Georgia Prosecutors Open Criminal Inquiry into Trump's Efforts to Subvert Election," *New York Times*, February 10, 2021.

4. Marc K. Landy and Sidney M. Milkis, *Presidential Greatness* (Lawrence: University Press of Kansas, 2000).
5. Fred Greenstein, *The Presidential Difference: Leadership Style from FDR to Barack Obama*, 3rd ed. (Princeton, NJ: Princeton University Press, 2009).
6. See also John P. Burke, Fred I. Greenstein, Larry Berman, & Richard Immerman, *How Presidents Test Reality: Decisions on Vietnam, 1954 and 1965* (New York: Russell Sage Foundation, 1989).
7. James David Barber, *The Presidential Character: Predicting Performance in the White House* (London: Routledge, 2020); Paul Quirk and Stephen Skowronek, "Resolved, Presidential Success and Failure Are Better Explained by Political Time and the Strength of Governing Coalitions Than a President's Character and Leadership Qualities," in *Debating the Presidency: Conflicting Perspectives on the American Executive*, ed. Richard J. Ellis and Michael Nelson (Washington, DC: CQ Press, 2019), chap. 7.
8. Aaron Levin, "Goldwater Rule's Origins Based on Long-Ago Controversy," *Psychiatric News* 51, no. 17 (September 2016): Accessed Dec 16, 2020 at: http://psychiatryonline.org/doi/10.1176/appi.pn.2016.9a19.
9. Amanda Bittner, *Platform or Personality? The Role of Party Leaders in Elections* (Oxford: Oxford University Press, 2011); Bruce Buchanan, *Presidential Campaign Quality: Incentives and Reform* (Upper Saddle River, NJ: Pearson, 2004); Stefan Müller, "Media Coverage of Campaign Promises throughout the Electoral Cycle," *Political Communication* 37, no. 5 (September 2020): 696–718; Thomas E. Patterson, "News Coverage of the 2016 General Election: How the Press Failed the Voters" (HKS Working Paper No. RWP16-052, Harvard University, Harvard Kennedy School, Cambridge, MA, December 2016), https://doi.org/10.2139/ssrn.2884837; Elizabeth Bent, Kimberly Kelling, and Ryan J. Thomas, "Electoral Reckonings: Press Criticism of Presidential Campaign Coverage, 2000-2016," *Journal of Media Ethics* 35, no. 2 (April 2020): 96–111; John Carey, "How Media Shape Campaigns," *Journal of Communication* 26, no. 2 (June 1976): 50–57.
10. Paul Quirk, "The Presidency: Donald Trump and the Question of Fitness," in *The Elections of 2016*, ed. Michael Nelson (Thousand Oaks, CA: CQ Press, 2018), 189–216; George T. Conway, "Unfit for Office," *Atlantic*, October 3, 2019; Glenn Thrush, "A Former Top Military Commander under Trump Is among 489 Security Leaders Who Say He Is Unfit for Office," *New York Times*, September 24, 2020.
11. Edward-Isaac Dovere, "Why Biden Won," *Atlantic*, November 8, 2020; Chris Cillizza, "The Remarkable Humanity of Joe Biden," *Washington Post*, June 1, 2015.
12. Luke O'Neil, "'I Am a Gaffe Machine': A History of Joe Biden's Biggest Blunders," *Guardian*, April 25, 2019.

13. Glenn Kessler, "The Sexual Allegations against Joe Biden: The Corroborators," *Washington Post*, April 29, 2020.

14. Greg Sargent, "Joe Biden and the Empathy Gap," *Washington Post*, June 6, 2020; Gabriel Debenedetti, "Biden's Strategy Right Now? Hang Back and Be a 'Normal Person,'" *New York Magazine*, October 6, 2020.

15. John Hendrickson, "Stuttering through It: How a 13-Year-Old Boy Delivered the Best Speech of the Democratic National Convention," *Atlantic*, August 21, 2020.

16. Colleen J. Shogan, "The Contemporary Presidency: The Political Utility of Empathy in Presidential Leadership," *Presidential Studies Quarterly* 39, no. 4 (2009): 859–77.

17. Ian Prasad Philbrick, "Why Does America Have Old Leaders?," *New York Times*, July 16, 2020.

18. Mark Fisher, David L. Franklin, and Jerrold M. Post, "Executive Dysfunction, Brain Aging, and Political Leadership," *Politics and the Life Sciences* 33, no. 2 (April 2015): 93–102; Jena McGregor, "Fewer Companies Are Forcing CEOs to Retire When They Hit Their Golden Years," *Washington Post*, September 27, 2018.

19. Ryan Lizza, "Biden Signals to Aides That He Would Serve Only a Single Term," *Politico*, December 11, 2019.

20. Jeff Fishel, *Presidents & Promises: From Campaign Pledge to Presidential Performance* (Washington, DC: CQ Press, 1985); Elin Naurin and Henrik Ekengren Oscarsson, "When and Why Are Voters Correct in Their Evaluations of Specific Government Performance?," *Political Studies* 65, no. 4 (December 2017): 860–76.

21. Lauren Fedor, "How Bernie Sanders and His Supporters Made Peace with Team Biden," *Financial Times*, August 18, 2020; Rachael Bade, "Rep. Ocasio-Cortez's Convention Speech Serves as Warning to Democratic Establishment and Biden," *Washington Post*, August 18, 2020.

22. Ronald Brownstein, "How Pundits May Be Getting Electability All Wrong," *Atlantic*, September 12, 2019; Ed Kilgore, "The Case for Biden's 'Electability' Fades under Scrutiny," *New York Magazine*, July 14, 2019.

23. Nahal Toosi, "Joe Biden's First Diplomatic Fight Will Be at Home," *Politico*, October 9, 2020; Maggie Astor, Lisa Friedman, Dana Goldstein, Zolan Kanno-Youngs, Margot Sanger-Katz, and Jim Tankersley, "6 Takeaways from the Biden-Sanders Joint Task Force Proposals," *New York Times*, July 9, 2020.

24. Lisa Friedman, "What Is the Green New Deal? A Climate Proposal, Explained," *New York Times*, February 21, 2019.

25. Josiah Bates, "If We're Talking about Criminal Justice Reform, Then Show Some Justice," *Time*, November 16, 2020; Alexander Burns, "Joe Biden Had Close Ties with Police Leaders. Will They Help Him Now?," *New York Times*, October 24, 2020, sec. U.S.

26. David Smith, "Biden Plans to Reach across the Aisle—but Is He Walking into a Republican Trap?," *Guardian*, November 14, 2020.

27. James P. Pfiffner, "Presidential Transitions," in *The Oxford Handbook of the American Presidency*, ed. George C. Edwards III and William G. Howell (New York: Oxford University Press, 2009), 85–107; Joshua Zoffer, "The Law of Presidential Transitions," *Yale Law Journal* 129 (August 2019): 2500–572.

28. Elena Schneider and Alex Thompson, "Biden's Transition Team, Wary of Trump and COVID-19, Sets Massive Fundraising Goal," *Politico*, September 12, 2020.

29. Daniel Henninger, "Joe Biden's Cabinet of Diversity," *Wall Street Journal*, December 16, 2020; Michael D. Shear and Annie Karni, "Biden Faces Intense Pressure from All Sides as He Seeks Diverse Cabinet," *New York Times*, December 12, 2020.

30. Katrina Manson, "Joe Biden Faces Pushback over His Defence Secretary Nominee," *Financial Times*, December 8, 2020.

31. Kate Sullivan, "Harris on Her Working Relationship with Biden: 'We Are Full Partners in This Process,'" CNN, December 3, 2020.

32. George C. Edwards, *At the Margins: Presidential Leadership of Congress* (New Haven, CT: Yale University Press, 1990); George C. Edwards, *The Strategic President: Persuasion and Opportunity in Presidential Leadership* (Princeton, NJ: Princeton University Press, 2009).

33. Matthew Beckmann, "A President's Decisions and the Presidential Difference," in *Leadership in American Politics*, ed. Jeffrey A. Jenkins and Craig Volden (Lawrence: University of Kansas Press, 2017), 65–87.

34. Dylan Scott, "9 Questions about Budget Reconciliation You Were Too Afraid to Ask," *Vox*. January 25, 2021.

35. James M. Curry and Frances E. Lee, "Non-party Government: Bipartisan Lawmaking and Party Power in Congress," *Perspectives on Politics* 17, no. 1 (2019): 47–65; David R. Mayhew, *Divided We Govern: Party Control, Lawmaking, and Investigations, 1946–2002* (New Haven, CT: Yale University Press, 2005).

36. That polarization has occurred primarily through movement to the right among Republicans, with much less movement to the left among Democrats, is called "asymmetric polarization." See Jeffrey B. Lewis, Keith Poole, Howard Rosenthal, Adam Boche, Aaron Rudkin, and Luke Sonnet, "Voteview: Congressional Roll-Call Votes Database," 2020, https://voteview.com/data.

37. Drew DeSilver, "A Productivity Scorecard for the 115th Congress: More Laws Than before, but Not More Substance," Pew Research Center, January 25, 2019, https://www.pewresearch.org/fact-tank/2019/01/25/a-productivity-scorecard-for-115th-congress/.

38. Glenn Kessler, "When Did Mitch McConnell Say He Wanted to Make Obama a One-Term President?," *Washington Post*, January 11, 2017.
39. Jeff Stein and Sean Sullivan, "Long-Standing Ties between Biden and McConnell Could Shape Early Agenda," *Washington Post*, November 9, 2020; Carl Hulse, "Republican Resistance Looms in the Senate for Biden's Nominees," *New York Times*, November 20, 2020; Lauren Fedor, "Mitch McConnell: A Thorn in the Side of a Biden Administration," *Financial Times*, November 9, 2020.
40. Frances Lee, *Beyond Ideology: Politics, Principles, and Partisanship in the US Senate* (Chicago: University of Chicago Press, 2009).
41. Perry Bacon Jr., "What Democrats Can't Do As Long As the Filibuster Remains in Place—And What They Can," *FiveThirtyEight*, February 1, 2021.
42. Tami Luhby, Caroline Kelly, and Devan Cole, "Here Are 7 Trump Health Care Measures That Biden Will Likely Overturn," CNN, November 16, 2020; Madeleine Ngo, "Biden Plans to Roll Back Trump-Era Education Policies," *Wall Street Journal*, November 29, 2020; Marianne Lavelle, "Trump Rolled Back 100+ Environmental Rules. Biden May Focus on Undoing Five of the Biggest Ones," *Inside Climate News* (blog), November 17, 2020, https://insideclimatenews.org/news/17112020/trump-roll backs-biden-clean-cars-power-methane/.
43. Adam L. Warber, Yu Ouyang, and Richard W. Waterman, "Landmark Executive Orders: Presidential Leadership through Unilateral Action," *Presidential Studies Quarterly* 48, no. 1 (2018): 110–26.
44. Susan Webb Yackee, "The Politics of Rulemaking in the United States," *Annual Review of Political Science* 22, no. 1 (2019): 37–55.
45. Lisa Manheim and Kathryn A. Watts, "Reviewing Presidential Orders," *University of Chicago Law Review* 86, no. 7 (2019): 1743–1824.
46. Sharece Thrower, "To Revoke or Not Revoke? The Political Determinants of Executive Order Longevity," *American Journal of Political Science* 61, no. 3 (2017): 642–56; Connor Raso and Peter Fox, "What a Biden Administration Should Learn from the Trump Administration's Regulatory Reversals," Brookings, September 28, 2020, https://www.brookings.edu /research/what-a-biden-administration-should-learn-from-the-trump -administrations-regulatory-reversals/; Robert Roberts, "The Judicial Response to the Presidential Polarization of the Administrative State," *American Review of Public Administration* 49, no. 1 (January 2019): 3–20.
47. Lisa Heinzerling, "Unreasonable Delays: The Legal Problems (So Far) of Trump's Deregulatory Binge," *Harvard Law & Policy Review* 12, no. 1 (2018): 13–48; Fred Barbash and Deanna Paul, "The Real Reason the Trump Administration Is Constantly Losing in Court," *Washington Post*, March 19, 2020.

48. Matt Viser, Seung Min Kim, and Annie Linskey, "Biden Plans Immedi-
    ate Flurry of Executive Orders to Reverse Trump Policies," *Washington
    Post*, November 7, 2020.
49. "Joe Biden Terminates Much of Donald Trump's Legacy," *Economist*,
    January 30, 2021.
50. Joseph Bafumi, Robert S. Erikson, and Christopher Wlezien, "Balancing,
    Generic Polls and Midterm Congressional Elections," *Journal of Politics*
    72, no. 3 (July 2010): 705–19.
51. Geoffrey Skelley, "Republicans Are on Track to Take Back the House in
    2022," *FiveThirtyEight* (blog), November 12, 2020; Burgess Everett and
    John Bresnahan, "Republicans Dash to Defend Perilous 2022 Senate Map,"
    Politico, November 23, 2020.
52. Larry Bartels, *Unequal Democracy: The Political Economy of the New Gilded
    Age* (New York: Russell Sage Foundation, 2008); Michael Comiskey and
    Lawrence C. Marsh, "Presidents, Parties, and the Business Cycle, 1949–
    2009," *Presidential Studies Quarterly* 42, no. 1 (2012): 40–59.
53. Jeanna Smialek, "Fed Chair Says Economic Recovery May 'Stretch'
    through End of 2021," *New York Times*, May 17, 2020.
54. Betsy McKay and Jonathan D. Rockoff, "What Are Joe Biden's Plans for
    COVID-19?," *Wall Street Journal*, November 13, 2020; Nidhi Subbaraman,
    "Joe Biden's COVID Plan Is Taking Shape—and Researchers Approve,"
    Nature 587, no. 7834 (November 2020): 339–40.
55. Martin Sandbu, "Why Joe Biden Must Go Big," *Financial Times*, Novem-
    ber 12, 2020; David J. Lynch, "Biden's Economic Team Set to Prepare
    Ambitious Recovery Plan, Challenging Republicans' Renewed Debt Wor-
    ries," *Washington Post*, December 2, 2020.
56. David E. Sanger, "The End of 'America First': How Biden Says He Will Re-
    engage with the World," *New York Times*, November 9, 2020; Dan Balz,
    "America's Global Standing Is at a Low Point. The Pandemic Made It
    Worse," *Washington Post*, July 26, 2020; George Packer, "The President Is
    Winning His War on American Institutions," *Atlantic*, April 10, 2020.
57. Max Boot, "With His Foreign Policy Speech, Biden Begins to Repair the
    Damage that Trump Did," *Washington Post*, February 4, 2021.
58. Guian McKee, "Joe Biden's Health-Care Plan Is More Than a Half-Century
    in the Making," *Washington Post*, October 27, 2020; Amy Goldstein and
    Erica Werner, "Biden Presses to Expand Health Insurance on Uncertain
    Congressional Terrain," *Washington Post*, November 10, 2020.
59. Marianna Sotomayor, "What's In, and Out, of Biden's Health Care Plan,"
    NBC News, December 16, 2020, https://www.nbcnews.com/politics/meet
    -the-press/blog/meet-press-blog-latest-news-analysis-data-driving
    -political-discussion-n988541.
60. John Harwood, "Analysis: How Democrats Are Using the COVID Stim-
    ulus to Fight Income Inequality," CNN, February 15, 2021.

61. Jeff Tollefson, "Can Joe Biden Make Good on His Revolutionary Climate Agenda?," *Nature* 588, no. 7837 (November 2020): 206–7; Fiona Harvey, "Joe Biden Could Bring Paris Climate Goals 'within Striking Distance,'" *Guardian*, November 8, 2020.

62. That this failure has been largely the effect of such intimidation has been confirmed by extensive reporting. The prominent journalist Carl Bernstein provided names of twenty-one Republican senators who "show 'extreme contempt' for Trump . . . behind closed doors despite most displaying public deference to the president." Andrew Solender, "These 21 GOP Senators Show 'Extreme Contempt' for Trump in Private, according to Carl Bernstein," *Forbes*, November 23, 2020. Bernstein reported that he received these names from reliable, on-the-record sources. In 2019, former Republican senator Jeff Flake stated that "at least 35" Republican senators would vote to convict Trump in his impeachment trial if they could do so by secret ballot. Jonathan S. Gould and David Pozen, "The Senate Impeachment Trial Could Use a Little Secrecy," *Atlantic*, December 16, 2019. Trump certainly has true believers among congressional Republicans. But they may be a minority of those members.

63. Megan Cassella and Alice Miranda Ollstein, "Biden Confronts Staffing Crisis at Federal Agencies," *Politico*, November 12, 2020.

64. Jonathan Mahler, "Can America Restore the Rule of Law without Prosecuting Trump?," *New York Times*, November 17, 2020; "How to Fix Impeachment," *Politico*, December 6, 2019.

65. Joseph Marks, "The Cybersecurity 202: Biden Will Get Tougher on Russia and Boost Election Security. Here's What to Expect," *Washington Post*, November 9, 2020.

66. Sarada Peri, "Obama Couldn't Fix the System. Biden Must," *Atlantic*, August 5, 2020.

67. Ronald Brownstein, "The GOP Cheat Code to Winning Back the House," *Atlantic*, February 11, 2021; Chris Hayes, "The Republican Party Is Radicalizing against Democracy," *Atlantic*, February 8, 2021.

68. Eugene J. Dionne, "Democrats Are Faced with a Choice. Protect the Filibuster or Protect Democracy," *Washington Post*, January 29, 2021.

Congress

EVER MORE PARTISAN, POLARIZED, AND NATIONAL

GARY C. JACOBSON

LIKE THE TWO PREVIOUS federal elections featuring Donald Trump on the ballot or in the White House, the congressional elections of 2020 were notable for extreme levels of party loyalty, polarization, nationalization, and presidential influence on the vote choice—all, of course, tightly linked phenomena.[1] And as in 2018, they set new records for campaign spending, voter turnout, and women pursuing and winning congressional seats. If nothing else, Trump has been a peerless inspirer of civic engagement. Although Trump lost to Joe Biden by more than 7 million votes and a margin of 4.4 percentage points, Republicans gained seats in the House of Representatives; they lost control of the Senate, however, when Democrats won the two Georgia runoff elections held in January 2021. Like Trump, Republican congressional candidates performed considerably better than preelection polls projected and no doubt for the same reason, an inadvertent but systematic under-sampling of Trump Republicans.

The congressional results are summarized in table 1. Every Republican incumbent won, and court-ordered redistricting in North Carolina accounts for two of the three open seats they lost. Thirteen Democratic incumbents lost, and a Republican took one of the fourteen open Democratic seats. Republicans did not fully recover from the blue wave that had cost them control of Congress in 2018, but they undid some of the damage and are well within striking distance of a House majority in 2022. Democrats defeated four Republican Senate incumbents while losing one of their own, leaving the Senate divided 50–50 (the two independents vote to organize with the Democrats), with newly elected vice president Kamala Harris holding the tiebreaking vote.

TABLE 1. Membership changes in the House and Senate during the Trump era

	Republicans	Democrats	Independents
House of Representatives			
Elected in 2016	241	194	
Elected in 2018	199	235	
Before the 2020 election	201	233	1
Elected in 2020	213	222	
Incumbents reelected	165	205	
Incumbents defeated	0	13	
Open seats retained	34	13	
Open seats lost	3	1	
Senate			
After the 2016 election	52	46	2[a]
After the 2018 election	53	45	2[a]
After the 2020 election	50[b]	48[b]	2[a]
Incumbents reelected	14	10	
Incumbents defeated	4	1	
Open seats retained	3	1	
Open seats lost	0	0	

Source: Compiled by author.

[a] The Independents caucus with the Democrats.

The Trump Impact

The single most important shaper of the House and Senate elections was voters' reactions to Donald Trump and his presidency. Since his arrival on the national political stage, Trump has drawn sharply divergent partisan responses to virtually every aspect of his character and conduct on the way to becoming the most polarizing president on record. In the last Gallup poll taken before the 2020 election, 94 percent of Republicans but only 3 percent of Democrats said they approved of his performance, the widest partisan gap ever reported by Gallup. In all major polls taken in October, the figures averaged 91 percent among Republicans and 4 percent among Democrats, with very large majorities in both parties holding their opinions "strongly."

Democrats came to loathe Trump for what they see as, among other things, his misogyny, racism, narcissism, cruelty, mendacity, corruption, incompetence, authoritarian impulses, contempt for democratic norms and institutions, disparagement of traditional allies, and fondness for authoritarian rulers, as well as his policies on health care, the environment, regulation, taxes, and immigration. But none of the particulars that made Trump so repugnant to ordinary Democrats shook his support among ordinary Republicans. Most of them evidently share his opinions, grievances, and resentments, admiring what Democrats despise about him: his America-first nationalism, disdain for nonwhite immigrants and assertive minorities, attacks on mainstream news media as "enemies of the people," defiance of elite and expert opinion, mistrust of government institutions, contempt for Democratic leaders and their party, and blanket assault on Barack Obama's legacy. Trump convinced millions of disaffected Americans that he was on their side, that his enemies were their enemies, and that by attacking him they were attacking them. Even those Republicans who found his manner and character off-putting appreciated his policies on taxes, deregulation, trade, Israel, and immigration, as well as his stacking the federal courts with conservative judges. And before the coronavirus pandemic did its damage, Republicans could point to steady economic growth, very low unemployment, and a booming stock market as additional reasons to support him.

These deeply divergent views of Trump were reinforced by news coverage of his presidency, with mainstream news organizations quick to point out his lies, instability, trampling of democratic norms, alienation of allies, and incompetence in staffing and managing the executive branch. The implicit but unmistakable subtext of their coverage was that Trump was unqualified by character, temperament, knowledge, and experience for the presidency. Trump's response was to make mainstream news sources the target of his supporters' wrath, attacking them as "enemies of the people" and purveyors of "fake news" in a sustained effort to delegitimize their reporting and avoid answering for his actions. This effort largely succeeded among Republican voters, helped along by conservative news and opinion outlets led by Fox News, whose most popular personalities routinely delivered uncritical praise and support for Trump's words and actions along with constant disdain for his critics. The media ecosphere thus contributed importantly to the overwhelming polarization of opinions of Trump.[2]

Backed by his enthusiastic supporters, Trump executed a complete takeover of the Republican Party. Criticism from congressional Republicans, common while Trump was pursuing the 2016 nomination and still heard early in his presidency, grew exceedingly rare as critics departed, fell silent, or morphed into ardent defenders. No one facing a Republican primary electorate wanted to risk bruising his ego. Trump's influence over his party's public image and popularity was stronger (and therefore more polarizing) than that of any previous postwar president.[3] In short, Trump made himself the dominant focal point for the organization of political attitudes, and consequently both the House and Senate election results in 2020 were, with only a few exceptions, tightly bound to his popular standing and electoral performance in the districts and states. Despite the staggering sums spent to influence congressional contests, the results echoed the vote for the top of the ticket far more than any distinctive local considerations.

The House Elections

Endorsing Joe Biden at the Democratic convention, runner-up Bernie Sanders framed the upcoming presidential contest in apocalyptic terms: "The future of our democracy is at stake. The future of our economy is at stake. The future of our planet is at stake."[4] The sense that victory for the other side would be disastrous for the country was shared by a large proportion of partisans on both sides, with 89 percent of Trump supporters and 90 percent of Biden supporters agreeing that victory by the other party's nominee would "lead to lasting harm to the U.S."[5] Large majorities (80 percent of Biden supporters and 77 percent of Trump supporters) said Democrats and Republicans not only are at odds on policy issues but "fundamentally disagree on core political values."[6] Such political sentiments inspired record turnout, record high levels of party loyalty and straight-ticket voting, and an extremely close connection between presidential and congressional voting at both the individual and aggregate levels. Although election data are still incomplete, the available evidence indicates that 2020 was the most nationalized, partisan, and president-centered election yet observed.

Table 2 presents some of the evidence. The correlation between the presidential and House vote, which has been growing for two decades, reached its highest point in 2020 at 0.986. A simple logit model estimating the effects of the presidential vote on which party wins each seat predicted the 2020 results with 96.0 percent accuracy, only a tick below the even more remarkable 2018 figure.[7]

Another useful indicator of electoral nationalization is the standard deviation of the major-party vote swing from the previous election across stable, contested districts: the smaller the standard deviation, the more uniform the swing across districts, and thus the more nationalized the

TABLE 2. District-level presidential vote and House results, 2000–2020

House election year	Presidential vote year	House/ president vote correlation	% winners correctly predicted	Value of incumbency	Standard deviation of vote swing
2000	2000	.803	80.4	8.6	6.4
2002	2000	.805	86.2	8.5	
2004	2004	.839	86.4	6.8	5.5
2006	2004	.839	83.5	6.5	6.0
2008	2008	.851	80.7	7.1	6.0
2010	2008	.917	91.3	4.8	6.3
2012	2012	.952	94.0	2.5	
2014	2012	.942	94.3	3.7	4.3
2016	2016	.950	94.7	2.3	4.6
2018	2016	.974	96.1	2.1	4.3
2020	2020	.986	96.0	1.3	3.0

Source: Compiled by author.

election. The standard deviation of the swing between 2018 and 2020 is the smallest yet observed: 3.0.[8] As elections have become more nationalized and the presidential choice such a dominant electoral force, the value of incumbency, measured in vote shares, has dropped to levels last seen in the 1950s.[9] The estimated incumbency advantage for 2020 was a mere 1.3 percentage points, less than one-sixth what it was at the beginning of the century. For the same reason, the effect of candidate quality as measured by previous experience in elected office has also shrunk; its estimated value was only 0.9 percentage points in 2020, the lowest for the postwar period.[10] Although the incumbency advantage measured in votes was small, House incumbents were very successful in 2020, with Republicans winning all of their general election contests and Democrats winning 94 percent of theirs. This was not because they were incumbents, however, but rather because they ran in districts that favored their party in presidential voting. Nine of the thirteen losing Democratic incumbents represented districts won by Trump in 2020; six of the eight lost seats they had taken from Republicans in the 2018 blue wave. All three Democratic open-seat takeovers were in districts where Biden outpolled Trump, so that, altogether, thirteen of the seventeen seats that changed party hands in 2020 went to the party of the district presidential winner. Of the fifty-one open seats contested in 2020, the party of the presidential winner won fifty.

TABLE 3. National turnout and voting in U.S. House elections, 2014–20

	Turnout (%)	Democrats		Republicans	
		Votes (millions)	Share (%)	Votes (millions)	Share (%)
2014	36.7	35.6	45.5	40.1	51.2
2016	60.1	61.8	48.0	63.1	49.1
2018	50.0	60.6	53.4	50.9	44.8
2020	66.7	77.5	50.8	72.9	47.7

Source: Turnout: United States Election Project, reported at electproject.org; votes: 2014–18, official election returns; 2020, Cook Political Report, https://cookpolitical .com/2020-house-vote-tracker?

TURNOUT

One striking effect of Trump's genius for provoking extreme partisan dis-cord was the sharp increase in voter participation during his presidency, documented in table 3. Turnout in the 2018 midterm, at 50 percent of eligi-ble voters, was the highest in a century, and Democrats were the main beneficiaries.[11] The total vote for Republicans in 2018 was 10.7 million higher than in the previous midterm, 2014, but the Democratic vote was up almost 25 million, and consequently, the Democrats' vote share also rose sharply and they picked up a net forty-one seats (table 1). Trump's profoundly polarizing presence registered even more powerfully in 2020, inspiring the highest turnout in any national election since 1900. Demo-crats increased their total House vote by 17.0 million over 2018, but Republi-cans increased theirs by 21.1 million. Democrats still won a larger share of House votes than Republicans did in 2020, but their margin was nar-rower than in 2018, and the Republican turnout surge helped recover terri-tory they had lost in the midterm. Credit may be due to the Republicans' superior ground game in some states. Less concerned with the COVID-19 pandemic, Republicans did more face-to-face and door-to-door canvass-ing than Democrats, who were more observant of masking and social dis-tancing protocols.[12]

RECRUITMENT

Republicans also narrowed another gap that had widened dramatically in 2018. As table 4 reveals, Democrats have consistently fielded the greater

TABLE 4. Women candidates for Congress, 2000–2020

	House of Representatives				Senate		
	Republicans		Democrats		Republicans		Democrats	
	Ran	Won	Ran	Won	Ran	Won	Ran	Won
2000	42	18	80	44	2	2	4	4
2002	46	21	78	42	3	2	8	1
2004	53	25	88	46	1	1	9	4
2006	42	21	94	57	4	2	8	6
2008	37	17	95	62	3	1	4	3
2010	47	24	91	55	6	2	9	4
2012	48	20	118	62	6	1	12	9
2014	50	23	109	65	5	3	10	1
2016	47	25	120	64	4	1	12	5
2018	52	13	183	89	8	3	15	11
2020	96	30	200	89	9	6	12	2

Source: 2000–2018: Center for American Women and Politics, Rutgers University, https:// cawp.rutgers.edu/sites/default/files/resources/canwincong_histsum.pdf; 2020: compiled by author.

number of women running and winning congressional seats during this century, with gaps between the parties on both increasing dramatically in 2018. Fully half of the 254 nonincumbent Democrats who won House nominations were women; counting incumbent Democrats, 183 of the party's 427 nominees were women, a share 50 percent higher than in any prior election. About half of them won, and 35 of the 62 Democrats newly elected in 2018 were women. Fifteen of the Democrats' Senate nominees in 2018 were also women, including 11 winners, again record numbers. The remarkable burst of grassroots activism among Democratic women was a direct response to the shock they experienced with Trump's election in 2016 and his subsequent rhetoric, conduct in office, and actions regarding health care, immigration, reproductive rights, sexual harassment, and the environment.[13]

Republican leaders concluded that their relative dearth of women candidates was hurting their cause and in 2020 made a concerted effort to recruit and fund more of them. The effort paid off, nearly doubling their number of women candidates in the general election compared with recent years.[14] Eleven of the fourteen Republicans who took seats from

Democrats were women, including nine of the twelve who recaptured seats lost in 2018; four of them defeated incumbent Democratic women in the process. Democrats still fielded twice as many women as Republicans did in 2020, and a larger share of them won (44 percent versus 31 percent), but women's representation in the Republican conference in the 117th Congress will be their largest ever. As in past elections, candidates' gender had no systematic impact on the district vote once district partisanship (measured by the 2020 presidential vote) is taken into account; women's victories in both parties depended mainly on winning their party's nominations in districts favorable to their side. A couple of exceptions are instructive, however. The two women who retook seats in Orange County, California, in districts won by Hillary Clinton in 2016 and lost to Democrats in 2018's blue wave, Young Kim and Michele Park Steel, are Korean Americans. They are also experienced officeholders: Kim in the state assembly and Steel as county supervisor (a powerful position in California). Both districts went for Biden in 2020, so their victories show that Republicans with the right skills, characteristics, and local reputations could separate themselves sufficiently from Trump to win in Democratic-leaning districts. But such instances were exceedingly rare in 2020.

Republicans also fielded a larger than usual number of nonwhite House candidates in 2020: seventy-six, up from fifty-three in 2018. Twelve of them won, compared with four in 2018. Of the eleven Republican women who took seats from Democrats, four were nonwhite. Two of the other three Republican takeaways were accomplished by nonwhite men: Miami mayor Carlos Gimenez, born in Cuba, and in Utah, Burgess Owens, a Black former professional football player. The Democrats retained a wide lead in fielding nonwhite candidates (149, up from 131 in 2018) and in electing them (94, up from 92 in 2018), but Republicans made progress in diversifying their House delegation, with the proportion of white males dropping from 91.5 percent in 2018 to 82.2 percent in 2020 (among Democrats, the proportion is now 36.0 percent).

Expanding the representation of women and minorities in the party of Donald Trump, known for racist and misogynist rhetoric, is perhaps a curious development, but it stems from a deliberate effort by the Republican Party to adapt to changing demographics and to keep pace with the surge of nonmale, nonwhite Democratic representatives. Survey data find plenty of women who are attracted to Trump's America First nationalism and conservative social and economic policies, so finding women candidates comfortable in his Republican Party is not particularly difficult. Indeed, some have turned out to be Trumpier than Trump; two of the newly elected Republican women, Marjorie Taylor Greene of Georgia and Lauren Boebert of Colorado, endorse the crackpot QAnon conspiracy theory that Trump is engaged in a secret battle against the "deep state" and a ring of satanic sex-trafficking pedophile cannibals.[15] Diversity indeed.

PRIMARY ELECTION LOSSES

Although incumbents won the general elections at typically high rates in 2020, the number who were not renominated by their party was the highest for any non-redistricting year since 1974 (eight, as compared with an average of about three). Two fell victim to legal problems from violating campaign laws. Three Democrats and two Republicans lost to candidates who presented themselves as closer to their respective parties' increasingly divergent ideological mainstreams—Democrats on the progressive side, Republicans on the conservative side. The primary defeat of Dan Lipinski (D-IL) removed one of the few remaining pro-life Democrats from Congress. Denver Riggleman (R-VA) was denied renomination at his party's state convention after he presided over a gay marriage ceremony. These elections thus made another small contribution to widening the ideological divide in the House. The final loser was Steve King (R-IA), whose history of racist comments finally cost him his House committee assignments and local party support.

CAMPAIGN MONEY

The intense partisan fervor provoked by Trump's person and presidency also inspired huge increases in another form of political participation: contributing money to campaigns. As of the November 23 reporting date, spending by House candidates in 2020 averaged $1.8 million, a number sure to be higher when the final reports are in but already 9 percent more than in 2018 and twice as much as in 2016. Spending in support of candidates by outside groups, including political party committees, reported through November for 2020, averaged $822,000.[16]

Campaign contributions and outside spending are always concentrated in the most competitive districts. In 2018, the average combined spending by and for candidates in the seventy-one districts rated by the authoritative Cook Political Report as toss-ups or just leaning toward one of the parties was $8.9 million for Democrats and $6.6 million for Republicans, totals much higher than in any previous election. For the fifty-eight toss-up and leaning contests in 2020, the averages, even with incomplete data, were already $9.8 million and $8.2 million, respectively. In 2018, outside groups supplied about 43 percent of the Democrats' total spending and

48 percent of the Republicans' total spending; the proportions for 2020 were 49 percent and 60 percent, respectively. To what extent did such lavish spending affect the outcomes? High spending levels were strongly associated with Democrats' takeovers in 2018 and with the sharp increase in Democratic turnout that contributed to them; Democrats won twenty-three of the twenty-six Republican-held districts where total spending by and for their candidates exceeded $10 million.[17] However, sixteen of these districts had given a majority of their votes to Clinton in 2016. Overall, Democrats won fourteen of fifteen Clinton districts where spending on their side exceeded $10 million, but also eight of ten where it did not. Spending lavishly may have helped, but it also signaled a level of enthusiasm that drove Democrats to the polls in great numbers in all districts regardless of what the campaign spent.[18] In 2020, with Republicans as motivated to vote as Democrats, money could not protect Democrats in high-risk districts. In the fourteen Republican takeover districts, the average total spending by and for Democrats was $12.2 million; for Republicans, it was $10.5 million. The losing Democrats had greater financial backing in ten of these contests. In at least thirty-two other districts, Democrats invested more than $5 million in attempts to replace Republicans, but only one was successful. Despite unprecedented levels of spending in the district campaigns, the House results were dominated by the same national forces that shaped the presidential results. Perhaps saturation campaigns simply reinforce their exasperated target voters' partisan predispositions.

INDIVIDUAL VOTING

Preelection surveys accurately anticipated Trump's powerful influence on the individual vote in both the 2018 and 2020 elections. In 2018, preelection surveys found an average of 93 percent of voters reporting preferences consistent with their opinion of the president (for Republicans, approving of the president; for Democrats, disapproving). Such a high level of consistency is unprecedented; the previous record holder was Obama, at 87 percent; for George W. Bush, consistent party preferences for president and House member averaged 81 percent and for presidents from 1980 to 2000, 74 percent. In postelection surveys in 2018, about 93 percent of respondents reported votes aligned with their opinion of the president.[19]

Preelection polls projected that Trump's influence on the House vote would be at least as potent in 2020. Again, about 93 percent of prospective votes were consistent with views of Trump.[20] Pew's October survey found only 4 percent of voters planning to vote for either Biden and a House Republican or Trump and a House Democrat.[21] In the twenty-six weekly *Economist*/YouGov surveys that asked the same question between June and November, an average of 97.2 percent of respondents who reported preferences in both elections chose the same party in both.[22] The sophisticated academic surveys most useful for exploring the details of individual voting in 2020 are not yet available, but the first postelection *Economist*/YouGov poll (taken November 10–12) reported a straight-ticket voting rate of 96.8 percent among voters for major party candidates.

Straight-ticket voting was of course strongly associated with party loyalty. In the preelection *Economist*/YouGov polls, prospective defections among Democratic identifiers averaged only 3.7 percent for the president and 2.9 percent for the House; the respective figures for Republican identifiers were 5.3 percent and 3.3 percent. Similarly low defection rates were reported in other preelection polls. The postelection *Economist*/YouGov poll reported defection rates for the two offices of 3.1 percent and 1.9 percent among Democrats, 4.9 percent and 4.6 percent among Republicans. These are very low defection rates by historical standards; indeed, the overall defection rate reported in the 2020 exit poll, about 4.5 percent, was the lowest in any of the exit polls going back to 1972. In sum, 2020 is likely to set a new record for party loyalty as well as straight-ticket voting—one reason turnout was so important.[23]

Electoral Coalitions

High levels of straight-ticket voting in the *Economist*/YouGov survey meant that the demographics of the House parties' electoral coalitions matched that of their presidential candidates quite closely (table 5). Women were responsible for the Democrats' majority vote in both the presidential and House elections; the gender gap was about 10 points in House voting, 8 points in presidential voting. Whites favored Republicans, nonwhites Democrats, just as in the presidential election. The House vote also showed a strong age gradient, with the youngest cohort 21 points more Democratic than the oldest cohort. An education gradient, with more educated voters favoring the Democrats, was also evident, but the largest difference—37 points—was between voters in large cities and those in rural areas. These data confirm the image of the Republicans as the party of older, white, less educated, male voters residing outside metropolitan areas, and the Democrats as the party of younger, nonwhite, better educated, and female voters living in urban areas. Demographic differences in the parties' electoral constituencies serve to reinforce partisan divergence in

TABLE 5. Demographics of the House and presidential votes, 2020

	Vote for U.S. House		Vote for president	
	Democrat	Republican	Biden	Trump
All	52.7	47.3	52.7	47.3
Gender				
Men	47.5	52.5	48.3	51.7
Women	57.2	42.8	56.3	43.7
Race				
White	44.5	55.5	44.5	55.5
Black	93.1	6.9	93.7	7.6
Hispanic	69.2	30.8	65.9	34.1
Other	53.2	46.8	57.7	42.3
Age				
Under 30	65.3	34.7	67.1	32.9
30–44	57.3	42.7	54.7	45.3
45–64	53.4	46.6	53.2	46.7
65+	43.9	56.1	44.5	55.8
Education				
High school or less	47.0	53.0	46.0	54.0
Some college	52.4	47.6	52.0	48.0
College graduate	53.5	46.5	54.3	45.7
Postgraduate	59.8	40.2	60.4	39.6
Residential area type				
Large city	71.4	28.6	72.0	28.0
Suburb near large city	54.0	46.0	53.2	46.8
Small city or town	51.5	48.5	51.4	48.6
Rural area	34.2	65.8	35.2	64.8
Ideology				
Liberal	96.3	3.7	96.4	3.6
Moderate	60.8	39.2	61.0	39.0
Conservative	7.9	92.1	7.8	92.2

Source: Economist/YouGov Survey, November 10–12, 2020.

Congress because they map onto differences in self-reported ideology. The final set of data in table 5 shows just how sharply voters in this survey split along ideological lines between Republican conservatives and Democratic liberals.[24]

The Senate Elections

The 2020 Senate elections, like the House elections, were largely driven by reactions to the top of the ticket (figure 1). In 2016, for the first time ever, every Senate seat went to the party that won the state's electoral votes for president. The 2020 elections did not quite match that record; Maine Republican Susan Collins won handily in a state Biden won by more than 7 points, but after Democrats won the two Georgia runoffs, it was the only state delivering a split outcome. Despite Collins's off-diagonal performance, the correlation between the major party share of votes won by candidates for president and Senate was .95 in 2020, slightly higher than the previous record set in 2016 (.94). The other Republican Senate candidate who outperformed Trump significantly was Ben Sasse of Nebraska. Interestingly, Collins and Sasse had been at least occasional public critics of Trump, certainly more often than other Republicans seeking reelection to the Senate. Evidently, their votes from crossover Biden supporters more than offset any votes withheld by Trump supporters offended by their apostasy.

Senate Campaign Finances

The extent to which the Senate vote echoed the presidential vote is all the more remarkable considering the incredible sums of money spent to influence these races. Table 6 lists the contests and their results in descending order based on the total spent in the state by the candidates' campaigns and by outside organizations, including the parties, according to the preliminary data available in early January 2021. These numbers will be higher once the final data are published, but they already surpass any previous election by a huge margin. The current total is $3.43 billion, already 143 percent higher than the final total for 2018 ($1.41 billion), previously the highest ever. The 2018 midterm had produced six Senate contests in which combined spending exceeded $100 million; in 2020 there were at least twelve such contests, and in seven the total exceeded $200 million. Total spending in the two Georgia elections decided by January runoffs approached an astonishing $900 million.

In the ten most expensive Senate contests, more than half the spending was by outside groups on behalf of the candidates they supported.

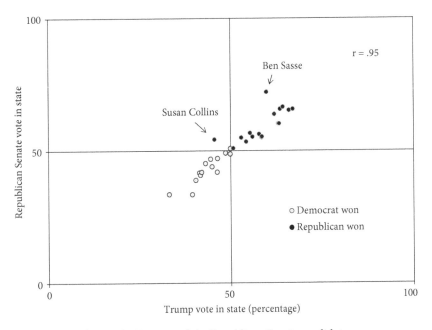

FIG. 1. Statewide vote for Trump and the Republican Senate candidate, 2020

Democratic groups and individuals, aided by the technology developed by ActBlue to channel funds to liberal candidates,[25] made lavish investments aimed at winning control of the Senate by taking out Republican incumbents in red and purple states. Republican donors responded generously in their defense, but the Democrat was supported by significantly more money in the nine of the first ten contests on this list, all but one involving Republican incumbents. They were successful in Georgia and Arizona; all of the other states (except Maine) went for Trump. The polls in most of these states had given them a false sense of hope by overstating the Democrat candidate's support, just as they had overstated Biden's support, and the outcomes ended up matching his margins. Overall, Democrats were better financed than Republicans in twenty-five states; of these, they lost the twelve states won by Trump and won twelve of the thirteen states won by Biden, the exception again being Maine, where by some accounts the tsunami of Democratic money, amounting to $125 per eligible voter, actually turned off voters and hurt their candidate's cause.[26] They also won the Georgia contest where their candidate was outspent, but Jon Ossoff's $226 million was evidently enough. The reality is that in every plausibly competitive contest, both sides had more than adequate resources to make

TABLE 6. 2020 Senate election results and campaign money

State	Candidate	% Vote	Candidate Receipts ($1,000s)	Outside Spending ($1,000s)	Total Spending ($1,000s)	$ Per Voter	% Outside
Georgia[a]	David Perdue (R)	49.4	89,126	181,271	270,397	30.7	67.0
	Jon Ossoff (D)	50.6	138,257	88,112	226,369	36.6	38.9
Georgia[a]	Kelly Loeffler (R)	49.0	92,136	106,440	198,576	26.9	53.6
	Raphael Warnock (D)	51.0	124,278	76,260	200,538	27.2	38.0
North Carolina	Tom Tillis (R)	48.7	25,341	100,699	126,040	16.2	79.9
	Cal Cunningham (D)	46.9	51,257	117,898	169,155	21.8	69.7
South Carolina	Lindsey Graham (R)	54.5	107,056	32,471	139,527	35.5	23.3
	Jaime Harrison (D)	44.2	130,609	17,018	147,627	37.6	11.5
Iowa	Joni Ernst (R)	51.8	30,198	75,612	105,810	45.6	71.5
	Theresa Greenfield (D)	45.2	55,601	96,862	152,463	65.7	63.5
Arizona	Martha McSally (R)	48.8	71,484	43,035	114,519	22.1	37.6
	Mark Kelly (D)	51.2	99,043	40,042	139,085	26.8	28.8
Maine	Susan Collins (R)	50.6	29,835	50,241	80,076	73.8	62.7
	Sara Gideon (D)	42.7	74,495	61,068	135,563	124.9	45.0
Michigan	John James (R)	48.2	48,156	47,039	95,195	12.6	49.4
	Gary Peters (D)	49.9	51,397	49,228	100,625	13.3	48.9
Kentucky	Mitch McConnell (R)	57.8	67,985	13,318	81,303	24.5	16.4
	Amy McGrath (D)	38.2	94,134	16,351	110,485	33.4	14.8
Montana	Steve Daines (R)	55.0	32,819	48,371	81,190	97.0	59.6
	Steve Bullock (D)	45.0	48,726	59,353	108,079	129.1	54.9
Colorado	Cory Gardner (R)	42.2	28,225	22,190	50,415	11.7	44.0
	John Hickenlooper (D)	53.5	42,908	15,568	58,476	13.6	26.6

State	Candidate						
Texas	John Cornyn (R)	53.5	33,924	12,017	45,941	3.0	26.2
	Mary J. Heger (D)	43.9	29,273	27,790	57,062	2.4	48.7
Kansas	Roger Marshall (R)	53.5	6,632	31,811	38,444	18.4	82.7
	Barbara Bollier (D)	41.6	28,519	20,436	48,955	23.4	41.7
Alabama	Tommy Tuberville (R)	60.1	8,549	4,150	12,699	3.4	32.7
	Doug Jones (D)	39.7	30,641	1,202	31,843	8.6	3.8
Alaska	Dan Sullivan (R)	54.0	10,463	139	10,602	20.2	1.3
	Al Gross (D)	41.3	19,363	14,133	33,497	63.7	42.2
Minnesota	Jason Lewis (R)	43.5	7,107	868	7,975	1.9	10.9
	Tina Smith (D)	48.8	16,230	655	16,885	4.1	3.9
New Hampshire	Corky Messner (R)	41.0	3,947	1,013	4,960	4.6	20.4
	Jeanne Shaheen (D)	56.7	19,353	329	19,682	18.2	1.7
Massachusetts	Kevin O'Connor (R)	33.3	912	684	1,596	0.3	42.9
	Ed Markey (D)	65.9	13,988	7,579	21,568	4.3	35.1
Virginia	Daniel Gade (R)	44.0	4,883	139	5,023	0.8	2.8
	Mark Warner (D)	56.0	17,217	7	17,224	2.8	0.0
Tennessee	Bill Hagerty (R)	62.1	11,701	1,547	13,247	2.6	11.7
	Marquita Bradshaw (D)	35.2	1,654	2,681	4,334	0.8	61.9
New Jersey	Rik Mehta (R)	41.1	587	1	588	0.1	0.2
	Cory Booker (D)	57.0	15,334	954	16,289	2.6	5.9
Mississippi	Cindy Hyde-Smith (R)	54.1	3,352	63	3,415	1.6	1.8
	Mike Espy (D)	44.0	12,201	642	12,842	5.8	5.0
New Mexico	Mark Ronchetti (R)	45.6	3,953	449	4,401	2.9	10.2
	Ben Ray Lujan (D)	51.7	8,936	1,813	10,749	7.1	16.9
Arkansas	Tom Cotton (R)	100.0	12,698	2	12,700	5.8	0.0

(continued)

TABLE 6 (continued)

State	Candidate	% Vote	Candidate Receipts ($1,000s)	Outside Spending ($1,000s)	Total Spending ($1,000s)	$ Per Voter	% Outside
Louisiana	Bill Cassidy (R)	59.3	11,346	1,195	12,541	3.7	9.5
Oregon	Joe Rae Perkins (R)	39.4	137	0	137	2.1	0.0
	Jeff Merkley (D)	56.9	11,235	0	11,235	3.4	0.0
Illinois	Mark Curran (R)	39.1	349	77	426	0.0	18.1
	Dick Durbin (D)	54.7	10,401	0	10,401	1.2	0.0
Oklahoma	James Inhofe (R)	62.9	5,901	9	5,911	2.1	0.2
	Abby Broyles (D)	32.8	2,072	25	2,097	0.7	1.2
West Virginia	Shelley Moore Capito (R)	70.3	5,748	11	5,759	4.1	0.2
	Paula Jean Swearengin (D)	27.0	2,047	0	2,047	1.5	0.0
Delaware	Lauren Witzke (R)	37.9	469	0	469	0.7	0.0
	Chris Coons (D)	59.4	7,120	50	7,170	10.0	0.7
Nebraska	Ben Sasse (R)	64.7	6,382	18	6,400	4.6	0.3
	Chris Janicek (D)	25.0	145	0	145	0.1	0.0
South Dakota	Mike Rounds (R)	65.7	4,751	1	4,752	7.3	0.0
	Dan Ahlers (D)	34.3	273	8	281	0.4	2.7
Idaho	Jim Risch (R)	62.6	3,322	0	3,322	2.6	0.0
	Paulette Jordan (D)	33.3	1,111	0	1,111	0.9	0.0
Wyoming	Mike Enzi (R)	73.1	2,970	851	3,821	8.9	22.3
	Cynthia Lummis (D)	26.9	552	0	552	1.3	0.0
Rhode Island	Allen Waters (R)	33.5	30	0	30	0	0.0
	Jack Reed (D)	66.5	3,998	0	3,998	5.0	0.0

Note: Incumbents are italicized.

Source: See footnote 22.

their cases, and the results, like those in House races, confirm that for the most part the very expensive campaigns mainly cemented Trump-dominated partisan loyalties.

Extraordinary levels of party loyalty were anticipated in preelection polls—only 4 percent of prospective partisan voters in Pew's October survey preferred the rival party's Senate candidate, the same as in House elections—and were confirmed by the statewide exit polls in the competitive states. Among the first ten states in table 6, the rate of partisan defection in exit polls averages 4.5 percentage points in the states besides Maine, where 13 percent of Democrats reported voting for Collins, and Arizona, where 12 percent of Republicans reported voting for Democratic challenger Mark Kelly. Like the House elections, the 2020 Senate elections extended the long-term trend toward ever more nationalized and president-centered elections that peaked with Trump on the ticket (table 7). The proportion of split outcomes is the second lowest on record, exceeded only in 2016. The correlation between the state-level vote for president and Senate is slightly higher than in 2016, when it was substantially larger than in any previous election. The number of senators representing states where their party won the most votes in the most recent presidential election reached an all-time high after the 2020 elections, ninety-four, and the number of states with split Senate delegations—one Republican and one Democrat—fell to six, the least since voters began electing senators. The separation of red and blue in the Senate now mirrors the separation of red and blue in presidential voting with great fidelity.

Unlike the House elections, the Senate elections produced no dramatic increase in the number of women candidates (table 4), and again with Collins the exception, their success depended on their party's presidential candidate's performance in the state. The two victorious Democratic women were incumbents, as were four of the five winning Republican women; the sixth, Cynthia Lummis, easily won the open seat in Wyoming, the reddest state of all in 2020. Loomis's win and defeats of Martha McSally's in Arizona and Kelly Loeffler's in Georgia left the party with seven women in the Senate; the Democrats will seat sixteen. The 2020 elections increased the Senate's ethnic diversity by two members. Kamala Harris's elevation from the Senate to the vice presidency was offset by the appointment of Alex Padilla as her replacement, the election of Democrat Ben Ray Lujan to New Mexico's open seat, and Raphael Warnock's victory in the Georgia runoff against Loeffler, raised the number of ethnic minority Senators to eleven (three Blacks, two Asian-Americans, six Hispanics).

TABLE 7. The nationalization of Senate elections, 1980–2020

Year	Same party victory (%)	Senate/president vote correlation	Senators from party of presidential winner	Split Senate state delegations
1980	61.8	.528	54	25
1984	48.4	.379	51	23
1988	48.4	.174	47	21
1992	70.5	.253	67	21
1996	70.5	.625	63	19
2000	70.5	.453	71	14
2004	79.4	.578	75	17
2008	80.0	.730	76	15
2012	81.8	.798	79	18
2016	100.0	.935	86	14
2020	97.1	.950	94	6

Source: Compiled by author.

The 117th Congress

The Trump presidency widened and deepened national political divisions, and even in defeat, Trump's legacy will make it very difficult for Joe Biden or anyone else to heal them. Biden assumed the presidency facing challenges even more daunting than those faced by Barack Obama, who took office in 2009 amid the deepest postwar recession to that date. The COVID-19 pandemic, largely ignored by the Trump White House during Trump's final months in office, grew increasingly severe during the fall of 2020, with records for new cases set almost daily; effective vaccines became available in December but were still many months away from distribution. In the meantime, measures needed to slow the disease's spread continued to disrupt and worsen the economic and social lives of millions of Americans. Biden also faced rising pressure to address the profound and persistent economic and racial inequities exposed by the pandemic and the police killings of unarmed Black citizens that sparked widespread protests in 2020. And he faced the increasingly ominous threat posed by global climate change, denied by Trump and aggravated by his administration's policies.

In meeting these challenges Biden could expect little, if any, help from the opposition. The newly elected Congress has a smaller Democratic

House majority than Obama enjoyed. The tied Senate gives the minority plenty of opportunity to obstruct; its leader Mitch McConnell, who on becoming Senate majority leader in 2011 said his top priority was to make Obama a one-term president, is not likely to be any more accommodating to Biden. Congressional Republicans hail from a world in which about 90 percent of their partisans approved of Trump's performance as president and an even larger proportion voted to reelect him. That Trump's grip on ordinary Republican voters did not end with his defeat is evident from their willingness to accept his delusional claim that Biden won only because of fraudulent votes and to cheer his attempts to overturn the result. In the *Economist*/YouGov poll taken a week after the election, only 14 percent of Trump's voters said Biden was the legitimate winner (compared with 99 percent of Biden's voters); 78 percent said Trump should not concede, 88 percent said he should pursue court cases aimed at throwing out Democratic votes, and 62 percent thought the court cases would change the outcome of the election. Three months later, the same poll found 74 percent of Republicans and 78 percent of Trump voters still denying Biden was the legitimate winner.[27]

Initially, very few congressional Republicans contradicted Trump's victory claim or congratulated Biden on his election; only a handful openly echoed Trump's charges of widespread fraud, but even fewer urged him to acknowledge Biden's win, and most reverted to their reflexive silence in the face of Trump's less defensible acts.[28] Even after a Trump-inspired mob vandalized the Capitol on January 6, 138 Republican representatives and eight Republican senators ended up supporting a last-ditch effort to derail Biden's inauguration by having Congress reject the normally-routine certification of his electoral college victory, demanding instead a review of the exhaustively debunked claims that vote-rigging in swing states had stolen the election from Trump. That so many Republicans chose to indulge rather than resist Trump's delusional and sinister attempt to subvert American democracy was both disturbing and a sign of how afraid they were to anger his supporters. Republicans who expected to face future primary electorates were understandably reluctant to get on Trump's wrong side out of fear of his solid support among ordinary Republicans, more of whom think of themselves as Trump supporters than as party supporters.[29] Trump's petty vindictiveness is well known, and given his postelection performance, not only disputing Biden's victory and inciting a mob to block its certification, but also refusing for weeks to cooperate in transition planning, there is every prospect that he will do all he can to torpedo Biden's presidency. This would include berating and threatening any congressional Republican collaborating with Biden or congressional Democrats, let alone joining them to impeach and convict him for provoking the Capitol riots. To remain in the public eye and retain his status as party leader, Trump is likely to make at least a pretense of running again in 2024, making cooperation with Biden and congressional Democrats even riskier for Republicans who might hope to inherit his following.

Cooperation between Biden and Congress will be difficult to arrange in any case. The congressional parties are polarized over what matters as well as what should be done about what they believe matters. Climate change, inequality, and social justice are not on the list of top priorities for Republican leaders or their voters, who remain ideologically opposed to many of the policies that might address them. Trump's "leadership" in the COVID-19 crisis managed to make the simple but necessary steps to curb the pandemic—wearing masks and social distancing in public spaces—into partisan issues. In Pew's postelection survey, only 16 percent of Trump voters wanted more COVID-19-related restrictions; 44 percent wanted less. Among Democrats, the preference was 66 percent more, 3 percent less.[30] Biden and congressional Democrats will thus face stiff resistance to any effort to organize an effective national response to the still dangerously high caseload that might require broad public cooperation. Congressional Republicans rejected an economic stimulus package large enough to make a difference before the election and are likely to revert to their politically convenient (when a Democrat is president) horror of deficit spending in the new Congress, limiting Biden and the Democrats' ability to address the economic devastation wrought by the pandemic. They no doubt anticipate that Biden will get the blame if the economy languishes.

Republicans will also act with an eye toward 2022, hoping to regain a House majority. Their chances are, by historical example, not bad but not a sure thing. The president's party usually loses House seats at the midterm (as in 2006, 2010, and 2018), but when it does not, the main reason is that it made paltry or no gains in the previous presidential year and has relatively few vulnerable seats to defend; 1998 and 2002 are examples. Democratic losses in 2020 put some limits on their vulnerability in 2022. They will defend only seven seats in districts won by Trump, while Republicans will be defending nine seats in Biden districts. But House districts will be redrawn for 2022, and as after the 2010 Census, Republicans will have the final say in the drawing of many more districts (188) than will Democrats (73) and will certainly try to use this to their advantage to add at least a few seats.[31] Democrats are in slightly better shape in the Senate, where all thirteen seats they will defend in 2022 were won by Biden; three of the twenty-two seats to be defended by Republicans were won by Biden, but by small margins (Georgia, Wisconsin, and Pennsylvania). Whatever happens in 2022, the Senate is likely to remain closely divided.

The prospect, then, is for considerably more conflict than cooperation between the parties during the 117th Congress. The gap between the average 2020 presidential vote in House districts won by Democratic and Republican representatives—an indicator of the gap between the preferences of their respective electoral constituencies—was 26.3 points, not far off the all-time record of 28.8 points set in 2016. The Senate is divided almost entirely into Democrats from Biden states and Republicans from Trump states. The parties represent demographically and ideologically divergent coalitions that remain deeply suspicious of the other side's aims and values. Insofar as members of Congress faithfully represent the people who elected them, intense partisan conflict with a high potential for legislative gridlock is likely to persist. This does not bode well for effective government in a time of national crisis.

Notes

1. Gary C. Jacobson, "The Triumph of Polarized Partisanship: Donald Trump's Improbable Victory in 2016," *Political Science Quarterly* 132 (Spring 2017): 1–34; Gary C. Jacobson, "Extreme Referendum: Donald Trump and the 2018 Midterm Elections," *Political Science Quarterly* 134 (Spring 2019): 1–30.
2. Gary C. Jacobson, "*Divide et Impera*: Polarization in Trump's America," in *Four Years of Trump: The U.S. and the World*, ed. Mario Del Pero and Paolo Magri (Milan: Instituto per gli Studi di Politica Internazional, 2020), 17–49.
3. Gary C. Jacobson, "Donald Trump and the Parties: Impeachment, Pandemic, Protest and Electoral Politics in 2020," *Presidential Studies Quarterly* (December 2020), in press.
4. Janet Hook, "Bernie Sanders Makes an Urgent Plea for Unity at the Democratic Convention," *Los Angeles Times*, August 17, 2020.
5. Michael Dimock and Richard Wike, "America Is Exceptional in the Nature of Its Political Divide," Pew Research Center, October 13, 2020, https://www.pewresearch.org/fact-tank/2020/11/13/america-is-exceptional -in-the-nature-of-its-political-divide.
6. Claudia Deane and John Gramlich, "2020 Election Reveals Two Broad Voting Coalitions Fundamentally at Odds," Pew Research Center, November 6, 2020, https://www.pewresearch.org/fact-tank/2020/11/06/2020-election -reveals-two-broad-voting-coalitions-fundamentally-at-odds/.

7. Logit is a variation on ordinary least squares regression that is more suitable for a dependent variable taking only two discrete values—win or lose.

8. All previous postwar election swings have larger standard deviations; it cannot be computed for years ending in "2," because redistricting destroys comparability.

9. The value of incumbency is estimated here by a modified version of the Gelman-King index that substitutes the district-level presidential vote in the current or, for midterms, most recent presidential election for the lagged vote, allowing years ending in "2" and districts redrawn between apportionment decades to be included; for details, see Gary C. Jacobson, "It's Nothing Personal: The Decline of the Incumbency Advantage in U.S. House Elections," *Journal of Politics* 77, no. 3 (July 2015): 861–73.

10. For comparison, see Gary Jacobson and Jamie Carson, *The Politics of Congressional Elections*, 10th ed. (Lanham, MD: Rowman & Littlefield, 2020), 66.

11. Turnout data are from Michael McDonald's United States Election Project, reported at electproject.org.

12. Susan Davis, "How the GOP Defied Expectations Down the Ballot," NPR, November 17, 2020, https://www.npr.org/2020/11/17/935455984/how-the -gop-defied-expectations-down-the-ballot.

13. In the June 2018 Pew survey, only 16 percent of Democratic women said that Trump respected women, while 79 percent of Republican women said he did. In the twenty-four YouGov surveys taken during the first half of 2018, 81 percent of Democratic women disapproved of how Trump was handling "women's rights," while only 9 percent approved; their opinions on his handling of health care, immigration, and the environment were nearly identical. In the 2018 Cooperative Congressional Election Study, 96 percent of Democratic women disapproved of Trump's performance, 89 percent strongly.

14. Li Zhou, "Why Republican Women Candidates Had Such a Strong Year," *Vox*, November 14, 2020, https://www.vox.com/21562289/republican-women -election-records.

15. Jacob Knutson, "11 GOP Congressional Nominees Support QAnon Conspiracy," Axios, July 12, 2020, https://www.axios.com/qanon-nominees -congress-gop-8086ed21-b7d3-46af-9016-d132e65ba801.html; Andrea Salcedo, "Marjorie Taylor Greene, Who Backs QAnon and Has Made Racist Remarks, Wins Congressional Seat," *Washington Post*, November 4, 2020.

16. Data on campaign spending are from "Congressional Races," Center for Responsive Politics, November 22, 2020, https://www.opensecrets.org /races.

17. Gary C. Jacobson, "Money and Mobilization in the 2018 Congressional Elections" (delivered at "Partisanship Reconsidered: A Conference to Honor David Magleby," Brigham Young University Provo, Utah, June 6–8, 2019).
18. Ibid.
19. Jacobson, "Extreme Referendum."
20. The average is from 114 surveys taken by five polling organizations analyzed by the author.
21. "Large Shares of Voters Plan to Vote a Straight Party Ticket for President, House, and Senate," Pew Research Center, October 21, 2020, https://www .pewresearch.org/politics/2020/10/21/large-shares-of-voters-plan-to-vote -a-straight-party-ticket-for-president-senate-and-house/.
22. The *Economist*/YouGov results are reported at https://today.yougov.com /topics/economist/survey-results.
23. Results of the 1972–2016 exit polls are available at https://www.nytimes .com/interactive/2016/11/08/us/politics/election-exit-polls.html; the 2020 exit polls are still in preliminary form and are available at https://www .nytimes.com/interactive/2020/11/03/us/elections/exit-polls-president .html.
24. In this survey, 30 percent labeled themselves liberal, 31 percent moderate, and 36 percent conservative.
25. Elena Schneider, "How ActBlue Has Transformed Democratic Politics," *Politico*, October 30, 2020.
26. Ellen Barry, "The Democrats Went All Out against Susan Collins. Rural Maine Grimaced," *New York Times*, November 17, 2020.
27. *Economist*/YouGov poll, February 6–9, 2021, at https://docs.cdn.yougov .com/rqqxdo2ujy/econTabReport.
28. Paul Kane, Mike DeBonis, and Rachael Bade, "Most Republicans Greet Trump's Push to Overturn the Election with Customary Response: Silence," *Washington Post*, November 20, 2020.
29. The NBC News / *Wall Street Journal* poll has asked Republican respondents in thirty-two surveys taken 2017–21, "Do you consider yourself to be more of a supporter of Donald Trump or more of a supporter of the Republican Party?" On average, 52 percent have said Trump, and 40 percent the Republican Party; Trump has been preferred in all but three of these surveys, with two ties.
30. "Sharp Divisions on Vote Counts, as Biden Gets High Marks for His Post-Election Conduct," Pew Research Center, November 20, 2020, https:// www.pewresearch.org/politics/2020/11/20/sharp-divisions-on-vote-counts -as-biden-gets-high-marks-for-his-post-election-conduct/. The other respondents in each group wanted restrictions to remain as they are.
31. David Wasserman, "The Cook Political Report's 2021 Redistricting Overview," January 26, 2021, at https://cookpolitical.com/analysis/house/redis tricting/cook-political-reports-2021-redistricting-overview.

The Meaning of the 2020 Election

FUNDAMENTALLY DIVIDED

Andrew Rudalevige

In 2016, when Donald J. Trump was elected president over Hillary Rod-ham Clinton, political science models grounded in the economic "funda-mentals" that help forecast electoral outcomes converged on a similar conclusion: it was a toss-up. And so it proved, with Trump earning an Electoral College victory on the basis of fewer than 80,000 votes (out of close to 15 million) spread across three key states even as he fell nearly 3 million votes short of Clinton's popular vote total nationally.[1]

In 2020, though, no one was sure such models would have any utility, given the COVID-19 pandemic and the recession it sparked. Usually, second-quarter growth—change in the gross domestic product (GDP) from April to June—is an excellent predictor of the electoral results in November. But in the second quarter of 2020, lockdowns prompted by the pandemic caused GDP to decline 9.5 percent, meaning that on an annu-alized basis the economy had shrunk by nearly one-third. Plugged into existing models, that off-the-charts result suggested Trump would win only 31 percent of the popular vote—a nearly impossible result in a two-person race.[2] Further, since the recession had been intentionally induced to combat the coronavirus crisis, Trump received little blame for the eco-nomic downturn.[3] That in turn caused forecasters to create off-the-cuff workarounds, deleting economic variables or even positing artificial "politically neutral" GDP growth of 2.5 percent to stand in for the actual (but also misleading) data.[4] As one political scientist quipped in April, "It's about the fundamentals—whatever those will be."[5]

Yet other indicators were more consistent. All elections involving an incumbent are a referendum on that incumbent's performance, and the 2020 election was stark in this regard. The president was eager to make the election about himself and to dominate the airwaves; with rare exceptions Trump pitched not his policies but his person, not "issues" but "attitude." For the first time the Republican National Convention did not bother to adopt a platform laying out the proposals it hoped to enact if the party won the election, merely asserting that it "has and will continue to enthusiastically support the president's America-first agenda," whatever that might prove to be.[6] For his part, Democratic challenger Joseph Biden, the former vice president, was happy to cede the limelight. He ran a low-key coronavirus counterpoint to William McKinley's 1896 "front porch" campaign even as Trump and his aides mocked him for "hiding in his basement."[7]

As he bid for reelection, however, Trump's public approval ratings had never surpassed 50 percent during his time in office. He won the presidency in November 2016 with just 46 percent of the national popular vote, compared with Clinton's 48 percent. He did not receive the usual inaugural "honeymoon" boost from the public, starting his presidency with 45 percent approval in January 2017. That figure proved remarkably stable. It dipped below 40 percent from time to time and occasionally rose as high as 49 percent. But by late October, it was again at 46 percent in Gallup's final preelection survey—and at 46.8 percent of the electorate on Election Day, November 3.[8]

By the same token, as early as July 2019 polls commissioned by NBC News and the *Wall Street Journal* showed Biden with 51 percent of the national vote in a projected matchup with Trump. In October 2019, that figure was 50 percent. In March 2020, a couple of weeks after Biden racked up big wins in the Super Tuesday primaries, it was 52 percent.[9] A year into the same polls' time series—by July 2020 tracking a real rather than hypothetical contest—Biden was at 51 percent. In September, at 51 percent. And on November 3, with voter turnout the highest in more than a century, Biden won 51.3 percent of the ballots cast across the United States, outpacing Trump by some 7 million votes. That was the highest percentage of the vote for someone challenging an incumbent president since Franklin Roosevelt won 57.4 percent in his landslide win over Herbert Hoover in 1932.

Although Trump did not carry any state he lost in 2016, Biden rebuilt the Democratic "blue wall" in the upper Midwest that had crumbled for Clinton, winning Michigan and Wisconsin as well as Pennsylvania. He flipped Georgia and Arizona too, albeit narrowly—the latter voting Democratic for only the second time since 1948. Biden outpaced Clinton's vote percentage in forty-four of the fifty states. That was enough for him to rack up 306 electoral votes as well, winning a comfortable majority and claiming the presidency.

One fundamental had indeed mattered: from the time Donald Trump announced his first candidacy in 2015 to the time he left office in early 2021, a majority of Americans never supported him.

Biden's play of the campaign cards thereby rested on the hand the president had dealt him, and it paid off. It took advantage of Trump's aggressive divisiveness, which was both effect and cause of America's deepening polarization. It stressed Trump's managerial failures with regard to the coronavirus pandemic. And it rested on Biden's own appeal: as not-Trump, as not-Hillary Clinton, as not-socialist—in short, as himself. Even so, that dichotomy did not always translate down ballot, where Republicans generally outran the top of the ticket and greatly exceeded preelection expectations. One important meaning of the election, then, is that the United States is deeply divided, with a perilous path to working as one even in the midst of crisis. The likelihood of gridlocked governance loomed over the incoming Biden administration.

A Divider, Not a Uniter

If the stability of the public's assessment of President Trump made the final tally unsurprising, that stability itself was somewhat shocking. As just noted, the shape of the November 2020 vote was visible in November 2019—yet the year in between was chock full of politically salient, even unprecedented, events. Just a sampling would have to start with accusations that Trump withheld appropriated military aid to pressure the president of Ukraine to criminally investigate the Biden family's business dealings in that country, Trump's subsequent impeachment by the House of Representatives, and his acquittal in the Senate. There were successive, massive waves of COVID-19, downplayed by the White House even though Trump himself became one of more than 9 million cases (though fortunately not one of the more than 230,000 deaths) in the United States as of Election Day. There were lockdowns that drove the economy into a deep recession, millions of people out of work, and huge increases in federal spending. There were widespread protests over racial justice sparked by the murder of an unarmed, prone Black suspect by Minneapolis police officers, marches that spilled over into violence and looting while also featuring the use of federal officers to attack even peaceful demonstrators in the name of "law and order." There was an array of natural disasters, including record numbers of destructive wildfires and hurricanes. Then, less than seven weeks before the election, iconic Supreme Court justice

Ruth Bader Ginsburg died—to be replaced by the far more conservative Amy Coney Barrett in extraordinarily rapid fashion six weeks later.

Theories of public opinion assume that opinion is driven by events. But the real-world dramatics seemed to have little effect on people's opinion of the president, or ultimately on their votes. In part, this reflected geographic sorting, in which people move to like-minded communities, surrounded by others who reinforce their ideologies. Sorting extends past the physical world to the virtual one as well, with the growth of news (or sometimes "news") ecosystems catering to preexisting beliefs. Either way, Americans have frequently chosen to live in "siloed echo chambers [which] increasingly prevented objective fact from penetrating."[10] As a result, people increasingly view the world through partisan-colored glasses. Consider that in the fall of 2016, with Barack Obama still in office and a Clinton victory expected, the Gallup Poll's Economic Confidence Index measured Democratic respondents' confidence at plus-18 and Republicans' at minus-31. In early 2017, however, with little actual change in the nation's economic performance, those ratings suddenly flipped: Democratic assessments dropped nearly 40 points, to minus-20, while Republicans' jumped almost 80 points, to plus-46. Such sentiments reversed again within a month of the 2020 election. Again, no real changes had occurred—indeed, markets shot up upon news of the Biden victory and its promise of administrative stability (and new federal stimulus dollars). But while in October 2020 just 4 percent of Republican identifiers said they expected to be worse off financially a year later, by late November that figure had increased tenfold, to 40 percent.[11]

This is testament to the fierce partisan polarization that has become a part of many Americans' very identity, extending the fierce tribal loyalty once reserved for sports teams to one's political affiliation. For much of the twentieth century, the Democratic and Republican Parties were both broad coalitions spanning a wide ideological range. But as the Democratic Party promoted civil rights measures during the 1960s, Republicans saw an opportunity to lure southern Democrats who opposed those measures; conversely, liberal Republicans in the North and Pacific West began to be displaced by Democrats. The upshot was that each party became internally homogenous, with little overlap and less incentive to respond to contrary opinion. Voters sorted themselves into those parties—which in itself fostered polarization even though the broad distribution of preferences across the electorate may not have dramatically changed. One upshot of this sorting is a rise in *negative* partisanship. Those for whom politics is

foremost among their group identities are increasingly driven less by positive fandom for their side than by disgust with the other team. This is more
consequential than the (obviously correct!) view that the Red Sox are good
while the Yankees are evil, since the need to churn up fear and loathing in
order to drive political activism then drives political discourse. As Ezra
Klein notes, politicians looking to activate their base must make appeals
that "border on the apocalyptic." In short: "You don't just need support.
You need anger."[12]

Anger and apocalypse were prominent in Donald Trump's skill set—
and the way he deployed them was one reason for the public's rock-solid
assessments of his performance, both positive and negative. In so doing he
departed from past efforts by incumbents running for reelection based on
bipartisan achievements. By 1996 Bill Clinton had worked with a Republican Congress to enact welfare reform and move toward a balanced budget.
In 2004 George W. Bush touted his management of the war on terror to
keep Americans safe in a dangerous world. In 2012 Barack Obama stressed
his successes in dealing with the challenges he inherited from his predecessor: "Osama bin Laden is dead, and General Motors is alive!" As Clinton put it, "The president is supposed to be a unifying force, not just in
rhetoric but in fact."[13]

To be sure, Clinton's "fact" is hard to achieve on the ground, even for
presidents who aspire to do so. Most presidential elections are close (just
40 percent of winning candidates since 1824 have won more than 52 percent
of the popular vote, with only a single instance since 1988). Thus, most presidents operate on narrow margins of popular support. Public approval of all
presidents over the past fifty-five years, since Lyndon Johnson took office in
1965, averages to 50 percent. And even that figure is polarized, with a huge
gap between Democratic and Republican respondents.[14]

Even so, Donald Trump marked the mathematical extreme of that
trend, both in result and intent—the stylistic mirror image of George W.
Bush's stated desire to be a "uniter, not a divider."[15] Gallup found that as of
late October 2020, 94 percent of Republicans approved of the job Trump was
doing—but just 4 percent of Democrats did.[16] On Election Day, those figures were confirmed at the ballot box.[17] Exit polls suggested that three-
quarters of voters had made up their minds well before Labor Day.[18]

Why? We might consider a brief alternate history of the Trump years,
in which the president did seek common ground. On this earth, January
2017 kicked off with the president-elect releasing his past tax returns and
corporate financial records, having divested entirely from the Trump
Organization. Trump also deleted his personal Twitter account and

turned down his daughter's and son-in-law's requests to join the White House staff, concerned about the message such nepotism would send. He demanded that the intelligence community investigate all efforts by Russia to interfere with the 2016 election. Trump's cabinet choices drew on preeminent policymakers across party lines—he even asked former first lady Michelle Obama to serve with him as the UN ambassador (she declined). "I am not beholden to any party or any interest and my administration will not be either," he proclaimed in his inaugural address, adding, "I pledge to every citizen of our land that I will be president for all Americans, and this is so important to me. For those who have chosen not to support me in the past . . . I'm reaching out to you for your guidance and your help so that we can work together and unify our great country."[19]

In office, alt-Trump quickly turned to a series of bipartisan policy proposals. He traveled to Oroville, California, where a failing dam had become a symbol of how crumbling infrastructure could become life-threatening, to roll out vast investments in American roads and bridges, dams and ports. This was to be paired with new programs aimed to support "human infrastructure" in both isolated rural areas and inner cities. California had provided the entire margin of Trump's popular vote loss to Hillary Rodham Clinton, a point Trump alluded to: "I know you didn't vote for me," the president said. "But I'm here to vote for you."

In keeping with his campaign pledges, Trump proposed tax increases on the wealthiest Americans in order to shore up Social Security and Medicare. Likewise, as promised, he proposed a replacement plan for the Affordable Care Act that expanded coverage, lowered premium costs, and protected those with preexisting conditions. An immigration compromise soon followed, with a new border wall quickly beginning to rise even as young "Dreamers" were given citizenship. "I've been on both sides of every issue during my career," the new president joked, realizing the freedom of action that being unencumbered by long political experience granted him. Trump even renominated Merrick Garland to fill the vacancy on the Supreme Court left by the death of Antonin Scalia nearly a full year before. The Senate majority leader, who had held up Obama's original nomination of Garland, received a scolding: "We all need to work together," Trump said, "and the court should be above ideology."

To Democrats' shock (and to the displeasure of many Republican partisans), Trump's call for unity after a bitter campaign seemed to produce just that. The president's approval ratings soared—to 61 percent upon his inauguration, which drew record crowds to Washington, DC, and to 72 percent when his first hundred days were marked by the successful passage of many of his legislative proposals. This set a tone for the administration that allowed Trump to build a center-right coalition that promoted an "America First" agenda even as it put Democrats on their heels by co-opting some of their main policy goals. "Midterm loss" was held to a handful of seats in 2018, and when the coronavirus arrived in the United States in 2020 the nation agreed on the need for shared sacrifice in the name of public health. The president made the threat clear from the outset. He elevated the role of independent scientists, consistently stressed that wearing a face mask in public was not a partisan matter, and won kudos for his management of the crisis.

And then? At the end of this dream sequence, we woke up. For of course that was not the path the president and the new administration chose. But it could have been.

Although the party sorting described above means that normally "all the pressures within each party come from the same side, pulling elected officials away from the electorally safer center ground," Trump could arguably have been immune from this dynamic, having created his own base.[20] He ran as a policy outlier in the GOP primaries, against international alliances, free trade, and immigration, and in favor of spending on infrastructure, raising taxes on the rich, universal health care, and maintaining Social Security and Medicare. The Republican establishment was not pleased with his heterodoxy, but many less ideological primary voters were.[21] Trump's ads regarding trade policy, for instance, were (ironically, given his 2016 opponent) very similar to Bill Clinton's in 1992.[22] Careful readers may have noticed that some of the words just attributed to the 2017 inaugural address were in fact spoken by President-elect Trump—on election night itself in 2016.

Yet that early outreach did not recur. Having pulled the Republican Party into his orbit, Trump never moved toward the middle. As a matter of tone, January 2017 found Trump already backpedaling from bipartisanship. Pre-inauguration tweets charged the intelligence agencies investigating Russian involvement in the election with "made up, phony facts" and suggested that their actions resembled "Nazi Germany." They also attacked Democrats and "head clown Chuck Schumer," as well as civil rights icon and congressman John Lewis, and for good measure targeted the media ("FAKE NEWS"), pollsters and polls ("phony," "rigged"), Hillary Clinton ("guilty as hell"), and even the cast of the hit musical *Hamilton*.[23] Trump's inaugural address likewise failed to build bridges. Its dark tone excoriated past political leadership and painted a bleak picture of the United States beset by a weak military, "the ravages of other countries," and "the crime and the gangs and the drugs."

Space does not permit a full recounting of the president's feuds, even those limited to social media. Trump's Twitter feed alone contained 24,685 entries from January 20, 2017, through Election Day 2020.[24] Its ethos barely changed from the 2016 campaign. As of May 2019, the *New York Times* tallied nearly 600 people and organizations attacked through that medium—not least the "failing *New York Times*" itself, an insult used 205 times by the president to that point.[25]

The media were a favored foil, but other thematic regularities aimed at categorizing Americans into distinct groups that were good or bad depending on their support of Trump himself. As political scientist Gary Jacobson observed, "Virtually everything he has said or done as president has catered exclusively to the coalition that elected him, its white national-ist segment in particular, but also small-government and religious conser-vatives."[26] His rhetoric created and constantly reinforced competing identities: "Republicans and real Americans" (as Trump tweeted in 2018) versus traitors to the "real" America. The former were concentrated in white, rural areas, while the latter were racially diverse and largely urban or suburban. Cosmopolitan elites and their world, Trump told his sup-porters, had victimized them. They needed to—quite literally—wall it off. Past leaders had not been smart. But he and they were.

The rally that officially kicked off Trump's bid for reelection in June 2019 provides a snapshot.[27] On stage in Orlando, Florida—in "MAGA, MAGA, MAGA, we're in MAGA country, that I can tell you"—the president touted the national economy, his immigration policy, and his judicial selections. But he focused less on policy than on shared victimhood. Their enemies were the "Deep State" and political correctness, the "great and illegal witch hunt" (the Mueller investigation), and "the Fake News Media and their part-ner in Crime, the Democrats." Together "they went after my family, my business, my finances, my employees, almost everyone that I've ever known or worked with, but they are really going after you. . . . Our Radical Demo-crat opponents are driven by hatred, prejudice, and rage. They want to destroy you and they want to destroy our country, as we know it." In his inaugural address Trump had invoked "American carnage"; the Orlando rally suggested a similarly bleak landscape. "A vote for any Democrat in 2020 is a vote for the rise of radical socialism and the destruction of the American dream," he told the crowd.

The president's policies and rhetoric regularly attacked not just Wash-ington Democrats but "Democrat cities" and other locales that dissented from his policies. Puerto Rico received far less attention (and more impor-tant, less money) from the administration after being hit by hurricanes than did Texas or Florida.[28] "Total DISASTER" Chicago "protected criminals," with shootings "totally out of control."[29] As for the nation's most populous state, "California is going to hell," Trump tweeted: it had too many homeless people, too many taxes, too much crime, too many wildfires and electrical brownouts. Responding to Black Lives Matter protests across the country, Trump declared in September 2020 that his administration would "not allow Federal tax dollars to fund cities that allow themselves to deteriorate into lawless zones."[30] The president directed his administration to identify "anarchist jurisdictions"—specifying New York, Seattle, Washington, and Portland, Oregon—and eliminate their grant funding; his political appointees, even in the Justice Department, dutifully complied.[31]

Such localized critiques frequently veered into more universal and racially tinged campaigns. "Issues like immigration, race, and Islam were central not only to Trump's election but also to his presidency," three political scientists concluded; "the debate over who is and can be an American" moved from the campaign trail to the White House.[32] The attacks on John Lewis and Atlanta were followed by tweets about another prominent Black congressman, Elijah Cummings, who represented parts of Baltimore: "Cumming [sic] District is a disgusting, rat and rodent infested mess. No human being would want to live there." He also adapted an old trope to demand that four nonwhite female members of Congress—three of whom were born in the United States—should "go back and help fix the totally broken and crime infested places from which they came" instead of criticizing his administration.[33] Trump had already made clear what he thought of those metaphorical places: "shithole countries" whose emigrants (if from Haiti) "all have AIDS" or (if from Nigeria) should "go back to their huts."[34] None of this, Fox News anchor Chris Wallace noted, required much imagination to see as "the worst kind of racial stereotype." As Wallace said, "I'm not reading between the lines. I'm reading the lines."[35]

Those lines traced others drawn throughout the administration with regard to the role of race in American history and memory. Early on Trump defended white supremacists who marched to protest the planned relocation of a Charlottesville, Virginia, statue of Confederate general Robert E. Lee; later he would support the so-called Western chauvinist Proud Boys hate group. Statues and symbols glorifying the Confederacy remained a flashpoint throughout Trump's term.[36] The 1619 Project, a journalistic initiative that stressed the centrality of slavery to American political history, also came in for criticism. Trump attacked it as overly critical and even unpatriotic, creating the 1776 Commission in response and holding a White House conference to "address [its] distortions."[37] Trump even created a task force "for building and rebuilding monuments to American heroes" and threatened to veto a defense authorization act that mandated renaming military bases named for Confederate military officers.[38] Most of these statues were erected during the Jim Crow era to commemorate white supremacy, and those who explicitly betrayed the United States and killed its soldiers in the name of slavery were hardly American heroes. The ahistorical claim that the Confederate flag represented "heritage, not hate" appealed to some (but hardly all) white southerners and was adopted by northern Trump fans too.[39] Indeed, dissolution of union was a key element of Trump's governing style. In short, as veteran journalist Ron Brownstein put it, "Trump has governed as a wartime president for red America, with blue America as his target."[40]

Trump's attacks aimed to rally his base, with a special emphasis on attracting white women living the "Suburban Lifestyle Dream." He pitched himself as "savior of the suburbs," asking "why would Suburban Women vote for Biden and the Democrats when Democrat run cities are now rampant with crime . . . which could easily spread to the suburbs." Worse, "they will reconstitute, on steroids, their low income suburbs plan!"[41] That "plan" was an Obama-era initiative seeking to "foster inclusive communities" through enforcement of the Fair Housing Act. Trump touted his rollback of that policy: reducing racial segregation, he pronounced, would increase crime and lower housing prices. "Low income housing" would be "hell for suburbia," he said. Indeed, it "would mean abolishing, ruining the suburbs."[42]

All of this did, certainly, drive voter turnout—including in the suburbs. As noted, a record number of eligible voters participated in the election, at a rate (some 66.5%) not seen since 1900. And Trump's base was indeed motivated, even fervent. Some thought that the nation's pre-COVID economic performance justified reelection. Even some who were harmed by administration policies—farmers who lost income as a result of the administration's trade wars, for instance—saw defending Trump's honor as a defense of their own invested emotions in his success. Some who had long bemoaned immorality in politics saw Trump as an imperfect but long-sought vehicle for anti-abortion and pro-Christian policymaking initiatives. Some simply saw decrying left-wing anger at Trump as the independently virtuous value of "owning the libs." The pull of the culture wars was potent—and broadly credited with Trump's notable gains among Latino voters, which cut into 2016 Democratic margins in seventy-eight of the one hundred U.S. counties with a Latino-majority population. Republican charges that Democrats

would "defund the police" and turn the nation toward socialism clearly res-
onated with a subset of conservative Latino voters, themselves a diverse
group reflecting the wider divisions of American politics along the lines of
religiosity and population density.[43]

The problem for Trump was that personalizing the vote drove turnout
in both directions. As one Floridian put it in 2018, "My vote is driven by
Trump 1,000 percent," with the punchline: "I just find him despicable."[44]
Overall, Trump's championing of policy positions made them less popular
over time; support for increased levels of immigration and favorable views
of immigrants, for example, rose sharply from 2017 to 2020, especially
among younger voters.[45] And it turned out that suburbs were already far
more diverse and tolerant places than in Trump's memory and rhetoric.
White suburbanites (especially women) saw the president's family separation policy as needlessly cruel, for instance, and protests supporting the
Black Lives Matter movement sprang up in a wide array of places with few
resident Black lives. There was far less concern about "anarchy" than about
school shootings, and Trump's warnings that "they want to take your guns
away" fell flat among suburbanites. Indeed, internal polling in both parties suggested that "Trump's law-and-order messaging alienated far more
women than it attracted."[46] His hectoring demeanor in the first 2020
debate—insulting, unwilling to allow others to speak, and too often fact-
free—didn't help either.

In the end, Trump held his own compared with 2016 in urban areas and
in "pivot counties" that had shifted to him from Obama. But he lost ground
dramatically in suburbs with large numbers of college-educated voters.
Election analyst Harry Enten went so far as to argue that the difference
between 2016 and 2020 was simply that "enough well-to-do white people
changed their votes from non-Dem[ocratic] in 2016 to Biden in 2020."[47]
That was especially true of well-to-do white women, as the gender gap
expanded to a chasm. In one October CNN poll, Biden led among female
voters by 24 points; exit polls ultimately suggested 15 points. Women also
rated him more favorably than Trump by large margins on multiple issues
the president saw as his strengths, including crime and safety, the economy, and nominations to the Supreme Court.[48]

The upshot was that Trump began his term as a minority leader,
cemented opinions about him, and drove away potential support. The lack
of movement in his approval ratings was the product of his lack of outreach to anyone new. Longtime political analyst Charlie Cook, more than a
year before the election, warned that Trump "seems unwilling or unable to
reach or even talk to those beyond [his] base, those situated between his

core support and the opposition camp."[49] And that opposition was energized and unified: any rifts in the Democratic coalition were quickly sealed by Trump's attacks.

Asked whether he needed to expand his base, Trump himself replied, "I think my base is so strong I'm not sure that I have to do that."[50] Yet this ran up against a simple fact: math. If—as one supporter whom Trump retweeted declared—"only true Americans can see that President Trump is making America great," the census of "true Americans" defined that way simply fell short of a winning coalition.[51] As GOP campaign guru Karl Rove wrote in his memoir, "A party's base is, by definition, part of a larger whole, which itself is only part of an even larger electorate. . . . Elections are about addition, not subtraction."[52]

In that spirit perhaps one hopeful meaning of the election is that aggressive efforts at minority factionalism are insufficient for electoral victory. Even Trump seemed to know this, though he expressed it through a distressing corollary as he opposed pandemic-inspired moves to simplify election logistics: that Democrats wanted "levels of voting that if you'd ever agreed to it, you'd never have a Republican elected in this country again." In other words, one way to avoid addition is through differential subtraction. As disgruntled conservative Bill Kristol responded, "Today's Republican Party spends far more time and effort trying to suppress voters than convince voters."[53]

Mourning in America

One might have expected the coronavirus pandemic to disrupt the pattern of divisiveness. There is a long history of the nation rallying around the president during crisis. At such times the president has a unique opportunity to simultaneously do good for the country and do well for himself— simply by doing the job. Trump told an interviewer in August that "George Washington would have had a hard time beating me before the plague came in."[54] But while the pandemic represented a huge challenge, it also presented a huge stage upon which Trump could have showcased his leadership and management skills and thereby unify the country. He did not. One result, as a 2020 ad attacking him put it, was "mourning in America."[55]

Far from forging consensus, Trump's reaction to the coronavirus pandemic wound up exacerbating polarization, from his attempts at blame shifting, to a flurry of falsehoods about the dangers the virus posed, to the politicization of public health measures. At times, to be sure, Trump seemed to realize the gravity of the situation and the need for presidential leadership.

In mid-March he said he viewed his role "as, in a sense a wartime president" against "an invisible enemy." He called for shared sacrifice, "because we are all in this together, and we will come through together."[56]

But this plea came after he publicly downplayed the severity of the virus, telling Americans in February it was no more serious than the flu and that American cases totaled "15 people, and the 15 within a couple of days is going to be down to close to zero, that's a pretty good job we've done."[57] Within a week of assuming the "wartime" mantle, Trump pivoted within a single press conference from asserting that "no force is equal to the strength of a . . . unified America, a united America" to attacking the Obama administration ("We inherited a broken, obsolete system"), congressional Democrats, China, and frequent critic Senator Mitt Romney, as well as stressing that his "incredible team" needed no help from past policymakers ("If I felt that if I called, I'd learn something . . . I would make the call in two minutes. But I don't see that happening"). Trump went on to complain repeatedly that his own sacrifices were unappreciated ("It cost me billions and billions of dollars to be president") and only attracted "nasty" questions.[58] Two days later, prompting alarm from medical experts, the president quickly pivoted to urging businesses and stores to reopen, promising "packed churches" at Easter in April: "We've got to get it open—our people want it open."[59]

As unemployment rose to levels not seen since the Great Depression, Trump's stress on easing lockdowns rather than preaching patient precautions grew more strident. He urged less testing for the disease in order to make case numbers appear low. He pushed unproven medical treatments, sidelined scientific guidance that recommended continued caution, and hired new advisers more ready to provide his preferred advice. And in mid-April he sent tweets attacking Democratic governors who had imposed lockdowns in their states: "LIBERATE MICHIGAN!" he demanded. "LIBERATE VIRGINIA! LIBERATE MINNESOTA!"[60] The war, in short, became one waged against those seeking to keep limits in place. And it came frighteningly close to becoming a shooting war. After hundreds of armed protesters stormed the Michigan state capitol to protest Governor Gretchen Whitmer's stay-at-home order—with signs that compared the governor to Adolf Hitler and threatened the "tyrant bitch" with "the rope"—Trump described them as "very good people."[61] In late fall a militia group was charged with plotting to storm the capitol, hold Whitmer and other state officials hostage, and carry out their televised executions.[62]

By then, the president himself had caught COVID, requiring hospitalization and supplemental oxygen, along with steroids and an experimental drug cocktail. The treatment was successful, but when Trump returned to the White House he did not take the opportunity to change his tone on the severity of the virus—instead, his message was that because he had recovered, the disease was not a threat. ("It affects virtually nobody," he said in September—only "elderly people with heart problems."[63]) The president was clearly done dealing with the disease as a public policy matter. He had long since returned to in-person campaign rallies and indoor events at the White House, at which numerous White House staffers and Trump associates became sick from the virus. Ten days before the election Trump blamed the media for their attention to a disease that by then had killed at least 230,000 Americans: "That's all I hear about now.... Turn on television, 'Covid, Covid, Covid Covid Covid.'" He soon claimed the disease would vanish from the airwaves on November 4, since "they want to make our numbers look as bad as possible for the election."[64] In fact, coverage accelerated after the election because deaths did too. By early December, more than 3,000 Americans were dying from the coronavirus each day—more than died on September 11, 2001, or in the 1941 Pearl Harbor attack.

Instead of inspiring national unity, then, Trump's reaction to the crisis played out along familiar, partisan lines. The president largely refused to wear a face mask and mocked those who did, making that safety measure a symbol of the culture wars. In September he inaccurately blamed the "tremendous death rates" in "blue states and blue state-managed" for the scope of the pandemic.[65] Conservative news outlets echoed the suggestion that the virus was effectively a "deep-state hoax," discounted the severity of the disease, and heavily promoted supposed cure-all treatments—at least one of which, hydroxychloroquine, turned out to harm patients more than it helped them. Polls found "stark partisan differences on hand washing, social distancing, travel and other pandemic-related behavior."[66] Even charity was not above the fray. After former president George W. Bush reminded Americans during a coronavirus relief fundraiser that "we are not partisan combatants; we are human beings," Trump responded by attacking Bush for his failure to rail against partisanship during "the greatest Hoax in American history"—namely, Trump's impeachment.[67] "In the past," observed Cook Political Report analyst Amy Walter, "when I was asked what it would take to break the partisanship and gridlock in Washington, I said I thought it was going to take something truly horrible happening.... But, here we are, almost a year into the worst pandemic this country has seen in 100 years, and this crisis, instead of bringing us together, has become yet another one which divides us."[68]

Political scientists like to talk about the "hand you're dealt" as a candidate. But as the incumbent president, Trump had the chance to stack the deck in his favor. That he did not baffled even political enemies. In May 2020, Obama adviser Ben Rhodes mused that "this is one of those moments where doing the job well would have political benefit."[69] But in the end it is hard to argue that the president did the job well. No national strategy was created to send clear public messages, to manage a reopening process, to procure or distribute medical equipment on an equitable basis, or for testing or contact tracing. Former White House aide James Fallows concluded unsparingly in late 2020 that "the coronavirus pandemic may represent the greatest failure of governance in U.S. history, and responsibility for the extent of its ravages falls squarely on Donald Trump."[70] One does not have to agree with the severity of this assessment to accept that better management of the crisis—in terms of organization, coordination, utilization of scientific expertise, communication—was a road mapped but never taken.[71]

Six decades ago, presidential scholar Richard Neustadt warned that the "presidency is no place for amateurs."[72] That hypothesis has been tested in various ways ever since. Perhaps experience is a necessary but not sufficient requisite for the office: certainly more than one president with a long professional pedigree in the political world has failed to meet the tests of leadership the office assigns. Donald Trump, the first president never to hold elected, appointed, or military office, did not make a strong case that Neustadt was wrong. As Trump himself put it, "I thought it would be easier."[73]

Biden, Blessedly Boring

Certainly when it came to Washington politics, Joe Biden was no amateur. One could argue that his longevity was a curse rather than a blessing, and Trump tried to frame it as such. "In 47 months, I've done more than you've done in 47 years, Joe," he said during their first debate. This was a reprise of 2016, when Trump successfully framed Hillary Clinton's long turn on the national stage as corrupting: "Hillary has experience, but it's bad experience."[74]

Yet 2020 was not 2016 and "Sleepy Joe" was not "Crooked Hillary." Trump's 2020 stump speech sought to ignore that he had been in the White House for four years, attacking events that occurred on his watch and touting himself as a nonpolitical outsider. Dark images of urban unrest only reminded viewers that they were scenes from Trump's own term in office. "The virus is stealing the show, but Trump is sticking with reruns," one observer quipped.[75]

One reason Trump was able to patch together victory in 2016 was that he faced a historically unpopular opponent. Gallup noted that Trump's 61 percent unfavorable score at the time was the worst for any candidate in presidential polling history, but that Clinton's 52 percent unfavorable score was second worst. Nearly a fifth of voters told exit pollsters they had dim views of both candidates. That group broke for Trump by more than 15 percentage points.[76]

Four years later few remained indifferent to Trump. Only 3 percent of respondents in the 2020 exit poll rated both candidates unfavorably this time, and only 3 percent liked both. Fifty-four percent said Biden had the right temperament to be president; only 44 percent said the same of Trump. And while polarization made acclamation unlikely, Biden's favorability ratings actually increased as the campaign wore on.[77]

The quick consolidation of the Democratic primary field around Biden helped his cause. Biden, who was seen as the clear front-runner at the outset of the 2020 campaign, stumbled early—finishing fifth in New Hampshire—only to score a dominant win in the South Carolina primary, the first contest to showcase a racially diverse electorate. The large Republican field in 2016, each of whose members fancied himself a superior candidate to Donald Trump, had failed to coordinate against him. Democrats in 2020 did the opposite, dropping out in quick sequence to endorse Biden. The remaining choice was between Biden and Vermont senator Bernie Sanders, pitting reassurance against revolution. Democratic voters chose reassurance, banking on Biden's status as the least common denominator in the field as a sign of his ultimate electability.

Trump tried hard to make the case that Biden was a crazed socialist. "The Radical Left Democrats, who totally control Biden, will destroy our Country as we know it," Trump tweeted. "Unimaginably bad things would happen to America." Biden would undermine public safety, the president said. He would dry up oil wells, "put China first and America last," "double and triple your taxes": "He's against God. He's against guns. He's against energy."[78]

But Biden, at seventy-eight, did not seem like a radical. He had blue-collar roots in blue-collar Scranton, Pennsylvania, and appealed to the "blue wall" states. He opposed the Green New Deal and "defunding" the police. He sometimes stuttered. Indeed, Trump's own nickname for him seemed to indicate somnolence rather than socialism. If Trump was exhausting—as longtime chronicler of the GOP Tim Alberta said, "It's impossible to quantify how tired Americans are of this presidency"[79]—Biden promised the chance to not worry about the White House for weeks at a time. Masked and socially distant, pledging "science over fiction," Biden seemed calm, boring, and, not least, in tune with the public: two-thirds of voters said masking was "a public health responsibility" rather than a "personal choice."[80] Experience and competence were, at least in 2020, back in vogue.

So was unity. Rhetorically disciplined in a way that belied his reputation for loquacity, Biden had few variations on that theme, over and over offering a clear contrast with Trump. "The current president has cloaked America in darkness for much too long. Too much anger. Too much fear. Too much division," began his speech at the Democratic National Convention. "I will be a Democratic candidate, [but] I will be an American president. I will work as hard for those who didn't support me as I will for those who did. That's the job of a president."[81] Closing the final debate between the candidates, he said much the same thing: "[If elected] I will say, 'I'm the American president. I represent all of you whether you voted for me or against me. And I'm going to make sure that you're represented."[82]

Splitting America but Not the Ticket? Hail, Gridlock

Trump split America and Biden capitalized on that split. But Americans did not split their tickets.

This seems counterintuitive. After all, while Trump lost by a margin larger than the one he deemed a "landslide" in 2016, many others in the GOP had a far better November. Although it did not prevent many Republicans from pretending the results of the presidential election were fraudulent, the party's down-ballot candidates outpaced predictions.[83] As in 2016 the national polls were broadly correct, but state-level polls frequently underestimated Republican support. In the House, Democrats expected to add to their majority. Instead they lost twelve net seats, leaving Speaker Nancy Pelosi steward of a majority of just four (222 votes in the 435-person chamber). Nor did Democrats win back key state legislative chambers they had targeted in states like Texas, with an eye toward controlling redistricting following the 2020 census. Democrats needed to net three seats for a working Senate majority (with Vice President Kamala Harris breaking tie votes) and hoped to vault well beyond that bar. But Democratic candidates fell far short in places they thought would be competitive, such as states like Kansas and Texas, and failed to capture two seats they thought certain, in North Carolina and Maine. That pushed the fate of the chamber to two January 5 run-off elections in Georgia. Here, ironically, Trump's continued attacks on the state's November results and its election officials demobilized Republican voters and sparked Democratic turnout, helping Democrats take Senate control by the narrowest of margins.

Even with unified government, though, the result was not the sharp repudiation of Trump's Republican Party that the president's critics—including "never Trump" Republicans—hoped for. The elections did not usher in a new "political time" of massive institutional reconstruction, with large Democratic majorities poised to make sweeping changes ranging from expansion of the Supreme Court to statehood for Washington, DC, and Puerto Rico.[84] And they led some to quickly declare that split-ticket voting had returned to American politics. How otherwise could Trump lose, while Republican House and Senate candidates won?

Obviously in some cases this was accurate. In the Maine Senate race, for example, embattled incumbent Susan Collins fended off her challenger with 51 percent of the vote even as Trump lost the state by 9 points. But Collins was a special case. Though she had frequently supported controversial Trump nominees and initiatives, she assiduously ignored the president during her campaign and was delighted to earn an insulting Trump tweet for her opposition to Amy Coney Barrett's ascension to the Supreme Court a week before the election. After twenty-four years in the Senate, Collins relentlessly touted her seniority and ability to bring home the bacon—in the form of navy shipbuilding jobs—and her constituent service. Because all the polls pointed to a Biden victory, her opponent's single-note insistence that Collins must be punished for slavish support of Trump perhaps seemed less persuasive. That also hampered other Democrats who ran explicitly as a check on Trump: voters didn't need a check on Trump if Trump was going to lose.

In this sense the stability of the presidential race soothed the sting for Trump's down-ballot copartisans. The results also reflected the GOP's new success in recruiting more diverse candidates, especially for key swing seats in Florida, Texas, and California. All told, Republican women won eleven of the fourteen races that Democratic incumbents lost and more than doubled their numbers in the GOP caucus.[85] In the Miami area, for instance, local television anchor Maria Elvira Salazar, the daughter of Cuban refugees, won in a district that four years earlier had favored Hillary Clinton by 20 points. The female membership of the incoming 117th Congress still skewed Democratic by a 3–1 margin. Still, it was harder to believe that Trump's sexism or racism infected the entire GOP when the local face of the party was female or Latino or both.

Even so, the final results reflected the dominant influence of partisan polarization, exacerbated by geographic sorting. Biden did well nationally—and Democrats won the aggregate national House and Senate votes too. But when wrenched through the prism of House districts and state-level Senate contests, their national majority did not translate into the same success. Maine was the only state where the Senate and presidential results diverged. Democratic hopes in Iowa, Kansas, Texas, and even South Carolina and Montana were a victim of straight-ticket solidarity; Nathaniel Rakich and Ryan Best of the website FiveThirtyEight went so far as to argue that "there wasn't *that* much split-ticket voting in 2020." They noted that the few places where Biden's vote diverged significantly from Democratic Senate candidates were explained by extremely local phenomena.[86] Few places that supported Biden supported a Republican congressional candidate, and vice versa: Biden won 223 congressional districts, and Democrats 222, with just half a percentage point separating their overall vote share.[87]

Thus, the results foreshadowed the continuation and even the rein-forcement of partisan gridlock, with tiny majorities in each chamber add-ing increased pressure for party unity. As Frances Lee has shown, minority legislators operating with narrow margins have little incentive to help the other party achieve anything of substance lest they reduce their own chances of winning a majority in the next election.[88] Biden trum-peted his administration's diversity and commitment to forging unity across the aisle. But many Republican legislators, taking their cue from Trump, refused to acknowledge Biden as president-elect, even as they began to oppose his proposals. Trump himself promised to keep his Twitter finger poised, and even to run again in 2024.[89] For that matter, left-leaning Democratic partisans indicated they too would demand sig-nificant policy concessions from a president they had supported largely as a pragmatic vehicle to defeat Trump.

Another meaning of the election, then, was that if it had restored nor-mality, it was the "new normal" of polarized division in which "confronta-tion and paralysis have become divided government's natural state."[90]

To be sure, governance in the American system is rarely easy. The structure of government itself anticipates and even encourages gridlock. In *Federalist* #73, Alexander Hamilton argued that we should "consider every institution calculated to restrain the excess of lawmaking, and to keep things in the same state in which they happen to be at any given period, as much more likely to do good than harm."[91] Those out of power are happy when the government finds it hard to act—"Hail, Gridlock!" read a sign held by a Tea Party activist in 2010.[92]

Yet though the framers distrusted "mutability," they hated incompe-tence more. Hamilton argued in *Federalist* #22 against what would become the Senate filibuster, noting that however appealing a supermajority approval process might seem on paper, "its real operation is to . . . destroy the energy of government." It would impose "tedious delays; continual negotiation and intrigue; contemptible compromises of the public good." Such a situation, he warned, "must always savor of weakness, sometimes border upon anarchy." And it was anarchy, not government, that posed the greatest threat to individual rights and freedoms.[93]

In that vein, consider Hamilton's attacks on the pre-constitutional Articles of Confederation, which created a central government that Hamilton saw as so weak to be paralytic. As he wrote as early as 1780, reforms were needed to "give new life and *energy* to the operations of government." Once properly constituted, "business would be conducted with dispatch, method, and system."[94] Dispatch, method, and system were crucial: government must be able to reach decisions, with some alacrity when needed; and it must have mechanisms for carrying out those decisions effectively and efficiently, without going back on its word. That implied certain institutional arrangements. Hamilton is best known for his advocacy of an independent presidency that would provide "energy in the executive," that energy in turn serving as "a leading character in the definition of good government."[95] He argued that "the true test of a good government is its aptitude and tendency to produce a good administration."[96]

Yet the notion of "energy"—and of unity, too—goes beyond the presidency, as James Madison pointed out. In *Federalist* #37, Madison argued that "energy in government is essential to that security against external and internal danger, and to that prompt and salutary execution of the laws, which enter into the very definition of good government." Good government, in that sense, required competence. Indeed, the very point of having an energetic government order was to be able to act in the long-term benefit of the people, exactly because of its structural ability to withstand their short-term disdain. This formulation squares the circle between conservative desires for stability and the need for energy. Energy is needed in the short term to achieve stability in the long run. "Confrontation and paralysis" undermines both.

This political prescription, in the *Federalist* and elsewhere, centers on administrative competence and—crucially—on the capacity of the system to make hard choices for the long term. And here the United States of the 2020s is on worrying ground. Its separate but power-sharing institutions require consensus, or at least consensual compromise, to move toward the general interest. But as currently constituted those institutions channel factional interests toward dissensus instead, echoing Hamilton's prescient caution: "The only enemy which Republicanism has to fear in this country is in the spirit of faction and anarchy. If this will not permit the ends of government to be attained under it, if it engenders disorders in the community, all regular and orderly minds will wish for a change, and the demagogues who have produced the disorder will make it for their own aggrandizement. This is the old story."[97] After the 2020 election, the national mood remained raw, further infected by President Trump's persistent—and flat-out false—claims of electoral fraud. A demagogue fanning disorder for his own aggrandizement? The old story is new again.

Better Angels, Worst Instincts

After the 2016 election, there was a certain sense in both parties that Trump had magical political powers that would transform dross to gold at the polls. Hillary Clinton's unexpected loss instilled PTSD in Democratic activists, and a faith-based sense of omnipotence in MAGA nation.[98] Yet it is perhaps not too simplistic to argue that Trump drew an inside straight in 2016, dealt himself a bad hand as president, and suffered the electoral consequences. "The stars might lie," as Mary Chapin Carpenter once sang—indeed, when it came to the outcome of the election, even the president might lie—"but the numbers never do."[99]

Much political science scholarship over the next decade will likely focus on the question, Was it the presidency, or just Trump? As the forty-sixth president, Joe Biden served as a restoration of sorts. He chose diverse, experienced, "normal" appointees for his administration, starting with a part-Black, part–South Asian woman as his vice president and partner in governance. In a Thanksgiving address, he renewed his theme of bipartisan, even supra-partisan, unity: "We're at war with a virus—not with each other."[100]

At the same time, the still-serving president of the United States chose to call into a cell phone speaker at a hotel on the outskirts of Gettysburg, Pennsylvania, urging that the results of the 2020 election be overturned. On Thanksgiving Day he claimed again that he had been robbed of his rightful win, that "there is NO WAY Biden got 80,000,000 votes!!! This was a 100% RIGGED ELECTION."[101]

For the record, Biden received 81,284,716 votes, as certified by fifty states and the District of Columbia. Trump's barrage of postelection lies were not different in kind from the more than 22,247 falsehoods the *Washington Post* fact-check team tabulated through August 2020—a total submitted in late October with apologies that its staff could simply not keep up with the president's rhetoric.[102] But because these particular lies attacked the United States' very foundation as a democratic republic, they were more dangerous. Trump consistently gave license to America's worst instincts rather than inspiring its better angels. In 2020, Biden won 306 electoral votes, well more than the 270 needed to clinch the presidency and by coincidence the same number captured by Trump four years earlier. Yet Trump and his sycophants claimed that Biden's win was a hoax, seeding doubt about democracy itself. At the end of his administration, Trump demanded fealty to yet another alternate reality, even as Facebook and Twitter began to add routine warnings "lest viewers actually believe what the president of the United States was telling them."[103] In a December rally in Georgia, Trump continued to preach the politics of persecution: "We're all victims. Everybody here, all these thousands of people here tonight, they're all victims. Every one of you."[104] This, because they had lost a free and fair election.

Trump's complaints might not have mattered had not a significant part of the Republican Party followed his lead. Seventeen states and more than 120 Republican members of Congress—60 percent of the GOP caucus—signed onto a Texas lawsuit claiming that state's right to enforce other states' election laws, a suit whose legal claims were so fanciful that the Supreme Court refused even to hear it. A month later, hundreds of Trump's followers would violently storm the U.S. Capitol in an ugly display of mob rule as they attempted to overturn the election results. For too many it appeared that the road to serfdom was a desirable byway if Donald Trump lay at the end of it.

Yet the broader point is perhaps not about this cult of demagoguery. As the United States diverged into open and closed, into urban and rural, into an economy in which more than 70 percent of national GDP is produced by less than 20 percent of American counties, so did the parties' paths to power diverge.[105] Republicans will, of necessity—having lost the national popular vote in seven of the last eight presidential elections—take advantage of institutions that benefit state-based representation, which is to say the Electoral College and the Senate.[106] But how long will those advantages hold, given the demographic and generational change already in progress? At some point the meaning of any election is played out in practice: both parties will need to recalibrate, seeking new coalitions based on a new combination of policy positions. But by rejecting Trump but not Trumpism, the 2020 election deferred this question—perhaps to 2024, perhaps beyond.

Notes

1. For a review, see Andrew Rudalevige, "The Meaning of the 2016 Election: The President as Minority Leader," in *The Elections of 2016*, ed. Michael Nelson (Washington, DC: Sage/CQ Press, 2018), 217–18.
2. Seth Masket, "Do Really, Really Bad GDP Numbers Mean a Really, Really Bad November for Trump?," *Mischiefs of Faction* (blog), July 30, 2020, https://www.mischiefsoffaction.com/post/really-bad-gdp. No major party nominee has ever received that small a share of the national vote in a two-way race.
3. See, for example, Alan Abramowitz, "It's the Pandemic, Stupid," *PS: Political Science and Politics* 54 (January 2021): 52–54.
4. For example, James Campbell, "The Trial Heat and Convention Bump Forecasts of the 2020 Presidential Election," Center for Politics, University of Virginia, September 17, 2020, https://centerforpolitics.org/crystal-ball/articles/the-trial-heat-and-convention-bump-forecasts-of-the-2020-presidential-election/; see generally the "2020 Presidential Election Forecasting Symposium," edited by Ruth Dassonneville and Charles Tien, *PS: Political Science and Politics* 54 (January 2021): 47–110.
5. Seth Masket, "It's about the Fundamentals, Whatever Those Will Be," *Mischiefs of Faction* (blog), April 22, 2020, https://www.mischiefsoffaction.com/post/covid-trump-fundamentals.
6. Bob Woodward quoted Trump son-in-law and White House aide Jared Kushner as saying of the president, "I don't think it's even about the issues. I think it's about the attitude." Woodward, *Rage* (New York: Simon & Schuster, 2020), 264; and see Reid Epstein, "The GOP Delivers Its 2020 Platform. It's from 2016," *New York Times*, August 25, 2020.
7. Glenn Kessler, "Trump Campaign Ad Manipulates Three Images to Put Biden in a 'Basement,'" *Washington Post*, August 7, 2020.
8. See Gallup's interactive Presidential Job Approval Center, available at https://news.gallup.com/interactives/185273/presidential-job-approval-center.aspx. For the popular vote totals, see the U.S. Election Atlas, collated by Dave Leip, available at https://uselectionatlas.org/RESULTS/.
9. All data in this and the subsequent paragraphs are from the same pollsters. See Q8 in Hart Research Associates / Public Opinion Strategies, "Mid-October 2020," Study #200870, October 9–12, 2020, https://www.documentcloud.org/documents/7231554-2200870Mid-October.html.
10. Michael S. Schmidt, *Donald Trump v. The United States* (New York: Random House, 2020), xi.
11. See Frank Newport, "Partisan Polarization and Ratings of the Economy," Gallup, February 28, 2020, https://news.gallup.com/opinion/polling-matters/287105/partisan-polarization-ratings-economy.aspx; Andrew Dugan, "Americans' Economic Confidence Positive in 2017," Gallup,

January 2, 2018, https://news.gallup.com/poll/224822/americans-economic
-confidence-positive-2017.aspx; Jim Tankersley and Ben Casselman, "After
Biden Win, Nation's Republicans Fear the Economy Ahead," *New York
Times*, December 2, 2020.

12. Ezra Klein, *Why We're Polarized* (New York: Avid Reader Press, 2020),
64. See also Marc J. Hetherington and Thomas J. Rudolph, *Why Washington Won't Work: Polarization, Political Trust, and the Governing Crisis* (Chicago: University of Chicago Press, 2015).

13. Quoted in Rudalevige, "Meaning of the 2016 Election," 232.

14. Barack Obama received 52.9 percent nationally in 2008. Electoral and
approval figures updated from calculations in Rudalevige, "Meaning of
the 2016 Election," 229–30.

15. Bush, too, failed to achieve this; see Gary C. Jacobson, *A Divider, Not a
Uniter* (New York: Longman, 2006).

16. See Gallup, Presidential Job Approval Center. By contrast, on Election Day
2016, the partisan gap in views of Barack Obama was "only" 80 percentage points.

17. At least according to exit polls, which, as discussed elsewhere in this volume, should be taken with a grain of salt given the huge turnout and multiple avenues for voting in 2020. However, CNN's report of more than
15,000 respondents suggests that 94 percent of Democrats voted for Biden
and 94 percent of Republicans voted for Trump. See the 2020 exit poll
results at https://www.cnn.com/election/2020/exit-polls/president/na
tional-results.

18. Ibid.

19. "Transcript: Donald Trump's Victory Speech," *New York Times*, November 9, 2016.

20. Morris P. Fiorina, *Unstable Majorities: Polarization, Party Sorting,
and Political Stalemate* (Stanford, CA: Hoover Institution Press, 2017),
106.

21. John Sides, Michael Tesler, and Lynn Vavreck, *Identity Crisis: The 2016
Presidential Campaign and the Battle for the Meaning of America* (Princeton, NJ: Princeton University Press, 2018), chap. 5.

22. For instance, see Clinton's ad "Morning," which focuses on layoffs in
Decaturville, Tennessee, available at http://www.livingroomcandidate.org
/commercials/1992/morning.

23. These tweets come, respectively, from January 12, 2017; January 11, 2017;
January 5, 2017; January 14, 2017; January 10, 2017 (and on eight other
occasions before the inaugural); January 13, 2010; and November 20,
2016. Trump tweets can be located via the search function (by subject or
date) at the invaluable Trump Twitter Archive, https://www.thetrumpar-
chive.com/.

24. Calculated from the Trump Twitter Archive.

25. Jasmine Lee and Kevin Quealy, "The 598 People, Places and Things Donald Trump Has Insulted on Twitter," *New York Times*, last updated May 24, 2019, https://www.nytimes.com/interactive/2016/01/28/upshot/donald-trump-twitter-insults.html. That doesn't include references to the *Times* as "dishonest," "weak," "dumb," "dopey," "irrelevant," "clueless," "stupid," "sad," "dying," "disgraced," "nasty," "phony," a "liar," or "fake news." See Philip Bump, "The Expansive, Repetitive Universe of Trump's Twitter Insults," *Washington Post*, August 20, 2019.

26. Gary C. Jacobson, "Extreme Referendum: Donald Trump and the 2018 Midterm Elections," *Political Science Quarterly* 134 (Spring 2019): 14.

27. A transcript of the Orlando rally is available at "Speech: Donald Trump Announces His 2020 Candidacy at a Political Rally in Orlando—June 18, 2019," Factbase, https://factba.se/transcript/donald-trump-speech-maga-rally-reelection-orlando-june-18-2019, accessed February 11, 2021.

28. Austin Weinstein, "Trump Tightens Aid for Puerto Rico as Turmoil Grips Island," Bloomberg, August 2, 2019, https://www.bloomberg.com/news/articles/2019-08-02/trump-tightens-aid-for-puerto-rico-as-turmoil-grips-island.

29. Tweets of July 6, 2020; February 23, 2017; and August 18, 2020.

30. President to Attorney General and Director of the Office of Management and Budget, "Memorandum on Reviewing Funding to State and Local Government Recipients That Are Permitting Anarchy, Violence, and Destruction in American Cities," White House, September 2, 2020, https://www.whitehouse.gov/presidential-actions/memorandum-reviewing-funding-state-local-government-recipients-permitting-anarchy-violence-destruction-american-cities/.

31. And were quickly sued. See Emma Fitzsimmons, "With Billions at Stake, New York Sues Trump over 'Anarchist' Label," *New York Times*, October 22, 2020.

32. Sides, Tesler, and Vavreck, *Identity Crisis*, 202.

33. Katie Rogers and Nicholas Fandos, "Trump Tells Congresswomen to 'Go Back' to the Countries They Came From," *New York Times*, July 14, 2019.

34. See Sides, Tesler, and Vavreck, *Identity Crisis*, 201–2.

35. Quoted in Woodward, *Rage*, 266–67. Wallace was talking about Trump's tweets regarding Cummings.

36. Fadel Allassan, "Confederate Monuments Become Flashpoints in Protests against Racism," Axios, June 7, 2020, https://www.axios.com/confederate-monuments-racism-flashpoint-07bd1074-5635-4939-9a55-e572543483b7.html; Eugene Scott, "Trump's Ardent Defense of Confederate Monuments Continues as Americans Swing the Opposite Direction," *Washington Post*, July 1, 2020.

37. Office of the White House Press Secretary, "President Donald J. Trump Is Protecting America's Founding Ideals by Promoting Patriotic Education,"

White House, November 2, 2020, https://www.whitehouse.gov/briefings
-statements/president-donald-j-trump-protecting-americas-founding
-ideals-promoting-patriotic-education/. To be sure, there were scholarly
critiques of the 1619 Project as well, but these were far less politically
charged.

38. Exec. Order No. 13934, 85 Fed. Reg. 41165 (July 3, 2020); Lindsay Wise and
Andrew Duehren, "Trump's Defense-Bill Veto Threat, Explained," *Wall
Street Journal*, December 11, 2020.

39. That the Confederate battle flag represents something other than slavery
meshes poorly with the historical testimony of the Confederacy's own
membership. "Our position is thoroughly identified with the institution of
slavery," said the Mississippi declaration of secession in early 1861. "There
was no choice left us but submission to the mandates of abolition, or a dissolution of the Union." "A Declaration of the Immediate Causes Which
Induce and Justify the Secession of the State of Mississippi from the Federal
Union," Avalon Project, Yale Law School, January 9, 1861, https://avalon
.law.yale.edu/19th_century/csa_missec.asp; see also James McPherson,
"Southern Comfort," *New York Review of Books*, April 12, 2001.

40. Ronald Brownstein (RonBrownstein), Twitter.com, October 7, 2020,
11:46 a.m., https://twitter.com/RonBrownstein/status/1313868309603872768.

41. Quoted in "Fact Check US: Would the Democrats 'Ruin the Suburbs' as
Donald Trump claims?," The Conversation, October 19, 2020, https://
theconversation.com/fact-check-us-would-the-democrats-ruin-the-sub
urbs-as-donald-trump-claims-147211; tweet of August 22, 2020.

42. Annie Karni, Maggie Haberman, and Sydney Ember, "Trump Plays on
Racist Fears of Terrorized Suburbs to Court White Voters," *New York
Times*, July 29, 2020; "Fact Check US."

43. Marc Caputo, "Culture Wars Fuel Trump's Blue-Collar Latino Gains,"
Politico, November 21, 2020; Marcela Valdes, "The Fight for Latino Voters," *New York Times Magazine*, November 29, 2020, 26.

44. Quoted in Lisa Lerer, "Trump Has Become a Midterms Rorschach Test,"
New York Times, October 25, 2018.

45. See "Immigration," Gallup, https://news.gallup.com/poll/1660/immigra
tion.aspx, accessed February 11, 2021; Bradley Jones, "Majority of Americans Continue to Say Immigrants Strengthen the U.S.," Pew Research
Center, January 31, 2019, https://www.pewresearch.org/fact-tank/2019
/01/31/majority-of-americans-continue-to-say-immigrants-strengthen
-the-u-s/.

46. Meredith Conroy, Amelia Thomson-DeVeaux, and Erin Cassese, "Why
Trump Is Losing White Suburban Women," FiveThirtyEight, October 20,
2020, https://fivethirtyeight.com/features/why-trump-is-losing-white
-suburban-women/; Nolan Weidner, "Crowds Show That This Time Black
Lives Matter in Central New York's White Suburbs, Too," *Syracuse*

Post-Standard, June 19, 2020; Robert Costa, "'They're Afraid': Suburban Voters in Red States Threaten GOP's Grip on Power," *Washington Post*, August 9, 2019; Tim Alberta, "Four Funny Feelings about 2020," *Politico*, October 6, 2020.

47. Harry Enten (forecasterenten), Twitter.com, Tweet of December 2, 2020, 1:32 p.m., https://twitter.com/forecasterenten/status/1334203877592354822.

48. CNN poll released October 28, 2020, available at http://cdn.cnn.com/cnn /2020/images/10/28/rel15.pdf.

49. Quoted in Jacqueline Alemany, "Trump May Still Be a Historical Underdog for Reelection," *Washington Post*, August 9, 2019.

50. Quoted in Paul Waldman, "Trump: I Can Win Reelection with Just My Base," *Washington Post*, June 20, 2019.

51. Tweet of September 17, 2017.

52. Karl Rove, *Courage and Consequence* (New York: Threshold, 2010), 70.

53. Sam Levine, "Trump Says Republicans Would 'Never' Be Elected Again If It Was Easier to Vote," *Guardian*, March 30, 2020; William Kristol (BillKristol), Twitter.com, October 31, 2020, 2:50 p.m., https://twitter.com /BillKristol/status/1322611839524589572?s=20.

54. Anthony Leonardi, "Trump: George Washington Would Have Struggled to Beat Me before Coronavirus," *Washington Examiner*, August 11, 2020.

55. Video available at https://lincolnproject.us/video/mourning-in-america/. The ad was inspired by a famous commercial from Ronald Reagan's reelection campaign in 1984—"Morning in America"—which the script subverted nearly line for line. Trump's response was not to defend his management of the pandemic. Instead, it was a post-midnight multi-tweet screed attacking the ad's creator, the Lincoln Project.

56. Caitlin Oprysko and Susannah Luthi, "Trump Labels Himself 'a Wartime President' Combating Coronavirus," *Politico*, March 18, 2020.

57. Quoted in Philip Bump, "Six Months Ago, Trump Said That Coronavirus Cases Would Soon Go to Zero. They . . . Didn't," *Washington Post*, August 26, 2020; Editorial Board, "Coronavirus Response Shows Donald Trump's Failure of Leadership," *USA Today*, October 29, 2020; Woodward, *Rage*.

58. Office of the White House Press Secretary, "Remarks by President Trump, Vice President Pence, and Members of the Coronavirus Task Force in Press Briefing," White House, March 22, 2020, https://www.whitehouse. gov/briefings-statements/remarks-president-trump-vice-president -pence-members-coronavirus-task-force-press-briefing-8/.

59. Philip Ewing and Barbara Sprunt, "Trump Sets Easter Goal for Reopening American Economy," NPR, March 24, 2020, https://www.npr.org /2020/03/24/820774378/trump-id-love-for-u-s-to-be-opened-up-by-easter -amidst-pandemic-response.

60. James Fallows, "2020 Time Capsule #15: Liberate," *Atlantic*, April 18, 2020.

61. Tweet of May 1, 2020.

62. Darcie Moran and Joe Guillen, "Michigan AG Details Extremist Plot to Kidnap Gov. Whitmer, Including Plan to Burn Capitol Building," *USA Today*, November 13, 2020.

63. Glenn Thrush, "'It Affects Virtually Nobody,' Trump Says, Minimizing the Effect of the Coronavirus on Young People," *New York Times*, September 22, 2020.

64. Tommy Beer, "Trump Predicted 'Covid, Covid, Covid' Would End after the Election. It's Worse Than Ever," *Forbes*, November 11, 2020.

65. Philip Bump, "Trump Blames Blue States for the Coronavirus Death Toll—but Most Recent Deaths Have Been in Red States," *Washington Post*, September 16, 2020.

66. Jay J. Van Bavel, "In a Pandemic, Political Polarization Can Kill People," *Washington Post*, March 23, 2020.

67. Peter Wehner, "The President Is Unraveling," *Atlantic*, May 5, 2020.

68. Amy Walter, "The Divides That Define Us," Cook Political Report, November 12, 2020, https://cookpolitical.com/analysis/national/national -politics/divides-define-us.

69. Quoted in Ashley Parker and Philip Rucker, "In Next Phase of Pandemic, Trump Appears Poised to Let Others Take the Lead," *Washington Post*, May 17, 2020; see also Jonathan Bernstein, "Does Donald Trump Want to Be Re-elected?," Bloomberg, May 15, 2020.

70. James Fallows, "How Biden Should Investigate Trump," *Atlantic*, January/February 2021; Fallows, "The Three Weeks That Changed Everything," *Atlantic*, June 29, 2020; Parker and Rucker, "In Next Phase of Pandemic." On the question of effective communication, conservative commentator Ed Whelan called Trump "the guy who turned White House press conferences on Covid into daily 90-minute nationally televised campaign ads for Joe Biden." See Ed Whelan (EdWhelanEPPC), Twitter.com, December 11, 2020, 8:47 p.m., https://twitter.com/EdWhel-anEPPC/status/1337574662952411137.

71. Indeed, the government possessed step-by-step playbooks for pandemic response developed during earlier crises. And a simulation exercise staged during the early 2017 transition period sought to familiarize the incoming administration with the ways to deal with a new and deadly disease arising in Asia, leading to the "worst influenza pandemic since 1918." See Nahal Toosi, Daniel Lippman, and Dan Diamond, "Before Trump's Inauguration, a Warning," *Politico*, March 16, 2020; Editorial Board, "Coronavirus Response."

72. Richard E. Neustadt, *Presidential Power* (New York: Wiley, 1960), 180.

73. One of his staffers told *Politico* that he had dismissed all the talk about experience—but that "this shit is hard." Both quoted in Sides, Tesler, and Vavreck, *Identity Crisis*, 203–4.

74. "Read the Full Transcript from the first Presidential Debate between Joe Biden and Donald Trump," *USA Today*, September 30, 2020, https://www.usatoday.com/story/news/politics/elections/2020/09/30/presidential-debate-read-full-transcript-first-debate/3587462001/; James W. Ceaser, Andrew E. Busch, and John J. Pitney Jr., *Defying the Odds: The 2016 Elections and American Politics* (Lanham, MD: Rowman & Littlefield, 2017), 112.

75. Lisa Lerer, "The Virus Is Stealing the Show, but Trump Is Sticking with Reruns," *New York Times*, July 15, 2020.

76. Lydia Saad, "Trump and Clinton Finish with Historically Poor Images," Gallup, November 12, 2020, https://news.gallup.com/poll/197231/trump-clinton-finish-historically-poor-images.aspx; the 2016 exit polls are available at https://www.cnn.com/election/2016/results/exit-polls.

77. See the 2020 exit polls at https://www.cnn.com/election/2020/exit-polls/president/national-results.

78. Tweet of July 19, 2020; Peter Wade, "Trump Nonsensically Says Biden Will 'Hurt God, Hurt the Bible,'" *Rolling Stone*, August 6, 2020.

79. Alberta, "Four Funny Feelings." See more generally Tim Alberta, *American Carnage* (New York: HarperCollins 2019).

80. 2020 exit polls cited above (see note 77). A Kaiser Family Foundation poll in the field in November and December found an even larger split, with 73 percent of respondents saying mask-wearing was a public health responsibility and just 23 percent a personal choice. See "KFF Health Tracking Poll—December 2020: COVID-19 and Biden's Health Care Agenda," Figure 9, https://www.kff.org/coronavirus-covid-19/report/kff-health-tracking-poll-december-2020/.

81. "Transcript: Joe Biden's DNC Speech," CNN Politics, updated August 21, 2020, https://www.cnn.com/2020/08/20/politics/biden-dnc-speech-transcript/index.html.

82. "Debate Transcript: Biden Final Presidential Debate Moderated by Kristen Welker," *USA Today*, October 23, 2020, https://www.usatoday.com/story/news/politics/elections/2020/10/23/debate-transcript-trump-biden-final-presidential-debate-nashville/3740152001/.

83. Apparently the vast conspiracy that could reprogram voting machines from beyond the grave (this was indeed part of the president's legal team's claims) had not thought to do so for Democratic congressional candidates. See Ali Swenson, "AP Fact Check: Trump Legal Team's Batch of False Vote Claims," AP.com, November 19, 2020, https://apnews.com/article/fact-check-trump-legal-team-false-claims-5abd64917ef8be9e9e2078180973e8b3.

84. See the writings of Stephen Skowronek on "political time"—for example, *Presidential Leadership in Political Time: Reprise and Reappraisal*, 3rd ed. (Lawrence: University Press of Kansas, 2020).

85. Rachael Bade, "GOP Women's Record-Breaking Success Reflects Party's Major Shift on Recruiting and Supporting Female Candidates," *Washington Post*, December 7, 2020.

86. Nathaniel Rakich and Ryan Best, "There Wasn't That Much Split-Ticket Voting in 2020," FiveThirtyEight, December 2, 2020, https://fivethirtyeight.com/features/there-wasnt-that-much-split-ticket-voting-in-2020/.

87. Rakich and Best, "Split-Ticket Voting"; Ronald Brownstein, "Democrats' Real Liability in the House," *Atlantic*, November 27, 2020.

88. See Frances E. Lee, *Insecure Majorities: Congress and the Perpetual Campaign* (Chicago: University of Chicago Press, 2016); Fiorina, *Unstable Majorities*, chap. 5.

89. However, Trump was banned from Twitter in January 2021 for inciting violence during the mob attack on the U.S. Capitol on January 6. That ban was made permanent in February. See Brian Fung, "Twitter CFO Says Trump's Ban Is Permanent, Even If He Runs for Office Again," *CNN.com* (February 10, 2021), https://www.cnn.com/2021/02/10/tech/twitter-trump-ban-public-office/index.html.

90. Klein, *Why We're Polarized*, 251.

91. See the online edition of the Federalist Papers provided by the Library of Congress, https://guides.loc.gov/federalist-papers/full-text.

92. Carl Hulse, "With Tea Party in Mind, Republicans Have Change of Heart about Earmarks," *New York Times*, November 15, 2010.

93. A longer discussion of this point is in Andrew Rudalevige, "'Hail, Gridlock'? Hamiltonian Energy, Madisonian Institutions, and American Dissensus," in *Broken Government? American Politics in the Obama Era*, ed. Iwan Morgan and Philip Davies (London: University of London Press, 2012), 13–18, on which this section is based.

94. Hamilton to James Duane, September 3, 1780, in *The Works of Alexander Hamilton*, ed. Henry Cabot Lodge, 12 vols. (Federal ed.) (New York: G.P. Putnam's Sons, 1904), Volume 1, p. 213, https://oll.libertyfund.org/title/lodge-the-works-of-alexander-hamilton-federal-edition-12-vols.

95. *Federalist #70*.

96. *Federalist #68*—and went on to famously add that "a government ill executed, whatever it may be in theory, must be, in practice, a bad government." *Federalist #70*.

97. Hamilton to Col. Edward Carrington, May 26, 1792, in Lodge, *Works of Alexander Hamilton*.Volume 9, p. 513.

98. Jonathan Martin, "Trump, Biden and the Myth of 'But 2016,'" *New York Times*, May 15, 2020.

99. Mary Chapin Carpenter, "I Feel Lucky," *Come On, Come On* (1992).

100. "Read: President-Elect Joe Biden's Thanksgiving Address as Prepared for Delivery," CNN Politics, updated November 25, 2020, https://www.cnn

.com/2020/11/25/politics/read-joe-biden-thanksgiving-address/index
.html.

101. Tweet of November 26, 2020.

102. Glenn Kessler, Salvador Rizzo, and Meg Kelly, "Trump Is Averaging More Than 50 False or Misleading Claims a Day," *Washington Post*, October 22, 2020.

103. Peter Baker, "Trump's Final Days of Rage and Denial," *New York Times*, December 5, 2020.

104. Max Boot, "Why the Republican Cult of Victimhood Is So Dangerous," *Washington Post*, December 11, 2020.

105. Mark Muro, Eli Byerly Duke, Yang You, and Robert Maxim, "Biden-Voting Counties Equal 70% of America's Economy," Brookings Institution, November 10, 2020, https://www.brookings.edu/blog/the-avenue/2020/11/09/biden-voting-counties-equal-70-of-americas-economy-what-does-this-mean-for-the-nations-political-economic-divide/.

106. Seth Masket, "The Conversation Republicans Don't Want to Have," *Mischiefs of Faction* (blog), December 8, 2020, https://www.mischiefsoffaction.com/post/gop-conversation.

Sixty Years of Elections

FROM JOHN KENNEDY TO JOE BIDEN

Gerald M. Pomper

> Raise a glass to freedom
> Something they can never take away
> No matter what they tell you
> —"The Story of Tonight," *Hamilton*

When John Kennedy won the 1960 election, he became the youngest man ever elected president. When Joseph Biden won the 2020 election, he became the oldest man elected president.

This change in the life cycles of men and American politics provides the foundation of this chapter's examination of sixty years of American political events and the extensive changes that occurred during that time in our national life.

These six decades (also comprising the professional lifetime of this author) are times of almost incomprehensible change, mutations that would seem to climax with the tumultuous election, administration, and defeat of Donald Trump. Think back to or imagine yourself at the beginning of this astonishing period, a fourth of America's lifetime since the Declaration of Independence. In 1960, no Catholic had ever served as president of the United States; no woman, no African American, no Latino, indeed no person other than a white male, had ever been given more than token consideration for the office; and even a white southerner had not been nominated for the position in a century.

In earlier years, presidential nominations were decided by party leaders and bosses, largely unrestrained by national laws or state primaries. Campaigns still exhibited candidate broadcasts of thirty minutes, labor unions composed a third of the workforce, venerable torchlight parades drew crowds, private rooms at conventions hosted negotiations that might become smoke filled while tobacco was legally consumed. But politics did *not* include televised debates, cable television, computers, cell phones, social media, or space satellites. The electoral rolls included a mere trace of nonwhites in most southern states and fewer women than men elsewhere, and only limited ranks of youths below the age of twenty-one, unmarried or non-Christian adults, or uncloseted homosexuals. The vocabulary of American politics included no entries for sexual harassment, gay rights, white nationalism, or even geographic sites in Vietnam, Afghanistan, or the moon's Sea of Tranquility.

American politics changed enormously, even unimaginably, by 2020. Of course, the election would be different from that of 1960; a new bride marking her first vote on a paper ballot for John Kennedy might well press an arthritic finger to a computer screen to record her preference for Donald Trump. She would vote along with 160 million other Americans, more than twice as many as cast ballots in her youth. Millions of her peers would be absent from the polls, having mailed their ballots to avoid the threat of contagious infection by the coronavirus.

Many of the established practices and even the rituals of American politics were altered in the 2020 election. Party conventions already had been reduced to celebrations without deliberations. This year, they essentially disappeared, becoming only television shows, with delegates functioning as either antiseptic cheerleaders for Donald Trump or unseen participants on virtual networks for Joseph Biden. Boisterous campaign rallies on packed streets were replaced by speeches before television cameras shared only electronically in Zoom sessions, exhausting airborne travel replaced by the revival of the sedate nineteenth-century "front porch campaign." Candidate debates, begun in 1960, were changed to bar any audiences at the debate sites. Turnout set records beyond the past 120 years, but the ballots were more likely to be "turned in" at post offices or early vote centers than cast at the polls. Concessions by the losers, grudging but usually gracious, were replaced by the bitter disdain of Trump, both as the loser in 2020 and even as the winner in 2016.

What has happened? How and why? And are we a better nation?

Changes in American Politics

American politics has passed through a series of party eras, each constituting one to two generations. In the twentieth century, they included periods of Republican supremacy (1876–1924) and the New Deal Realignment (1928–60).[1]

Kennedy's victory marked the transition from the last realignment to our own uncertain times. In the four elections of Franklin Roosevelt and the nearly eight presidential years of his successor, Harry Truman, the Democratic Party built a new majority coalition. By 1960, the dynamism of the New Deal system was largely spent. Domestically, Truman could not achieve any major new programs. Foreign policy focused on settling the framework of the post–World War II world, including rehabilitating former foes Germany and Japan, dissolving European colonialism, and containing the threat of an expansionist Soviet Union. When Republicans returned to power under Dwight Eisenhower, they largely accepted the Democratic programs of a federal welfare state and international leadership.

But new challenges to these uneasy foreign and domestic arrangements would soon arise. Assertive post-Stalin leaders of the Soviet Union and a dynamic communist China upset the world balance of power. Fidel Castro's revolution in Cuba undermined U.S. dominance of the Western Hemisphere. Arab regimes confronted traditional European and American hegemony in the Middle East. Africa's nations emerged from colonial status, with no assurance of political and economic stability in untested independence.

Political change within the United States carried impending significance. The war had given millions of young people new knowledge of their nation and world, including prairie-state Protestants meeting urban Catholics, women recruited to airplane manufacturing as their first paid jobs, and "Negroes" gaining job protection in northern cities. Veterans returned home to reap benefits from the GI Bill, enabling them to earn college degrees, qualify for better jobs and higher class status than their parents, and buy a modest home in new suburban tracts. Impatient to change their nation, this new electorate, whose choice in the 1960 presidential election was between two youthful veterans of the war, Kennedy and Richard Nixon, was also impatient to marry and to breed, quickly producing the baby boom that would vastly increase the national population, and vastly change its politics.

By their very size, the new generations would change American culture. Encouraged by the Supreme Court's ending of legally mandated school segregation in 1954, they led a civil rights revolution that would soon extend from integrating lunch counters in the American South to defiant enfranchisement of Blacks long excluded from polling booths. In separate mobilizations, women would challenge cultural habits, demand a fuller equality, and eventually become a majority of the active electorate. Within a decade, further resistance to established custom came from gays and lesbians, and reactive resistance emerged from a reputed "silent majority" of traditionalist and segregationist whites unwilling to yield their traditional positions. Violence became both more frequent and more evident as television coverage became universal. Assassination stalked political leaders, urban riots lay waste to cities, and threats of force turned nominating conventions and campaign rallies from exuberant affirmations to threatening confrontations.

CHANGE IN ELECTION OUTCOMES

The new era's politics become evident in changes in election outcomes.[2] The long period from Kennedy to Trump can be seen as an extended standoff between the two major parties, alternating power from time to time, but neither party able to establish a lengthy and pervasive dominance.

One vital measure of a stable party system is landslides in the presidential elections. Once common, they have largely disappeared. This change is evident in the historical record, going back a century to the twenty-six elections beginning in 1920. (See table 1.)

In the first ten elections in this sequence (1920–56), there were five Democratic and five Republican victories. The parties rotated wins by large margins: the average number of electoral votes won by victors was 375 out of a constant base of 531, and the average margin of victory was 342 electoral votes. This period includes only one close election, that of Truman in 1948. Landslides of over 400 electoral votes were achieved by unspectacular candidates such as Warren Harding and Herbert Hoover, as well as the imposing figures of Franklin Roosevelt and Dwight Eisenhower.

In the last ten elections (1984–2020), winning candidates have achieved an average of only 357 electoral votes from an enlarged base of 538 (now including Alaska, Hawaii, and the District of Columbia), and the average margin of victory has shrunk almost in half, to 175. Only Ronald Reagan in 1984 and his designated successor George H. W. Bush have won over 400 votes. The parties have split victories in these contests, each winning five times—yet the GOP lacked popular pluralities in two of its wins (2000 and 2016; see figure 2 in Mellow and Smith's chapter). Small minority victories still may have large consequences, as Donald Trump exemplified, but the claims he made of a popular mandate were illusory.

The same declines in electoral support are evident in the popular vote. In the earlier period, the median tally for the presidential winner was

TABLE 1. Presidential elections, 1920–2020

Year	Electoral votes		Winner%total
	Dem	Rep	
1920	127	404	60.3
1924	136	382	54.0
1928	87	444	58.2
1932	532	59	57.4
1936	523	8	60.8
1940	449	82	54.7
1944	432	99	53.4
1948	303	189	49.6
1952	89	442	55.1
1956	73	458	57.4
1960	303	219	49.7
1964	486	52	61.1
1968	191	301	43.4
1972	17	521	60.7
1976	297	241	50.1
1980	49	489	50.7
1984	13	525	58.8
1988	112	426	59.2
1992	370	168	43.0
1996	379	159	49.2
2000	267	271	47.9
2004	252	286	50.7
2008	365	173	52.9
2012	332	206	51.1
2016	232	306	46.1
2020	306	232	51.3

Source: Compiled by the author.

Note: Votes by individual "faithless electors" are attributed to the popular winner of the state.

56.2 percent of the overall national vote, a solid endorsement. Only one of the ten winners failed to get a national majority. Even that exception, Truman in 1948 at 49.6 percent, came within a rounding count of half the country's support.

Popular endorsement declined considerably in the six transitional elections between these periods (1960–80), when four of six winners—Kennedy,

Nixon in 1968, Carter, and Reagan in 1980—lacked a convincing national majority. Then, in the ten most recent contests, the median winning percentage fell to only 50.7 percent, a thin margin. Moreover, four of ten winners fell short of a national majority, and three others—George W. Bush (2004) and Barack Obama (2012) in their second terms and Biden in 2020—barely scraped above half the national total. The absence of clear popular support has become accepted as a structural condition of presidential elections. Trump not only won in 2016 while gaining only 46 percent of the national popular vote; he almost wriggled to reelection with a similar count.

These patterns are not important because of statistical differences. Their significance may be the important change they represent in the legitimacy of presidential elections owing to the absence of policy mandates. The pattern of the earlier period advantaged the winning party and candidate in subsequent policy disputes. They had the rhetorical wind to their backs by virtue of the solid endorsement of the electorate in their landslide margins. Moreover, being large, these victories carried immunity against charges of election fraud or maladministration.

President Warren Harding, for example, relied on this democratic premise in his inaugural address. Renouncing any American involvement in the League of Nations, he invoked the presumed message of the election of 1920: "We turned to a referendum, to the American people. There was ample discussion, and there is a public mandate in [the] manifest understanding, intelligent, dependable popular will of America." A dozen years later, Franklin Roosevelt would also invoke a popular call for a very different program: "The people of the United States have not failed. In their need they have registered a mandate that they want direct, vigorous action. . . . They have made me the present instrument of their wishes. In the spirit of the gift I take it."[3]

Contrast this relationship of voters and parties in the current period. With narrower margins between Republicans and Democrats, even winning politicians cannot claim much of a mandate, while losers become more tempted to dispute the meaning, accuracy, and even the legitimacy of ballot tallies. What plausible mandate could Bill Clinton claim with 43 percent of the popular vote in 1992, George W. Bush with a margin of four electoral votes in 2000, or Donald Trump with a deficit close to 3 million popular votes in 2016?

In earlier periods, landslide elections fostered legitimacy and the claim to popular mandates. In our current politics, elections evidence division, offsetting directions in the vote, and partisan polarization and deadlock.

In this system of conflictual politics, the dialogue of democracy often becomes an indecipherable babble of loud and contradictory voices.

CHANGE IN GEOGRAPHICAL COALITIONS

The 1960 election also marked the emergence of another change in national politics: the realignment of the geographical bases of the major parties. The change had already begun and would not reach full development until future decades, but the Kennedy candidacy spurred the transition to a new political map.

By the time of the Kennedy-Nixon contest, demographic and attitudinal changes were transforming regional and national politics. Southern segregation was crumbling under attacks first by the Supreme Court, then from mass protests and voting drives by Blacks, and then in Lyndon B. Johnson's landslide election in 1964 and the major egalitarian legislation that followed.

Whites also changed, shifting residences and businesses from the older industrial regions toward the southern and western states, making California the fulcrum of America's economic and political change. Undermining southern traditionalism, many moved to work or retire in the region's warmer climes as dense urbanized areas replaced uncrowded rural counties. Kennedy's election validated the American legitimacy of Catholicism, even as its adherents became more numerous and more educated and were transformed from the working-class environment of their parents to exemplars of middle-class achievement. Manufacturing and farming declined, service and professional employment rose. At the same time, women entered offices and workplaces, changing from a distinct minority of wage earners to holders of close to half of all jobs. Income at first rose for all groups, so that the middle class received 62 percent of the nation's total income by 1970, more than twice the 29 percent share of the upper class. The trend then reversed during the rest of the twentieth century and beyond, so that the middle class share dropped to 43 percent, surpassed by the 48 percent received by the upper class in 2018.[4]

Political realignments inevitably reflected these vast changes. They are clearly evident in figure 1. This map shows the partisan vote of the states at the start of this period (Kennedy's miniscule victory in 1960) and, with Obama's second win in 2012, at its pre-Trump end point by a larger but still small Democratic margin.

Kennedy's minimal coalition of 302 electoral votes was built from the older industrial states with large Catholic populations, allied with the diminishing traditionalist loyalties in states of the old Confederacy. When

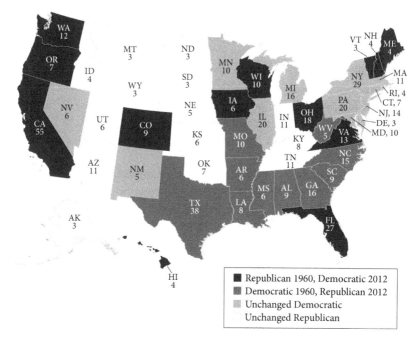

FIG. 1. The changing electoral map, 1960–2012
Source: Adapted by the author from official reports of the electoral vote in 1960 and 2012.

Obama won two terms, he drew a very different political map. By then, the former Confederacy had abandoned the Democrats' solid secessionist South for a more congenial Republican foundation. Kennedy carried eight of the eleven Confederate states as well as the Border states of Missouri and West Virginia. Obama carried two of his party's former domains— Virginia and Florida—but lost all the other contests.

Between these bookend elections, party allegiances changed considerably. A bare majority of states demonstrated the same party loyalty— fourteen states remained Republican, principally in the Plains and Mountain regions, and thirteen remained Democratic, principally in the urban Northeast. Nearly half, twenty-three of the fifty states, switched loyalties—thirteen from Republican to Democratic,[5] ten in the opposite direction. These shifts were so considerable that the correlation of the parties' state votes in 1960 to 2012 is only 0.23.

Those changes foreshadowed the Trump drama. By the time of the 2016 election, these redefined fault lines broke the Obama coalition, with the loss of five states in the industrial heartland, as well as all the

Confederate and Border states except Virginia. This pattern also appears in the Trump defeat of 2020. The South again largely repudiated its historical ties to the party of the Confederacy. New England and the Great Lakes states, the mid-nineteenth-century birthplaces of the Republicans, emerged as the foundation of the Biden victory, while the Pacific states, once solidly Republican, became the Democrats' bulwark.

Another characteristic of elections relates not to individual states but to the interstate similarity, or coherence, of the vote across states, reflecting the degree of consensus among voters. In a coherent election, the margins in each state would be relatively similar, indicating that a common mood affected voters throughout the nation. To measure coherence, we compare the inter-party margin of victory or defeat in each state with the national Democratic vote, identifying areas where the party's candidate ran above or below the national Democratic percentage by 5 percentage points or less.

In 1960, the election results are coherent. Most of the states—thirty-two of the fifty—were close to the national two-party vote for Kennedy, 50.1 percent. The Democrats gained outsize victories in only seven states and lost heavily in eleven Republican states. Even in these atypical states, the average margins were not catastrophic—7.1 percent where Republicans walked to victory, 11.4 percent when Democrats had easy wins.

The election of 1960 was tantalizingly close. The important point is that it was not only close overall but close throughout the country, so that it was a truly coherent national decision. The median state was won or lost by 0.7 percent of the vote. There were some runaway contests, but relatively few. In all regions, Kennedy surprisingly won some states by a hair—New Jersey, Illinois, New Mexico, Texas—as Nixon did in Florida, Ohio, Montana, and Oregon. In sum, over four-fifths of the country's population were in states close (within 5 percent) to the national division, and therefore worthy of politicians' attention as they designed their presidential campaigns. In a hallmark of a more national party system, the Kennedy-Nixon contest came close to a communal judgment of two well-matched candidates and, implicitly, their programs.

By contrast, in 2012, one-sided results marked thirty-seven states and the District of Columbia, each voting more than 5 percentage points above or below the national Democratic percentage. Some two-thirds of the national population lived in those states, meaning that the candidates could ignore two-thirds of the electorate who were surely for them or against them.

The results were hardly different in 2020, when thirty-five states (and the District of Columbia) were more than 5 percentage points above or below the national Democratic percentage. Outcomes near the national average (a median of 49% for each party) came in only fifteen states—all but three went for Biden. Republicans won most of the oversize victories, twenty-two, compared with thirteen (and D.C.) for the Democrats. In these one-sided states, each party fared a lot better or worse than in the nation generally (a median vote of 59%).

These disparities had less impact on the electoral vote. Democrats actually won more electoral votes in the runaway states, by a count of 182–150. However, the disparity is somewhat illusory, resulting from the huge effect of California's plunking its king-size fifty-five electoral votes for Biden, and the bare statistical inclusion of Texas, casting its thirty-eight electoral votes for Trump, as a marginal state (just shy of the 5% dividing line). The overall distribution shows a current strategic advantage for Republicans. They have a largely secure base and can concentrate on winning a handful of competitive states, even if they do not achieve a national popular vote majority. Democrats have fewer certain states and must campaign more extensively.

These are huge differences between the two partisan areas. They represent not only differences but also geographical polarization. By 2020, as the electoral map (see figure 2 in Mellow and Smith's chapter) shows, the nation had two concentrated Democratic areas in its northeastern quadrant and western/southwestern sprawl, a large Republican opposition through its vast middle, and a small region of close competition bordering the Great Lakes. The presidential election was not a national choice but a battle between two armies camped in separate fortifications while mobilizing for conflict on a distant field. The parties were not engaged in a national debate but in a limited war. Perhaps paradoxically, national partisanship has an increasing impact within states (as Jacobson shows in his chapter), but this common partisanship widens the differences among the states.

The nation is now close to settling into an electoral deadlock. Landslide victories have become rare, foreclosing the possibility of claimed mandates. An era of stable party dominance—such as the periods of Republican supremacy and then the New Deal realignment in the twentieth century—would at least provide predictability in the lives of politicians and citizens. Observers have forecast such stability for the past sixty years, predicting both an "emerging Republican majority" and an "emerging Democratic majority."[6]

Yet neither vision has come to pass. Instead, recent battle lines mark hardened entrenchments between impassioned foes, with neither party able to achieve coherent policy goals. Republicans have not won a popular majority for their presidential candidate in seven of the last eight elections, the longest such stretch of any party in history. Democrats, even while taking the presidency in half of the elections from 1984, have won only one large popular majority (Obama's first election in 2008). Yet the alignments set before 2012 have persisted since then.[7] These are signs of a new stability but not of a new political calm. The American political reality has become close elections, frequent turnovers in control of the White House and the chambers of Congress, divisions in power, increasing hostility between the parties and the separate branches, and decreasing capacity of government. There is no balance of harmony, but instead a stability of hostility.

Change in Individual Voting Behavior

The divisions that have developed among states have also developed among citizens. Changes in the voting preferences of different groups have made the contemporary parties different from those that existed from the New Deal, as seen in the trends presented in table 2, which summarizes the contribution of major groups to the Democratic coalition at the beginning and end of the 1960–2016 period.

A group's contribution is simply the number of votes it brings to the presidential party. It grows or diminishes by simple arithmetical measurement of complex change. A group that grows in *size*, or raises *turnout*, or increases the Democratic *share* of its vote will boost its *contribution* to the party. Contributing less inevitably decreases its importance to the party. Table 2 presents these figures in the second, third, and fourth columns.

We see major changes in the Democratic coalition during this period, as the party shifts away from its traditional base in the white working-class, rural areas in the South, and Catholics. Incorporating the transformations from the civil rights movement, Blacks and other nonwhites became critical supporters, rising from only a small proportion of the Democratic coalition in 1960 (4% for Blacks, the only nonwhite group measured) to a critical component (20% for all nonwhites) in 2016. Their increased weight comes from all the potential sources of change. Their size in the national population grew, their turnout exploded with the invalidation of legal segregation and racist voting laws, and political events spurred added loyalty to the Democratic Party. In this same period, Democrats lost support among other groups: men; both professed Catholics and Protestants, especially white Evangelicals; and rural residents.

A parallel and more striking change in the period after 1960 was electoral shifts in the parties reflecting—as both cause and effect—the

Table 2. The Democratic Party coalitions

Group/Year	% of total electorate	% vote for Democrat	Democrat vote (millions)	% contribution to coalition
Whites 1960	95	48	15.6	46
Whites 2016	70	37	17.2	30
Blacks 1960	5	74	1.3	4
Blacks 2016	12	88	7.0	11
Nonwhite 2016	27	75	13.5	20
Women 1960	50	47	8.0	24
Women 2016	52	54	18.7	28
Men 1960	50	52	8.9	26
Men 2016	48	41	13.1	20
Catholic 1960	21	82	5.9	17
Catholic 2016	23	45	6.9	10
Protestant 1960	71	37	9.0	26
Protestant 2016	52	39	13.5	20
College graduates 1960	34	1.3	4%	11
College graduates 2016	49	10.4	16%	32
Non-college 1960	33	52	5.9	17
Non-college 2016	18	45	5.4	8
Urban 1960	26	60	5.3	16
Urban 2016	34	59	13.3	20
Suburban 1960	49	44	7.4	22
Suburban 2016	49	45	14.7	22
Rural 1960	25	47	4.0	12
Rural 2016	17	34	3.8	6

Source: 1960: ANES Continuity Study; 2016: NEP exit polls, washingtonpost.com.

Note: "Democrat vote" is the product of multiplication of total Democratic vote for president in the designated year (1960: 34.15 million, 2016: 66.51 million) by "% of total electorate" and "% vote for Democrat." "% contribution to coalition" is this figure divided by the total party vote for president in the designated year.

ideological stances of their supporters. When Kennedy was elected and for most of the next two to three decades, the parties were different in their policy directions, but not dramatically distinct in their ideologies. Starting in the 1990s, polarization in attitudes becomes evident among both officeholders and their followers.

This change is presented in table 3, which shows the ideological leanings of different partisans: those strongly committed to the Democratic

TABLE 3. Party and ideology, 1972 and 2016

	Liberal	Moderate	Conservative
1972			
Strong Democrat	30.4%	60.8%	7.8%
Independent Democrat	22.5%	68.2%	7.3%
Independent Republican	3.8%	79.0%	17.2%
Strong Republican	3.3%	58.6%	38.2%
2016			
Strong Democrat	56.2%	40.0%	3.7%
Independent Democrat	34.2%	61.4%	1.5%
Independent Republican	1.4%	65.2%	34.7%
Strong Republican	0.6%	22.0%	77.3%

Source: ANES surveys 1972, 2016, recalculated by author. The original liberal-conservative scale records respondents' self-classifications on a 7-point scale. In this table, "Liberal" is defined as positions 1,2, "Moderate" as positions 3,4,5, "Conservative" as positions 6,7 on the ANES scale.

and Republican Parties and those self-proclaimed Independents who admit to a "leaning" toward one of the two major parties. We look at their ideological identifications in two years. The first is 1972, when party attachments were still based on tradition and a hazy attachment to policy issues.[8] The second year is 2016, as ideology became the basis for party attachment, and Trump became the emblem of sharp party differences.

In the first grouping in the table, there is a significant proportion of liberals among strong Democrats, but moderates are the modal group, an identification that is even greater among Independents who lean toward the Democrats. Similarly, among Republicans, there are many conservatives, but moderates predominate.

By 2016, when Trump took over the leadership of the Republicans, the party had become overwhelmingly conservative, and there is only a bare trace remaining of liberals among Republican voters or their allies among Independents. Democrats have moved in the opposite ideological direction—liberals are now a majority of their party base and have increased among their Independent allies, while conservatives have essentially disappeared.

This change in the basis of partisanship culminates decades of increased ideological commitment by the voters. In classic studies of American electoral behavior, coherence in political ideology was absent in the minds of most voters, who instead relied on the cues of traditional loyalties to parties and social groups or judgments about the "nature of the times" or the personal characteristics of candidates. By 2016, and continuing in 2020, average voters displayed a coherence in their political beliefs that matched that of the "elites" of earlier times. That coherence was undergirded by the rising effect of two attitudes. Racial resentment, always present in American history, has become newly significant. Negative partisanship—that is, hostility toward the opposition party—has become a stronger motivation than a voter's traditional loyalty to his or her own party. Analyzing these trends, Alan Abramowitz astutely foretold the path to 2020: "The Trump years are likely to witness the most intense partisan hostility in modern American history."[9]

This review of the past sixty years leads to a dim forecast for future American politics. A series of close and indecisive elections provides no basis for a mandate to resolve policy issues. The changing geography of these elections has fractured the country into opposing areas of hostile partisans, leaving the electoral outcome to a few battlegrounds. Neither major party has a voting coalition that can provide sufficient popular thrust toward meeting the nation's problems, as ideological coherence precludes political compromise. Neither the former Republican dream of an "electoral lock" nor the Democratic reliance on an ensured "blue wall" of supportive states has been realized. Political moderation has diminished among both officeholders and voters. Partisan consistency in elections—whether for the House of Representatives, Senate, or state legislatures—reduces the checks and balances of national institutions or federalism.

The total effect of these changes is the current status of political polarization, reflecting the fierce partisanship of political leaders—the elites that Marc Hetherington[10] identifies as prime movers in these developments but who now show little ability or interest in resolving the resulting conflicts. In 2020, the partisan divide was glaringly evident on the floor of Congress, in the massive voter turnout, in the bitter differences and quarrels among neighbors and within families, and eventually in Republicans refusing to acknowledge Trump's evident defeat even after he trailed Biden by 7 million popular ballots and 74 electoral votes.

The Campaign of 2020: A Series of Unfortunate Events

Although the tone of politics in 2020 was strident, the contestants did agree on one premise: the election was fought as an existential decision for the nation. Lara Trump, the president's daughter-in-law declared, "This is not just a choice between Republican and Democrat or left and right. This is an election that will decide if we keep America America—or if we head down an uncharted, frightening path towards socialism."[11] Former president Obama also saw the election as an apocalyptic struggle: "You can give our democracy new meaning. . . . But any chance of success depends entirely on the outcome of this election. This administration has shown it will tear our democracy down if that's what it takes to win."[12]

American voters also believed the election was critical. In a Gallup poll, 77 percent of registered voters said the outcome mattered more to them than in previous election years.[13] The opinion was shared by Democrats (85%) and Republicans (79%). These sentiments were not routine patriotism—barely more than 40 percent offered the same answers in 2000. In 2020, voters followed through on their determination by casting ballots in difficult and dangerous circumstances, setting records of participation not seen since the dawn of the twentieth century. They cast their ballots after a campaign that was historically conflictual and foreboding for the American future.

An Election of Magic and the Apocalypse

The political life and presidency of Donald Trump had been almost magical. Despite a history of adulterous liaisons, crude comments about women's looks and intelligence, and boastful sexual assaults, he won a majority in 2016 among white women voters. Despite behavior contrary to basic democratic norms, including verbal attacks on news correspondents and banishing critics from the White House, 30,000 documented lies, and threats to order military responses to protests, he came close to majority approval in some national polls. A two-year investigation by a special counsel, and Trump's own efforts to enlist foreign leaders to sully his leading Democratic opponent, eventually brought impeachment by the House but quick acquittal by the Senate with only one Republican in each chamber supporting the charges. Trump had created a political Teflon to shield himself against the heat of government and public opinion.

Then came a turn of history: a plague of biblical proportions arose in China, traveled like locusts to Europe, then swarmed to the United States. A pandemic darkened the planet, killing over two million of the world's men and women, with the pestilence reaching its highest numbers in the United States—over 24 million cases and over 400,000 American deaths by the end of Trump's presidency. His response was inadequate, even uncaring, as he wrongly assured the nation that this novel threat would be gone in days. But even if he were as wise as Moses, he was as likely to defeat the coronavirus as the ancient Pharaoh was to end the Egyptian plagues.

The pandemic brought a second, human assault. As some Americans died, others were laid off and sent home to shelter in place to ward off contamination. As businesses closed and consumers hunkered down, the economy collapsed. Most governors issued emergency orders closing businesses and requiring residents to stay at home in lockdowns isolated from work or social contacts. As 22 million workers lost their jobs, the official unemployment rate quadrupled to nearly 15 percent, reaching the worst level since the Great Depression and wiping out all the touted job gains of the Trump years. A third of the lost jobs did return in May and June, but others were lost after new outbreaks of the coronavirus, with unemployment still at a crisis level of 11 percent at the end of the summer.

Trump himself initiated few actions, leaving most operational decisions to public health and state officials, as he looked toward an economic recovery through the reopening of workplaces. He acted more like a cheerleader, urging people to gather in churches on Easter (where they would be more subject to contagion), or as a patent medicine salesman, suggesting ingestion or injection of chlorine bleach to ward off infection (a dangerous and useless treatment). Still, politically, Trump came close to riding out the onslaught. By the end of March, his approval rating rose to its highest level in the more than three years since his inauguration.[14]

Then, on May 25, a different kind of assault occurred: the murder of George Floyd, a young African American man, through police violence in Minneapolis. For the next two weeks, protests, overwhelmingly peaceful and often held by crowds with white majorities, swept the nation. Marches filled streets in over 2,000 cities throughout the nation,[15] engaging millions of Americans. Startling symbolic acts ensued, including stripping the traditional picture of "Aunt Jemima" from pancake syrup bottles, assuming the prayerful pose of "taking a knee" at athletic events, and removing the names of Confederate officers from military installations. In response, the president emphasized "law and order," interpreted by him as forceful "domination" of protest, including armed repression by elite combat troops ordered to Washington.

The president had suffered three huge onslaughts: the pandemic wave, the economic collapse, and the racial protests. His political Teflon had seemingly been burned away. His polled disapproval rating neared a four-year high, and his favorable evaluations fell almost below the politically catastrophic level of 40 percent. Preelection polls showed Biden leading him on average by over 8 percent nationally, and ahead in virtually every battleground state. Yet still searching for renewed magic, Trump would try to repeat his first miraculous victory.

The Conventions and the Campaign

The active general election campaign began with the national conventions in July, then went into high gear in September. While the candidates jousted, the world whirled. By September 1, COVID-19 had infected 6 million Americans and killed 184,000; the pandemic's economic impact sent 39 million to the unemployment rolls; urban protests, retaliations, and police actions brought violence and dissent to scores of cities; children, parents, workers, and college students were confined to their homes for months. Institutions such as national party conventions withered; political communication was transformed from human speech to electronic artifice; the language of campaigning changed from dialogue to vituperation.

Amid all these massive changes in American lives, a different kind of magic appeared. The year 2020 loomed as one of unparalleled catastrophe, but the campaign seemed both virulent and frozen. Despite the apparent coming of an apocalypse, voters hardly changed their intentions, remaining impassioned, opinionated, and yet collectively unmoving in their commitments. A chart (figure 2) of their presidential preferences at the beginning of each month from April to November pictures a steady, slowly rising Democratic lead. According to polls, Biden held an early but not overwhelming lead of 6–7 percent, rising in October to 8–9 percent. There were daily perturbations and a summer bump and subsequent slump for Biden, but the overall trend was essentially a straight line over the full campaign. Pundits, practitioners, and political scientists pondered every turn of events, every strategy and speech of Trump and Biden, like picnickers wary of scattered raindrops. Yet voters seemed like distant observers of a tornado—fascinated, sometimes fearful, but seemingly fixed in their opinions. Voters had already made up their minds, it seemed. The outcome of the election appeared already determined.

The campaign tested established models of voter behavior. Incumbency is normally an advantage for presidents seeking reelection; they had won all but three of thirteen such contests since 1936. Trump used the large powers of his office to advance his campaign—for example, by staging partisan rallies on rent-free sites such as the White House, Fort McHenry, and Mount Rushmore. But he still presented himself as an outsider criticizing the "Washington swamp" and the "Deep State" that he now commanded, his four years replete with attacks, defections, and firings of career officials and many of his own appointees.

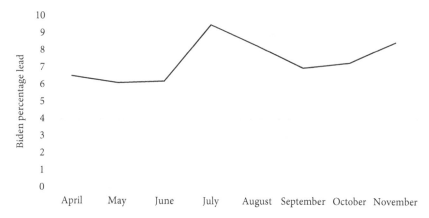

FIG. 2. Biden lead in presidential polls
Source: Adapted by author from daily reports of "Who's Ahead in the National Polls?,"
fivethirtyeight.com.

Another common gauge of presidential elections is the relative emphasis on the past or the future. Retrospective evaluations are common in electoral behavior, because voters have direct empirical knowledge of past events, while the future is always difficult to predict.[16] The nominating conventions of both parties centered on the incumbent president. The emphasis was stark when Biden delivered his acceptance speech on the last night of the Democratic convention, focusing on the past four years of the Trump administration: "If he's given four more years, he'll be what he's been the last four years," he said, "a president who takes no responsibility, refuses to lead, blames others, cozies up to dictators and fanned the flames of hate and division. . . . [He] will wake up every day thinking the job is all about him, never about you."[17] The president's failures, particularly in dealing with the coronavirus epidemic, became the focus of the Biden campaign.

Trump's supporters quipped that the two words most frequently voiced by the Democrats in 2020 were "Donald" and "Trump." That personal emphasis was even more evident in the Republicans' own programming. Unconcerned with political tradition and wary of the pandemic, Trump shuttled the location of the party convention among Charlotte, Jacksonville, and Washington, then minimized the roles of most delegates. The president appeared every night of their four-day conclave, shattering all precedents. The speakers included most members of his family—his wife, four of his adult children, two of their spouses or partners, ideological allies among party officials and citizens, but no former Republican presidents or nominees.

For all the attention he received, however, Trump said little about his goals in a second term. Instead of the normal party platform including pledges of future action, the GOP simply republished its 2016 document, adding only a single page of bullet points, largely repetitions of past programs, and a specific ban on any new declarations of policy until 2024. Trump's emphasis instead was on the gloomy future that he foresaw in a Democratic administration. Attacking from Biden's hometown of Scranton, Trump warned, "If you want a vision of your life under [a] Biden presidency, think of the smoldering ruins in Minneapolis, the violent anarchy of Portland, the bloodstained sidewalks of Chicago, and imagine the mayhem coming to your town and every single town in America."[18] He combined that vision of "American carnage" with virulent personal attacks. Trump cited (and attacked) Biden by name forty-one times in his acceptance speech. Biden, while certainly extremely critical of the president, never mentioned the word "Trump" at his own convention, the name itself a blasphemy to his supporters.

Trump made many aggressive moves, looking for events and a strategy that would put him on a path to reelection. But each of his early efforts floundered, as possible themes failed to catch fire, including alleged corrupt behavior by Biden's son, scurrilous hints that Biden was physically feeble or mentally impaired, and depictions of Biden as a "radical socialist" controlled by left-wing Democrats such as Senator Bernie Sanders.

On September 18, another option opened for Trump when Supreme Court justice Ruth Bader Ginsburg died after a long series of illnesses. Trump saw a golden opportunity to add a conservative to the court, believing that right-wing voters would rally to his own cause. All but two Republican senators quickly fell into line, and he did ultimately achieve confirmation of his choice, Judge Amy Coney Barrett. But there was no electoral gain as liberal opponents flooded Democratic coffers with contributions of $300 million.

The first scheduled presidential debate followed, another chance for Trump to subdue his challenger. But he overplayed his hand, aggressively berating Biden, violating debate rules by speaking beyond time limits, interrupting and attempting to loudly overwhelm his opponent, and giving Biden openings for his own jabs, smirks, and disdain. Asked to reject groups that advocated "white supremacy," Trump whiffed at the easy pitch and appeared to share their extreme conspiratorial constructs and programs. Biden, while not spectacular, easily refuted the whispered attacks on his health simply by being competent and coherent.

Two days later, the president revealed that he had contracted the coronavirus disease, required treatment at Walter Reed hospital for three days, and returned to campaigning even while his physical condition was still uncertain. Vital campaign support was lost in these critical days when major Republican figures contracted COVID-19 during and after a celebration of Barrett's nomination, including the chair of Trump's campaign, his coach for the television debates, three Republican senators, the chair of the Republican National Committee, three leading White House policy advisers, the president's press secretary, and his wife, youngest child, and eldest son.

Additional scheduled television events gave Trump a chance to revive. He rejected new rules for a remote rather than in-person second debate, which would foreclose direct attacks on Biden. Instead, the candidates held their own town halls on different networks, drawing a diminished combined audience of about 27 million on television, a sharp decrease from the 73 million predicted for a direct confrontation. The intended third debate went ahead as scheduled, less than twelve days before Election Day, and weeks after millions of ballots had already been cast in early and absentee voting.

Events turned against Trump as relentlessly as they had favored him until the election year. He fired his campaign manager of three years' standing, who had mismanaged the party's finances, leaving the affluent Republicans with shrunken resources. The economy showed some signs of revival in the summer—another possible magical intervention for Trump, but reports in the fall revealed an increase in unemployment claims and new business losses. Four days before the country voted, as the president got the good news that the economy had strongly improved in the third quarter of the year, the welcomed report was offset by the bad news that new coronavirus cases had reached a record daily high, over 100,00 nationally.

Trump had put much hope and much government money into a vigorous medical effort to achieve the ultimate "October surprise," announcing the "miracle" of a proven vaccine to stop the spread of COVID-19 before "a certain day," November 3. The research effort was impressive, but scientists cautiously extended trials, announcing the successful tests of a vaccine six days *after* all ballots were cast—evoking Trump's clear resentment of the delay.

Looking beyond the discouraging polling, Trump refused to accept the legitimacy of the vote. He denounced absentee mail balloting and attempted to hinder the procedure through reduced funding for the Postal Service. He tentatively suggested that the election be postponed, or that ballot counting end on the night of November 3, so that mailed ballots would not be tallied.

The president prepared to challenge any apparent defeat through court suits and refused to commit himself to the minimal promise of "the peaceful transfer of power." Instead, untiring to the last day, he made a stalwart personal effort, frenetically rushing to close the polling gap at multiple mass rallies in battleground states, presaging his later desperate efforts to reverse his electoral defeat. His targets combined his two campaigns, a reprise of his attacks on Clinton in 2016 and a continued denigration of "Sleepy Joe Biden" and "monster" Kamala Harris. For all his foes, he had the same threatening incitement: "Lock 'Em Up."

The Voters Decide

As early and mail voting began at the beginning of October, the rhetoric of the campaign deteriorated further. Conspiracy theories spread, fueled by reports of imagined secret plots to steal the election. From the Left, an article in one of the nation's most distinguished magazines warned of imminent efforts by Trump designed, for example, at "recruiting 50,000 volunteers in 15 contested states to monitor polling places and challenge voters they deem suspicious-looking" and alerted readers that Trump "might invoke the Insurrection Act of 1807 [and] deploy the United States military to Democrat-run cities in order to protect life and property . . . bypass election results and appoint loyal electors in battleground states where Republicans hold the legislative majority."[19]

If these forebodings showed exaggerated worries about the future, they were more than matched by fears expressed by Trump supporters. On the internet, fantastic theories abounded, including one that blamed his hypothetical loss on "a cabal of satanic pedophiles." Sidney Powell, a lead lawyer for Trump, "laid out an elaborate conspiracy theory about efforts by the former Venezuelan president Hugo Chávez, who died in 2013, to essentially rig elections in the United States" by using corrupted voting machines.[20]

The president joined the challenges to reported voting results, although with less imaginative objections. A day after the close of in-person voting, he announced at the White House both that he had won the election and that the prevailing Biden count was fake. For weeks, he repeated various suspicions of fraudulent ballots, including voting by dead people, inclusion of ballots sent after established deadlines, theft of mailed Trump ballots, exclusion of Republican poll watchers, and false tabulations.

When the media reported a winning Biden majority, he refused to accept defeat, as detailed below. After a handful of Republican senators demurred and Republican state politicians certified Biden victories, he finally allowed transition planning but defiantly said he would "never concede" and insisted that Biden had won only a "rigged election." As his hopes shrank, he prepared new strategems while promising to mount a four-year comeback before the next election, 2024.

Turnout

By November 3, Election Day, turnout was already impressive even before the customary polling stations opened. More than 101 million had voted early or by mail, more than thrice the number in 2016. While Democrats led in early and mailed ballots, the flood of voter participation continued on Election Day. Trump still clung to his belief—eventually confirmed—that a strong countervailing vote on November 3 would result from direct local canvassing among the diminishing minority of in-person voters.[21]

The overall result was a record turnout, near 160 million, an increase of about 15 percent over 2016. Nationally, two-thirds of the eligible population voted, achieving the highest voting rate since 1900. Participation reached record levels throughout the country—in nineteen states more than 70 percent of the eligible population cast votes, while only five were below 60 percent, and a majority cast ballots in every state. These turnouts, in contrast to the earlier eras of the nation, included groups once excluded from the voting rolls: women, Blacks, Asian Americans, persons younger than twenty-one, and disabled individuals unable to reach inaccessible sites. By this standard, the election of 2020 was the most democratic ever held in the United States, a historic outpouring of the largest number of participants in a free election in any country other than India at any time in human life.[22]

Moreover, despite the strong passions held by voters on the opposing sides, their nightmares were abandoned—at least temporarily—to the dark. Whites were not assaulted by urban Blacks, Trump did not mobilize the Department of Justice or armed troops to halt the election, judges were uncorrupted by party loyalties, election administrators did their jobs. Balloting was largely peaceful, free of violence and obstruction, accurately reported, and conducted with scarce fraud or illegal balloting. Voting was simpler and faster than in the primaries, bolstered by procedural improvements in many states and extensive recruitment of volunteers—including tens of thousands of tech-savvy teenagers who filled vacancies among poll workers, often elderly, who were more vulnerable to COVID-19 and less familiar with computer technology.

The Final Results

Meeting its constitutional duty on December 14, the Electoral College delivered the final electoral votes: 306 for Biden, 232 for Trump, exactly the reverse of the 2016 counts for Clinton and Trump. The former vice president won exactly half of the fifty states as well as the District of Columbia, with five states flipping from Republican to Democratic and none going in the opposite direction. Biden made gains in different regions, narrowly extending the blue Democratic map to include Arizona and Georgia, while restoring it to former party bastions on the Great Lakes.

Biden led in the total popular vote by 4.4 percentage points, 51.3 to 46.9. Winning the largest vote of any presidential candidate in U.S. history, his plurality over Trump was 7 million, close to three times greater than that of Clinton over Trump in 2016. Biden's margins in critical states, however, were much narrower. Trump had won four years earlier by only 77,000 combined votes in three states. He could have won a second term as a minority president if he had secured the right combination of another 125,000 votes in four close states—Wisconsin and Pennsylvania in the industrial Midwest, and Georgia and Arizona in the Sunbelt.[23] Instead, Trump joined the short list of defeated incumbent presidents, losers in their bids for reelection. Biden's success was clear and sufficient—but as Wellington famously said of his historic victory over Napoleon at Waterloo, it was "a close-won thing."

The results, while definite, were not decisive. With the vital exception of Trump's removal, the political balance remains frozen in partisan deadlock. The most important election, for president, did provide Biden with the immense power of the office and removed a flawed and failed incumbent. But Biden had no landslide, only an attenuated mandate, and few new fellow partisans with whom to share the victory. Democrats netted only one additional Senate seat before victories in two runoff elections in Georgia brought them to slim control of the chamber where the new vice president would cast a tie-breaking vote. In the House, they barely retained control, their fragile margin now reduced to single digits. The party took over no new state legislative chambers, remaining vulnerable to Republican gerrymanders after the 2020 census results are reported.

Explaining these results requires analysis of the views of individual voters, using opinion polls during the campaign and exit polls of actual voters.[24] When polled early in the year, voters generally said they would do as they did in 2016, as seen in figure 3, choosing Trump again or simply replacing Democrat Clinton with Democrat Biden. Change would come

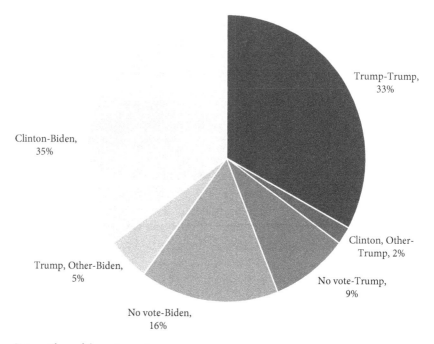

Fɪɢ. 3. Flow of the vote, 2016–20
Source: Author's calculation of data from the American National Elections Studies, 2020 Pilot Study.

primarily from new voters—those who had abstained, chosen a third party, or were too young to participate four years earlier.

Later, when ballots were actually cast, that same stability—or immobility—was also evident in the limited shifts among demographic groups. (See table 4.) The party lines hardened a bit, ideological conservatives rallied more fervently around Trump and liberals around Biden, while Independents and moderates moved significantly toward the Democrats (a 12-point shift in both groups), demonstrating the party's politically astute nomination of a reputed centrist. There were apparent slight declines in the other groups favoring Democrats. Trump gained among ethnic minorities, and the fabled "gender gap" was smaller because, as women held their support steady, men moved toward Biden. College graduates gave an edge to Biden, offset by nongraduates' backing of Trump.

To a limited extent, Biden did resuscitate the older Democratic coalition. Women maintained their support, a larger portion of Catholics backed the potential second Catholic president, Biden gained a sliver of

TABLE 4. Voting patterns in the presidential vote

Group	% Share of Voters	Biden % 2020	Trump % 2020	Democratic % Change 2016-20
White men	35	38	61	+8
White women	32	44	55	+2
Black men	4	79	19	−9
Black women	8	90	9	−9
Latino men	5	59	36	−8
Latina women	8	69	30	−5
Asian, Other	8	58	38	−7
Democratic ID	37	94	5	+5
Republican ID	36	6	94	−1
Independent, Other ID	26	54	41	+12
College grads	41	55	43	+3
Non-college grads	59	48	50	+4
White grads	32	51	48	+6
White non-grads	35	32	67	+3
Nonwhite grads	10	70	27	−1
Nonwhite Not college grads	24	72	26	−2
White women grads	14	54	45	+3
White women Not college grads	17	36	63	+2
White men grads	16	50	50	+7
White men Not college grads	16	30	67	+2
Protestant/Christian	43	39	60	−1
White Evangelical	28	24	76	+6
Catholic	25	52	47	+6
No religion	22	65	31	−3
Most important issue				
Coronavirus pandemic	17	81	15	
The economy	35	17	83	
Crime and safety	11	27	71	
Health care	11	62	37	
Racial inequality	20	92	7	

Sources: National Election Poll, conducted by Edison Research, as reported at: washingtonpost.com/elections/interactive/2020/exit-polls/presidential-election-exit -polls/; cnn.com/election/2020/exit-polls (accessed November 11, 2020); for 2016, .pewresearch.org/fact-tank/2016/11/09/.

additional support from Evangelicals, young voters gave him over 60 percent of their new votes, and Blacks increased turnout in the critical states.

Further insight comes from the actual recorded vote, facilitating reliable "ecological inference" from voters' residential location. The party vote held steady at the population extremes: large cities again gave Democrats three of every five votes, and rural counties and small towns held or marginally added to their recent Republican majorities of 60–70 percent. The areas crucial for Biden's victory were the suburbs—particularly college towns, retirement communities, and exurbs—which moved toward the Democrats by more than 4 percent.[25]

But the election had no clear policy focus. Biden supporters concentrated on the pandemic or health care, Trump backers on the economy. The antagonists even used different terms for the same issue, whether "racial inequality" (Democrats) or "crime and safety" (Republicans).

Future voting patterns are uncertain. Demographic change provides no sure Democratic foundation. Groups constituting the Republican base have diminished in size; groups voting Democratic have increased. The ranks of college graduates, both white and minorities, will expand. Suburbs will grow, and rural areas will decline. As the nation becomes more urban and suburban, diverse and secular, the Republican Party may decay.[26]

But demography is not destiny. Groups may change their loyalties, as some members of minority ethnic groups did in 2020. Dynamic new leaders—like a new Trump or even the defeated but resurrected original version—may revive Trump's siren calls to the voters. As it was in 2020, the future of their political system is ultimately in the hands and minds of the American electorate.

Conclusion: An Uncertain Future

Relieved optimists saw the defeat of Trump as the electoral repudiation of an authoritarian attack on American liberties, the basic political norms of constitutional democracy, and moral decency. But worried pessimists pointed to Trump's four-year violation of established standards, his rejection of the principle of a "peaceful transfer of power," and his unremitting denunciation of the election as fraudulent and illegitimate—the last claim endorsed, even as late as Inaugural Day, by 70 percent of Republican voters.[27]

These attitudes were exacerbated, not created, by the Trump presidency. Trump legitimized antidemocratic behaviors, such as derision and threats of imprisonment and violence toward opponents and the deliberate stoking of racist sentiments. Whether or not he makes a political comeback, these practices may well be repeated by other, more competent politicians. "The weakening of our democratic norms is rooted in extreme political polarization—one that extends beyond policy differences into an existential conflict over race and culture," warn leading experts on antidemocratic trends.[28] The discordant results of the election of 2020 only underline the threat that "the evolving ways we're polarized—by age, geography, sex, class and faith—are still the more powerful forces, dragging us ever back toward stalemate.[29]

Although the results showed a clear Biden victory, these concerns were not resolved by the election of 2020. Instead, the threats were increased as Trump, enraged by his defeat, pursued his phantom dream of a landslide victory for eleven weeks, eventually provoking a violent insurrection against the democratic process of the United States.

His acts[30] included the administration's five-week delay, contrary to statute, in establishing transitions from the outgoing to the new administration. On his own, Trump denounced the "rigged" election results repeatedly, even farcically and possibly corruptly, focusing his ire on election officials who confirmed his narrow losses in the battleground states. He summoned Michigan state legislators to the White House to urge that the Republican state legislature declare the election invalid, and replace the popular vote for Democratic electors with a Republican slate. He denounced the Republican governors of Arizona and Georgia, who certified Biden as their states' winner, and, in the face of Georgia's hand recount of five million ballots, secretly urged its Secretary of State to "find" enough ballots to turn the outcome in his favor. Recruiting unprepared lawyers, he pursued sixty lawsuits charging electoral fraud or unlawful practices, but won none of significance. Appealing to the Supreme Court, he filed a nonsensical suit to invalidate the election result in three states won by Biden, a plea the Court unanimously rejected in a single sentence. In final desperation, he unsuccessfully urged Vice President Mike Pence to violate the Constitution by rejecting the reported electoral results at the formal counting by Congress on January 6, two weeks before Inauguration Day.

When Congress convened on that day, Trump took his final step to maintain power. Having summoned his supporters to attend a "wild" mass rally, he denounced Pence's reluctance to ignore the official tally while urging thousands of rowdy protestors to "march to the Capitol" to force a reversal. They raucously followed his lead, breaking doors and windows to take control of the halls and chambers of Congress for nearly four hours, threatening the lives of Pence, Speaker Nancy Pelosi, and fleeing senators and representatives. Their riot led to the death of five people, including three members of the Capitol Police.

The nation was shocked, frightened, uncertain. Congressional leaders of both parties attempted calm, and both House and Senate reconvened to ratify Biden's victory—although a majority of House Republicans and eight Republican senators still stood with Trump. Not until the next day did Trump join the country's denunciation of violence. The House moved quickly to impeach Trump a second time, indicting him for "Incitement to Insurrection." But, although judged guilty by a Senate majority of 57–43, he escaped conviction by the required two-thirds vote as most Republicans stayed loyal to their departed leader.

All Americans now agree that the United States needs more unity and more comity. With victorious words that later became the theme of his inaugural address, President Biden acknowledged "how deep and hard the opposing views are in our country on so many things. But I also know this, as well. To make progress, we have to stop treating our opponents as enemies. We are not enemies. What brings us together as Americans is so much stronger than anything that can tear us apart."[31]

Biden's outreach echoed Abraham Lincoln in his first inaugural address, facing the Civil War: "We are not enemies, but friends. We must not be enemies. Though passion may have strained, it must not break, our bonds of affection." And Biden also reiterated the historic appeal of Thomas Jefferson, taking office after the first peaceful transfer of power through popular election in human history: "Let us, then, fellow-citizens, unite with one heart and one mind. Let us restore to social intercourse that harmony and affection without which liberty and even life itself are but dreary things."[32]

Benjamin Franklin provides a final hopeful interpretation of the election of 2020. While he waited to sign the proposed new Constitution in 1787, he remarked that he had often gazed at the sun painted on the chair of George Washington, the presiding officer. Franklin admitted he had been distracted by "the vicissitudes of my hopes and fears . . . without being able to tell whether it was rising or setting." At the final ceremony, the oldest delegate came to an optimistic judgment: "But now at length I have the happiness to know that it is a rising and not a setting Sun."[33]

Perhaps the American sun will still rise. Perhaps.

Notes

I dedicate this chapter to Sandra Bergelson, "New angel mine, unhoped for in the world."

I thank Tyler Cheatle, an outstanding Rutgers student, for his insightful help in the data analyses.

1. There are many—and conflicting—interpretations. Classic studies include Walter Dean Burnham, *Critical Elections and the Mainsprings of American Politics* (New York: Norton, 1970) and James Sundquist, *Dynamics of the Party System*, 2nd ed. (Washington, DC: Brookings Institution, 1983).

2. The material in this section is drawn from my article "Landslide Elections and Policy Mandates," Sabato's Crystal Ball, University of Virginia Center for Politics, June 11, 2020. centerforpolitics.org/crystalball. I thank the editors for their permission.

3. The quotations are from their respective inaugural addresses in 1921 (avalon.law.yale.edu/20th_century/harding.asp) and 1933 (avalon.law.yale.edu/20th_century/froos1.asp).

4. Pew Research Center, Juliana Menasce Horowitz, Ruth Igielnik, and Rakesh Kochhar, January 9, 2020, pewsocialtrends.org/2020/01/09/trends-in-income-and-wealth-inequality/.

5. Hawaii is included as a Republican state in 1960, on the basis of its original reported vote. In a later reversal, its electoral vote was officially awarded to Kennedy.

6. Kevin Phillips, *The Emerging Republican Majority* (New York: Arlington House, 1969); John Judis and Ruy Teixeira, *The Emerging Democratic Majority* (New York: Simon & Schuster, 2002).

7. The state-by-state correlations reach high values of 0.85 for 2012–16 and 0.98 for 2016–20.

8. It is also the year that the American National Election Studies fully used its refined 7-point "liberal-conservative scale" to assess the effect of ideology on voting choices.

9. Alan Abramowitz, *The Great Alignment* (New Haven, CT: Yale University Press, 2018), chap. 7 and p. 173. See also Matthew Levendusky, *The Partisan Sort* (Chicago: University of Chicago Press, 2009).

10. Marc J. Hetherington, "Resurgent Mass Partisanship: The Role of Elite Polarization," *American Political Science Review* 95 (September 2001): 619–31.

11. James Hohmann, "The Daily 202," washingtonpost.com, August 27, 2020.

12. cnn.com/2020/08/19/politics/barack-obama-speech-transcript/index.html.

13. Willem Roper, "2020 Election Matters More Than Previous Years, Voters Say," Statista, October 20, 2020, statista.com/chart/23235/.

14. Data from daily presentation, "Who's Ahead in the National Polls?," FiveThirtyEight.

15. *New York Times*, June 16, 2020, A16–A17, nytimes.com/interactive/2020 /06/13/usgeorge-floyd-protests-cities-photos.html.

16. Morris Fiorina, *Retrospective Voting in American National Elections* (New Haven, CT: Yale University Press, 1981); Anthony Downs, *An Economic Theory of Democracy* (New York: Harper & Row, 1957), chap. 12.

17. Dan Balz, "Biden Offers Sharp Attack on Trump as a Dark Force and Promises to Be 'an Ally of the Light' as President," *Washington Post*, August 21, 2020.

18. *New York Times*, August 20, 2020, p.A1.

19. Barton Gellman, "The Election That Could Break America," *Atlantic*, November 2020.

20. Maggie Haberman and Alan Feuer, "Trump Team Disavows Lawyer Who Peddled Conspiracy Theories on Voting," *New York Times*, November 22, 2020.

21. "Voter Turnout," at: electproject.github.io/Early-Vote-2020G/index.html (November 2, 2020).

22. Turnout estimates are from the authoritative source of the United States Election Project, November 16, 2020, electproject.org/2020g.

23. Arithmetic speculation can lead to other imagined outcomes. If Trump had gained only 44,000 votes in three states—Wisconsin, Arizona, and Georgia—he would have achieved a 269–269 tie in the Electoral College, leaving a final decision to the new Congress. There, the possible result could be either the choice of Trump by the House or the designation of Speaker Nancy Pelosi as Acting President. Or, to extend the guesswork, a recount might have resulted in Biden winning additional electoral votes in Maine or North Carolina or Florida.

24. This analysis was done expertly in earlier chapters, especially the chapter by Hetherington and that by Mellow and Smith. In the treatment here, I use only a small portion of these data. The unusual problems in this year's surveys are examined well by two expert pollsters: David Hill, "The Dirty Little Secret Pollsters Need to Own Up To," *Washington Post*, November 19, 2020; and Nate Cohn, "What Went Wrong with Polling? Some Early Theories," *New York Times*, November 11, 220, A12.

25. Richard Florida, Marie Patino, and Rachael Dottle, "How Suburbs Swung the 2020 Election," Bloomberg City Lab, November 17, 2020, bloomberg .com/graphics/2020-suburban-density-election.

26. George F. Will, "Trump Will End His Presidency as He Began It: Whining," *Washington Post*, October 21, 2020; George F. Will, "The Coming Decade of Democratic Dominance," *Washington Post*, October 28, 2020.

27. Patrick Murray, "National: Majority Support Trump Impeachment," Monmouth University Poll (January 25, 2021), at www.monmouth.edu/polling.

28. Steven Levitsky and Daniel Ziblatt, *How Democracies Die* (New York: Crown, 2018), 9.

29. Ross Douthat, "Will the 2020 Election Be Decisive?," *New York Times*, November 4, 2020, A31.

30. For a fuller account, see Jim Rutenberg et al., "77 Days: Trump's Campaign to Subvert the Election," nytimes.com/2021/01/31/us/.

31. Katie Glueck and Thomas Kaplan, "Biden, Now President-Elect, Calls for End to 'Grim Era of Demonization'," *New York Times*, November 7, 2020, A1.

32. Abraham Lincoln, First Inaugural address, at: avalon.law.yale.edu/19th _century/lincoln1.asp; Thomas Jefferson, First Inaugural Address, at: avalon.law.yale.edu/19th_century/jefinau1.asp.

33. James Madison, *Notes of Debates in the Federal Convention of 1787* (Athens: Ohio University Press, 1966), 659.

CONTRIBUTORS

MICHAEL NELSON is the Fulmer Professor of Political Science at Rhodes College and a senior fellow at the University of Virginia's Miller Center. His book *Resilient America: Electing Nixon in 1968, Channeling Dissent, and Dividing Government* won the American Political Science Association's Richard E. Neustadt Award for the outstanding book on the Presidency and Executive Politics published in 2014, and the Southern Political Science Association conferred its 2009 V.O. Key Award for Outstanding Book on Southern Politics on Nelson and coauthor John Lyman Mason for *How the South Joined the Gambling Nation: The Politics of State Policy Innovation*.

MARJORIE RANDON HERSHEY is professor emerita of political science and philanthropic studies at Indiana University. Among her books and articles about political parties and elections, her book *Party Politics in America* is now in its eighteenth edition.

MARC J. HETHERINGTON is Raymond Dawson Bicentennial Professor of Political Science at the University of North Carolina–Chapel Hill. His research centers on public opinion, with particular focus on polarization and trust in government.

CHARLES R. HUNT is an assistant professor of political science at Boise State University and the author of the forthcoming book *Home Field Advantage: Roots, Reelection, and Representation in the Modern Congress*. His scholarship focuses on congressional elections, representation, and campaign finance.

GARY C. JACOBSON is Distinguished Professor of Political Science Emeritus at the University of California, San Diego. He specializes in the study of U.S. elections, parties, interest groups, public opinion, and Congress. His most recent book is *Presidents and Parties in the Public Mind* (2019).

WILLIAM G. MAYER is a professor of political science at Northeastern University. He is the author or coauthor of twelve books, including the forthcoming *Uses and Misuses of Politics: Karl Rove and the Bush Presidency*.

NICOLE MELLOW is a professor of political science at Williams College and the author of *The State of Disunion: Regional Sources of Modern American*

Partisanship and *Legacies of Losing in American Politics*, with Jeffrey K. Tulis. Her current research focuses on eugenics and American nation-state development.

GERALD M. POMPER is Board of Governors Professor of Political Science (Emeritus) at Rutgers University. His twenty-one books include *Ordinary Heroes and American Democracy*, *Voters' Choice*, *Elections in America*, *Passions and Interests*, and collaborations on studies of presidential elections from 1976 to the present work.

PAUL J. QUIRK is Phil Lind Chair in U.S. Politics at the University of British Columbia. He studies the presidency, Congress, public opinion, and public policy and is editor of *The United States and Canada: How Two Democracies Differ and Why It Matters*.

ANDREW RUDALEVIGE is Thomas Brackett Reed Professor and chair of the Department of Government and Legal Studies at Bowdoin College. His books include *The New Imperial Presidency*, *The Politics of the Presidency*, and *By Executive Order*, as well as edited volumes on the Bush and Obama administrations.

CANDIS WATTS SMITH is associate professor of political science and African American studies, and she is the Laurence & Lynne Brown-McCourtney Early Career Professor at Penn State University. Her books include *Racial Stasis: The Millennial Generation and the Stagnation of Racial Attitudes in American Politics* and *Stay Woke: A People's Guide to Making All Black Lives Matter*.